Financial Exchanges

The recent global economic crisis has drawn a spotlight on the world of finance. Financial exchanges are changing, and this insightful new book examines the manner and reasons for these changes.

Financial Exchanges: A Comparative Approach offers an in-depth analysis of this sector. Surveying thirty different financial exchanges, including stock, derivative, commodity, and offshore exchanges, this book examines the challenges they face and the ways in which they are adapting. The book includes a pertinent chapter on the dominance of derivatives, examining a number of derivative exchanges in detail.

Taking in a host of international exchange powerhouses, including those in Hong Kong, Shanghai, London, New York, and the Persian Gulf, this book will benefit students taking courses on financial markets and institutions, as well as professionals interested in international financial markets.

Francis A. Lees is Professor of Economics and Finance at the College of Business Administration at St. John's University, New York, USA.

Financial Exchanges

A Comparative Approach

Francis A. Lees

Routledge
Taylor & Francis Group
NEW YORK AND LONDON

First published 2012
by Routledge
711 Third Avenue, New York, NY 10017

Simultaneously published in the UK
by Routledge
2 Park Square, Milton Park, Abingdon, Oxon OX14 4RN

Routledge is an imprint of the Taylor & Francis Group, an informa business

Library of Congress Cataloging-in-Publication Data
Lees, Francis A.
Financial exchanges: a comparative approach / Francis A Lees.
p. cm.
Includes bibliographical references and index.
1. Stock exchanges. 2. Capital market. 3. International finance. I. Title.
HG4551.L347 2011
332.64—dc22
2011006547

ISBN: 978–0–415–89243–8 (hbk)
ISBN: 978–0–415–89244–5 (pbk)
ISBN: 978–0–203–80589–3 (ebk)

Typeset in Garamond
by Swales & Willis Ltd, Exeter, Devon
Printed and bound in the United States of America on acid-free paper by
Edwards Brothers, Inc.

Contents

Figures and Tables

Figure

Tables

Preface

This book is the product of research carried out over the period 2006–10. Originally my objective was straightforward: describe how leading financial exchanges are restructuring, to become a new investor owned business sector. But, as the research progressed, it became clear that a deeper and more complex process was taking place affecting exchanges, markets, and the entire financial landscape.

This more complex process required that the following difficult questions be answered. First, trading has taken on an importance and life of its own. It is transforming the financial services business, pushing aside older structures and methods, leading to the creation of a new paradigm. How are these fundamental changes affecting financial exchanges? Second, how will the struggle taking place as exchanges fight for survival and success be resolved? Finally, will the role of financial exchanges expand or diminish? Will exchanges become more or less important?

Financial exchanges are complicated parts of the institutional framework. Often we fail to appreciate their sensitivity to the environment in which they operate and, more important, their many contributions to the well-being of the overall business system.

Exchanges have become key parts of our financial system. We often fail to appreciate their role in concentrating market liquidity and price discovery. That is because they are so visible and transparent. They function at such a pace that we fail to see the efficiency level at which they perform.

As we observe throughout the eleven chapters, exchanges are experiencing rapid change, and challenges to their competitive position. Researching this subject leads me to an inescapable conclusion. We need new approaches to the regulation and public policy support of these market institutions.

In the 1930s the United States created a regulatory system designed to protect less informed and sophisticated investors, and to provide a level playing field in public securities markets. Today we have many more types of traders and investors using the exchanges and other market venues to service their needs. We observe an escalating number of venues on which investors can trade securities and gain information. Trading systems function in different ways. As we move from one venue to another, markets can react in unexpected ways. The flash crash of May

2010 gives testimony to the potential for instability when a single large trader goes into panic mode.

Financial markets have become more closely intertwined and interconnected. Pressures on one venue can spill over and generate unforeseen impacts on other market sectors. Regulatory responsibility should be capable of limiting the spread of destabilizing pressures across the trading system. It is hoped that this book will shed additional light on these and related issues.

Acknowledgments

Researching and writing this book has been a challenge. The financial landscape in which stock exchanges and derivative exchanges operate is broad, diverse by nation, and changing at a fast pace. The exchange sector is in a period of accelerated restructuring, owing to the growing importance of trading as an essential component of financial services. Global geopolitics is experiencing shifts in the balance of power. Exchanges have discovered they must anticipate these shifts and respond quickly.

My own work in this project represents a small part of the collective knowledge and understanding of many professionals and specialists close to the subject. I thank all who aided and abetted me in efforts to write this book.

The officers and staff of exchanges constitute a first and necessary information and knowledge source. These professionals at leading exchanges provided information, insights, and written materials, responded to queries, and encouraged further investigation. Most especially, I wish to acknowledge the help of those at the London Stock Exchange and at the London Metal Exchange, who generously provided me with a clear understanding of the operations and challenges faced by these organizations.

Regulatory agencies play a key role in monitoring the activities of financial exchanges. Correspondence with SEC Commission Chairman Mary Schapiro and Branch Chief Gloria Smith-Hill proved to be most helpful.

An interview with Edward Whitley, Chief Executive at London-based International Financial Services, provided extremely useful data concerning London's role as a leading financial center. At other times interviews with London-based financial executives provided valuable information and deeper perspective. These include: Keith Mullin at IFR Thomson, Ed Baker at Alliance Capital, Hugh Baxter at Standard & Poor's, Jason Hollands at ISIS Asset Management, Jeremy Palmer at UBS Wealth Management, Eric de Bodard at Moody's, Catherine Claydon at Goldman Sachs, and Liselotte Burdorf-Cook at the UK Financial Services Authority.

Library research cannot be adequately acknowledged. I wish to thank the several reference library staff at the Huntington Public Library (Long Island) for providing help and assistance in finding and securing a vast number of books and documents covering the research requirements for this project.

My word processing technician Roberta Kuhr demonstrated unbounded patience in working through numerous revisions.

Finally, the greatest debt is to my wife Kathryn, who has been a patient friend and supporter through this and other projects.

Acronyms

Abbreviation	Meaning
ADB	Asian Development Bank
ADIA	Abu Dhabi Investment Authority
ADR	American depository receipt
AGM	annual general meeting
AIG	American International Group
AIM	Alternative Investment Market
AMEX	American Stock Exchange
ArcaEx	Archipelago Exchange
ASX	Australian Stock Exchange
ATS	alternative trading system
BGI	Barclays Global Investor
BIFFEX	shipping and freight index (LIFFE)
BIS	Bank for International Settlements
BM&F	Bolsa Mercadorias e Futuros (Brazil)
BME	Bolsas y Mercados Españoles
BOVESPA	Sao Paulo Stock Exchange
BOX	Boston Options Exchange
BRIC	Brazil–Russia–India–China
BSE	Boston Stock Exchange
BSX	Bermuda Stock Exchange
CAGR	cumulative average growth rate
CBOE	Chicago Board Options Exchange
CBOT	Chicago Board of Trade
CBSX	CBOE Stock Exchange
CCP	central (clearing) counterparty
CDS	credit default swap
CEF	complex event processing
CFTC	Commodity Futures Trading Commission
CIC	China Investment Corporation
CISX	Channel Islands Stock Exchange
CMA	Capital Markets Authority (Saudi Arabia)
CME	Chicago Mercantile Exchange

CMM	competitive market maker
COMEX	The Commodity Exchange
CSD	central securities depository
CSRC	China Securities Regulatory Commission
DCE	Dalian Commodity Exchange
DFM	Dubai Financial Market
DIFX	Dubai International Financial Exchange
DJIA	Dow Jones Industrial Average
DPMM	designated primary market maker
DR	depository receipt
DTB	Deutsche Termin Börse
DTCC	Depository Trust and Clearing Corporation
EAM	electronic access member
ECN	electronic communications (or computer) network
EMH	efficient markets hypothesis
ETF	exchange traded fund
FCM	Futures Commission Merchant
FICC	fixed income, currencies, commodities
FSA	Financial Services Authority
FTA	free trade area
FTSE	Financial Times/Stock Exchange
GAAP	Generally Accepted Accounting Principles
GCC	Gulf Cooperation Council
GDP	gross domestic product
GDR	global depository receipt
GEB	Growth Enterprise Board
GEM	Global Exchange Markets
GEM	Growth Enterprise Market
GMT	Greenwich Mean Time
GNMA	Government National Mortgage Association
GNP	gross national product
HFT	high frequency trading
HFTs	high frequency traders
HKEx	Hong Kong Exchanges and Clearing
HKFE	Hong Kong Futures Exchange
HKMEx	Hong Kong Mercantile Exchange
IAS	International Accounting Standards
ICE	Intercontinental Exchange
IFRS	International Financial Reporting Standards
IMF	International Monetary Fund
IMM	International Monetary Market
IOSCO	International Organization of Securities Commissions
IPE	International Petroleum Exchange
IPO	initial public offering
ISE	International Securities Exchange

ISX	Irish Stock Exchange
JADE	Joint Asian Derivatives Exchange (Singapore)
JGB	Japanese government bond
JSE	Johannesburg Stock Exchange
KCBT	Kansas City Board of Trade
KIA	Kuwait Investment Authority
KIB	Kuwait Investment Board
LBO	leveraged buyout
LCE	London Commodity Exchange
LCH	London Clearing House
LDP	Liberal Democratic Party (Japan)
LIFFE	London International Financial Futures Exchange
LME	London Metal Exchange
LMM	lead market maker
LNG	liquefied natural gas
LSE	London Stock Exchange
M&A	mergers and acquisitions
MiFID	Markets in Financial Instruments Directive
MOU	memorandum of understanding
MSCI	Morgan Stanley Capital International
MTF	multilateral trading facility
MTP	multilateral trading platform
NASD	National Association of Securities Dealers
NASDAQ	National Association of Securities Dealers Automated Quotations
NGLs	natural gas liquids
NMS	national market system
NNM	NASDAQ National Market
Nomad	nominated adviser
NSE	National Stock Exchange of India
NSSF	National Social Security Fund (China)
NYBOT	New York Board of Trade
NYMEX	New York Mercantile Exchange
NYSE	New York Stock Exchange
OCC	Options Clearing Corporation
OECD	Organisation for Economic Co-operation and Development
OFT	Office of Fair Trading
OMX	OM Exchange
OTC	over the counter
PCX	Pacific Stock Exchange
PhilEx (or PHLX)	Philadelphia Stock Exchange
PMM	primary market maker
PRC	People's Republic of China
QFC	Qatar Financial Centre

QFII	qualified foreign institutional investor
QIA	Qatar Investment Authority
QIB	qualified institutional buyer
QUEST	Quotation and Execution System for Trading
RBS	Royal Bank of Scotland
REIT	real estate investment trust
S&P	Standard & Poor's
SAMA	Saudi Arabia Monetary Authority
SEAQ	Stock Exchange Automated Quotations
SEATS	Stock Exchange Alternative Trading System
SEC	Securities and Exchange Commission
SES	Stock Exchange of Singapore
SESDAQ	Stock Exchange of Singapore Dealing and Automated Quotations
SETS	Stock Exchange Electronic Trading System
SFE	Sydney Futures Exchange
SGX	Singapore Stock Exchange
SIMEX	Singapore International Monetary Exchange
SMEs	small and medium enterprises
SMEB	Small and Medium Enterprise Board (China)
SMX	Singapore Mercantile Exchange
SOFFEX	Swiss Options and Financial Futures Exchange
SOX	Sarbanes–Oxley Law
SSE	Shanghai Stock Exchange
SWF	sovereign wealth fund
SWX	Swiss Stock Exchange
TAIFEX	Taiwan Futures Exchange
TOCOM	Tokyo Commodity Exchange
TOPIC	Teletext Output of Price Information by Computer
TSE	Tokyo Stock Exchange
TSX	Toronto Stock Exchange
UAE	United Arab Emirates
UBS	Union Bank of Switzerland
WCE	Winnipeg Commodity Exchange
WSJ	*Wall Street Journal*
WTO	World Trade Organization
ZCE	Zhengzhou Commodity Exchange

1 World Capital Markets

Over the past four decades world capital markets have been expanding at a pace double that of the real economy. By the year 2010 it could be said that global capital markets had grown to achieve hegemonic status. They engulf us in all of our daily activities, and exert a control over our destinies never before experienced. This chapter outlines the broad trends in global capital market development and evolution, and how financial exchanges have benefited from and contributed to this process.

Broad Trends

Since 1970 we have experienced a golden age in financial markets. This is illustrated in: a) the growing importance of free and competitive capital markets to achieve optimal allocation of the world's capital; b) creation of the single currency (the Eurozone) as a means of promoting capital efficiency across Europe; c) growing interest in minimizing the role of government in business via fiscal reforms and privatization; and d) a drive by emerging market nations to develop larger and more efficient financial markets.

In the following we chronicle key developments in Europe, the Americas, and Japan that have supported expansion of world capital markets, beginning with Europe and the Thatcher revolution.

European Initiatives

Here, we describe European initiatives that provided incentives for accelerated capital market development. The Thatcher revolution was a turning point in UK political economy, emphasizing the importance of competitive capital markets to achieve economic success.[1] Twenty years later, formation of the European single currency led to vast changes in the integration and development of capital markets on the continent.

Thatcher's Revolution

From 1979 onward, when Margaret Thatcher became the first woman prime minister of the United Kingdom, we have observed a steady shift away from government ownership and regulation of economic activity. This shift has been tempered by the world financial crisis of 2008–09. The Thatcher government first tackled exchange controls, unifying the dollar trading market in London and removing uncertainties associated with a volatile investment dollar market. This action brought the UK corporate sector and financial markets into more direct alignment with their counterparts in Europe, North America, and other parts of the globe. At once, British companies could acquire, or be acquired by, their counterparts in other countries. Portfolio investors could enter or leave the UK financial markets at will, their actions based primarily on investment incentives, no longer dependent on the size of the premium on investment dollars.

The Thatcher government reduced tax rates paid by individuals and corporations. This had a positive impact on equity investing, share ownership, and stock market turnover.

Thatcher put in motion a privatization program, geared toward reducing the burden of inefficient state enterprises, generating fiscal revenues, and removing government deficit finance. As we note below, some of the largest capitalization companies now traded on the London Stock Exchange (LSE) were privatized in the period during and following Thatcher's government. Many other countries have launched successful privatization programs following the UK example. Privatization in the UK created many new retail shareholders, and fostered growth of the LSE on both the demand and supply sides of the stock market.

The London Stock Exchange benefited from the Thatcher initiatives. First, tax reduction provided a positive incentive to share ownership and trading. Equally important, a unified foreign exchange market brought foreign investors to London, to trade on the LSE. The rise in trading put pressure on dealers, brokers, and the stock exchange to modernize its structure and trading system. As a result, in 1986 a Big Bang reform of the LSE expanded the role of brokers and dealers, brought more trading capital to market makers, and introduced flexible commissions on trades. A shift into electronic trading allowed LSE to expand rapidly, and capture a rising share of French, German, and other Continental share trading.[2]

Europe's Single Currency

Creation of the Eurozone in January 1999 had as one of its primary objectives the unification of European capital markets into a larger, more efficient structure. From early 1999 onward the following was achieved:

1. European equity markets took on a horizontal rather than a vertical structure, facilitating competition and more precise equity valuation. Pan-European industry sectors became the focus, rather than country-currency sectors.
2. Government bond markets demonstrated a greater cross-substitutability between issues of participant countries.

3 Corporate bond issuance, nearly invisible prior to 1999, became a major source of company financing, displacing relationship bank lending with a more transactional finance.
4 High yield bond financing developed into an important alternative for below investment grade borrowers.
5 A Euro-denominated money market evolved, based on European Central Bank guided practices, and a rapidly developing repo market.

Launch of the single currency was preceded by participating countries bringing their government debt levels and fiscal budgets into conformity with European Union target levels. Stability and Growth Pact guidelines, as they were referred to, constituted the fiscal policy side of the single currency approach toward overall economic stabilization.[3]

The Americas

Here we examine the role of the United States as a pace-setter in the hegemonic expansion of global capital markets. From the early 1970s American financial institutions and markets carried out initiatives and innovations that were followed around the world, setting in motion reorganization of stock exchanges and creation of novel derivatives securities, and generally raising the level of financial market competition.

Two changes took place in the first half of the 1970s: introduction of innovative financial futures on the Chicago derivatives exchanges, and flexible trading commissions on the New York Stock Exchange. The new financial futures covered foreign currencies, short interest rates, and long interest rates. These innovations were the beginning in the creation of a long series of new instruments, giving derivatives exchanges twice the growth power of the more traditional stock exchanges.

Introduction of flexible or negotiated commissions on the New York Stock Exchange (NYSE) permitted this exchange to recapture trading that had been shifting to off-exchange trading markets. More important, it created a more competitive environment that has challenged exchanges, trading platforms, and market makers to respond.

Latin America also participated in the growth and expansion of capital markets. The debt crisis of the 1980s was ended when debtor countries in that region adopted liberal economic policies that opened their markets to foreign trade and investment. This became the groundwork for debt restructuring that pulled the region out of the debt quagmire that had endured for many years.

Brady debt restructuring took place in the period 1989–95. This debt restructuring was named after the US Treasury Secretary Nicholas Brady, who sponsored an exchange of bank debt owed by countries like Brazil, Argentina, Mexico, and others for Brady bonds issued by the central governments of these debtor nations. Brady bonds were collateralized by zero coupon US Treasury securities. This restructuring initiative had three important positive results. First, the debt crisis problem became a thing of the past. Second, Brady bonds became a core component of a revitalized market for bond trading—the emerging country bond market. Third, many countries became more creditworthy, which allowed their financial markets to operate in a more expansive manner.

Japan's Bubble

In the thirty-year period leading up to 1989 Japan's economy appeared ready to become number one. A high growth rate, success in export competitiveness, and expanding domestic wealth all seemed to be working together toward an inevitable conclusion. Japan, ranked second in the world GDP league, eventually could take the lead. Asset owners in Japan shared in this prosperity.

Japan experienced an extreme asset price bubble in the 1980s, with real estate and stock market values rising at a strong pace. This was accentuated by a weak dollar, giving yen-based assets a further boost in relative valuation. Over the period 1985–89, for example, the dollar (market capitalization) value of Japanese equities advanced from $978 billion to $4,392 billion, more than four times the 1985 level. In the same period the market capitalization value in the US equity market advanced from $2,324 billion to $3,505 billion. Japan's equity market enjoyed a higher valuation than the US equity market for a full three-year period (1987–89).

However, 1989 proved to be a peak year for Japan's equity market. One year later (December 1990) its market capitalization had fallen to $2,917 billion, or by 33 percent, now below the US market value. Table 1.1 provides us with an overview of these trends. In 1985 Japan's equity market accounted for 21.8 percent of the world equity market total. In 1988 this had risen to 42.2 percent, but by 1994 had fallen to 28.1 percent. Table 1.1 reflects the fact that in the decade of the 1990s Japan suffered a severe market downturn.

Over the past two decades structural factors have been at work in Japan that inhibit financial development and stock market performance. These include a lack of business investment, a savings rate that exceeds investment financing needs, and an aging population. Uncertainties regarding government policy retard consumer spending and business investment. Big business, the long powerful Liberal Democratic Party (LDP), and civil servants have constituted an "iron triangle" that makes change in economic policy a difficult task. Japan has a high public debt to GDP ratio close to 180 percent.[4] This debt likely will rise as spending on an

Table 1.1 Three Largest Stock Markets: Percentage Share of Global Equity Market Capitalization (1985–94)

	1985 %	*1988* %	*1994* %
Japan	21.8	42.2	28.1
United States	56.7	30.2	38.3
United Kingdom	7.3	8.3	9.1

Source: M. Eng, F. Lees, and L. Mauer, *Global Finance*, Addison Wesley, 1998, p. 530.

increasingly older population must increase. We discuss Japan's stock market and financial system in closer detail in Chapter 9.

Higher Intensity of Trading

Trading securities has become an industry in its own right. Large banks engage in proprietary trading to generate profit from this source. As a result, Basel II regulates bank capital required relative to the level of securities trading by individual banking institutions. This elevated importance of trading brings opportunities as well as challenges. Financial exchanges experience higher trading growth, but they attract rival competition seeking to take trading revenues.

Equity Markets

World stock market capitalization and trading have increased as a percentage of world GDP. This can be observed in Table 1.2. Over the period covered in the table, stock market capitalization rose from 52 percent of GDP in 1990 to 109 percent in 2005, but declined in the recent (2008) financial crisis. Similarly, stock market turnover rose from 29 percent to 117 percent of world GDP in the same period to 2005. In 2007–08 the value of share trading was elevated owing to market volatility related to the crisis period.

We can observe the increasing importance of securities trading in Table 1.3. Here we present comparative growth rates of the real economy, equity market capitalization and trading, and derivatives contract innovation and trading. A wide gap in growth rates separates the real economy and equity trading. World equity market trading has grown two to three times as quickly as real GDP in developed countries. A still wider gap separates real economic growth and derivatives innovations and trading. Derivatives trading has expanded at four to five times real GDP in emerging countries (Table 1.3).

The intensity of securities trading has experienced a discernible upward shift. This is related to several changes in world finance. These include: higher levels of wealth and income, adoption of benchmark investing via indexation,[5] the growing importance of new institutional trading entities including hedge funds and sovereign wealth funds, and development of a new paradigm in securities

Table 1.2 World Stock Market Capitalization and Turnover Value as a Percentage of World GDP (1990–2005)

	1990	*1998*	*2005*	*2007–08*
World stock market capitalization to GDP	52%	82%	109%	97%
World stock market turnover to GDP	29%	79%	117%	72%

Source: Standard & Poor's, and World Bank.

Note: Both statistics expressed as a percentage of world GDP.

Table 1.3 Comparative Growth Rates of Real Gross Domestic Product, Stock Markets, and Derivative Activities (1988–2008)

		Annual percentage growth rate
I	Real economy (GDP)	
	Developed country GDP growth	3–5%
	Emerging country GDP growth	4–8%
II	World stock markets	
	Capitalization value	6–9%
	Value of turnover	8–12%
III	Derivatives activities	
	Innovations (new contracts)	20–30%
	Derivatives trading	30–40%

Sources: Standard & Poor's, Annual *Stock Market Factbook*; World Bank, *World Development Report*; Bank for International Settlements, *Annual Reports*.

market trading—high frequency trading (HFT). These are described in subsequent chapters.

Bond Markets

Parallel to the impressive growth and development taking place in equity markets, government bond markets have expanded at a steady pace. More important, the expansion and growing liquidity in government bond markets, especially in key countries of the G7 group, have provided numerous benchmarks for pricing and issuing a widening range of bond types. These include: corporate bonds, which were not plentiful outside the United States prior to the launch of the single currency, mortgage bonds, emerging market bonds, high yield bonds, and asset-backed securities. Growth of bond issuance by amount and type has been strongly supported by expansion of over the counter swaps markets used for hedging interest rate and credit default risks.

Most G7 countries have well-developed and sizeable government bond markets (Table 1.4). Trading generally takes place on over the counter markets. Table 1.4 demonstrates the comparative size and scale of these markets in G7 countries at yearend 2006. Five currency areas are included in the table, namely the yen, US dollar, Eurozone (Italy, France, and Germany), pound sterling, and Canadian dollar. Interestingly, the sterling government bond market is the smallest relative to GDP, owing to successful privatization and revenue capture, economic reforms which constrained budget deficits, and North Sea petroleum development which expanded the government revenue base. Japan ranks first among the G7 countries in amount of debt outstanding, and when we compare government debt to GDP. With the world recession in 2008–09, the G7 countries have experienced a surge in government debt levels.

The preceding sections evidence creation of a new financial economy that has been developing over the past quarter-century. This financial economy is over and above the real economy, and the financial superstructure (financial system)

Table 1.4 Government Bond Markets in the G7 Countries (2006)

	Amount outstanding *$*	*Percentage of G7 total* *%*	*Government debt as percentage of GDP* *%*
Japan	6.6	37.9	139.0
US	5.9	33.3	48.7
Italy	1.5	8.1	96.1
France	1.3	7.5	71.5
Germany	1.0	6.0	41.8
UK	0.8	4.7	41.2
Canada	0.6	3.3	61.8

Source: Deutsche Bundesbank, "Current Trends and Structural Changes in the Public Bond Market," *Monthly Report*, October 2006, pp. 29–44.

Note: Amounts in US$ trillions.

needed to provide financing and capital mobilization. This "third economy" we label "financial trading." Financial trading differs from the financial superstructure in several ways. First, it basically does not add value to the operation of the real economy. Rather it facilitates trading activities. Many analysts consider securities trading a zero sum game. Second, it provides added incentives for creating innovative financial instruments. Third, it supports more intensive trading levels in capital market sectors. Some of this incremental trading can be termed "speculative," possibly adding to systemic risk.

The new financial economy provides opportunities for increased trading on financial exchanges as well as over the counter. For example, exchange traded funds (ETFs) have expanded the scope of trading on financial exchanges, probably not adding in any clear manner to systemic risk. Where financial exchanges can service the trading of new instruments in transparent markets, and without excessive leverage, such innovations most probably add to the overall effectiveness of the financial system. We return to this question in later chapters.

Regional Shifts

Over the past decades financial markets in the United States led the world in growth, diversification, and innovation. As a result, the US achieved a high level of capital market penetration, or ratio of private debt and equity to GDP. Below we describe how political and other leaders in the United States view this status and seek initiatives to maintain it.

Is the United States in Relative Decline?

In the period 2004–06 New York was prosperous and Wall Street was booming, but could these successes continue? Traditionally, London was the chief competitor in financial services, but, as the diffusion of wealth and technology took place, barriers to the flow of capital weakened, and other centers such as Dubai, Hong Kong, and Singapore became important challengers in the battle for financial service business.

In 2006 Mayor Michael Bloomberg of New York City commissioned the well-known McKinsey Report, which was published and released in early 2007. The Report tackles difficult questions, such as: 1) is the United States in relative decline as a financial services provider to the world? 2) what are the reasons for rising competitive challenges facing New York as a world financial center? and 3) what can be done to alleviate or stem such competitive pressures?

The Report notes that US financial markets are still the world's largest and most important. US financial markets are well ahead of Europe, Japan, and the rest of the world. Also, the US's financial stock is larger than that of other regions (Table 1.5). With a financial stock of $51 trillion, far more than that of Europe ($38 trillion) and Japan ($20 trillion), US leadership appears healthy. However, the Report notes a disparity in cumulative average growth rates (CAGR) between the US and other regions enjoying higher rates of growth (Table 1.5).

The Report sees several threats to the US (and New York City) lead position. These include evolving technology and communications, which allow real-time trading from virtually anywhere. Other regions are building market liquidity, and enhancing efficiency and competitive position. Further, IPOs now occur around the globe, depending less on the placement power of New York institutions. Fast-growing derivatives markets signal the more rapid diffusion of financial innovations. As New York launches new financial instruments, they are replicated elsewhere.

The McKinsey Report offers a number of suggestions to maintain US financial market competitiveness. These include: assuring a steady flow of trained professionals to adequately staff financial services companies; improving the legal environment—especially the high cost litigation that raises the cost of legal services; and achieving better regulatory balance.

Capital Markets Penetration by the EU

Financial markets outside the United States are growing faster than those in North America. Many regions compete for international capital. Differential economic

Table 1.5 US's Financial Stock Larger Than That of Other Regions, but Growth Is Lower

	Financial stock ($ trillions)		*(% total)*	*Cumulative growth rate (CAGR)*
United States	51		42	6.5%
Europe	38		31	
UK		$8		8.4%
Eurozone		$30		6.8%
Asia (excluding Japan)	13		10	15.5%
Japan	20		17	7.5%
	$122		100%	

Source: *McKinsey Report*, January 2007.

Note: Data refers to yearend 2005. CAGR refers to cumulative average growth rate.

growth rates influence the ability of regions to attract capital and grow their respective capital markets. Capital market penetration, measured as the ratio of private debt and equity to GDP, is used in the McKinsey Report to compare countries and regions.

The capital market penetration ratio allows us to distinguish nascent markets from emerging and mature markets (Table 1.5). The Report places China, India, Brazil, and Russia among countries with nascent markets. Spain, South Korea, and Taiwan rank along with numerous emerging markets. Singapore finds itself on a line separating emerging and mature markets. The United States, Switzerland, and several European Union countries are identified as mature by their relatively high rates of penetration and their per capita GDP.

The European Union has come close to catching up with the US in revenue generated by capital markets players, including banks, asset managers, and other large institutions. But the EU still lags in penetration ratios.

The McKinsey Report suggests that US based financial exchanges will continue to face competitive challenges. In the following section we conclude this chapter with a description of the contributions financial exchanges provide to the functioning of capital markets, and challenges faced in the near future.

Contribution of Stock Exchanges

The following chapters describe how leading financial exchanges function around the globe. While no two exchanges are very much alike, they all provide the financial and business system with specific benefits and advantages over alternative market structures. We describe these below. Also, we explain why financial exchanges must be encouraged to expand their scope of operations.

Gains From Exchanges

Financial exchanges make important positive contributions to the operation and functionality of markets. We describe these as eight distinct factors.

First, exchanges provide liquid trading markets, as they consolidate buy and sell orders on their platforms. This concentration of liquidity enhances the ability of exchanges to engage in price discovery, and leads to participants enjoying fair prices as they trade.

Second, financial exchanges generally tend to be the most liquid marketplace for the securities listed and traded. This reinforces their ability to provide superior price discovery, with equal access to all on the exchange trading platforms. All traders, small and large, tend to be assured of fairness in transacting.

Third, exchanges tend to manage trading systems with a view toward achieving the lowest transaction cost for participants. This includes: the aggregate of bid–ask spreads, brokers' commissions, price impact costs, and market timing cost.[6]

Fourth, exchanges provide assured clearing and settlement services. This removes or reduces counterparty risks, especially when the exchange operates as a central counterparty vis-à-vis buyers and sellers.

Fifth, exchanges generally provide self-regulatory functions, by monitoring actions of brokers on trading platforms, and reviewing trading patterns, price behavior, and other metrics related to maintaining fair and honest trading.

Sixth, exchanges provide maximum transparency of price, volume, volatility changes, and other important data and information.

Seventh, exchanges contribute importantly to the effective and efficient allocation of risk capital. This applies to the sectors and companies that need and receive funds.

Finally, exchanges facilitate proper operation of the corporate finance life cycle. This life cycle contains four phases: startup company, venture capital financing, initial public offering (IPO), and mature company. Stock exchanges float IPOs, contributing to the success of venture capital, and implementing the third phase. With effectively operating equity markets (and stock exchanges), companies are able to obtain needed equity financing and make the transition through the four stages of the life cycle.

Challenges Ahead

In the future the world's capital markets face numerous challenges. These include: more intensive rivalry from big institutions seeking to expand market reach; a continuing need to achieve structural reforms; and the growing urgency for improved regulation.

In particular, the period 2007–10 witnessed the appearance of new challenges for financial exchanges and the capital markets. Fragmentation of equity trading poses a threat to the ability of exchanges to provide certainty and assurance in price discovery. Lack of transparency in large over the counter swaps markets makes it difficult to evaluate institutional exposures and investor risk. The flash crash in the US equity markets on May 6, 2010 attests to weaknesses in market structure and operational stability in markets dominated by algorithmic trading.[7] We discuss these specific issues in detail in subsequent chapters.

The need for structural reforms became apparent in the period 2008–09. The failure of several large banking institutions can be traced back to difficulties in clearing over the counter swaps and lack of transparency in high growth market sectors. With this, regulators pressured swaps traders and dealers to shift clearing of these instruments to transparent trading platforms where a central counterparty could assure fail-safe completion of the transaction at no risk to market participants. Also, regulators have been demanding there be improved transparency in such markets.

Large institutions seek to provide a more complete range of services to clients. In September 2009 one of the largest money managers, BlackRock, announced plans to create its own global trading platform. The asset manager would cross trades of customers without going through Wall Street service providers. Broker-dealers and exchanges could be marginalized from this practice.

BlackRock's plan to develop a world class global trading platform follows its acquisition of Barclays Global Investors (BGI), one of the largest asset managers globally.[8] The platform would realize cost efficiencies across all asset classes. The money monopoly could cross trades for customers without use of dealers, brokers, and exchanges, and possibly save clients transaction costs.

Proposals to reform regulation of capital markets multiplied in the crisis period 2008–09. One proposal has been to tax financial transactions that are considered not socially productive. Lord Turner, chairman of the UK Financial Services Authority (FSA), suggested a global tax on such financial transactions. Some years earlier James Tobin, a well-known American economist, had recommended a tax on global foreign exchange trading.

According to Lord Turner, a tax on financial transactions would curb excessive trading and act as a disincentive where financial executives have encouraged speculative and highly leveraged securities trading. We should note that such tax proposals are highly controversial, and meet with aggressive counter-arguments. For example, W. Buiter admits there are problems of excessive issuance and trading of credit default swaps, but suggests alternate solutions such as tougher bank capital requirements.[9]

Clearly there are numerous challenges in the years ahead regarding the structure, efficiency, and functioning of world capital markets. As we observe in the following chapters, these challenges most certainly relate to and potentially impact the operation and success of global financial exchanges.

2 Financial Centers and Exchanges

Over 250 financial exchanges operate around the world. These exchanges are based in over 100 countries, with the largest and most important operating in a dozen leading financial centers. These exchanges make vitally important contributions to securities traders including businesses, financial institutions, individual investors, and government entities. In this chapter we focus on the role played by two dozen leading financial centers housing the largest financial exchanges.[1]

This and the following chapters consider and answer pivotal questions regarding these financial centers and the exchanges they host. How important are the financial centers and the exchanges located within their jurisdictions? To what extent does the status of the financial center affect the ability of the exchange in that center to operate in a successful and competitive manner? Why are exchanges experiencing an ownership and business transformation? What are the main ingredients of this transformation?

In the following section we review trends in the status of the leading centers and exchanges. Then we look at the leading centers and analyze their strengths and weaknesses. Subsequently, we analyze the leading financial centers around the globe, and consider five perspectives on their future.

Financial Centers and Their Exchanges

Financial exchanges do not operate in a vacuum, and their success can be influenced by the status of the financial center in which they are based. A good illustration of this is the Tokyo Stock Exchange (TSE). For the past fifteen years this exchange has fallen on hard times. Much of this can be attributed to the weak performance of Japan's economy and financial markets. This is demonstrated by very low interest rates, a high level of government debt, reluctance on the part of Japanese investors to shift into riskier asset classes, depressed equity prices, and weak growth in incomes. Japan's weak financial markets have been a reflection of slow growth, an aging population, and labor markets that offer fewer lifetime jobs and dismal real wages.[2] By contrast, China's stock market has flourished and enjoyed higher market valuations, spurred by high economic growth and a competitive export sector. Financial centers shape the conditions and broad environment in which their respective stock exchanges operate.

Overview of Centers and Exchanges

Here we analyze and describe nineteen financial centers and their respective exchanges (Table 2.1). These centers host over three dozen exchanges, including stock exchanges, derivative and commodity exchanges, and offshore exchanges. Five distinct types of financial centers are included in this discussion: world, regional, large national, emerging market, and offshore. As noted below, some centers deserve several category designations. For example, Singapore is a regional center and also an offshore financial center.

London and New York rank at the top as world centers hosting some of the largest exchanges. London in particular hosts the London Stock Exchange (LSE), London Metal Exchange (LME), LIFFE derivatives exchange, Baltic Exchange (for ship contracts), and energy trading market (formerly identified as the International Petroleum Exchange (IPE), now owned and operated by ICE). New York also enjoys a range of exchange types. While the stock exchanges in New York are considerably larger than the London Stock Exchange, New York does not cover quite as many areas of trading activity as London.

We include three regional centers, two in Asia (Hong Kong and Singapore), and Zurich. The Asian centers and their exchanges are discussed in considerable detail in Chapters 9 and 10. Zurich hosts the SWX Swiss Exchange, described in Chapter 4. SWX lists domestic and foreign securities, and facilitates a large trading volume in bonds issued by Swiss and non-Swiss issuers.

Four large national centers include: Tokyo (described in Chapter 9), two European centers (Frankfurt and Paris), and Sydney. The Australian Stock Exchange is analyzed in detail in Chapter 9. The Frankfurt center hosts Deutsche Börse, one of the largest exchanges by revenue and profitability (Chapter 4). Paris hosts the Euronext exchange, a union of several European exchanges. Euronext merged with NYSE Group in 2007.

Five emerging financial centers are included in Table 2.1. Four are from the so-called BRIC countries (Brazil, China, India, and Russia). Most of these are discussed in detail in later chapters. The Gulf Emirates cover all six Gulf Cooperation Council (GCC) countries, each having a prosperous stock market and banking system. The GCC and its capital markets are discussed in detail in Chapter 11.

Finally, we include several offshore centers in our overview. Offshore centers largely service non-resident entities and wealth holders, and their stock exchanges list and trade companies based in other political jurisdictions. We describe the offshore centers and their exchange markets in detail later in this chapter. Their respective financial exchanges are described in detail in Chapter 4.

Large Centers Provide Support

Financial centers can provide a positive environment in which financial exchanges can flourish and prosper. Alternately, financial centers can present exchanges they host with problems and issues that retard development of the respective financial

Table 2.1 Selected Leading Financial Centers and Exchanges

Financial center	*Stock exchange*	*Derivative and commodity exchange*
I World financial centers		
A London	LSE	LIFFE[1]
		Baltic Exchange
		LME
		IPE[2]
B New York	NYSE	NYMEX[3]
	NASDAQ-OMX[4]	ICE[2]
C Chicago		CME[3]
		CBOE
		CBOT[3]
II Regional centers		
D Hong Kong	HKEx	HK Futures
E Singapore	SGX	SIMEX
F Zurich	SWX	Eurex[5]
III Large national centers		
G Tokyo	Tokyo SE	Tokyo Futures
H Frankfurt	Deutsche Börse	Eurex[5]
I Paris	Euronext[6]	LIFFE[1]
J Sydney	Australia SE	[7]
IV Emerging market centers		
K Shanghai	Shanghai[8]	[9]
L Moscow	Micex and RTS[10]	
M Mumbai	National Stock Exchange	[11]
N Sao Paulo	SP Stock Exchange	BM&F
O Gulf Emirates	Dubai, Abu Dhabi, Qatar, Oman, Bahrain, UAE, Saudi Arabia, Kuwait	
V Offshore centers[12]		
P Luxembourg	Luxembourg SE	
Q Bermuda	BSX	
R Channel Islands	CISX	
S Dublin	Irish Stock Exchange	
T Other	[13]	

Notes

1 LIFFE merged with the Euronext Exchange.
2 International Petroleum Exchange (IPE) now is part of Intercontinental Exchange (ICE) based in Atlanta.
3 In 2007 CME merged with CBOT, and later with NYMEX.
4 OMX is based in Sweden; it merged with NASDAQ in early 2008.
5 Eurex is partly owned by Deutsche Börse (80%) and SWX (20%).
6 Euronext group includes: Amsterdam, Brussels, Lisbon, and Paris stock exchanges, plus the LIFFE derivatives exchange.
7 Derivative exchange now part of stock exchange group.
8 Also should include Shenzhen Stock Exchange.
9 China operates three large commodity exchanges.
10 Trading on these Russian exchanges takes place both in rubles and in hard currency.
11 A number of relatively small commodity–derivative exchanges are being established in India.
12 The offshore centers provide trading in a range of instruments generally not listed on other financial exchanges.
13 These include: Barbados, the Cayman Islands, Panama, and several other offshore centers.

exchanges residing at these centers. In the following sections we illustrate these points in detail.

Most of the financial centers in Table 2.1 provide a positive environment for exchanges located there. In the following sections we describe how centers support and influence their respective exchanges, and the role played by the exchanges in adding to the attractiveness of the center.

London and New York

In the twenty-year period 1987–2007 both London and New York offered positive operating environments for their respective exchanges. Both centers offer a pro-business climate, efficient infrastructure, a reasonable and declining tax burden, and a full range of related financial services (insurance, banking, asset management). Both centers focus on servicing a large and diverse client base, with a somewhat different makeup. Historically, London has served a global client base, including foreign banks and investors, foreign exchange trading, and international companies. By contrast, New York has a more domestically rooted client base.

As can be seen in Table 2.1, London and New York host close to a dozen leading financial exchanges, only three of which are stock exchanges. The other exchanges fulfill trading in specialized areas. London in particular hosts specialized and unique exchange markets. In the past New York has provided low cost capital market opportunities for corporate and other borrowers. Also, New York attracts global investors, allowing this center to recycle capital efficiently. London also attracts global investors, and plays a role in recycling capital, with its merchant banks, foreign exchange market, and Eurocurrency operations. Chicago complements the role of New York as a domicile for the largest derivative exchanges.

London provides certain institutional advantages relative to New York. These include the London Stock Exchange, with highly diversified foreign company listings. Also, London hosts the London Metal Exchange, where non-ferrous metals, steel, and plastics are traded on a worldwide basis. According to Edward Whitley, chief executive officer at International Financial Services, London, in most respects London holds an edge over New York and most other financial centers in a range of services and share of market (Table 2.2).

Table 2.2 provides data covering the period 2004–07, indicating the financial market share of the UK, US, and other centers that provide eight distinct financial services. London leads in six of these services (cross-border bank lending, foreign equities trading, foreign exchange turnover, over the counter derivatives trading, secondary trading of international bonds, and marine insurance). New York (plus Chicago) leads in two areas (exchange traded derivatives, and hedge fund assets managed). Japan is a close second (marine insurance) and third (foreign exchange trading) in two of the eight service areas.

Over the period 2000–08 London appeared to be gaining relative to New York, as evidenced in Table 2.2. But in the following two years a financial crisis dealt severe setbacks to both New York and London. A global financial centers report

Table 2.2 International Financial Services Provided in Five Leading Centers (Percentage Share)

	London	*New York*	*Tokyo*	*Paris*	*Frankfurt*	*Others*
1 Cross-border bank lending	20	8	7	7	10	48
2 Foreign equities trading	40	30	—	—	3	27
3 Foreign exchange trading	31	18	8	3	5	35
4 Derivatives turnover:						
exchange traded	6	32	2	2	11	47
over the counter	42	24	3	10	3	18
5 International bonds secondary trading	80	7	—	—	—	13
6 Marine insurance	15	10	14	8	10	43
7 Hedge fund assets	20	60	2	2	—	16

Source: International Financial Services, London. Data averages cover period 2004–07.

from Z/Yen Group consultants released early in 2010 showed London had lost its lead over New York, leaving the twin centers at approximately the same level.[3]

Regulatory changes in the US and UK are likely to tip the balance, and it is difficult to anticipate how that may play out. Paul Volcker, former chairman of the Federal Reserve and a key consultant to the government in Washington, DC, has called for stiffer regulation and downsizing of complex financial institutions. It is believed this initiative, if acted on, could result in a leakage of corporate finance business from North America to Europe. But it remains to be seen whether American and European financial regulation will focus more on prohibitions or on tax and fee levies imposed on banking institutions. Where the balance will fall between the two financial centers (New York and London) is difficult to predict at this point in time.[4]

Regional and Large National Centers

We describe three regional centers that play a unique role, and host leading financial exchanges. Zurich attracts large offshore funds from Europe and beyond, which are invested through the SWX Swiss Exchange and through the large Swiss banks. At times, large Swiss banks provide liquidity to the Swiss bond market, where international issuers place debt securities. Alternately, Swiss banks recycle funds into the Eurocurrency markets or to New York for investment. Finally, the Swiss banks play a key role in asset and wealth management, directing investable funds to whatever financial center lists and trades the desired asset class.

Hong Kong and Singapore fulfill a similar role in Asia, but also have enjoyed other financial service functions. Singapore has provided trade-finance entrepot functions for Southeast Asia. Therefore, the Singapore exchange has enjoyed rising levels of liquidity for trading and investment. In recent years Singapore has been actively developing asset management and wealth management business, seeking to attract the wide range of service providers.

Hong Kong's status as a financial hub continues to climb as it welcomes the decision by HSBC, the large British bank, to relocate its chief executive from London to Hong Kong, and as it closes the gap on London in competitive rankings among the world's leading financial centers. The Global Financial Index computed by the Z/Yen Group is based on a survey of financial professionals, and effectiveness of functions in areas including office rents, tax rates, and airport service satisfaction. The survey results of second half 2009 rank Hong Kong as high as or higher than London and New York. Hong Kong is Asia Pacific headquarters for large investment banks, and the main gateway to Mainland China.

Table 2.1 also describes four large national centers: Tokyo, Frankfurt, Paris, and Sydney. Paris has led other European centers in introducing new methods and financial technology. It was the first after London to modernize the stock exchange and introduce flexible commissions, and an early developer of derivative trading on the Matif market. In the early 1990s Frankfurt was busy integrating the numerous regional stock exchanges, as German banks sought to create a Finanzplatz Frankfurt. At this time the Deutsche Börse was created, which in turn launched its Termin Börse for derivative trading. The Termin Börse later became Eurex, owned 80:20 by Deutsche Börse and SWX respectively.

In the decade 1999–2009 the single currency appeared to be a plus for London's role as a global financial center. France and Germany appeared to have kept to a subtle and behind-the-scenes agreement, the "widget–cheese–finance" standoff. This unspoken deal inside the EU allowed the French to keep control of their cheese, the Germans produced widgets, and hedge funds, private equity firms, and investment banks continued to operate in London.[5]

With two years of economic downswing and financial market crisis, the widget–cheese–finance pact is falling apart. It is becoming clear that Paris is set on gaining more Eurozone financial business, and German political leaders appear less willing to tolerate the volatility inherent in Anglo-Saxon type finance. It remains to be seen how doggedly the UK government will fight to retain its hold on financial service business. Frankfurt and Paris were ranked 13 and 20 by the Z/Yen survey in 2010, which suggests they are some distance from encroaching on London's financial business. Germany's ability to move ahead in financial services may reside more in how the Eurozone and its currency work through the sovereign debt crisis that severely undercut the status of the euro in 2010. According to a report by an authoritative German research firm, "the success and internationalization of Germany's financial sector is looking inseparable from the question of the long term stability of the Euro."[6]

Sydney has been catapulted into a world class financial center by unification of regional stock and derivative exchanges in Australia. But Sydney also benefits from a mandatory pension scheme that aggregates demand for securities investment into competitive pension fund managers. Underpinning Australia's economic prospects and favorable financial environment is its diversified commodities industry, ranging across meat, grains, iron ore, and numerous other commodities. Australia's financial exchanges are discussed in detail in Chapter 9.

Tokyo stands in contrast to these and other national financial centers. Japan delayed its stock exchange Big Bang for too long, and has been slow to bring about reforms and investment in stock market technology. In Chapter 9 we analyze these factors underlying Tokyo's slow development as a financial center.

Emerging Market Centers

We restrict our analysis of emerging market centers to the four BRIC countries, plus the constellation of Gulf Emirates. These centers are developing steadily, owing to high economic growth and large population bases in the four BRIC nations, and enormous oil and gas wealth concentrated in the Gulf Emirates. Over the period 2002–10 the Moscow financial center has enjoyed rapid development, spurred by resource based exchanges notably in oil and gas, iron and steel, non-ferrous metals, and precious metals.

Shanghai is expanding as the main financial center of China, despite the continued use of capital controls by the Communist government. Hong Kong provides a necessary and useful escape valve in this system of capital controls. A high savings rate in China feeds growth of the financial system, especially banks and the stock market.

The Sao Paulo financial market benefits from a diversified economy, including industrial, agricultural, and resource based sectors. The BM&F derivative exchange in Sao Paulo benefits from Brazil's role as a largest or second largest producer of numerous agricultural and commodity products. Recent offshore petroleum discoveries add to this advantage enjoyed by Brazil in commodities trading. These discoveries have led to Petrobras carrying out the largest equity capital raising in the form of a $67 billion offering in 2010.[7]

The Indian economy similarly appears poised for economic expansion. India enjoys a large population that is quite young. At least one-quarter of Indian people speak English, providing an enormous positive human resource advantage.

Offshore Centers

Offshore financial centers provide specialized and unique services that differ from those available in larger national centers. These are described below. But several offshore centers operate as regional centers (Hong Kong and Singapore), providing services that compete more directly with New York and London.

Offshore financial centers come in at least three varieties, offshore banking centers, tax havens, and financial-investment centers. Offshore banking centers are located where banks are permitted to maintain and service external accounts that extend beyond the banking activity typical and needed for the local economy. Generally offshore banks are organized as branches or subsidiaries of their respective parent bank. These offshore offices enjoy a large measure of freedom from host country regulation.

The International Monetary Fund (IMF) identifies the Bahamas, Bahrain, the Cayman Islands, Hong Kong, the Netherlands Antilles, Panama, and Singapore as major offshore banking centers (Table 2.3, Column B). When the US Federal Reserve imposed reserve requirements on foreign branch advances of eurodollars to the respective US parent, it also made it easier for smaller US banks to establish so-called "shell" branches. Shell branches could be based in an offshore location, but manage funds from the American head office.

Hong Kong and Singapore offices of American and other large banks are not designated shell branches, since these banking offices actively participate in the local bank operations and the Asian dollar market. The latter is a subset of the London centered eurodollar market.

Tax haven centers enjoy low corporate income tax and withholding tax rates on passive income (defined as interest and dividends). Tax havens are useful locations for large corporations, which establish a wholly owned subsidiary based in the offshore center. In turn, this subsidiary could own operating subsidiaries of the same corporate group. Essentially, the tax haven subsidiary would serve as a pass-through for corporate cash flows, shielding them from tax liabilities.

Tax haven centers are identified by their low tax rates on corporate income received from operating subsidiaries. Also, they enjoy low withholding tax rates on distributions of passive income (Table 2.3, Column A). As can be observed in Table 2.3, several countries provide a zero tax rate on corporate income (the Bahamas, Bahrain, Bermuda, the Cayman Islands), while others have tax rates of 36 percent or lower. Several centers enjoy tax treaties with the United States, affording low withholding on dividend and interest income.

Offshore financing and investment centers provide a mix of services needed by participants on both sides of the capital markets. On the financing side, companies, governments, and other entities can obtain financing at low cost in offshore centers. For example, Luxembourg and Switzerland operate bond markets which facilitate low cost financing for borrowers. Offshore centers possess money markets (Singapore, Hong Kong) where Asian dollars and local fund borrowings can be facilitated. Several of these centers have stock markets that facilitate issuing, listing, and trading of equity and other securities. Ten of the offshore centers identified in Table 2.3 have stock exchanges that support the financing and trading of securities.

Offshore centers provide services required by fund managers. These include: securities trading on exchanges, hosting hedge fund and other alternative asset class entities, and the listing and trading of specialized investment funds that cater to specific needs of portfolio investors.

Several of the centers in Table 2.3 provide all three services (banking, tax haven, financing-investment), including: Bahrain, Hong Kong, Panama, and Singapore. Luxembourg and Switzerland play unique roles in this respect, which are further described elsewhere in this chapter.

Luxembourg is an important tax haven. Also, Luxembourg has a withholding tax treaty with the United States. For this and other reasons Luxembourg is an attractive destination for investors and wealth holders in the United States and

Table 2.3 Leading Offshore Centers, Financial Services Provided

Financial center	A. Tax haven			B. Offshore banking center[2]	C. Financing-investment centers					
	Corporate income tax rate[1]	Withholding tax[1]								
		Interest	Dividends		1. Operates significant financial exchange	2. No. of listed companies	3. Percentage listed companies foreign	4. Equity turnover as percentage market capitalization	5. Bond and loan financing available	6. Innovation fund management
1 Bahamas	0			X						
2 Bahrain	0			X	Yes	45		12		
3 Barbados	36	5	15							
4 Bermuda	0				Yes					Yes
5 Cayman Islands	0			X						
6 Channel Islands:										
Jersey	20				Yes					Yes
7 Guernsey	20				Yes					Yes
8 Hong Kong	17.5			X	Yes	1,017	1	76	Yes	Yes
9 Ireland: Dublin	12.5	0	15		Yes	58	17	85		
10 Liechtenstein	20									Yes
11 Luxembourg	22.8	0	15		Yes	34	80	2	Yes	
12 Netherlands Antilles	34.5			X						
13 Panama	30			X	Yes	31	[3]	4		
14 Singapore	20			X	Yes	455	15	101	Yes	Yes
15 Switzerland: Zurich	30	0	15		Yes	253	31	141	Yes	Yes

Sources: Standard & Poor's, *Global Stock Markets Factbook*, 2009; PricewaterhouseCoopers, *Corporate Tax Summaries*, various issues.

Notes

1 Percentage rate of tax.

2 Based on IMF designation.

3 Most listings in Panama are foreign owned companies.

other countries. The operation of Luxembourg's financial exchange is detailed in Chapter 4.

Asia on the Rise

While London and New York continue to lead financial centers, Asian centers are narrowing the gap. Hong Kong is the lead candidate to catch New York and London, but Singapore is advancing steadily.[8]

Singapore has demonstrated a renewed aggressiveness to catch up with Hong Kong on several fronts:

- Singapore is promoting a new, foreign owned financial exchange, the Singapore Mercantile Exchange, to compete with the existing exchange.
- Singapore continues to improve tax breaks for corporate headquarters and manufacturing plants.
- Singapore offers low cost telecommunications and English language services.
- Singapore is close to India, where the business sector is expanding across Southeast Asia. Indian companies find Singapore a comfortable and appealing financial center.

Meanwhile, Hong Kong seeks to broaden the range of its financial services and to capture the attention of international companies. Rusal, the large Russian metals company, has listed its stock on the Hong Kong exchange.[9]

What Makes a Leading Financial Center?

Below we analyze the economic and locational factors that underlie the competitive status of leading financial centers. Twelve centers are included in this analysis. Eight factors are utilized for this purpose. Second, we examine the time zone location of these centers.

Analysis of Eight Factors

Eight economic and cultural factors exert a strong influence over the development and competitive status of financial centers. The eight factors are identified from an iterative process in which lead centers are identified, their positive and negative factors are identified, and a winnowing process is applied in which eight main factors are isolated.

The results of this analysis are summarized in Table 2.4, where twelve centers and eight economic and cultural factors constitute a matrix where forty-three cells are identified as reflecting positive, five cells are identified reflecting negative, and forty-eight cells are evaluated as non-significant. The eight factors and the frequency of their showing a positive effect are: 1) economic growth (4); 2) large internal market (5); 3) industrial base (5); 4) commodity base (3); 5) financial and

Table 2.4 Eight Factors Underlying Financial Center Status

Center	*Economic growth*	*Internal market*	*Industrial base*	*Commodity base*	*Regulation*	*Entrepreneurialism and innovation*	*Wealth status*	*Trading and entrepot*	*Favorable*	*Unfavorable*
New York		X	X		X	X	X		5	—
London			X		X	X	X	X	5	—
Paris		X	X				X		3	—
Frankfurt		X	X				X		3	—
Hong Kong	X				X	X	X	X	5	—
Tokyo		X	X		—	—	X		3	2
Zurich					X		X	X	3	—
Toronto				X	X	X			3	—
Singapore					X	X	X	X	4	—
Sydney	X			X		X			3	—
Gulf Emirates	X	—		X			X		3	1
Shanghai	X	X			—	—	X		3	2
Totals:										
Positive	4	5	5	3	6	6	10	4	43	
Negative		1			2	2				5

other regulation (6); 6) entrepreneurialism and innovation (6); 7) wealth accumulation (10); and 8) entrepot and trading status (4).

Three centers can claim five factors as having a positive influence. These are London, New York and Hong Kong. Singapore is a close fourth, with four positive factors. In this analysis, centers located in much larger countries enjoy fewer positive factors than Singapore (e.g., Paris, Frankfurt, and Tokyo).

The analysis in Table 2.4 includes negative ratings for three centers (Gulf Emirates, Tokyo, and Shanghai). Both Tokyo and Shanghai suffer from adverse regulatory systems and cultural and other impediments to entrepreneurship and innovation. The Gulf Emirates suffer from small internal markets in a majority of the six countries.

In the case of the Gulf Emirates, considerable foreign exchange earnings have enabled rapid wealth accumulation. This is discussed in detail in Chapter 11. In the case of Shanghai, central government policy aims at the development of this center as the focal point for financial markets and services.

Early in 2009 the government of China reiterated its intention to turn Shanghai into an international financial center by 2020 that would rival New York, London, and Hong Kong. Chinese officials acknowledge the huge gap now existing between the Shanghai and other capital markets. Shanghai trails Hong Kong in financial talent, an important disadvantage. But the most significant and important disadvantage lies in Shanghai lacking a vibrant entrepreneurial base (Table 2.4).[10] Shanghai has much to learn from the successful development of other centers over the past sixty years. For example, Li Ka-Shing, the world's most successful entrepreneur, started his business making plastic flowers. At this time (the 1940s) other Chinese industrialists migrated to Hong Kong, converting that center into a textile manufacturing powerhouse. These entrepreneurs gradually moved into manufacturing machinery, electronics, and providing professional services.

In the 1960s and 1970s huge British merchant houses like Jardines dominated Hong Kong's commercial and industrial landscape, but local Chinese entrepreneurs more than matched their colonial counterparts and, by the end of the 1980s, had surpassed them. If Shanghai is to match Hong Kong's success it must discover how to enable skilled entrepreneurs like Li Ka-Shing to compete in a system not bound by regulatory constraints and impediments.

Time Zone and Physical Location

Time zone location exerts a proximity oriented advantage or disadvantage for financial centers. In the following we describe and analyze the time zone locations of seventeen financial centers, and give each a rating based on: a) weighted average proximity, and b) number of other centers within operational simultaneity.

Twenty-Four Time Zones

A system of international time-keeping divides the world into time zones utilizing 24 standard longitudinal meridians, each 15 degrees apart (360 divided by 24).

Time is measured in each zone as a certain number of hours ahead of or behind the time at the Greenwich meridian (Greenwich Mean Time or GMT). For example, when it is 12 noon GMT (Greenwich and London), it will be 2 p.m. in Zambia, Romania and Poland. Similarly, when it is 4 p.m. GMT, it will be 11 a.m. in Peru and New York.

GMT has been the internationally accepted basis for calculating solar time since 1884. The Greenwich meridian corresponds to 0 degrees of longitude. The International Dateline is an imaginary line that extends from pole to pole, corresponding to 180 degrees of longitude. This dateline arbitrarily marks calendar days. Moving from east to west across this dateline, a traveler will need to set his/her calendar back one day.

Based on this system, financial centers find themselves located in distinct time zones. In some cases (Tokyo and Sydney), distant centers (in the Northern and Southern hemispheres) find themselves operating within the same time zone, with business and banking hours in these centers enjoying full business day time of operation overlap. In other cases there may be no time of operation overlap, since some centers are located at the most remote distances from one another (New York and Tokyo). Fortunately, most leading financial centers enjoy some time of operation overlap with other centers, allowing commercial and financial transactions to proceed during their common hours of operation.

Time Zone Proximity

The ability of a financial center to operate successfully hinges on several factors. In a broad perspective these factors include: a) economic factors discussed previously and detailed in Table 2.4, and b) proximity to other financial centers. In the following we analyze the time zone proximity of leading world financial centers.

In Table 2.5 we consider seventeen financial centers. We measure the "distance" between financial centers located in a number of time zones. With 24 different time zones, the maximum distance between any two financial centers will be 12 and the minimum zero.

If we consider London, for example, it is ten time zones away from Tokyo and Sydney, and eight time zones from Hong Kong, Shanghai, and San Francisco. But as a financial center London is located quite close to European financial centers (Frankfurt, Zurich, and Paris), South Africa, Sao Paulo, and the Persian Gulf Emirates. Little wonder that London effectively challenges New York for a leading role as world financial center.

By contrast, New York is located more remotely from financial centers than London. New York is located nine or more time zones from seven of the seventeen financial centers included in Table 2.5.

In Table 2.5 we measure distance of financial center from other financial centers in two ways. These include weighted average proximity to other centers, and number of centers located four or fewer time zones apart. Centers with the lowest weighted average proximity enjoy closer proximity to other centers. Centers with

Table 2.5 Time Proximity for Seventeen Leading Financial Centers

	1. Weighted average proximity	*2. Number of centers four or fewer time zones apart*
I Most proximate:		
South Africa	5.14	6
Frankfurt	5.21	7
Paris	5.21	7
Zurich	5.21	7
Gulf Emirates	5.28	9
Mumbai	5.36	8
II Moderately proximate:		
London	5.60	6
Singapore	5.64	6
Hong Kong	5.71	6
Shanghai	5.71	6
Sydney	6.28	4
Tokyo	6.28	4
III Least proximate:		
Sao Paulo	6.78	7
New York	7.21	4
Toronto	7.28	4
Chicago	7.28	4
San Francisco	7.57	3

Note: Hong Kong enjoys a median position with respect to both rankings in the table. The Gulf Emirates and Mumbai enjoy a strong strategic position, given their relatively low distance (Column 1) from other centers, and top ranking in number of centers that enjoy half-day business hours overlap.

the greatest number of other centers four or fewer time zones apart also enjoy closer proximity and ability to transact with other centers at least half of daily operating hours or longer.

In Table 2.5 we rank centers in descending order of their average proximity to other centers (Column 1). Three European centers and South Africa are the top ranked in this respect, with weighted average proximity of 5.14 and 5.21. This number measures the average number of time zones a given center is apart from other centers included in the table.

A second measure is found in Column 2 of Table 2.5. This indicates the number of centers four or fewer time zones apart from the financial center being measured. For example, San Francisco has the highest weighted average distance (in time zones) from all others, or 7.57. Also, San Francisco finds itself "reasonably close" to only three other centers in the table. By contrast, London is "reasonably close" to six other centers (including New York), but New York is "reasonably close" to only four other centers.

We should note that emerging country financial centers (Gulf Emirates and Mumbai) enjoy most proximate status in Table 2.5. Therefore, they benefit from considerable business day overlap with nine and eight other centers respectively.

Is New York Maintaining its Relative Position?

The January 2007 McKinsey Report describes the challenges facing New York's financial services sector.[11] This is one of several studies searching for answers to the changing status of New York as a global financial center, problems faced, and measures needed to strengthen New York's position. Given the rising status of London and other centers, there is growing concern in the United States over New York's competitive status. Following the McKinsey Report there has been considerable analysis concerning the status of New York. In the following we consider five perspectives on this issue.

Five Perspectives on Financial Markets

A debate opened up in the period 2006–09 over whether the United States is losing its competitiveness in global capital markets. This debate operates at three levels: 1) Has the US really lost competitiveness? 2) If so, what are the reasons? 3) What can and should be done?

One group led by NYSE Group former CEO John Thain points out that twenty-two of the twenty-five largest IPOs in 2006 globally were not listed on US financial exchanges.[12] This group agrees that America's financial markets and exchanges have lost competitiveness, that enactment of Sarbanes–Oxley (SOX) in 2002 is partly responsible, and that the harshest and most costly aspects of SOX should be eliminated.

Thain and others have a *reformist* perspective, believing that regulation and cost-increasing measures of overzealous regulators should be reversed. They see tort reform as a vital part of the changes required to revive venture capital activity. Also, they defend the existing new issue underwriting system that enables investment banks to allocate shares to institutional investors who agree to purchase additional shares in the IPO after-market.

Juxtaposed against this view are those who would *stay the course.* They advocate doing nothing, and include defenders of Sarbanes–Oxley like former SEC chairman Arthur Levitt.[13] They point out that the US stock market has performed well, and that US market competitiveness may be increasing as investor confidence rises. This perspective welcomes increased transparency of markets, and measures to achieve deeper market liquidity (Table 2.6).

A third perspective views the *shifting competitiveness* of financial markets as inevitable. According to Robert Pozen, the main factor in market selection for global IPOs is the country where the issuer has its headquarters. Of the ten largest IPOs globally in 2006, eight were headquartered in China and Europe, so they launched in the Hong Kong and European markets.[14]

Preference by these Asian and European issuers for nearby markets is facilitated by Securities and Exchange Commission (SEC) Rule 144a, which allows foreign companies to raise capital from US institutional investors without an SEC registration. According to Pozen, in 2006 foreign companies raised a record $10.5 billion via SEC registered offerings, but a much larger $133 billion from US markets under Rule 144a.

Table 2.6 Five Perspectives on US Financial Markets

Perspective	*Description*
1 Reformist	Over-regulation and poorly considered reforms have raised the cost of issuing and trading securities in the US. Government reforms and financial market initiatives are required to reverse these problems.
2 Stay the course	Emphasizes the role of investor protection, and need for adequate regulation. Asserts SOX restores investor confidence.
3 Inevitable shift in competition	Rise of large issuers in Asia and Europe, along with preference for nearby markets, leads to inevitable rise in these regional stock markets. Also, differences in regulatory approach can shift issuance to more familiar markets.
4 Entrepreneurial	View venture capital IPOs as lifeblood of American economy. Loss in this area threatens the technology leadership of American financial and business system.
5 European perspective	The single currency allows Europe to play a key role in global finance. In Europe an appropriate balance is required between the efficiency of financial markets, social stability, and market volatility.

Created in 1990, the Rule 144a market is strictly limited to so-called qualified institutional buyers (QIBs). These are financial institutions with at least $100 million in investable assets. Qualified buyers are free to trade securities of both US and foreign companies that have never offered their shares to the investing public. Companies that issue stock under Rule 144a can access America's deep and liquid capital markets without submitting to public company accounting rules or becoming subject to Sarbanes–Oxley reporting.[15] The Rule 144a market has grown rapidly over the period since being established.

In 2006, for the first time more capital was raised in the US via the Rule 144a channel than through IPOs on all the major stock exchanges combined. With the expansion of this market, NASDAQ proposed a project called Portal. Portal aims to be a central clearing house for buyers and sellers of Rule 144a securities. Only QIBS are to trade on this network, and the number limits on institutional participants would continue to apply.

Foreign financial markets have developed and modernized their technology platforms, while maintaining lower underwriting spreads and listing fees than New York. In particular, London gives strong protection to minority stockholders that appears more effective than that provided in the United States.

When asked about factors that keep them away from US markets, foreign executives often cite litigation costs. These non-US executives are concerned with the volume and size of class action claims against publicly traded companies in the US. In Europe shareholders rarely sue. As a result, provisions for directors' and officers' liability insurance in the US are six times as high as similar coverage in Europe.

Pozen holds that the rise of large global issuers in Asia, the easy access of US institutions to non-US IPOs, and the enhanced attractiveness of the London markets are irreversible forces that will prevent the US from regaining its formerly dominant position of the mid-1990s.

A fourth perspective is *entrepreneurial*. This entrepreneurial perspective sees many decades of venture capital companies providing a job creating engine for the US economy. A study by the consulting firm Global Insight, released by the National Venture Capital Association in 2007, notes that since 1970 enterprises backed by venture capital now employ 10 million workers in the US, and in 2005 generated sales of $2.1 trillion. These companies employ over 9 percent of the US private sector workforce and account for 16.6 percent of GDP.

According to this perspective "we are killing the job-creating engine with a combination of high transaction costs and tremendous friction."[16] This is the unintended consequence of a range of regulatory measures, all of which seemed like good ideas at the time but that in total have turned out to be a disaster. These include decimalization of NASDAQ, and the SEC's Regulation Full Disclosure (FD). Those were followed by then New York Attorney General Eliot Spitzer's "global settlement" which separated investment banking from equity research and made certain that analysts' compensation could not be a function of their winning underwriting or merger advisory mandates for their Wall Street firms.

The abandonment of small cap research and market making by underwriting firms, and upward shift in costs for small cap issuing companies have raised the bar for companies (and their breakeven size) that go public on NASDAQ. According to Grady, in 1996 the average deal size of a NASDAQ IPO was $34 million, and average market capitalization $133 million.[17] Ten years later the average IPO deal size was $113 million and the average market capitalization was over $330 million, a size only a much larger company can sustain.

A fifth and final perspective can be found in *Europe*. In the period 1999–2008, the Eurozone financial market became a real financing alternative to the US dollar based capital markets. Euro denominated international bond issues have come to challenge and equal dollar denominated issues. The Eurozone stock markets now enjoy a common currency of denomination, horizontal rather than vertical stock markets reflecting contested sectors rather than national divisions, and greater liquidity.

European regulators and investors have experienced concern with certain aspects of Anglo-American capital markets. In particular they reject the high degree of short-termism in the United States, reflected by quarterly reporting, its dampening influence on the ability of American companies to emphasize investment spending for long term profitability, and the short term focus of hedge funds. Peer Steinbrück, formerly German finance minister, called for German companies to resist the short-termism of American corporate reporting, insisting that the focus should be "how to keep a company competitive in the medium to longer term."[18]

Steinbrück is anxious that the German economic model should retain its traditional features. This means investing more in research and development, which may not be consistent with the aspirations of hedge funds pushing for special dividend payments.[19]

Europe's reform proposals following the 2008–09 global financial crises continue to reflect an approach toward capital market evolution that differs from that in the United States. European governments favor limits on short selling, and a tax on banks that could be used to stabilize that sector should a banking crisis manifest itself.

Evaluation

The five perspectives described above reflect differing views concerning the role of US capital markets in world finance, whether their competitive status is eroding vis-à-vis other financial centers, and what measures might be considered appropriate to correct perceived shortcomings.

The reformist and entrepreneurial perspectives are closely overlapping, holding that investment banks and financial exchanges should receive light regulatory treatment, and retain maximum flexibility to innovate and issue securities. The stay the course perspective defends Sarbanes–Oxley as necessary to restore investor confidence, and holds that the regulatory initiatives designed to remove abuses should be continued.

An alternate view holds that an inevitable shift in competitiveness has been taking place. High Asian growth and creation of the Eurozone give support to new financial centers of gravity in Europe and Asia. Privatization and going public activity inevitably give rise to higher volumes of new securities issues and listing of shares. As a result, Hong Kong, Singapore, Shanghai, and other financial centers are expanding and attracting financial business. Not unexpectedly, regional financial exchanges benefit from these trends.

Finally, a European perspective gives equal emphasis to financial market development and the social economy. Europeans are concerned with the potentially destabilizing influence of activist investors (hedge funds), and the potential loss of jobs from the private equity restructuring of companies. Continental Europe is adopting an equity culture, but it is not quite the same as the equity culture found in London and New York. On the Continent residual concerns remain quite high over social stability and potential job losses resulting from company restructuring.

Clearly, financial exchanges around the world are experiencing a shift in their competitive status. Concern in the United States takes expression through a variety of perspectives, some of which are more inclined to be protective of financial exchanges than others. In the chapters which follow we consider in greater detail this shifting environment, how stock exchanges in the United States and other countries are reacting to these pressures, the design of new business models and wholesale restructuring by exchanges, and the growing importance of derivatives and derivative exchanges.

3 Changing Exchanges

Financial exchanges find themselves in a dynamic time period. Change is the order of the day. At leading exchanges, chief executive officers understand they operate in a financial world where old methods and paradigms must yield to new. They must adapt their operating modes and revise business models. In this chapter we describe how financial exchanges have revised their organization structures and become for-profit companies. We analyze the drivers of change. Also, we provide a model of stock exchange growth and analyze the shifting composition of equity trading.

A Transformed Sector

The Economist described the 2005 New York Stock Exchange purchase of the electronic exchange Archipelago as "transformational." The merger would change the 212-year-old floor based, not-for-profit mutual company into one of the world's modern financial markets.[1] By converting to a for-profit company, NYSE would have to manage a difficult transformation in its relationship with Wall Street brokerage and investment banking firms.

The transformation of NYSE that followed is detailed in later chapters. The NYSE experience is simply one part of a larger story about a sector that continues to adapt and evolve. In the following sections we describe the demutualization and early consolidation that took place in the period 1993–2006.

Demutualization

The Stockholm Stock Exchange was the first to demutualize in 1993. Subsequently, other exchanges followed this route, including Borsa Italiana (1997) and the Australian Stock Exchange (1998). By 2004 twenty-two stock and derivative exchanges had demutualized. These include: the London Stock Exchange (2000), NASDAQ (2001), the Chicago Mercantile Exchange (2002), the Tokyo Stock Exchange (2001), the Hong Kong Stock Exchange (2000), and the Singapore Stock Exchange (1999).

Prior to the 1990s financial exchanges were non-profit mutual associations owned by members. The members were brokers, or broker-dealer firms engaged in trading securities and derivatives. These firms conducted their trading business on the exchange trading floor. When exchanges were first organized, the concept was a membership club that extended exclusive trading privileges to participants. These participants or members brought trading orders from their clients to the exchange trading floor for execution.

As we describe below, equities trading expanded into a larger and more complex business, and a wider range of services and needs emerged. Also, regulatory rules were created to protect investors from sharp trading practices. These rules further complicated the responsibilities and operations of exchanges.

Demutualization gave recognition to the fact that some differences were emerging between the members and the exchange itself. Also, as we describe in a later section, exchanges were interacting with a clientele becoming more diverse. Finally, exchanges were in need of financing investment in electronic trading systems. This is expensive technology, and it would require a for-profit company to be able to raise capital for sizeable investment expenditure in technology.

The transformation to for-profit company status led to the listing (and initial public offering) of stock exchange companies. By the year 2006 at least twenty exchanges had become for-profit, publicly owned companies, with their shares listed for trading.

This rapid organizational transformation of stock and derivative exchanges is unparalleled.[2] It is the manifestation of a number of innovations and deregulatory events that have taken place in recent decades. As a result, in 2006 approximately 70 percent of world stock market capitalization value was listed and traded on for-profit and publicly owned exchanges (Table 3.1, Column D, Line 2). Exchanges in the Western Hemisphere were leaders in this shift to for-profit status, but exchanges in Europe were quick to follow and are closing the gap.

In 2006 the market capitalization value of companies listed on the world's stock exchanges was in excess of $44 trillion (Table 3.1, Column D, Line 4). Of this, 47 percent was in Western Hemisphere located exchanges, and 31 percent in European, Middle Eastern and African located exchanges. Asia and Oceania

Table 3.1 World Stock Exchanges: Organizational Structure 2006 (Percentage and Amount of Stock Market Capitalization Value)

		A. Western Hemisphere	*B. Europe, Middle East, Africa*	*C. Asia, Oceania*	*D. World total*
1	Demutualized and not listed	5%	19%	55%	19%
2	Listed exchanges	94%	67%	26%	70%
3	Other	1%	14%	19%	11%
4	Market capitalization*	$20.7	$13.7	$10.0	$44.4
5	Percentage of aggregate	47%	31%	22%	100%

Source: R. Aggarwal and S. Dahiya, "Demutualization and Public Offerings of Financial Exchanges," *Journal of Applied Corporate Finance*, Summer 2006, p. 97.

Note

* Amounts in US$ trillions.

accounted for the remaining 22 percent of market capitalization value. The bulk (94 percent) of Western Hemisphere market capitalization was listed on for-profit exchanges. At the same time 67 percent of the market capitalization on exchanges in Europe, the Middle East, and Africa was on listed exchanges. The smallest percentage of market capitalization of companies traded on for-profit and listed exchanges is found in Asia and Oceania, 26 percent. On a worldwide basis, 70 percent of aggregate market capitalization of public companies was listed and traded on for-profit exchanges. Listed exchanges now dominate the financial landscape in terms of the market value of listed shares.

Early Consolidation

The decade of the 1990s witnessed rapid transformation among European financial exchanges. By 2001 six European exchanges had become for-profit and listed companies. The six North American exchanges that took on this status made this transformation in the period 2002–06. Similarly, the eight Asian exchanges that became for-profit and listed did so in the period 2000–05, somewhat ahead of their North American counterparts. In the following sections we describe the new organizational imperative and two significant and early exchange consolidations in Europe.

New Organizational Imperative

Demutualization of financial exchanges in the United States followed a similar process in other financial service sectors: insurance, savings banks, and savings and loans. By 1990 demutualization had swept across the American life insurance and savings bank sectors. This led to for-profit status and mergers between shareholder owned entities searching for ways to unlock greater value for owners. Financial exchanges were destined to carry out parallel changes in their structure.

First round consolidations between exchanges brought relatively small entities into a larger tent. This tent, or holding company, was larger, had greater financial capacity, and provided better diversification of listings and revenues. The initiative to consolidate, described below, was not a surprise. What was surprising was the high level of success achieved in these consolidations.

Euronext Consolidation

One of the earliest and most interesting mergers of financial exchanges was the formation of Euronext. During the decade of the 1990s considerable attention was given in Europe to the need for modernization and greater efficiency in equity trading. At least four broad motivations underscored the need for Continental Europe to consolidate its equity trading. First, the Big Bang in London had elevated the London Stock Exchange ahead of Continental bourses in competitive efficiency. Following Big Bang, trading of French, Belgian, and other Continent-based company shares had shifted to London, owing to lower commission and trading costs. Continental exchanges responded with their own Little Bangs over the period 1987–95, but also came to the realization that size and scale of market played a role in the competitive equation. These could be achieved by consolidation of Continent-based exchanges.

Second, the NYSE was attracting European blue chip listings, with share trading shifting to North America.[3] Third, the basic rationale of the European Union was to enhance the efficiency of resource allocation, especially productive capital. What better way to accomplish this than by strengthening the efficiency of stock exchanges via merger?

Finally, preparation for the coming of the single currency compelled European exchanges to analyze their own business models. This led to demutualization and, in the case of the German exchanges, a wholesale restructuring and consolidation in the period 1990–98. In this period the German exchange developed high technology trading platforms and established its own derivative exchange, eventually named Eurex. Aggressive action on the part of the Deutsche Börse compelled other European exchanges to follow suit.

By 2000 the initial steps to organize Euronext had been completed, leading to the Paris, Amsterdam, and Brussels exchanges consolidating into a unified entity. Four years later the LIFFE derivative exchange also became part of Euronext.

By 2005 Euronext could report a more diversified revenue mix. Revenues from derivatives trading was its largest revenue source (34.5 percent), followed by cash trading (22.4 percent) and information services (20.3 percent).[4]

The OMX Group

In 1998 the Stockholm SE and OM Group merged. This brought together the largest financial exchange in Scandinavia with a company possessing expertise in computerized trading systems. The merger brought the most advanced electronic trading capabilities into a system with high technology capabilities. By 2006 OMX Group was adding three Baltic exchanges to its trading system. In its 2005 annual report, OMX noted that its "strategy in the Baltic region is to minimize the differences between the three national exchanges and make these markets a clear and attractive part of OMX's Nordic Exchange offering." This included expanding liquidity and developing more uniform market trading. OMX owned the exchanges in Latvia, Estonia, and Lithuania, as well as the central securities depositories.[5]

By 2006 OMX Group could boast a number of technology breakthroughs spanning the globe. These included providing computer systems for Borsa Italiana's derivatives market, IDEM, since 1994. In this case OMX was supplying core systems infrastructure and surveillance. OMX also was assisting the recently established and rapidly growing International Securities Exchange (ISE) in its efforts to redefine US options trading. By 2006 ISE had grown to handle average daily volumes of 2.5 million contracts. Also, OMX was supporting the Saudi Stock Market, the largest in the Middle East. This service responsibility includes everything from design to implementation of the trading system in Saudi Arabia.[6]

In its 2007 annual report, OMX provides a detailed analysis of its vision for the future of its industry sector, and how global trends are influencing the strategy which it follows in running its business, to conform with these evolving patterns. Trading markets are viewed as becoming more regional than national, regulatory changes in Europe and elsewhere are creating new business opportunities, and technology has become a key ingredient for competitive success. Therefore, OMX is developing technology to best meet the changing trading patterns of clientele. The company is gearing itself in a way that allows it to serve markets that are becoming more interconnected and unified.[7]

Drivers of Change

The past three decades are marked by deregulation of stock exchanges, promoting greater competition in securities trading. In the United States the elimination of fixed commissions, referred to as May Day 1975 for the NYSE, and the Big Bang in London in 1986, increased the scope of this competition. While in 1970 virtually all trading in NYSE listed shares took place on the exchange's floor trading platform, currently trading in these shares has become fragmented. Alternative trading venues include internalized trades serviced by large securities broker-dealers and investment banks, trading on exchanges other than the one holding the primary listing, and trading on electronic computer networks (ECNs). In the following sections we consider the driving forces that explain the motives behind demutualization and the shift toward for-profit status. These include the changing clientele of exchanges, technology, and the creation of alternative trading systems.

Changing Clientele

The clientele of stock exchanges and derivative exchanges has become more diversified. With this change in clientele, exchanges have found it necessary to restructure, to give greater voice and control to particular clientele groups, and to shift toward a governance system that rebalances the power and expression of interest of different clientele. In the following we examine how the clientele of exchanges has fragmented, and how a new governance structure evolved to rebalance the needs, interests, and power of each segment of exchange clientele. Also, we pay close attention to the specific needs of other groups of clientele, including market facilitators, brokers and dealers, investors, companies listing their shares, and shareholders in publicly owned and listed financial exchanges (Table 3.3).

The Investor

A mutual organization, by the title, implies a close overlap and identity of interests. When stock exchanges were first established, members followed very similar objectives, facilitating trades for buyers and sellers of securities. In most cases traders of securities were well-to-do businessmen, but over time markets grew and the needs of buyers and sellers became more diverse. The democratization of investment and expansion of equity culture created different types of individual investors, including wealthy landowners seeking diversification, successful industrialists, robber barons wanting control, and relatively small middle class individuals with less sophisticated appetites for risk. In the postwar period following 1945, institutional investors became more important in the equity markets. The growth of defined benefit pension plans in the United States and United Kingdom, and the appearance of investment trusts in the UK and mutual funds in the US institutionalized the equity markets. Since 1960 institutional investors have become a dominant investment group.

The preceding does not give due consideration to the increased role of alternative forms of investment, which are more global in their focus and outreach. A McKinsey study published in 2007 notes sovereign wealth funds have become powerful investors across global markets. These funds are one element in what can be described as the "four power brokers," a term used in the McKinsey Report. The four include: Asian central banks, petrodollar investors, hedge funds, and private equity. Collectively these four amassed $8.4 trillion in assets in 2006.

Governments in the Middle East and Asia are channeling a large part of these assets through sovereign wealth funds, which we discuss in close detail in Chapter 11. All four of the power brokers lack transparency in their investing activities, and are enjoying high growth in assets available for investment. As we observe in Table 3.2, petrodollar assets represented the largest type power broker in 2006, with at least $3.7 trillion in assets managed. This category is projected to be overtaken by funds held by Asian central banks, and in 2012 the Asian funds should exceed $7 trillion. However, private equity managed assets are expected to grow at the highest rate, 270 percent in the period 2006–12 (Table 3.2).[8]

The McKinsey Report notes that more aggressive investment initiatives by the four groups into alternative assets could reshape patterns of world investment. It remains to be seen how the growing role of these four will alter the balance and composition of stock exchange clientele in the future.

Market Facilitators (Brokers and Dealers)

The preceding describes the growth, diversification, and fragmentation of investors who buy and sell equities on and off the exchanges. Now we examine market

Table 3.2 The Four Power Brokers—Assets Under Management (2006–12)

	2006	*2012*	*Percentage change*
Petrodollar assets	3.7	6.9	86%
Asian central banks	3.1	7.3	135%
Hedge funds	1.3	4.6	253%
Private equity	0.7	2.6	272%
Total	8.8	21.4	143%

Source: Joanna Chung, "Quartet of Global Interests That Are Reshaping Trends in Financial World," *Financial Times*, October 9, 2007, p. 27.

Note: Amounts in US$ trillions.

facilitators, brokers and dealers who represent the original clientele that organized to establish exchanges, with a strong mutuality of interest. Over the past quarter-century, investment banks have become transformed. The largest investment banks operate integrated and complex businesses, and introduce many different clients of their own onto trading markets. Often an investment bank will represent and service conflicting interests in the equity market. For example, an investment bank might operate as a broker on a given stock exchange, own shares in that exchange, own an ECN that competes against that exchange, and carry out internalized trading of shares listed on that exchange. Also, it may trade futures and options in substitution for the underlying equities it trades on the exchange or in internalized trading.

Clearly investment banks are competitive vis-à-vis financial exchanges, and this competitive relationship is intensifying. At the same time, investment banks and financial exchanges enjoy some community of interest. Investment banks conduct much of their business on financial exchanges and rely heavily on exchanges for valuation and price discovery, liquidity, and other necessary services.

Companies Listing Shares

Not all but an increasing number of exchanges benefit from cross-listing of shares. Earlier we described the services exchanges provide for shareholders and companies. Companies have become a key part of the increasingly complex clientele of financial exchanges.

Companies generally initiate a listing on their domestic stock exchange at a suitable point in their corporate finance evolution. Further along in time such companies may deem it important to cross-list these shares on a stock exchange located in another country. Companies based in emerging market countries must consider such cross-listings very carefully, since there are several benefits that can be derived from cross-listing. Benefits derived from cross-listing for companies in developed countries may differ from those gained by companies based in emerging market nations. The following describes these benefits without any commentary regarding whether they are more beneficial to companies based in developed or emerging market countries:

1 improved valuation and pricing;
2 a more liquid market;
3 the reputational benefit from listing on an exchange with well-regarded governance and regulatory standards;
4 the ability to use shares in mergers and acquisitions in the country where they are listed.

These advantages are valuable, especially in an era when companies based in emerging markets have taken on a more aggressive posture in their global plans and strategies.

Large exchanges based in key financial centers (New York and London) regard it as essential to attract foreign blue chip company listings. Alternately, special exchange platforms have been developed (AIM, London) to attract a different company clientele: smaller and more venture capital type listings.

As clients, companies have become more willing to cross-list on exchanges where they perceive big institutional investors may discover the benefits from holding their securities in diversified portfolios. However, big institutional investors have become more mobile, and are able and willing to execute trades on home markets of companies, especially if the trading market (or exchange) offers needed services (liquidity and low trading cost).

Shareholders of Exchanges

Shareholders of exchanges are the newest component of exchange clientele. They came into existence beginning in 1993, and have grown in number and sophistication. They have shared in the run of mergers between exchanges since 2000. Also, shareholders appear to be satisfied with the general performance of globally listed shares. Exchanges are almost completely devoid of debt, a condition most favorable to shareholders. Finally, as we note in detail in Chapter 4, financial exchanges enjoy a high degree of operating leverage. Consequently, a small increase in business volume translates into a magnified rise in profitability.

From One to Many

Financial exchanges are evolving, each at its own pace. As this evolutionary process moves forward, exchanges learn from one another and reach out to embrace and service new clientele. In Table 3.3 we present a simplified description of this dynamic process. Four stages of exchange evolution and related clientele changes are specified. We label the four stages as: 1) early stage operations, 2) mutual association, 3) demutualized company, and 4) for-profit shareholder owned. As exchanges evolve in this manner, they experience a parallel increase in the number of clientele groups which they must service.

Initially there is a single clientele, the broker-dealers who organize the exchange, each participant sensing a common interest. At this stage the primary objective is to facilitate efficient trading for members. As the exchange experiences a growth in the number of companies whose shares are listed and traded, retail investors come to play a more important role in the success of operations. The exchange now comes to realize that more investors can be attracted for trading as more companies become listed for trading. We now have a mutual association with at least three distinct clientele groups (Table 3.3).

Demutualized exchanges appear when institutional investors achieve an important trading position and foreign company listings are a growing source of listing and cash trading. For-profit shareholder owned status comes into play as the exchange recognizes the need to attract listings from foreign blue chip firms, and as the institutional trading base expands to include non-domestic traders, and active institutional traders such as hedge funds.

Table 3.3 Evolution in Stock Exchange Clientele

Early stage operations	*Mutual association*	*Demutualized company*	*For-profit shareholder owned company*
Broker-dealers	Broker-dealers Domestic companies Retail investors[1a]	Broker-dealers Domestic companies Retail investors[1b] Institutional investors[2] Foreign firms needing capital	Broker-dealers Domestic companies Retail investors Institutional investors[3] Foreign firms needing capital Foreign blue chips[4] Shareholders of exchanges Active traders[5] Far-flung investors[6]

Notes

1a The NYSE moved away from fixed commissions in 1975 following pressure from the SEC and concern over third market growth.

1b Big Bang at LSE in 1986 in part aimed at retail investors. SEAQ platform begins operation.

2 LSE established SETS platform, for faster and more cost efficient trading.

3 More exchanges view institutional investors as a logical clientele. They are moving toward trading systems that meet the needs of this demanding clientele group.

4 NYSE enjoyed patronage of blue chip company listings well before it demutualized. However, other exchanges now are finding it necessary to restructure to retain listings of local blue chip companies that have cross-listed on exchanges in major centers.

5 Active traders include hedge funds and other proprietary traders. These clients generate a growing share of market trading, on and off exchanges.

6 As more stock markets become part of the world stock exchange indices, they must be ready and able to service far-flung investors. More and more investors apply index approaches to investment and fund management.

As we note in Table 3.3, leading financial exchanges now regard as their clientele a wide range of investors, companies listing shares, and other exchange participants. As a result the exchange must adapt under a business model that facilitates better servicing of this diverse clientele. We analyze these changes in exchange business models in the following chapters.

Technology

Over the past two decades high tech trading systems have impacted financial markets in a big way and continue to do so. These impacts are particularly significant for financial exchanges in at least three contexts. First, they create systems delivering trading improvements related to cost, speed of execution, and anonymity. Second, they shift the balance between fixed and variable costs at exchanges. Finally, they ultimately determine where or on what market venues trading takes place.

It is clear that the move toward automated, computer-style trading of stocks and other securities requires that exchanges increase fixed costs related to purchase and installation of computer systems, and reduce variable (labor) costs. Consequently, financial exchanges have experienced a rise in operating leverage. This rise in operating leverage mandates that exchanges find ways to expand trading volume and revenues. This elevates the incentives for new product development and consolidation.

Systems Development

If in the year 2000 you had been asked "Where can I trade a large company common stock?" you might have had the following possibilities:

1 on the primary listing market for the company shares;
2 on a regional stock exchange;
3 on electronic trading systems (some of the most important at that time were Instinet, Island, Archipelago, Bloomberg Tradebook, and POSIT);
4 on the so-called third market, where large dealers make markets;
5 on the equities block trading market;
6 on large non-US stock exchanges;
7 on options exchanges, including the CBOE, the American Stock Exchange, and the Philadelphia Stock Exchange;
8 on futures markets or exchanges, in the form of indexes on well-known baskets such as the S&P 500;
9 at investment banks that write tailored synthetic derivative contracts for clients.

Alternative trading systems (ATSs) have been growing in number and variety for over two decades. While not long ago traders bemoaned the lack of alternatives to NYSE and NASDAQ, currently there exist several dozen exchanges, ECNs, and alternative trading systems through which to route orders. Many of these ATSs are known as ECNs. Generally, these are order-driven securities trading systems that are not regulated or treated as exchanges. They may be owned by brokerage firms, dealers, or large investment banks. ECNs that have become important market venues include Instinet, Island, Archipelago, and Bloomberg Tradebook. Island and other ECNs have become successful in providing an electronic limit order book for equity securities traded on NASDAQ's electronic quote driven system, but less successful in competing for NYSE listed company equity trading. Often ECNs such as Archipelago charge different fees for market orders and limit orders. While these fees are paid by the brokers routing orders to the ECN, the differential will be reflected in commissions that traders pay for different types of executed orders.

Crossing networks are order driven markets that do not function as auction markets. In a crossing network trades take place at prices determined in other markets that trade the same instruments. These networks do not discover prices. Rather, the network discovers whether traders are willing to buy or sell at the crossing prices. Important crossing networks in the US include POSIT, Instinet's Global Instinet Crossing, and the NYSE After Hours Crossing session. Crossing networks often are referred to as dark pools, discussed in a following section.

Servicing Institutional Needs

Institutional investors have grown to dominate securities trading. A typical institutional investor probably needs to buy or sell no less than $10 million of any equity security it includes in its portfolio. If average daily trading of this stock is 16,000 shares, and the stock is priced at $40, average daily turnover is $640,000, only 6.4 percent of the typical institutional trade. To accumulate the $10 million investment position requires getting around several hurdles. These include: 1) adverse price impact on the market from placing large orders, 2) elevating price volatility and trading cost spreads, and 3) possibly revealing the buyer's (or seller's) identity, leading to more difficult trading. No single market structure is ideal in all circumstances. Therefore, to improve execution and lower transaction costs, institutional investors use a variety of ATSs, which provide complementary execution venues to traditional exchanges. Some pay liquidity providers (order flow consisting of limit orders) and charge liquidity takers (market orders). Others utilize prices on exchanges to negotiate crossings. Still others bring institutional traders together who want to trade a given security (Liquidnet).

Liquidnet is an institutional equity broker that operates an electronic ATS. Clients interface their orders into Liquidnet, which brings buyer and seller for a given stock into a negotiation regarding price. If they agree to price and quantity, they report the trade to Liquidnet, which then crosses the trade, so that neither trader ever knows the identity of the other party. At one point Liquidnet was charging each trader two cents per share commission. Liquidnet Trading is completely confidential, and traders do not need to submit orders to it.[9]

US Treasuries Go Electronic

Some of the best success in electronic trading has been in US Treasury securities. The proportion of institutions trading Treasuries electronically grew to 65 percent in 2006, and the proportion of their trading executed electronically advanced to 35 percent. This is based on data provided by Greenwich Associates.[10]

Overall, screen based trading in bonds has enjoyed only patchy success. In Europe, government bonds also are frequently traded on-screen. However, in the less actively traded sectors of the bond market (corporates and municipals), barely one-quarter of trades are done electronically. Less liquid sectors still are traded on opaque, over the counter markets. Here dealers are "market makers" and investors are "market takers."

The largest stakeholders in the bond market have few incentives to move to electronic trading with price transparency and a more level playing field. Dealers do not want to give up lucrative franchises that bankroll global operations. Buy-side firms are satisfied with the status quo, and regulatory officials tend to address only highly visible issues.

An example of how brokers have capitulated to a slow pace of change in the United States is the merger of credit derivatives interdealer brokers Creditex and Creditrade in 2006. Created in 1999, Creditex is entrenched as a leading electronic platform for credit derivatives in the European market, whereas Creditrade operates a larger business in North America and Asia. The merger combined Creditex's strength in electronic trading with Creditrade's strength in voice brokering of the securities indices. The combined group now is able to handle transactions entirely electronically.

The piece-by-piece shift toward electronic bond trading has left an opening for traditional exchanges. What is required is a platform dedicated to fixed income instruments. Existing electronic platforms servicing trading of US Treasuries, and the European MTS platform which is part of the London Stock Exchange and Borsa Italiana Group also offer such possibilities.

Dark Pools and Multilateral Trading Facilities

In October 2007 *Business Week* published an article "Big Traders Dive Into Dark Pools." This article noted that large institutional traders obtained a range of benefits from these venues, including low transaction cost, anonymity, and fast execution. Shortly after, the *Financial Times* ran a story "Banks Begin to Dip Into Dark Pools," commenting on the competitive challenges facing stock exchanges. Dark pools, or alternative trading systems, are unique in that they do not display quotes in a traditional manner. The price on a trade taking place on a dark pool is determined in the US by the National Market Bid–Offer spread, with execution taking place in the dark.[11]

Dark Pools

Dark pools are crossing networks that provide large institutional investors with the ability to trade anonymously, quickly, and at relatively low cost (Table 3.4). They have become an important competitive challenge for exchanges, and in some respects a pace-setter in equities trading. In the short period 2002–08 the number of such pools multiplied to forty in North America and at least a half-dozen in Europe. Writing in 2008, Mittal projected that by 2010 trading volume would

Table 3.4 Advantages Offered by Dark Pools to Institutional Traders

Benefit provided	*Components of benefit*	*Comments*
1 Anonymity	a. Limits information leakage. b. Allows repetitive transactions.	Minimize or delay any impact on trading price.
2 Speedy execution	a. Trade ahead of market impacts. b. Maintain asymmetric knowledge edge.	Large orders need more time for full execution. Difficult to prevent information leakage in case of large orders.
3 Low cost	a. Efficient system and trading engine. b. Fee structure rewards liquidity provider.	With high fixed costs, volume becomes important driver of cost reduction.

reach 1.5 billion shares, with a growth rate of 40 percent.[12] Dark pools service a range of trading participants, including well-informed and other institutions, retail investors, proprietary traders, and others. These pools enable market participants to engage in block trading and high frequency trading.

Dark pools have multiplied in number and importance for several reasons. These include: the growth of proprietary algorithmic trading; the fragmentation of order flow and competition to rebuild liquidity pools; and the desire of investment banks to expand into areas formerly held by financial exchanges and to create trading platforms that respond to the specific needs of institutional investors.

Late in 2007 the NYSE announced it would invest in a joint venture with BIDS, another dark pool. In this case NYSE's spillover order flow would be able to interact with the BIDS dark pool. Dark pools clearly present a threat, but perhaps also an opportunity, for exchanges. Earlier in 2007 Catherine Kinney, president of the NYSE, stated at a Securities Industry Association conference that shares crossed in the dark do not assist the market in determining a fair or accurate price. Only auction type markets can generate or find that fair price.

Regulatory initiatives have prompted dark pool expansion. The number of new dark pools operated by securities brokers reflects their ability to improve execution quality, reduce exchange fees, and increase commissions. Regulation NMS promulgated by the SEC in 2005 went into effect in late 2007. Its Equal Access Rule assures traders equal access to markets, and its Order Protection Rule prohibits trade-throughs of displayed, automated, and accessible quotations. The latter requires all market participants (including broker-dealers) to establish, maintain, and enforce written policies and procedures. Trade-throughs are purchases or sales of stock (during regular trading hours) at a price outside of the protected bid and ask spread.

The emergence of dark pools allows market participants to execute large blocks of shares in sizeable chunks at currently prevailing prices. This adds value to traders facing rapidly changing market conditions. The cost is fragmented execution and the related charges for using dark pools.

Multilateral Trading Facilities

Since 2006 a new form of ECN, multilateral trading facilities (MTFs), has emerged. These electronic trading platforms are owned and operated by groups of investment banks and hedge funds. Chi-X, an MTF launched early in 2007 by a group of banks, was reported early in 2008 to have taken 11 percent of LSE's market share in large stocks, and a very large percentage (31 percent) of trading in Cadbury.[13] Several new MTFs were scheduled to compete for LSE trading (late 2008 and early 2009). These include: BATS, Project Turquoise, and a pan-European platform from NASDAQ OMX.

BATS was organized in 2005 and initiated its services in 2006. It provides electronic order matching at low cost. BATS has been successful by creating a trading system that extends across several parallel matching engines. It continually re-engineers the platform, to respond to changing requirements and to ensure growth capacity. BATS constantly defines new order types and routing strategies.

BATS' success is based on being faster and offering cost and rebate incentives, customized services, and innovative billing. The BATS system measures order responsiveness in milliseconds (1/1,000 of a second). BATS pays liquidity adders and charges liquidity takers. These charges are adjusted flexibly to balance growth and liquidity consolidation. Innovative billing compensates liquidity adders on a weekly basis, not monthly. In 2008 BATS announced plans to convert to a financial exchange status. This status was realized early in 2009.

In 2008 BATS was matching a high percentage (82–87 percent) of orders on large cap stocks such as Microsoft, Cisco, and Dell (Table 3.5). Also, it accounted for 10–12 percent of trading in these equities.

No Two Are Alike

Dark pools vary in type and characteristics. We describe four types in Table 3.6:

1 public crossing networks;
2 internalization pools;
3 exchange based pools;
4 consortium based pools.

Public crossing networks are the longest operating, most launched by agency brokerages to generate commission revenues. These pools do not enjoy proprietary flow from the pool operator (Table 3.6, Line II). In each case a successful operating model assures generous liquidity flow. The oldest of these (POSIT, Liquidnet) hold a large institutional client base and can afford the luxury of steering away from commodity pricing (Table 3.6, Line III).

Generally these pools are continuous crossing markets, with buy and sell orders executed at a system midpoint price. Orders are not displayed, assuring anonymity and low and delayed information leakage, and avoiding or at least delaying market impact trading costs (Table 3.6, Lines IV–V).

Table 3.5 BATS' Performance in Selected Large Cap Stocks (January 2008)

Equity share	*BATS percentage matched*[1]	*BATS percentage of market traded*[2]
Microsoft	86.5	12.2
Oracle	87.9	12.1
Cisco	86.8	11.6
Dell	82.3	10.5
Yahoo	86.3	10.4

Source: BATS Trading.

Notes

1 Percentage of BATS volume matched on BATS book for respective security.

2 Percentage of total market volume traded at BATS for respective security, including matched and routed volume.

Table 3.6 Four Types of Dark Pools and Their Main Characteristics

Type pool	*1. Public crossing network*	*2. Internalization pool*	*3. Exchange based pool*	*4. Consortium based pool*
I Ownership	Agency brokerages	Bulge bracket broker-dealers	Financial exchanges	Consortiums of bulge bracket broker-dealers
II Type trading participants	Customer	Customer	Customer, proprietary trader	Customer, investor, and proprietary trader
III Pricing	Low to high	Low to medium	High	Low
IV Reason for creation	Generate commissions	Cost reduction,	Generate commissions, alpha generation	Generate commissions and order flow
V Main pools	POSIT, Pipeline, Liquidnet	Credit Suisse Crossfinder, UBS Pin, Goldman Sachs Sigma X	NYSE MatchPoint, NASDAQ Cross, Direct Edge	BIDS LEVEL

Source: Adapted from H. Mittal, "Are You Playing in a Toxic Dark Pool?" *Journal of Trading*, Summer 2008, pp. 20–33.

Internalization pools are more recent, and are designed to internalize trading flow for the broker-dealer. Goldman Sachs's Sigma X was one of the earliest. While originally designed to internalize trade flow and lower cost, most subsequently competed for both buy-side and sell-side business. Internalization pools differ from public crossing networks, enjoying a trade flow consisting of retail customer orders, institutional order flow, and proprietary flow. Incentives are broader, including cost savings, alpha generation (from interacting with proprietary flow), and commissions generated from offering dark pool liquidity to buy-side traders. Further, brokerage services can be more easily marketed to buy-side institutions.

Exchange based pools include two sub-categories: dark pools registered as market platforms by regulated exchanges (such as NYSE MatchPoint and NASDAQ Cross), and hidden pools (Table 3.6, Line V). Hidden pools contain hidden order liquidity supported by trading of ECNs and exchanges. Pricing on exchange registered pools is similar to other dark pools, on a per-share basis. Pricing on hidden order pools is based on a supplier–taker model, more typical on exchanges and ECNs. The customer receives a rebate for supplying liquidity, and pays (more than the rebate) a fee when taking liquidity. Hidden orders can interact with regular displayed orders.

Consortium based pools are owned and operated by groups of bulge bracket broker-dealers. Mittal characterizes these as a hybrid mix of public crossing networks and internalization pools. They tend to offer a more transparent business model, and are available to all sell-side firms. These pools often serve as a second-step venue, following the broker-dealer's first attempt to utilize its own internalization pool. Therefore, these pools may lack the first-step liquidity enjoyed by internalization pools.

How They Operate

Dark pools are so named because of the widespread belief they do not leak order information. These pools are expected to not make order information available to the general marketplace. This is achieved when order flow is not displayed. But, with execution, some market signals may become accessible to those in search of trading information.

When a trader "hits the tape" other traders become aware that an order (or partial order) has been placed into the flow and traded. Is there more, and how much more, of that order? Characteristically, dark pool orders are broken down over time and into smaller trading lots. For example, an original order to sell 100,000 shares of a given stock may be broken into four separate orders of 25,000 shares, to be placed as orders every twenty minutes. Further, each of these separate orders may be broken down into five smaller lots of 5,000 shares each. If the first lot of 5,000 shares is traded, and a four-minute interval exists to the second lot, the question becomes "What is the residual order size?" Smart traders engage in fishing, to deduce residual order flow information.

Information leakage may occur in the case of advertisement based public crossing networks. These pools place controls on information, reducing access to certain types of customers. Information flow in dark pools can be asymmetric, where one trader sends an order to the pool and the entire order information is made available to another trader (on the other side of the market) in a black box.

In general, execution prices in dark pools come from the national open market. Midpoint (of bid–ask spread) pricing is used. This supports the expectation that price impact trading costs tend to be low or non-existent (Table 3.4). However, hidden orders can result in execution away from the midpoint price. Further, information leakage can affect order execution in several ways. A price impact can exist when the dark pool moves away from the order. Some traders may game the system with information about order flow. Finally, adverse selection can operate when the order execution is conditioned on how the stock price moves.

Dark pools service a wide range of customer types. These range from the limited information customer (some buy-side institutions and retail investors), in which case the "other side of the trade" enjoys an excellent opportunity to trade without problems, to the dark pool trader or proprietor, which may be servicing trades of the broker-dealer, which could lead to bad trading outcomes.

Dark pool aggregators offer institutional investors a one-stop service, linked to other dark pools, much like internet search engines. One-Pipe, an aggregator launched in 2008 through a joint venture between Weeden & Co., a brokerage firm, and Pragma Financial, a New York financial software provider, gives access to twenty-five dark pools. Similarly, Liquidnet's H20 dark pool is open to outside orders. NASDAQ initiated routing orders to a number of dark pools, allowing the exchange to participate in trades shifting to other market venues.[14]

Regulatory Oversight

In 2009 regulatory bodies were giving dark pools increased attention. Several concerns enter into this increased attention by regulators, including fair and equal treatment for all investors, and proper functioning of markets.

Mary Schapiro, SEC chairwoman, has asked her staff to investigate the impact of dark pool trading venues that do not display quotes and their trading data to the public. A lack of transparency could undermine public confidence in the capital markets. Schapiro stated that the SEC is considering what regulatory action may be warranted to ensure adequate investor protection and better market integrity.[15]

Analysts observe that the lack of information concerning trades executed in dark pools could promote speculation about market price movements. Defenders of dark pools hold that large institutions are the dominant market participants in these pools, and their need to trade large blocks of shares can be best served in this type of market venue. While large orders are sliced into smaller, easier to execute trades in dark pools, a similar process has been going on at exchanges. The average size of a trade on the New York Stock Exchange is 300 shares. However, before being sliced, a typical order on a dark pool could be as large as 50,000 shares.[16] A large order coming into the order book of an exchange immediately is visible to rival traders, putting the trade in jeopardy. That is why, in dark pools, prices are visible only to traders participating in the dark pool trading system. Alfred Eskandar, a director at Liquidnet, notes that the initial purpose of dark pools was to protect a dark order from predatory traders.

SEC concerns extend to a potential diversion of liquidity away from stock exchanges so large it would be difficult for ordinary investors to determine whether the prices they observe on traditional exchanges are truly representative. At mid-year 2009 less than 9 percent of US equities trades were done on dark pools.

A Model of Stock Exchange Growth

Stock exchanges are a product of their economic system, financial market structure, and national wealth culture. Development of each nation's stock market has followed a unique course, dictated by factors described below.

Country Factors

A country's economic system can vary between capitalist, socialist, and some in-between status. Most capitalist systems foster public ownership of companies, facilitating external financing. Alternate forms of company ownership, for example family controlled and owned firms, are important in many European and Asian countries.

Financial markets supply equity and debt capital to companies operating in growth sectors of the economy. By definition, public ownership allows open capital markets to supply funds to finance the growth of companies.

The national wealth culture plays an important role by setting standards of performance which are used by owners of securities. We can label this set of performance standards the "equity culture." Before the single currency (the euro) appeared in Europe in 1999, many countries (Germany, Italy) possessed only a limited equity culture. Since 1999, the equity culture in these nations has grown steadily, motivated by wider interest in investing in common stock and mutual funds, and through more active trading of government bonds on European financial markets.

Financial market structures are important to stock market evolution. Key features include the existence of alternative trading channels such as ECNs, and availability of derivatives trading, in lieu of trading the underlying securities.

In the following we present a simplified model that explains the growth of stock exchange turnover within a national market structure.

Determinants of Turnover

Most stock exchanges derive a considerable portion of their operating revenues from equity trading. In Chapter 4 we analyze and compare revenue composition from trading and other sources for twelve leading exchanges around the world. Here we present a model that highlights the role of the key factors driving turnover levels in different stock markets.

Basic Model of Turnover

As we observe in Table 3.7, turnover is a function of three distinct factors: 1) number of shares listed, 2) valuation of shares, and 3) the intensity of trading. The number of shares listed is the sum of domestic shares and foreign shares listed.

Share valuation depends on two different sets of factors. First is the level of free cash flows companies can generate now and expected into the future period. But equally important are the qualitative and risk factors surrounding how these cash flows are generated, reported, and utilized. Underlying the qualitative considerations are how well corporate governance is executed by company directors and executives, transparency as reflected by financial and other disclosures regarding company activities, and the efficiency of overall company management as earnings and cash flows are reinvested to fund expansion and strengthen competitiveness.

Table 3.7 Determinants of Stock Exchange Turnover

1	Turnover (trading volume)	=	No. of shares listed	×	Valuation (price)	×	Intensity of trading
2	No. of shares listed	=	No. of domestic shares listed	+	No. of foreign shares listed		
3	Valuation is a function of (governance, liquidity, transparency, and efficiency) and corporate cash flow						
4	Intensity of trading	=	Percentage of market capitalization traded	=	$\frac{\text{Turnover value}}{\text{Market capitalization value}}$		

Finally, intensity of trading measures the turnover ratio on a given stock exchange. Trading intensity varies directly with the monetary value of turnover, and inversely with market capitalization (Table 3.7). In effect, turnover answers the question "On average, how many times was each stock traded over the past year?"

Domestic and Foreign Share Listings

Domestic company share listings result from broad economic and socio-political forces that control the balance between private (family) ownership, state ownership, and public ownership. The proportional content of these three types of ownership varies widely from country to country. In Table 3.8 we present estimates of ownership patterns for several selected countries. The first column presents stock market capitalization as a percentage of GDP. The US and UK exhibit relatively high ratios, reflecting an ownership system favoring publicly owned (listed) companies. State ownership has not been important in the United States. In the United Kingdom state ownership expanded in the decades following World War II, but during the Thatcher period (1979 onward) state ownership was reduced with large scale privatizations.

Germany and Italy offer a sharp contrast, with low ratios of public ownership (41 percent and 43 percent of GDP respectively). The Mittelstand occupies a large component of Germany's industrial sector, accounting for 98 percent of German companies, hiring 80 percent of employees, and responsible for a significant share of exports.[17] Privately owned, the Mittelstand companies offer potential stock market expansion, should a number of these opt for public ownership status.

Italy also reports low stock market capitalization relative to GDP, but for reasons somewhat different from those applicable to the case of Germany. First, Italy has endured a long period of state ownership of a significant share of its industrial

Table 3.8 Stock Market Capitalization as Percentage of GDP (2005–06), and Estimated Value of State Owned Enterprises and Privately Owned Enterprises (Percentage of GDP)

	Stock market capitalization as percentage of GDP	*Value of state owned plus privately owned companies as percentage of GDP*
United States	126	74
Germany	41	159
Italy	43	157
Japan	96	104
United Kingdom	126	74
China	29	171
Brazil	53	147
India	62	138
Switzerland	221*	

Source: Author's estimates.

Note

* The high valuation of 221 percent is due to extensive international operations of many publicly owned Swiss companies, particularly in food processing, confectionery, pharmaceuticals, and banking.

base. This operated in the interwar years (1920s and 1930s) and persisted long after World War II. At one point state ownership exceeded 60 percent of the productive economy. Preparation for entry into the single currency, and European Union competition policies led to privatization of a number of sectors, including energy and telecoms.

Italy provides a unique ownership condition owing to the size distribution of enterprises. A bimodal distribution reflects a large concentration of small size firms (family owned) and a smaller number (but important because of size) of large companies. The large companies are: 1) publicly owned and listed, and 2) state owned enterprises. The lack of midsize companies reflects a weakness in the Italian business system for growing companies through the so-called corporate finance life cycle. In turn, this translates into a gap at the venture capital stage of development.

In July 2005 the Italian Ministry of Economics and Finance carried out an offering of 9.5 percent of the electric utility ENEL, raising $4.9 billion. Four months later the state controlled Alitalia launched a company reorganization, with a rights offering that raised $1.25 billion. These transactions were the culmination of a twelve-year privatization program of seventy-five major deals that raised over $125 billion. Included in these transactions were Telecom Italia, ENI, Banca di Roma, Banca Nazionale del Lavoro, and Autostrade.

The privatization program had a massive impact on the market capitalization and trading volume of Italy's stock and bond markets. Market capitalization on Borsa Italiana grew from less than $150 billion in 1992 to over $770 billion at yearend 2000, and $800 billion in 2005. The number of listed companies on the Borsa Italiana rose by one-third. An even larger gain was recorded in stock market trading volume. In the period 1992–2005 the value of shares traded rose from under $100 billion to $1,300 billion. Privatized firms accounted for 41 percent of market capitalization, and 33 percent of trading volume in 2002.[18]

The second column in Table 3.8 reflects the "estimated" value of state owned plus privately owned companies relative to GDP. The reader can observe that for each country the two column numbers aggregate to 200 percent, a proxy for the "value" of all enterprises in the productive sector, irrespective of ownership. The exception is Switzerland, where a number of Swiss multinational companies generate enormous revenues on a worldwide basis. Hence, their valuations far exceed the capacity of the domestic economy.

Cross-Listing

Stock exchanges gain listings when non-domestic companies decide to cross-list their shares on the domestic exchange. During the past two decades we can observe a significant rise in this phenomenon. The basic reasons for cross-listing are complex, and are discussed in detail in Chapter 4.

Several stock exchanges have gained significant increases in listings from foreign companies listing their shares. These include NYSE, the Luxembourg Stock Exchange, the London Stock Exchange, and the Singapore Exchange.

De-equitization

An increasing phenomenon in world equity markets is de-equitization. De-equitization is a reduction in shares outstanding and trading in the market, which results from several different trends. These include private equity buyouts which convert publicly owned companies to private ownership, and company share repurchases. Both can lead to significant withdrawals of shares from the available supply trading in public markets.

The value of companies taken private experienced a strong uptrend in the period 2003–06, reaching close to $150 billion in 2006. The New York and London stock markets felt the brunt of this process. In 2006 the New York Stock Exchange saw a net withdrawal of listed capital of $38.8 billion, while NASDAQ suffered a net withdrawal of $11 billion.[19]

A report in the *Wall Street Journal* described the possible disappearance of US companies from public markets, given the amount of money used in share repurchases. According to the report, in 2007 Exxon repurchased $31.8 billion of its shares, five times the amount spent in 2003. This helped raise earnings per share, as the number of shares outstanding declined. Overall earnings exceeded $40 billion in 2007. The report noted that, if Exxon continued its buyback program, its last share of publicly traded stock would disappear in fifteen years. Clearly, buybacks constrain stock exchange growth, and could diminish market capitalization if they persisted at high levels.

The London Stock Exchange outperformed nearly every other financial exchange in 2006 in IPO activity. While the LSE experienced substantial delistings in this period, the value of LSE new listings was more than double its de-equitizations. London relies on foreign business. Nevertheless, a Citigroup analysis shows the LSE shrinking about 3 percent in 2006, as a result of company share buybacks and buyouts, something not seen previously.

Regional differences are important when we analyze de-equitization. Continental stock exchanges (Euronext and Deutsche Börse) bucked the de-equitization trend. In 2006 some $24.5 billion was raised through fifty-three equity issues on Paris-based Euronext, 60 percent more than the previous year. IPOs on Deutsche Börse totaled thirty-nine, raising $8.5 billion. Both exchanges enjoyed sustained growth in IPOs over the three years ending 2006. Privatization has helped boost this IPO activity.[20]

Also, global IPO volume ($123 billion in 2006) underlines the growing importance of China and Russia. Companies in these countries were responsible for $65 billion of IPOs in 2006, with virtually no offsetting buyout activity. Russian and Chinese companies are much like American companies thirty to forty years earlier. They hold enormous IPO scale and potential. Continued high GDP growth and profitable operations translate into expanding equity market capitalization.

By contrast, in the US and UK private equity has at times become a dominant force. Private equity funds can find value where the public equity markets cannot. It is possible that extended high levels of buyout transactions will yield persistently high amounts of de-equitization in US equity markets. Growth in company share repurchases and leveraged buyouts may pose challenges for the future status of exchanges. De-equitization is only a recent phenomenon; nevertheless it could become an important issue facing financial exchanges in the future.

Where Is Equity Trading?

In this section we explore growth trends in equity trading, capacity across alternative trading venues, and related shifts in the locus of equity trading. To analyze equity trading capacity, it is important to consider services offered by an enlarged equity trading complex. This equity trading complex consists of several distinct instruments, each offering different risk, cost of trading, and style of investing characteristics. Below we describe how the equity trading complex has become much larger and more diversified.

The changes described here result from emergence of new investor types, whose needs with respect to trading risk and cost vary considerably. For example, pension funds and other institutions are shifting their equity exposure to better capture alpha, using swaps and futures. Meanwhile, hedge funds steadily increase their use of derivatives to reinforce short-lived investor positions. Seeking cost efficiency, individual investors are shifting to index products offering low cost tradability, such as ETFs. Meanwhile, the expansion of quantitative strategies has increased activity levels in portfolio trading. Access to lower cost electronic execution allows faster and higher turnover.

Equity trading has become more complex, owing in part to the more diverse service needs of market participants. Also, the availability of alternative equity type instruments allows traders to blend risk and hedging positions, as well as seek faster or more anonymous trading methods. As we observe below, only part of trading activity takes place on listed stock exchanges.[21]

Relative Growth of Equity Products

Over the period 1997–2006 the growth in trading equity products on exchanges was 294 percent (Table 3.9). This includes: shares, futures, ETFs, and index options. This compares with growth in trading shares of only 173 percent. While share trad-

Table 3.9 Global Equity Product Volume, 1997–2006 (Daily Average in US$ Billions)

	1997	*2002*	*2006*	*Percentage growth 1997–2006*
Stocks	48	100	131	173%
Index futures	61	97	273	347%
ETFs	0.4	7	29	314%*
Index options	22	20	86	291%
Total	131.4	224	519	294%

Source: J.M. Hill, "Equity Trading Capacity Revisited: Growth, Fragmentation, and Fluidity," *Journal of Trading*, Spring 2007, p. 23.

Note
* Covers growth in the 2002–06 period only.

ing represented $48 billion (36 percent of overall equity trading) in 1997, by 2006 it had receded in importance to $131 billion or 25–26 percent of overall equity trading (Table 3.9). Derivatives and ETFs represent a growing share of exchange trading of equity products. Further, the growth in OTC equity trading indicates that the ratio of equity derivatives to stock trading was approaching 4 to 1 in 2006.

Table 3.9 exhibits the average daily trading volume of shares, options, ETFs, and index futures on global exchanges over the period 1997 to 2006. As can be observed, in 2006 listed equity volume exceeded $519 billion a day, shares representing approximately one-fourth of this. Only four years earlier (2002) the total activity level for equity products was slightly over $220 billion a day, with shares representing close to half of the total. Further, the velocity of equity markets has surged, providing liquidity needed for hedging as well as basic trading and investor positioning.

Derivatives markets reinforce liquidity, functioning as a means of hedging risk for liquidity providers. Over the past decade stock market liquidity has been expanded from several sources, including global index futures and index options. Over the decade to 2006, stock trading has doubled as a percentage of market capitalization, but futures trading value has more than tripled, representing a substantial increment to liquidity and risk management capacity.

Equity Derivatives and ETFs

The surge in equity derivative trading followed a four-year equity bear market, and the realization by asset managers that they needed new methods of structuring investment strategies. This would include greater use of technology and quantitative tools. Hill pinpoints the key factors driving these innovations in equity strategy and use of derivatives and other equity products:[22]

1 Trading beta directly as a distinct component of equity. This is associated with intensified interest in separating alpha skill from beta exposures. This results in using derivatives to establish long and short exposure in indexes. Further, hedge funds which are total return oriented have been growing their assets, and employing derivatives to implement view-based strategies.
2 Growth in shorting and hedging equity risk. Derivatives are traditional tools for risk reduction. Hedge funds actively employ long–short strategies, and pensions have taken on larger components of equity risk. Index products and basket trades now are widely used in risk control.
3 Shift to electronic trading and quantitative investment strategies. Increased access to lower cost electronic trading, and employment of quantitative trading tools have increased turnover and desire to capitalize on smaller price movements. This represents a partial shift away from fundamentally based and toward portfolio and electronic trading techniques.

Associated with these drivers are falling trading costs, greater competition, and lower market volatility. This has fostered use of higher turnover strategies using algorithms and quantitative tools. Further, more traders follow shorter horizons in benchmarking returns and in adjusting strategies.

Dealers view their equity risk exposure in aggregate. Global equity trading positions now are both long and short. Also, leverage is more commonly accepted. Finally, trading positions can be more balanced in size.

An Evolving Equity Trading System

We now enjoy a range of equity products that increasingly serve as substitutes for one another. As substitutes, these products take on increasingly interrelated pricing dynamics. As a result, market makers can more easily experiment and add new products to their technology platforms, at lower marginal cost.

This is evidenced with respect to financial exchanges. The shares representing ownership of financial exchanges have enjoyed significant price appreciation over the period 2006–08. Also, mergers between these exchanges are clear examples of profit-seeking on their part, via tapping into the demand for additional sources and types of liquidity: hence the mergers of NYSE and Euronext, NASDAQ and OMX, LSE and Borsa Italiana, and CME and CBOT.

Regional Comparisons

Regional comparisons provide useful insights concerning the relative development and diversity of the equity product complex. Table 3.10 summarizes the

Table 3.10 Global Equity Product Volume by Region, 2006 (Daily Average in US$ Billions)

	United States	*Europe*	*Pacific*	*Emerging*	*Total*
A	Daily average				
Stocks	$73	$33	$25		$131
Index futures	119	103	51	10	283
ETFs	28	0.8	0.3		29.1
Index options	49	28	9		86
Total	269	164.8	85.3	10	529.1
B	As percentage of total region				
Stocks	27.1%	20.0%	29.3%		
Index futures	44.3	62.4	59.9		
ETFs	10.4	0.7	0.3		
Index options	18.2	16.9	10.5		
Total	100	100	100		
C	As percentage of equity type				
Stocks	56%	25%	19%		100%
Index futures	43	37	18	2	100
ETFs	96	3	1		100
Index options	57	33	10		100

Source: J.M. Hill, "Equity Trading Capacity Revisited: Growth, Fragmentation, and Fluidity," *Journal of Trading*, Spring 2007, p. 23.

size and composition of the equity product complex in four regions of the world. Clearly, the United States dominates in all four components. The US is the only region with a well-developed ETF component.

The United States has a clear lead in stock and index option trading. However, Europe is close behind the US in index futures, and the Pacific region enjoys a sizeable volume of index futures as well. Index futures represents the solitary area in which emerging markets exhibit a high development and share of world trading. Finally, the lower absolute and relative status of index options reflects differential cost structures. Europe has much catching up to accomplish in stocks trading.

4 Business Models

In the preceding chapter we described how powerful forces have exposed financial exchanges to rising competition. In this chapter we examine financial exchanges more closely, and consider main features of their business models including profitability, sources of revenue, their geographic reach, and post-trade services. Also, we compare and contrast the basic types of financial exchanges.

Why Business Models are Important

In the past financial exchanges enjoyed the luxury of operating fairly simple business models. With a fairly homogeneous clientele requiring efficient execution and transparency, and the ability to concentrate trading on a single platform, stock exchanges enjoyed a semi-monopolistic position within a large comfort zone. In Table 4.1, we label this phase the public utility period. This contrasts with the current situation, where a diverse clientele is more demanding of improved services,

Table 4.1 Evolution of Business Models at Financial Exchanges

Time period	*Phase*	*Clientele needs and exchange initiatives*	*Main characteristics of securities trading*
1 Prior to 1970	Public utility	Stable.	Fixed commissions.
2 1970–90	Competitive	Exchanges undergoing Big Bang and other changes.	Flexible commissions, declining transaction costs, growth of third market trading.
3 1990–2005	Demutualization and for-profit status	Demutualize, shift to for-profit status.	Growing mobility and diversity of clientele. Growth in rival ECNs. Focus on trading speed and anonymity.
4 2005 onward	Consolidation	Use of mergers and acquisitions, and alliances.	Fragmentation of equity trading. Growing role of debt and derivative trading, algorithmic trading.

Note: These four elements form the building blocks of any business, including financial exchanges.

where speed of execution can be vital, and in which multi-platforms must be used to satisfy traders with different execution priorities.

Evolution of Business Models

Over the past four decades, financial exchanges have evolved their business models through four distinct phases. Until 1970 most exchanges operated as public utilities, vested with natural monopoly status. It was considered important for financial exchanges to operate in a non-competitive atmosphere, so without fail they could service investors requiring trade execution at market prices. However, in the United States and elsewhere, institutional investors were displacing individual investors and demanding lower trading costs. As a result the public utility model began to give way. In the 1970s and 1980s, leading exchanges adopted a more flexible model in which brokerage commissions and trading costs became subject to negotiation and competitive pressure.

This competitive phase (Table 4.1) endured for close to twenty years, and in quick succession exchanges experienced "Big Bangs" and "Little Bangs." Trading fees and commissions became subject to negotiation, and exchanges experienced shifts in trading volume from one exchange to another. A third phase commenced in the 1990s, as exchanges demutualized and assumed "for-profit" status as listed companies. In part this shift was motivated by the appearance of new competition, in the form of electronic communications networks (ECNs). But other forces of change were at work, including the desire of securities firms and investment banks to internalize trading into their own trading rooms, deregulation, and a more global perspective in securities trading and investment.

As we describe in a later section of this chapter and in Chapter 5, financial exchanges came to understand they needed to expand their geographic reach. This is accomplished in several ways, including attracting listings of foreign companies, and merging with exchanges based in other countries. Further, exchanges can list and trade index products (futures, options, and exchange traded funds) that track market sectors of securities listed in other countries.

Today financial exchanges service diverse investors, rapidly changing needs of listing companies, and evolving trade execution requirements. At the same time, exchanges must compete successfully vis-à-vis alternative market systems. To be successful in this regard they must continually analyze their business model with respect to the following:

1 improving and revising the revenue mix;
2 designing and adopting trading venues and platforms that service the needs of clientele;
3 improving and updating technology trading systems;
4 providing services that attract domestic and foreign listings; and
5 utilizing mergers and alliances with other exchanges.

We discuss the first four of these below. We reserve discussion of the fifth to Chapter 5.

Managing Business Models

According to Johnson, Christensen, and Kagermann, an effective business model contains four interlocking elements. Taken together, these should constitute a model allowing the firm to create and deliver value.[1] The four elements are:

1. maintaining a customer value perspective;
2. following a blueprint that defines value for the company;
3. identifying and utilizing key resources for maximum success; and
4. applying established processes to deliver services at an expanding scale of operations.

The first element translates into a financial exchange revising its trading platform, and creating better platforms on which clients may trade at low cost and also enjoy other benefits (speed of execution, anonymity). The second element seeks an optimal revenue mix, cost control, and cost rebalancing (fixed versus variable) to achieve operating leverage and diversify revenue sources.

The third element requires consideration of how to invest in systems technology for maximum benefit. This requires simultaneous balancing of competitive issues and operational capacity questions. In this regard, exchanges must consider scalability. That is, they must be prepared to service possibly huge changes in trading volume. When achieved, these shifts in volume can exert magnified effects on revenues and profit margins.

Exchanges have incorporated scalability into their business plans. This relates closely to the central importance assumed by technology systems. Having shifted from floor trading to electronic, exchanges need to more closely manage their fixed costs. This is associated with investment in high performance electronic trading systems. Fixed costs have replaced variable costs. As a result exchanges now seek scalability in their business models, and the ability to service high growth in transactions on a given trading platform at accepted levels of efficiency, combined with high operating leverage.

Finally, service oriented processes must be designed so that they can deliver value when the exchange succeeds in capturing rising business volume.

Comparison of Stock, Commodity, Derivative, and Offshore Exchanges

According to a study by Clayton, Jorgensen, and Kavajecz, published in 2006, there were 256 financial exchanges operating, based in 101 countries. Clayton et al. examine the economic environment associated with the existence of a financial exchange in a given country, and consider the factors related to a country having multiple exchanges. Second, they analyze factors determining choice of trading mechanisms used. Third, they investigate the long run relation between the presence of a financial exchange and the domestic economy.[2] They report details on 209 financial exchanges, indicating that 143 of these trade equities, 63 trade derivatives, and 3 trade "other" securities. Close to half of the 209 exchanges analyzed are based in developed countries, and one-fourth each in emerging and frontier countries.[3]

The Clayton et al. study notes that countries with exchanges tend to have larger economies with developed banking systems and civil law legal systems. Also, they are more open to foreign trade and investment. Multiple exchanges tend to be found in countries with larger economies and little if any government intervention. Trading mechanisms that rely on market participant liquidity (auction markets) are used more often in civil law countries and larger countries. This suggests a hierarchy of trading mechanisms, with those driven by market maker liquidity being easier to implement and sustain in smaller, less developed financial economies.

Clayton et al. find that exchanges serve as a vehicle for market participants to diversify their wealth in liquid assets. The creation of liquid financial assets made possible by financial exchanges serves to make cash less of a necessity for wealth holders.

Stock Exchanges

We begin our analysis and comparison with stock exchanges. They are the most common, the largest in number, and often the first to be established in a country.

The first stock exchange was established in 1773 in Antwerp, at that time part of the Netherlands. Not long after, the Philadelphia Stock Exchange (1790) was organized. Over the next sixty years, stock exchanges enjoyed a flourishing growth, most major cities in North America and Europe possessing their own exchange. But in the period 1850–1900 this trend was reversed as capital markets became national systems, and the benefits of concentrated liquidity became apparent.

In the twentieth century, stock trading became concentrated onto the largest exchange markets in New York, London, Tokyo, and several other cities, but during the decade of the 1990s the number of stock exchanges worldwide nearly tripled. This was related to initiatives in emerging market countries to establish more orderly financial markets and hasten development of national capital markets. Also in the 1990s stock exchanges began to demutualize, become for-profit companies, and list their own shares.[4]

We compare stock exchanges with other types of financial exchanges in Table 4.2. In this table we observe that stock exchanges trade primarily cash equities and, more recently, exchange traded funds (ETFs). A majority of these exchanges utilize auction markets.

Several exchanges use specialists to assemble the buy and sell book, and carry out trades that maximize a "clearing of the market." With electronic trading most exchanges now conduct automated auctions, without need for a specialist. A smaller number of stock exchanges use market makers, who buy and sell for their own account, serving as dealers. As we observe in Chapter 7, the London Stock Exchange SEAQ platform operates in this way. In both types of market (auction and dealer), brokers bring customer buy and sell orders to the trading system.

Growth and profitability tend to be low on stock exchanges. Annual trading growth and profit margins characteristically are much lower on stock exchanges

Table 4.2 Comparison of Stock, Commodity, Derivative, and Offshore Exchanges

	A. Stock exchange	*B. Commodity exchange*	*C. Derivative exchange*	*D. Offshore exchange*
1 Instruments traded	Cash equities; exchange traded funds (ETFs)	Futures contracts for commodities	Futures contracts for currencies; interest rates and indices	Stocks and bonds, and alternative investment funds
2 Trading system	Auction and dealer	Electronic auction	Electronic auction	Electronic and alliances with other exchanges for access
3 Contract specification	Share round lots; ETF index	Physical specificity and fixed delivery points	Standardized contracts with notional value	All types
4 Innovation	Low	Moderate to high	High	High
5 Clientele	Wide range, and increasingly HFTs	Natural hedgers, and portfolio diversifiers	Portfolio hedgers, and active managers	Wealth managers; holders of alternative assets
6 Growth and profitability	Low	High	Very high	Moderate to high
7 Clearing and settlement	Wide range used	Internal system	Internal system	Wide range used

Source: Wide range of sources utilized, including many of those cited throughout this chapter.

as compared with commodity and derivative exchanges. One reason for lower growth on stock exchanges is the more limited scope for innovation.

The disparity in revenue growth between stock and derivative exchanges is outlined in Table 4.3. Revenue growth at many derivative exchanges can be two to three times as large as at stock exchanges. Further, this higher growth translates into a significant disparity between operating profit margins, in favor of derivative exchanges (Table 4.3).

Some stock exchanges have attempted to neutralize this disadvantage by acquiring derivative exchanges. This explains in part the Euronext acquisition of LIFFE, the London derivative exchange. It also helps explain why more recently Deutsche Börse acquired the International Securities Exchange (ISE), one of five equity options exchanges operating in the United States. Other stock exchanges have

Table 4.3 Growth and Profitability of Stock and Derivative Exchanges

	Stock exchanges	*Derivative exchanges*
Revenue growth	10–15%	20–30%
Operating profit margin	15–20%	40–60%

Source: Author's estimates, including statement by Terry Duffy, chairman of the CME Group at the Midwest Finance Association luncheon, March 6, 2009, in Chicago, Illinois.

developed a derivatives business and/or merged with the domestic derivative exchange (Hong Kong, Australia, Toronto, Singapore).

Derivative exchanges generally do not view stock exchanges as attractive merger targets. Such a merger would average down revenue growth and, more importantly, profit margins (Table 4.3). As we describe in detail in Chapter 8, there has been a flow of mergers between derivative exchanges, but not a single case of a large derivative exchange acquiring a stock exchange.

Stock exchanges enjoy a widening clientele base. This includes high frequency traders (HFTs). However, commodity and derivative exchanges also benefit from a widening clientele base, including asset managers who use index futures for commodities and derivatives as essential components of their investing strategies.

Stock exchanges use a wide range of structures for clearing and settlement. In the US, clearing of equity trades is processed by the Depository Trust and Clearing Corporation (DTCC). In Europe and Asia some exchanges utilize in-house clearing services (Deutsche Börse) or an external service provider (LCH.Clearnet).

Commodity and Derivative Exchanges

Commodity and derivative exchanges differ from stock exchanges according to the instruments listed and traded, clientele served, ability to innovate, and growth prospects. These exchanges list and trade standardized futures contracts, where the initiative to create the contract lies with the exchange itself. Commodity exchanges seek to create and list new futures contracts which they believe will generate large trading volume and revenue. Derivative exchanges seek to create futures contracts that possess intellectual property rights protection and therefore cannot be copied by rival exchanges. Thus the S&P 500 Futures provides the exchange listing such a contract with protection from close rival products.

Futures contracts are traded by hedgers, speculators, and more recently investors seeking protection from adverse price movements in broad segments of the capital markets. Commodity and financial futures contracts provide such protection.

Those seeking to buy or sell futures contracts go through a broker referred to as a futures commission merchant. The customer order (buy or sell) goes to the futures commission merchant, and to the market for execution. Buyers of futures contracts take long positions, and sellers take short positions. When a trade has been completed, the buyer and seller participants are each obligated to the exchange until the contract reaches expiration or either party executes an opposite or offsetting trade.[5]

In recent years derivative exchanges have become more innovative than commodity exchanges in creating new tradable contracts. In the United States the surge in new futures contracts came after 1985. According to Gorham and Singh, new futures contracts created in the US remained under ten contracts per year until the 1980s. In the mid-1980s it averaged ten per year and in the mid-1990s twenty per year; in 2002 there were fifty new futures contracts created, in 2003 forty new contracts, in 2004 seventy-eight new contracts, and in 2005 120 new contracts.[6] In 2005 over 360 futures contracts were trading in the US, close to half of these financial futures. As of 2007, the three largest financial futures trading contracts were the EMini S&P 500, the Eurodollar Futures, and the US$/Euro FX contract, all listed and traded on the CME.

Futures transactions bring two parties together, buyer and seller. When the trade is fixed, the two parties to a futures contract have no responsibilities to one another, but they maintain a responsibility to the exchange itself. The exchange becomes the counterparty to the buyer and the seller, until the contract expires. The futures exchange operates its clearing and settlement process by carrying out the following functions:

1 It documents what trades have taken place with the respective futures commission merchants.
2 Margin deposits are determined, as a percentage of the (notional) value of the transaction.
3 An exchange of cash for initial margin, and follow-up cash exchanges for maintenance margin are administered by the clearing and settlement department of the exchange.
4 At contract expiration cash balances in the accounts of the buyer and seller are released for their use.

Offshore Exchanges

Offshore exchanges provide specialized and unique services that differ from those available in larger stock exchanges. The four exchanges described below, Luxembourg, Dublin, Channel Islands, and Bermuda, all fulfill increasingly important roles. They offer products and services not generally available in larger financial exchanges. Offshore exchanges in effect complement their larger heavyweight cousins in ways that suggest the future of financial exchanges will be one in which two distinct types of exchanges are likely to prevail. There will be large heavyweights (resulting from mergers such as that of NYSE and Euronext), and smaller niche players such as those based in offshore locations. To survive in an increasingly competitive world, it is important for offshore exchanges to specialize and offer complementary platforms and products not readily available on the larger exchanges.[7]

Most offshore exchanges enjoy certain advantages compared with their larger cousins. They operate in a more limited regulatory regime and face lighter tax burdens. Operationally, they provide expertise in specific securities and investment instruments and offer a wider range of listed instruments at low cost. We describe the competitive strengths of offshore exchanges in Table 4.4. Two of these exchanges, the Irish Stock Exchange (Dublin) and the Luxembourg Stock Exchange, are subject to European Union rules and regulations. Listing on a market subject to EU regulation can satisfy specific company needs. Luxembourg offers an efficient and competitive listing venue. Companies choosing to list in Luxembourg (or Dublin) bond to a well-accepted regulatory system. At the same time, their securities may also list and trade on the London Stock Exchange, which provides a liquid and low cost trading venue.

Table 4.4 Competitive Advantages of Four Offshore Stock Exchanges

	Competitive strengths/ advantages	*Channel Islands Stock Exchange (CISX)*	*Bermuda Stock Exchange (BSX)*	*Dublin (ISX)*	*Luxembourg Stock Exchange*
1	Subject to European Union rules/ regulations; gives its investors sense of safety			X	X
2	Technology trading platform partnership and collaboration with larger partner			X[1]	X[2]
3	Geographic location		X[3]		
4	Innovative and flexible approach to listing				
	a. First mover	X[4]			
	b. Broad range of instruments		X[5]		
	c. Attract hedge fund listings via extensive data service			X[6]	
	d. Special platform for corporate debt				X[7]
5	Specialized services for small company IPOs and pre-IPO listings for high growth companies		X		
6	List alternative fund structures	X[8]			
7	Flexibility in accounting and financial reporting	X[9]			

Notes

1 Dublin has a technology collaboration with Deutsche Börse until 2012.

2 In 2009 Luxembourg Stock Exchange and Euronext formed a partnership where securities listed on Luxembourg Stock Exchange are available on the Euronext platform.

3 Bermuda's geographic position gives it access to trading with New York and London markets for several business hours on a daily basis.

4 First exchange to list limited partnerships. Also facilitates low cost private equity acquisitions.

5 BSX lists hedge funds, debt, structured products, and synthetic derivative products.

6 ISX works closely with hedge funds to codify best practice, a form of quasi-regulation. ISX works closely with investor groups to apply principle-based criteria for listing.

7 Luxembourg has worked carefully to make itself the premier listing exchange. As part of a developing cooperation, Euronext has adopted the SAGE services and listing tools used by the Luxembourg Stock Exchange for listing corporate debt instruments.

8 CISX typically is used for listing a range of alternative fund structures, including property, hedge funds, and private equity funds.

9 CISX has established a strong role, even while located outside of European Union jurisdiction. There are no requirements to prepare accounts according to International Financial Reporting Standards (IFRS). Issuers have the choice of using US or UK GAAP. This allows CISX to offer a low cost alternative.

Offshore exchanges have initiated technology and trading platform alliances. For example, Dublin extended its seven-year technology collaboration with Deutsche Börse in equities trading and clearing to 2012 (Table 4.4, Line 2). The Luxembourg Stock Exchange and Euronext signed a partnership agreement whereby securities listed on Luxembourg are available for trading on the Euronext platform. This gives Euronext members access to 45,000 securities listed on the Luxembourg exchange. This includes 30,000 bond issues of over 4,000 issuing entities based in over 100 countries. In 2007 the Luxembourg Stock Exchange added over 13,000 new securities to its official list.[8]

The Bermuda and Channel Island exchanges list and trade hedge funds and private equity partnership shares. Given the opacity of how these funds operate, it would be difficult to envisage their listing in locations where high levels of transparency are required, such as the United States.

The Bermuda Stock Exchange (BSX) is geographically well positioned, midway between London and New York, two of the largest and most liquid financial markets. The BSX also offers a broad range of listed instruments for trading, including hedge funds and synthetic derivatives (Table 4.4, Line 4b). The Channel Islands Stock Exchange (CISX) also takes an innovative and flexible approach toward listing. CISX is one of the first exchanges to allow listing of interests in limited partnerships, and provides a tax efficient way for private equity investors to finance acquisitions (Table 4.4, Line 4a). The Irish Stock Exchange has played a key role as a listing base for hedge funds. As an exchange subject to EU oversight, it offers a high degree of comfort to investors. Adherence to best practice and cost containment, and close consultation with hedge funds' management have given the Dublin Exchange an advantage in gaining hedge fund listings (Table 4.4, Line 4c).

The Luxembourg Stock Exchange ranks first in listed international bonds in Europe (Table 4.5).[9] It was the first exchange to list a Eurobond in 1963. In 2010 over 71,000 international bond issues were listed for trading on leading European stock exchanges, with the Luxembourg Stock Exchange accounting for 42.5 percent of these.

Listing on the Luxembourg Stock Exchange is attractive for several reasons. There is a choice between two market venues, both in compliance with official

Table 4.5 Listing of International Bonds on European Exchanges, 2009

Exchange	*No. of bond issues*	*Percentage of total*
Luxembourg Stock Exchange	30,604	42.5
Irish Stock Exchange	17,592	24.3
Deutsche Börse	12,449	17.2
London Stock Exchange	6,071	8.4
NYSE Euronext	3,371	4.6
Others	2,193	3.0
Total	72,280	100.0%

Source: Luxembourg Stock Exchange, *The Luxembourg Stock Exchange: A Prime Location for Listing*, PricewaterhouseCoopers, 2010, pp. 2–3.

listing legislation. The main market is EU regulated. However, the exchange regulated market, the Euro MTF, is a multilateral trading facility in compliance with the Markets in Financial Instruments Directive (MiFID), launched in 2005 to satisfy the needs of issuers requiring greater flexibility in the preparation of financial information.[10] Equally important, Luxembourg Stock Exchange lists all types of securities and financial vehicles. A cross-membership agreement with NYSE Euronext allows access to the latter's market platform.

The Luxembourg Stock Exchange has developed as the premier listing exchange around the world. Four categories of securities each have their own requirements for listing and fee structure. These include: fixed income, warrants, equities (including depository receipts), and share units of investment funds. Fee structure and low cost facilitate efficient incentives to attract thousands of listings from all over the world. The Luxembourg exchange initiated a partnership with NYSE Euronext covering 1) cross-membership and 2) technology transfer. Members of the Continental European financial exchanges (Amsterdam, Brussels, Lisbon, and Paris) are able to activate cross-membership rights to the Luxembourg Stock Exchange. Conversely, members of the Luxembourg Stock Exchange may take advantage of their own cross-membership rights.

The partnership provides for all products listed on the Luxembourg Stock Exchange markets to be made available on NSC, the trading platform for NYSE Euronext. All members of the Luxembourg exchange may access the trading system of NYSE Euronext cash markets.

Revenue Sources and Profitability at Leading Exchanges

Financial exchanges generate revenues from a number of different activities. In the following we analyze the revenue sources of the twelve largest stock exchanges, covering the period 2005–06. These twelve exchanges are identified in Table 4.6,

Table 4.6 Revenues, Profitability, and Profit Margins of the Twelve Largest Exchanges (2005–06)

Exchange	*Total revenue*	*Rank in total revenue*	*Profit margin*	*Rank by profits*
Deutsche Börse	2,450	1	36%	1
NYSE	2,345	2	9%	5
NASDAQ	1,625	3	8%	8
Euronext	1,470	4	34%	2
LSE	725	5	50%	3
Tokyo	580	6	27%	6
OMX	518	7	25%	9
Hong Kong	500	8	61%	4
BME	340	9	45%	7
Borsa Italiana	320	10	23%	12
SWX	290	11	39%	10
TSX	260	12	37%	11
Median profit margin			35%	

Source: *Journal of Trading*, Winter 2008, p. 126.

and are listed in descending order according to their total revenues. This table also indicates the rankings of these exchanges according to total profits, and notes profit margin as a percentage of revenues.

Profitability

Deutsche Börse ranks first in Table 4.6 according to total revenues, and first also based on level of profits, but sixth in profit margin. The two New York based exchanges (NYSE and NASDAQ) ranked second and third based on revenues but exhibit low profit margins. Euronext and LSE ranked second and third according to profit levels. The Hong Kong, LSE, and BME exchanges ranked first, second, and third in profit margins.

Clearly, size of national economy is only loosely related to revenues, profits, and profit margins. In fact, NYSE and NASDAQ enjoyed the lowest profit margins of all twelve exchanges, and did not rank high in levels of profit. This can be attributed to their operating in highly competitive financial market environments.

Most interesting in Table 4.6 is the information on profit margins. Three exchanges stand out in enjoying profit margins far above all others. These are Hong Kong, LSE, and BME. All three exchanges have enjoyed high growth in trading volume, important as a supporter of profitability. In the case of Hong Kong, it has gained listings and expanded trading from Mainland China, including large privatization deals. LSE enjoys a large share of the listing and trading of foreign company stocks and is a most important listing venue for overseas companies. The Spanish BME is supported by a highly successful economic upsurge in that country, and a rising level of stock market transactions supported by corporate restructuring, mergers, and rising wealth levels.

Revenue Sources

Even more revealing concerning the detailed operation of financial exchanges is the breakdown of revenue sources. In Table 4.7, we identify six specific revenue sources, as well as an "other" category. Further, the table reveals sharp differences in the ability of each exchange to develop specific sources of revenue and to develop a more diversified business model. The table supports the view that "No two exchanges are alike."

Listing and trading are core activities of exchanges. Five of the exchanges in Table 4.7 have developed a substantial share of revenues (over 60 percent) from listing and trading (NASDAQ, NYSE, TSX, LSE, and Tokyo). Competition between exchanges for new listings, including cross-listings, has escalated as a greater number of these marketplaces possess the liquidity to host large cross-border IPOs.

Other exchanges enjoy more diversified revenues. Four exchanges in Table 4.7 generate considerable revenues from derivatives trading (Deutsche Börse, Euronext, SWX, and Hong Kong). In the case of Deutsche Börse and SWX, both are owners of Eurex, the third largest derivative exchange globally. Euronext merged

Table 4.7 Revenue Sources of the Twelve Largest Exchanges (2005–06)

Exchange	*Listing*	*Trading*	*Derivative trading*	*Clearing*	*Information products*	*Technology systems*	*Other*
Deutsche Börse	2	14	34	38	7	5	—
Euronext	6	26	33	—	11	17	7
SWX	6	34	39	—	8	—	13
BME	10	43	8	21	10	8	—
OMX	10	23	12	—	20	35	—
Borsa Italiana	11	19	7	39	15	—	10
Hong Kong	11	31	18	31	10	—	—
NYSE	14	57	—	—	9	6	14
NASDAQ	14	76	—	—	10	—	—
LSE	18	45	4	—	30	—	3
Tokyo	19	43	—	16	12	10	—
TSX	30	40	—	—	25	—	5

Source: *Journal of Trading*, Winter 2008, p. 126.

with LIFFE, the London-based derivative exchange, accounting for one-third of Euronext revenues.

All twelve exchanges indicate that they derive some revenues from information products. In only three cases is the contribution to revenues from this source in excess of 15 percent (TSX, LSE, and OMX). In the case of LSE, it is understandable that the third largest country stock market should be able to develop a sizeable revenue flow from information products. Most institutional investors around the globe research and trade securities on the London markets. Financial exchanges often work with commercial data providers such as Thomson-Reuters or Dow Jones to process and market stock exchange related data. Half of the exchanges in Table 4.7 report revenues from technology systems. OMX Group and Euronext report 35 percent and 17 percent revenue contributions respectively from this source. In this area of business OMX services over sixty major securities trading organizations, some of which are exchanges, large investment banks, and institutional investors, all needing the capability to interface active market trading throughout the day.

Fewer than half of the exchanges in Table 4.7 report revenues from clearing and settlement. Deutsche Börse and Borsa Italiana report substantial revenues from this source, and in each case clearing revenues constitute the largest single revenue source. In a later section of this chapter we discuss clearing and settlement in detail.

The four exchanges with the most diversified revenues are Borsa Italiana, BME, Euronext, and OMX. Exchanges with the most concentrated revenues are NASDAQ, TSX, and LSE. Tables 4.6 and 4.7 cover the period 2005–06. Subsequent to this time period several mergers took place, including exchanges in the top twelve. For example, NYSE and Euronext merged, as did NASDAQ and OMX Group. Similarly, LSE and Borsa Italiana merged. In later chapters we comment on the diversification objectives of these mergers. The reader may examine Table 4.7 and note the likely diversification benefits to be gained in these three merged entities.

Geographic Reach

Financial exchanges have employed numerous strategies designed to expand the geographic reach of their businesses. These include providing favorable listing and trading opportunities for domestic and foreign companies, extending trading session hours to facilitate more convenient market venues, creating alliances and mergers with other exchanges located in different time zones, and facilitating cross-listing by non-resident companies. Below we discuss these strategies. In Chapter 5 we analyze the role of mergers and acquisitions.

Initial Public Offerings

In this and the following section we analyze data measuring global initial public offerings provided by Thomson-Reuters. Also, we examine cross-listings. There can be considerable overlap in IPO and cross-listing data.

In the early 1980s we have an interesting example of the overlap between IPOs and cross-listings. When British Telecom was privatized by the Thatcher government in the UK, the projected market value of this telecoms behemoth indicated an international offering would be required. It was beyond the capacity of the not-as-yet restructured London Stock Exchange to carry out the entire offering. Branches were placed in the UK, North America, and Europe. Therefore, the BT offering simultaneously was an initial public offering, a series of cross-listings, and a near-global issue.

The point from this is that considerable overlap can exist between IPOs and cross-listings. They are not mutually exclusive. We need to remember that IPOs can be generated as young venture capital companies go public, when mature companies formerly taken private in a leveraged buyout (LBO) exit from buyout status, when large conglomerates spin off an attractive operating unit, and when state enterprises (such as British Telecom) are privatized.

IPOs are important to stock exchanges. They fuel the expansion in listings and tradable shares. We present data on global IPOs in Table 4.8, covering the period 2002–07.

Over the short period 2002–04, it would appear that financial exchanges in the Western Hemisphere were maintaining their competitive edge in generating and

Table 4.8 Money Raised Through IPOs by Region (US$ Billions)

	Western Hemisphere	*Europe, Middle East, and Africa*	*Asia Pacific*	*World total*
2002	21	20	25	66
2003	9	9	32	50
2004	44	33	48	125
2005	44	71	52	167
2006	50	105	91	246
2007 (H1)	32	51	40	124

Source: *Financial Times.*

attracting initial public offerings (Table 4.8). During the 1990s a technology based boom resulted in creation of venture capital enterprises, and their growth and public offering of shares. The business slump of 2000–02 damaged this sector, and venture capital IPOs related to technology failed to recover to former highs. As we observe in Table 4.8, there was a strong recovery in IPOs in the Western Hemisphere in 2004. However, in the next several years, the Europe, Middle East, and Africa, and Asia Pacific regions improved their share of the world total.

Some observers read the IPO trend in 2002–07 as reflecting a loss in competitive status for US financial markets in general and New York based financial exchanges in particular. As can be observed in Table 4.8, in 2005 and 2006 Western Hemisphere IPO levels remained below those of other regions. In 2006 and first half 2007 other regions increased their lead over the Western Hemisphere in IPO amounts. Little surprise that early in 2006 Mayor Michael Bloomberg of New York City commissioned the well-known McKinsey Report, released in January 2007 and commented on in earlier chapters. The period 2006–07 was one in which observers in New York expressed deep concern over the competitive challenges facing the US financial markets, from European and Asian rival centers and exchanges. This concern was given expression by mergers carried out by NYSE and NASDAQ, discussed in detail in the following chapters.

Europe's competitive strength in initial public offerings in 2005–07 was commented on frequently by the financial press. For example, at midyear 2007 the *Wall Street Journal* reported the European continent's position as an increasingly attractive home for companies looking to go public.[11] The *WSJ* went on to note that companies in emerging markets such as Kazakhstan and Russia were listing on the London Stock Exchange, an attractive marketplace for firms seeking to escape or avoid the regulatory rigors of a US listing. Also, the volume of initial public offerings by European issuers on that region's exchanges outpaced that of any other.

Russian company issuance leaped forward in 2006–07, reaching a level of $14.3 billion in first half 2007, pushing the country to third rank in the world, compared with seventh rank a year earlier. Across Europe, London was the prime beneficiary of rising IPO levels in 2006–07. Analysts reported that the LSE lead in listing came from a very light regulatory apparatus, most especially with respect to the second tier Alternative Investment Market (AIM).

In the Asia Pacific region, rising levels of IPOs can be attributed to high economic growth and large privatization issues from Mainland China. Few of the resulting IPOs found their way to North America. Large Chinese privatizations generally were listed in China, including the Hong Kong market. This is analyzed in detail in Chapter 10.

The year 2007 was a peak one in global IPO volume for the decade 2000–09. In 2008–09 IPO volume declined sharply, and the US share also fell. Asia was an exception to these trends, as its share of global IPO activity increased in 2008–09. Favorable trends continued for Asia into 2010. In the first three quarters of 2010 the Shanghai and Hong Kong stock markets each realized over $23 billion in initial public offerings, compared with only $11 billion on the NYSE and $7 billion on the LSE. At yearend 2010 Hong Kong was recognized as a standout performer in attracting IPO issuers from a wide range of countries. According to a *Financial Times* report, "Hong Kong is now firmly established as a major global listing venue—it's the place any issuer has to seriously look at."[12]

The future is likely to produce larger size IPOs. In September 2010 Petrobras, the Brazilian petroleum company, launched a $67 billion equity offering, the largest ever. The Petrobras issue was $31 billion larger than the second largest ever IPO, by NTT in 1987. Factors supporting larger IPOs include the greater global mobility of capital, the rising investment power of sovereign wealth funds, and the favorable status of companies such as Petrobras and NTT which enjoy the strong support of their respective governments.[13]

Cross-Listing

Perhaps the clearest manifestation of the battle of the bourses is in the distribution of cross-listings. Stock exchanges compete in a highly aggressive way to gain an edge in listing foreign company shares. These tend to be listings of successful companies, large blue chips or high tech and high growth enterprises. Many reasons are offered for cross-listing. These reasons apply differently to each exchange as well as across time periods. For example, in the 1990s the New York Stock Exchange attracted a large number of European cross-listings, but this source of listings probably has been exhausted. Therefore, we observe a smaller number of new European company cross-listings on the NYSE in the decade 2000–09.

The following have been cited as the most important reasons for cross-listing, from the company perspective:

1 Bond to a better regulatory system, assuring improved transparency and company reporting.
2 Bond to a better corporate governance regime, assuring protection of minority stockholders.
3 Achieve lower cost of capital, and higher wealth benefits.
4 Signal high product quality and expand markets.
5 Develop acquisition currency for mergers and acquisitions in country where cross-listed.
6 Rebalance ownership.

From the perspective of stock exchanges, cross-listing is a revenue builder in the core business. Success in this department gives the exchange strong "bragging rights." At least three patterns or strategies are apparent among financial exchanges that compete for cross-listings. These are: 1) full service strategy, 2) step-up-the-ladder, and 3) listing venue.

Main boards of the NYSE, LSE, and SGX have followed the "full service" strategy. They each seek to become the main cross-listing exchange in their respective regions. Also, they offer a full range of services including listing, trading, and data provision. The New York and London based exchanges have been developing in this way for many years. Singapore is a relative newcomer, but has enjoyed moderate success. We analyze SGX in Chapter 9.

The step-up-the-ladder strategy often utilizes a second board to attract cross-listings from companies based in other nations. Exchanges following this strategy include LSE (its AIM board), Hong Kong's market for smaller companies, and Tokyo's "Mothers" market. A successful company may be expected to outgrow the lower tier or second market, and move up to the main market in the future.

The third strategy, to operate as a listing venue, is demonstrated by the Luxembourg Stock Exchange. This exchange stands out among financial markets for several reasons. First, Luxembourg is an offshore financial center, and this lends its stock exchange the advantage of attracting investors, traders, and companies that want to list their securities. Second, the Luxembourg Stock Exchange has attracted an unusually large number of listings, especially considering the fact that it is located in a very small political entity. Third, the Luxembourg Stock Exchange at yearend 2007 boasted over 45,000 listings. It is doubtful any other exchange comes close to that figure.

Most of the listings on the Luxembourg Stock Exchange (68 percent) are bonds or fixed income instruments. In Table 4.9 we observe that over 31,000 listings represent fixed income instruments, and a similar proportion of turnover comes from trading fixed income. This exchange has developed its own unique business, which differs from other trading markets we are more familiar with. Given the relatively small size of the domestic economy it should not be a surprise that share listing and trading represent a smaller component than bonds and debentures.

The Luxembourg Stock Exchange has effectively developed a sizeable listing business. Nine pages of its annual report are needed to describe procedures for listing, prospectus approval, and listing fees for different categories of securities.[14]

On the equity side, over 200 foreign depository receipts are listed on the Luxembourg exchange. These include companies from South America, Asia, the Middle East, offshore centers, and Europe. A large number of companies are listed from India, Taiwan, and South Korea.[15]

We now return to cross-listing data to analyze trends and the competitive position of exchanges. Two sets of data are used for this purpose. The first data set

Table 4.9 Listings and Turnover on Luxembourg Stock Exchange (2007)

	Number of listings	*Turnover (million euros)*
Bonds	31,469	448.3
Stock	292	176.8
UCIs	7,372	27.0
Warrants	6,440	0.9
Total	45,573	653.0
Percentage bonds	69.1%	68.8%

Source: Luxembourg Stock Exchange, *Annual Report 2008*, pp. 58–59.

Note: Data excludes the Euro MTF trading platform.

comes from the World Federation of Stock Exchanges. It indicates global total cross-listings and the country markets accounting for these listings. The second data set comes from banks active in custody, depository receipts, and clearing–settlement of cross-border trading.

The first data set compares 1998 and 2005 cross-listing according to the country of the exchange hosting the listing. In 1998 three New York based exchanges (NYSE, American Stock Exchange, and NASDAQ) together accounted for close to 31 percent of all foreign listings around the globe (Table 4.10). The London Stock Exchange Main Market and Alternative Investment Market (AIM) held 16 percent, and no other exchange held more than 7 percent. Changes in cross-listings in the period 1998–2005 brought London's share of foreign listings to 19 percent, whereas the US market share declined to 29 percent.

Conventional wisdom among government leaders and the press is that in the period 2004–06 London became more competitive in attracting cross-listings than New York. In the following we examine cross-listing and what changes if any

Table 4.10 Global Distribution of Cross-Listings, 1998 and 2005

Host market	*1998*		*2005*	
	No.	*Percentage*	*No.*	*Percentage*
London Main Market	466	16	334	11
NASDAQ	441	15	332	11
NYSE	392	13	452	15
Luxembourg	227	7	206	7
Deutsche Börse	210	7	116	4
Swiss Stock Exchange	193	6	116	4
Amsterdam Exchange	146	5	*	
Paris Stock Exchange	183	6	*	
Brussels Stock Exchange	122	4	*	
AMEX	61	2	100	3
Australian Stock Exchange	60	2	71	2
New Zealand Stock Exchange	58	2		
Tokyo Stock Exchange	52	2		
TSX Group	49	2	39	1
Euronext			293	10
London AIM			220	8
Mexican Stock Exchange			176	6
Singapore Stock Exchange			122	4
Subtotal	2,660	89	2,577	86
Other	329	11	421	14
Grand total	2,989	100%	2,998	100%

Source: C. Doidge, G.A. Karolyi, and R. Stulz, *Has New York Become Less Competitive in Global Markets? Evaluating Foreign Listing Choices Over Time*, NBER Working Paper, 2007, p. 46.

Note
* These exchanges merged into Euronext prior to 2005.

may have taken place in relative competitive position of New York and London. Some analysts take the position that the flow of new listings is itself evidence that London has wrested leadership away from New York. We take a more middle view. Listings involve complicated decisions. They generate benefits and costs for listing companies. Also, each time period is unique. Listings initiated in one decade may not happen in another time period, owing to different conditions prevalent in each decade.

London listings and New York listings are not the same. If we refer back to our list of six reasons offered for company cross-listings, we can attribute certain advantages to New York, but somewhat different ones to London.

If we consider a New York listing, two of the key advantages are: 1) to develop an acquisition currency for mergers and acquisitions (M&A), and 2) to signal product quality and expand markets. The fact that the US is the largest consumer market in the world warrants a non-US company listing on a New York market. The first advantage, developing an acquisition currency, relates to several prominent listings in New York. Daimler-Benz listed in New York in the mid-1990s for both of the above reasons. Daimler subsequently acquired Chrysler Corporation, and expanded its market position in the United States.

A study published in 2005 in *Financial Management*, a leading research journal, supports the "acquisition currency" rationale. It is well understood that cross-listed stock provides a potentially useful form of payment for cross-border merger transactions. The *Financial Management* study finds that "one of the motives for European companies to cross-list in the US markets . . . is the need for a viable M&A currency." The study focuses on 326 non-cross-listed and 221 cross-listed European companies. The authors report that European firms that cross-list in the US are significantly more likely to acquire US firms than their European counterparts that do not list in the US. Once cross-listed, the European company continues with larger US acquisitions. Companies that already are active acquirers in the US are the ones that choose to cross-list. Cross-listings do not cause acquisitions, but rather increase the tendency to acquire in US markets.[16]

If we consider a London listing, two key advantages are: 1) to bond to a better corporate governance and regulatory system, and 2) to rebalance ownership. The world-respected Cadbury Code of governance implemented in the UK provides a significant advantage over the US in corporate governance. UK companies have more independent boards of directors than US companies, separate the CEO and chairman positions, and include comprehensive reporting on governance matters in annual reports.

Equally important, a London listing gives investors from a wide range of countries the ability to enjoy protection on a premier market. This benefit accrues to minority as well as other shareholders. In many cases a foreign firm has a controlling shareholder, and in the home country it is possible for control shareholders to benefit at the cost of minority shareholders. Thus, there can be a governance benefit from a UK cross-listing.

Shifts in Cross-Listing

There is the perception that cross-listing is a growing phenomenon. Table 4.10 suggests little or no increase in cross-listing. However, the data was not assembled for the purpose of recording trends in the incidence of cross-listing, but more to reflect changes in the ability of different markets and financial centers to attract such listings. Cross-listings can take place on different types of market venues, including an exchange's main market, the second level market (e.g., AIM in London), over the counter, or via a private placement. Also, the cross-listing can take several structures, including a listing of common shares, an American depository receipt (ADR), and shares not admitted to general public trading (private placement under Rule 144a in the US). In the US private placements have expanded rapidly, accounting for 312 cross-listings in 2005 (Table 4.11). This further complicates measure and evaluation of cross-listing.

Table 4.10 indicates significant shifts in a relatively fixed total of global cross-listings. The main components of these shifts are:

1. The US share declined (from 31 percent to 29 percent) whereas the UK share increased (from 16 percent to 21 percent). London's gain was concentrated in the Alternative Investment Market, where numerous smaller companies list, including technology, mining, and early stage enterprises. The US overall loss consisted of gains by NYSE and AMEX, and losses by NASDAQ.
2. Asian countries such as Singapore came onto the radar and now are important host countries. We discuss Singapore in detail in Chapter 9.
3. Emerging market countries gain as their stock markets become more liquid. For example, Mexico shows 176 companies cross-listed, reflecting the expansion of its stock exchange.

Emerging countries also have increased in importance as their domestic companies have initiated cross-listings. This is good news for the more liquid markets in developed nations. A research paper published in 2007 focuses on the worldwide depository receipt (DR) market. Using Bank of New York data, Peng et al. report that 1,912 depository receipt programs from 173 countries were available to investors at yearend 2005. This form of cross-listing catches the attention of investors as well as companies seeking capital.

Taiwan plays an important role in the DR market. Its first DR took place in 1992 and, from that date to 2005, 135 Taiwanese companies issued $32.7 billion of DRs.[17] In the period 2003–05 Taiwan ranked at the top globally in the amount of capital raised in DRs. Taiwanese firms engaged in cross-listing tend to be high tech oriented, with higher market value and growth potential, higher profitability, and lower financial risk. Analysis of buy and hold strategy indicates shares of these cross-listing firms enjoyed abnormal positive returns when compared with their benchmarks. The study concludes that cross-listing by Taiwanese firms in the period covered was value creating. Most of the Taiwanese firms that cross-listed did so in London and Luxembourg.

Cross-Listing in the UK and US Compared

We obtain a different understanding of trends in cross-listing from the information in Table 4.11. This data comes from a wide range of sources, including large banks that operate in this business, stock exchanges, market related trade information (Pink Sheets, CRSP), and company annual reports. Between 1990 and 2005 the number of cross-listings increased sharply in the US, and moderated in the UK. This is summarized in Table 4.11. This data reflects at least four trends. First, stock exchanges in the US experienced a near tripling of cross-listings in the period covered. Second, UK cross-listings shifted away from the LSE Main Board toward the Alternative Investment Market. Overall, London cross-listings expanded by 50 percent. Third, in this period London became a significant depository market. Depository receipts had played very little role fifteen years earlier. Fourth, American OTC and private placement type cross-listings surged, tending to give the US a commanding lead over London in number of cross-listings.

By yearend 2005 the US hosted 2,087 cross-listings, compared with 569 in the UK. Taking the UK and US together there was an increase of 1,838 cross-listings over the period 1990–2005, of which 1,605 were listed by US markets and 233 by UK markets. It would appear that the size and liquidity, along with the diversity of market venues, have given US markets an advantage over UK markets in the global competition for cross-listings. However, data for the period following 2005 provides a less favorable picture for the United States.

Why Foreign Firms Delist

How do explanations for cross-listing apply in the case of foreign firms deciding to delist? In a study published by the National Bureau of Economic Research, Doidge, Karolyi, and Stulz investigate SEC deregistrations by foreign firms.[18] They cover the period following passage of the Sarbanes–Oxley Act (SOX) in 2002 through 2008. In 2007 the SEC adopted rule 12h-6. Under the old rules, firms wanting to deregister from US exchange listing had to have fewer than 300 registered US shareholders. The change in 2007 removed this head count requirement. With the SEC easing these procedures, there was a short upward spike in deregistrations of foreign company listings that did not extend into 2008.

Table 4.11 Firms Cross-Listed in the US and UK (1990–2005)

	US cross-listings			*UK cross-listings*		
	Rule 144a	*OTC*	*Exchange*	*AIM*	*Depository receipt*	*Ordinary listings*
1990	15	139	328	0	3	333
1995	172	449	606	2	27	394
2000	296	764	960	29	122	363
2005	312	909	866	242	111	216

Source: *Journal of Trading*, Winter 2008, p. 126.

Doidge et al. observe that firms that deregister grow more slowly, need less capital, and experience poor stock return performance compared to other US listed foreign firms that do not deregister. They test two different explanations of deregistration: 1) loss of competitiveness, possibly from SOX and other regulatory developments that make US capital markets less competitive to other markets, and 2) bonding, where control shareholders of foreign firms have bonded to US laws and institutions. By bonding they become able to raise capital cheaply, but when growth opportunities slacken they quit US markets.

Based on share price behavior when foreign firms announced they were deregistering, Doidge et al. find that companies with better growth opportunities and larger financing deficits saw their stock prices fall much more significantly, which is consistent with the bonding theory. Foreign firms list shares in the US to raise capital at the lowest possible cost to finance growth. When these opportunities disappear, listing becomes less valuable.[19]

Overcoming Home Bias

Home bias is a phenomenon in search of a theory. Those analyzing international portfolio investment "observe" home bias when they compare the ownership patterns of equity investors with the relative size and importance of national equity markets. It can be hypothesized that a normal and well-diversified equity portfolio should contain equity securities from each country in proportion to how large the market capitalization of that country is to the world total. For example, if the US stock market accounts for 39 percent of world stock market capitalization, investors in the US and elsewhere should weigh the US domestic equity component at 39 percent.

Home bias is discovered when we realize that most US investors on average hold over 85 percent of their equity investments in domestic shares, and similarly that investors in other countries hold larger proportions of home country shares in their portfolios than is warranted by the ratio of their nation's stock market capitalization to the world total. Home bias is widespread, and it is doubtful that any country avoids the "sinful" practice. But over the years it has been reduced as investors learned the risk reducing benefits of international diversification. An important reason for home bias is the increased cost to investors of cross-border equity investment. This takes the form of information costs, currency exchange costs, trading costs on foreign stock markets, and the cost of monitoring and hedging risk of investments in other countries.

Home bias affects financial exchanges in several ways. First, it confines trading to domestic markets and securities issued by local entities. Second, it impedes the expansion and diversification of exchange listing and trading of foreign securities. This second effect is subject to question. Home bias may cause some companies to cross-list their equity securities, to gain access to investors based in other countries, given the expectation these investors will not "migrate" to trade in foreign stock markets.

According to the Deutsche Bundesbank, since introduction of the single currency (the euro), there has been a reduction in the home bias of German investors.

The share of domestic investments in German investor portfolios has declined from 79 percent at the beginning of monetary union to 58 percent at yearend 2007. At both of these dates German securities (stocks and bonds) made up 6 percent of the global portfolio of stocks and bonds. The decline in home bias of German investors has coincided with a growing preference for securities from the rest of the euro area (rising euro area bias). Similarly, the percentage of German securities held by non-residents has increased. When the euro was introduced in 1999, only 27 percent of German securities were held by non-residents. By 2007 this percentage had risen to 47 percent.[20]

Leading financial exchanges have struggled to overcome home bias. This is reflected in the cross-listings discussion in the preceding section. Exchanges employ a range of measures for this purpose. These include offering attractive listing fees, lowering trading costs, providing special time-of-the-day trading sessions, alliances with other exchanges, and mergers.[21]

Clearing and Settlement

We have learned that leading financial exchanges generate varying levels of revenue from clearing services. In this section we lay out the basic issue of how clearing should be provided, describe the several structures used by which clearing services are provided, examine how clearing may impact the competitive balance, and consider current efforts to bring about a more efficient clearing service.

One Part of a Process

Securities trading generally follows a six-step process, outlined in Table 4.12. All six steps are required, irrespective of the type of market venue (exchange trading, over the counter, or electronic platform) utilized for the trade.

Post-trade services include clearing and settlement, and are provided via four different structures. They include using an arm's-length or competitive supplier

Table 4.12 Six-Step Process in Securities Trading

Step		*Description*
Step 1	Order	Investor instructs broker to initiate a trade.
Step 2	Execution	Trade carried out on a financial exchange, over the counter, or on an ECN.
Step 3	Matching	Brokers on each side of the trade confirm details of the trade, and confirm trade complies with original order.
Step 4	Netting	Considerable reduction in value/volume of securities for settlement can be achieved by netting or offsetting cash and security flows. A single central counterparty can maximize potential for netting.
Step 5	Clearing	Positioning of securities and arrangement of payment prior to settlement.
Step 6	Settlement	Final transfer of securities and related cash settlements.

such as LCH.Clearnet, which services a number of European exchanges, the public utility model applicable in the United States for equity and equity options, stock exchange (vertical silos) operated clearing systems (used in Germany and Italy), and a safe-haven clearing model utilized in futures exchanges owing to the highly leveraged transactions common to most futures contract transactions (Table 4.13).

Early in 2008, Clara Furse, then chief executive at the London Stock Exchange, noted: "one of the pillars of London's market structure is its separation of trading revenues from post-trade services. London exchanges have used the services of a separate clearing provider . . . LCH.Clearnet . . . an independent, neutral and pro-competitive manner."[22] Since the merger with Borsa Italiana, the LSE has shifted toward the use of an exchange owned clearing service. This was operated by Borsa Italiana prior to merger with the London Exchange.

Alternatives to the competitive model are: 1) vertical silos where an exchange provides its own separate clearing services, and 2) the public utility model applicable in the United States (Table 4.13). In the US the DTCC and the Options Clearing Corporation (OCC) enjoy monopoly status, in return for which the market gains low cost service and absence of counterparty credit risk.

Europe enjoys both the horizontal or competitive model (LCH.Clearnet) and vertical clearing models. Deutsche Börse operates its own clearing, which generates substantial revenues (Table 4.6), but at high cost. Derivatives (futures)

Table 4.13 Alternative Clearing Models

Type		*Description*	*Where applied*
1	Vertical silo	Exchange owned and operated clearing service. Considered anti-competitive.	Deutsche Börse, Borsa Italiana.
2	Public utility model	Monopoly operation allowed to gain efficient, low cost clearing service. Depository Trust and Clearing Corporation does all equity clearing, and Options Clearing Corporation does all equity options clearing.	All US equity and equity options.
3	Competitive model	LCH.Clearnet competes for clearing as an external service provider.	Exchanges in Europe.
4	Safe-haven internalized (exchange operated)	Futures exchanges operate own internal clearing, owing to highly leveraged nature of trading in futures contracts, and need to assure integrity of process via margin and maintenance margin, and mark to market daily requirements.	Futures exchanges in US and Europe.

exchanges supply their own clearing services, considered essential to protect the integrity of the trading operation, which is highly leveraged. This is implemented by daily mark to market valuation of client trading accounts, and enforcement of initial and maintenance margin requirements.

Clearing Issues

As noted above, in 2008 Clara Furse warned of an anti-competitive trend if United Kingdom regulators failed to require competition in the provision of securities clearing. Throughout 2008 three questions were repeatedly discussed and debated in Europe concerning how to structure and deliver securities clearing and settlement:

1. What competitive balance is needed to allow European exchanges to operate effectively vis-à-vis North America, and prevent large scale migration of trading to US and other markets?
2. What clearing model best suits the widening range of clients of exchanges and other types of trading platforms?
3. How can trading and clearing of OTC derivatives be made more transparent, and achieve post-trade services free of counterparty credit risks?

Exchanges in London have used LCH.Clearnet for clearing services since 1888, when London Clearing House (LCH) was founded to clear commodity contracts. In the 1990s, LCH initiated clearing of contracts traded on the International Petroleum Exchange (IPE), the London International Financial Futures Exchange (LIFFE), and London Metal Exchange (LME). In 1995 LCH took on the clearing of cash equities, followed by cash bonds, repos, interbank interest rate swaps, and energy. In 1996 LCH restructured. In 2003 LCH merged with Clearnet, the latter established four years earlier to clear contracts traded on the Paris commodity markets. Clearnet later became part of Matif, the French futures exchange, and finally was merged into Euronext. LCH.Clearnet guarantees contract performance by becoming the central counterparty to all contracts registered in the names of its clearing members. It becomes the buyer to every seller, and the seller to every buyer, assuring that individual obligations will be fulfilled. It is the leading independent central counterparty group in Europe.[23]

Whither Clearing?

In 2008 the chief executive of LSE warned that an anti-competitive threat faced European exchanges. If UK regulators did not intervene, structural changes would be introduced and shift the landscape toward a growing number of small, in-house, and high cost clearing facilities. Clara Furse criticized moves by NYSE Euronext to distance itself from LCH.Clearnet and set up another clearer, as well as plans by the Intercontinental Exchange (ICE) to set up its own clearer in London.[24] At the same time as Furse issued these statements, the UK Office of Fair Trading (OFT) had completed its review of the ICE proposal to establish a London clearing facility, and referred these findings to the British Treasury.

Charlie McCreevy, the European Union's internal markets commissioner, has criticized delays in establishing effective links between clearing infrastructures. The EU "code of conduct" calls for interoperability between infrastructure providers, and effective competition across Europe's capital markets. Interoperability aims to encourage exchanges, clearing houses, and settlement plans in cash equities to link with one another to help lower post-trade costs across Europe. Also, it allows investors greater choice in where their trades are cleared and settled. The stakes are high. Should Brussels or the private sector dictate the coming shape of Europe's exchanges, clearing, and broader market structures as the EU struggles to compete with a powerful US capital market?[25]

The European Commission would have Europe's nationally based settlement systems and clearing houses, some owned by exchanges, open their services to each other, allowing free competition in providing post-trade services. This would stimulate competition and lead to reduced costs in trading and clearing. There have been close to eighty requests by exchanges, clearers, and central securities depositories to open up to each other, but little has resulted on the clearing side. In part this is due to the belief by clearers that the loss in clearing revenue would be substantial.[26]

LCH.Clearnet has been caught in the debate over clearing stock and derivatives trading in Europe. On one side, Brussels authorities call for competition within an open model. Alternately, some exchanges believe the future lies in exchanges owning their own clearing houses. In April 2008 LIFFE indicated it would set up its own in-house clearer, leaving LCH.Clearnet with a much diminished role. Meanwhile ICE, which operates a London based commodity futures business cleared by LCH.Clearnet, is campaigning to move clearing from LCH.Clearnet to a new clearer in London built by ICE.

One possible solution for LCH.Clearnet could be a partnership with the larger DTCC. This would create a pan-European post-trade service platform, supported by an array of market users, including banks and exchanges.

The largest users of exchanges and trading platforms, the banks, hold that Europe would benefit from a single clearer and settlement provider. Mirroring the US model, service costs could be brought much lower.[27] The question of whether centralized clearing should apply to OTC derivatives, especially credit default swaps, is discussed in Chapter 8.

Trading Beyond Equities

Earlier sections of this chapter comment on: 1) the slower growth of stock exchanges contrasted with derivative exchanges, 2) strategies employed by exchanges to improve and enhance their business models, and 3) wide disparities in profitability, revenue sources, and profit margins between exchanges.

Financial exchanges face challenging years ahead. To meet these challenges, exchanges must maintain high growth in revenues and achieve greater diversification in sources of revenue. This can be accomplished in part by moving toward trading beyond equities.

Stocks, Bonds, and Derivatives

Stocks, bonds, and derivatives offer three major routes toward increased trading volume. All leading stock exchanges have focused on providing better and more varied platforms for equities trading, but few have focused on bonds and derivatives.

Bonds Can be Better

At present only two leading financial exchanges have developed meaningful bond listing and trading. These are the Swiss Stock Exchange (SWX) and the Luxembourg Stock Exchange. Both exchanges operate in low tax environments and are loosely referred to as "offshore" exchanges. That is, a major part of their clientele is domiciled in other countries, and a large proportion of trading is in foreign or international securities.

We describe the composition of Luxembourg Stock Exchange listing and trading in an earlier section of this chapter. There we noted that listing of bonds accounts for 69 percent of aggregate listings, and bond turnover represents 68 percent of the total. The SWX reflects a similarly dominant role for fixed income securities. Table 4.14 provides a breakdown of trades (by number) and turnover.

Table 4.14 indicates that SWX turnover is dominated by bonds (56 percent of turnover), with equities (30 percent) and derivatives (10 percent) taking second and third rank. The "Trades" column in the table suggests a more important role for equities than bonds, but this reflects the tendency for equity trading to be crowded by higher frequency clientele. By contrast, fixed income trading consists more of institutional (wholesale) clientele. Swiss franc denominated bond trading accounts for 90 percent of fixed income transactions.

Table 4.14 Turnover and Trading on the Swiss Stock Exchange (Percentage of Total)

Instrument	*Turnover*	*Trades*
Equities:	30%	66%
Swiss equities	28	62
International equities	2	4
Bonds:	56%	10%
Swiss CHF	24	2
Foreign CHF	27	4
International bonds	5	4
Derivatives	10%	22%
Closed end funds	1%	1%
Exchange traded funds	3%	1%
	100%	100%

Source: SWX, *Annual Report 2005*, pp. 38–39.

In recent years aggregate turnover on the SWX has been in the range of US$250–320 billion, and exceeds Swiss GDP by a sizeable margin. The SWX has developed a substantial international trading business. If the SWX were reduced to trading domestic equities, we can observe from Table 4.14 that its turnover could be less than 30 percent of its current size. Bond trading, derivatives, international equities, and specialized funds add a dimensionality to SWX rarely matched by other financial exchanges.

Derivatives are Becoming Important

Eight of the stock exchanges described in Table 4.7 provide trading in derivatives. As observed in Table 4.7, four exchanges derive 18 percent or more of revenues from this source. Owing to the fact that growth in derivatives trading has exceeded that of equities, it seems likely that derivatives will become a more important revenue generator in future. Stock exchanges that focus on innovations in the form of 1) bringing existing OTC derivatives onto exchanges or 2) creating new derivative products certainly could experience an increase in the revenue share from this source.

New Instruments

In 1993 the first exchange traded fund was created and traded on the AMEX to replicate the S&P 500 performance. Since then, several hundred ETFs have been launched by Barclays Global Investors (iShares), Vanguard, and others. Most of these are structured to mimic the performance generated by a component of the Morgan Stanley Capital International (MSCI) Index. ETFs trade like common stocks, enjoy liquid markets, and provide within-day liquidity and price transparency.

New type trading instruments such as ETFs provide a key source of growth for stock exchanges. ETFs based on equity indices provided a needed spur to stock exchange trading growth in the period 1993–2008. In a parallel way, ETFs based on fixed income indices may well provide similar growth impetus in the coming decade.

Reporting in 2008, Mazzilli, Maister, and Perlman note the US bond market exceeds $27 trillion and is the largest in the world.[28] By contrast, the US equity market is $16 trillion. More importantly, the US fixed income market includes Treasury and agency, mortgage backed, corporate, municipal, and asset-backed securities. Reflecting the large and diversified fixed income market, the fixed income ETF market has been growing rapidly since 2002. Table 4.15 reports the size and expansion of fixed income ETFs available to investors in 2008.

Barclays Global Investors issued the first US listed fixed income ETFs in July 2002. Three tracked Treasury indices, while a fourth tracked the investment grade corporate bond index. By mid-2008 over sixty such ETFs were listed and traded on American exchanges (Table 4.15). Index-linked ETFs with over $43 billion in assets serve as attractive investment structures to gain exposure to fixed income sectors. Advantages of fixed income ETFs include diversified exposure,

Table 4.15 Fixed Income ETFs, 2008

Investment objective	*Number of ETFs*	*Total assets US$ millions*
Broad market	7	10,529
Treasury	16	16,048
Leveraged inverse	2	53
TIPS	2	6,780
Treasury/investment grade	5	1,312
Mortgage	1	594
Corporate investment grade	4	4,366
High yield	3	1,108
Preferred	3	1,546
National municipal	8	117
Single state municipal	6	164
International development	2	886
International emerging markets	2	139
Total	61	43,642

Source: P. Mazzilli, D. Maister, and D. Perlman, "Fixed Income ETFs: Over 60 ETFs Enable Portfolios of Bonds to Be Traded Like Stocks," *Exchange Traded Funds*, Institutional Investor, 2008, p. 59.

competitive returns, low cost, provision of regular income, and constant duration. These ETFs trade like equities, closely track net asset values and benchmark indices, and are not leveraged. The disadvantages of these instruments are lack of progression in maturity (constant duration), possibility of lower yield, possibility of inferior performance relative to individual bond issues for buy and hold investors, and possible exposure to tracking error risks.

Fixed income ETFs have become a widely accepted instrument. As this market sector matures we can expect to see a wider range of types of instruments becoming available, offering investors still wider choices for investment and trading.

5 Restructuring via Mergers

Financial exchanges face serious threat from competing trading systems and market makers. Exchanges have been pressed to adopt more flexible and responsive trading systems and migrate to electronic trading. Demutualization has given exchanges greater operating and governance flexibility. By converting further to public ownership, exchanges have undertaken more extensive restructuring by entering into mergers with other exchanges, by acquiring stakes in others, and by forming strategic alliances.

The business model of financial exchanges has become more controlled by fixed costs, as these enterprises have replaced trading floors and people-power with computerized systems. But, after the large fixed investment is made in modern high speed trading systems, the incremental cost from adding more trading volume is quite low. These factors have become strong incentives for exchanges to merge and combine their trading systems and platforms.

In this chapter we analyze the motives for merger of exchanges, including growing a larger business, achieving greater geographic spread, rebalancing the competitive equation, and creating a business model with optimal portfolio characteristics. We analyze merger and acquisition strategies as they apply to the financial exchange sector. Also, we analyze early mergers in this sector that led to a steady consolidation process. We provide a wide range of merger illustrations and examples, by type of merger as well as according to the different time periods in which these mergers have taken place. Table 5.1 outlines six merger variants, and describes the specific mergers that offer examples of these variants. These are discussed in detail throughout this chapter and in the following chapters.

Merger Analysis

Why do mergers take place? Are mergers the quickest and most flexible way to achieve corporate restructuring? Do most mergers turn out to be successful? These and related questions have puzzled analysts of business strategy and management for decades. We continue to find new answers to these questions. As new sectors and challenges move onstage with the recent and ongoing spate of mergers between financial exchanges, we need to rewrite these questions and frame them in a way that helps us explain and better understand this phenomenon.

Table 5.1 Six Merger Variants

Type of merger or consolidation	*Stock exchanges*	*Derivative and commodity exchanges*
1 Within-nation consolidation	Toronto Stock Exchange (2004)	CME–CBOT (2007) CME–Nymex (2008)
2 Cross-border regional	OMX Group (2003)	
3 Acquiring ECNs	NYSE–Archipelago (2006) NASDAQ–Instinet (2006)	
4 Pan-European	Euronext Group (2000) LSE–Borsa Italiana (2007)	Euronext–LIFFE (2004)
5 Transatlantic	NYSE–Euronext (2007) NASDAQ–OMX (2007)	Deutsche Börse–ISE (2007)
6 Acquiring stakeholdings and alliances, joint ventures	NYSE–National Stock Exchange of India (5 percent) Tokyo Stock Exchange –Singapore Stock Exchange (5 percent) Singapore Stock Exchange –National Stock Exchange of India (5 percent) Tokyo Stock Exchange –LSE joint venture to develop second tier market in Tokyo	Singapore (SGX) and OMX new clearing system for SGX derivatives Taiwan Futures Exchange (TAIFEX) signed memorandum of understanding (MOU) in March 2009 with NASDAQ OMX Group to partner in product development, operations, and derivatives

Source: Author's compilation; annual reports of financial exchanges.

Five Drivers

Bruce Wasserstein, a successful investment banker in the field of mergers, cites "elemental forces . . . which drive the merger process." These include: 1) regulatory and political reform, 2) technological change, 3) fluctuations in financial markets, 4) the role of leadership, and 5) tension between scale and focus.[1] Many mergers and acquisitions (M&A) in active sectors, such as media and telecommunications, financial services, and health care, have been stimulated by deregulation or other political change. We can point to regulatory change in the United States and Europe, which mandated greater competition among exchanges, and between exchanges and other trading venues.[2]

Technology change is discussed in Chapter 3 as important in driving exchanges to revise their business models and consider merger as a means of achieving larger volume on newly put-in-place electronic trading platforms. The propensity for financial market prices and trading volumes to fluctuate provides another incentive for exchanges to merge, to achieve more diversified and hopefully more stable revenue flow. Financial markets appear prone to episodes of volatility and changing circumstances. This volatility affects revenue flow of financial exchanges to a high degree.

Leadership at major financial exchanges has played a central role in energizing these for-profit companies to seek and negotiate mergers (Thain at NYSE,

Théodore at Euronext, Greifeld at NASDAQ) or to resist merger proposals when they appeared unattractive and following an organic restructuring seemed preferable (Clara Furse at LSE).

Finally, the interplay between scale and focus has risen to prominence in the exchange sector. Investment in high capacity trading networks gives urgency to widening the range of instruments eligible for listing and trading. Consequently, financial exchanges are becoming more like omnivorous search engines, taking on bonds, options, ETFs, and other tradable instruments. Here, the economics of scale and scope operate in a positive way.

To summarize, it appears that all five of Wasserstein's drivers of change are helpful in explaining the rising level of M&A activity in the financial exchange sector.

Three Levels of Analysis

Any merger analysis requires consideration of financial, business, and strategic impacts. Each follows a distinct criterion, and is answered by a specific question.

The financial criterion requires that the merger should generate short term benefits to the new entity. The specific question becomes: what is the balance between the premium paid to acquire another exchange and synergy realized from the merger? Also, are there tax benefits from the transaction, and can immediate earnings improvement be achieved?

The business criterion considers the ongoing rationale for merger. The key question is: Has this merger enhanced the business model? How? Finally, the strategic criterion considers how the merger can transform the participating entities toward an increased ability to compete and succeed on a long term basis. The specific question is: What transformation is accomplished? The transformation might bring broader geographic market reach, utilization of a single trading system for a wider range of security types, or blending equity and derivative trading on a single electronic platform.

Portfolio Analysis

Two approaches can be applied in analyzing whether particular mergers can produce favorable outcomes. These are the fundamental analysis and the portfolio approach. Fundamental analysis seeks to estimate or measure real synergies from merger. The portfolio approach considers the company entities as components of a portfolio, which possesses return–risk correlation metrics. In this section we consider the portfolio approach.

In an analysis of seventeen financial exchanges which have been publicly traded companies since 2001, Miller and Pagano use portfolio theory to consider "what-if" scenarios. They examine seventy-eight possible mergers between pairings of these seventeen exchanges, to identify the "best" and "worst" merger pairs. The criteria applied are risk–return and correlation patterns, therefore excluding consideration of potential merger synergies related to economies of scale or scope.[3]

Miller and Pagano examine combinations of exchanges that already have taken place (NYSE–Euronext) and potential pairings such as the NASDAQ Market and the London Stock Exchange. To gain a sense of the risk–return characteristics of the aggregate securities exchange industry, Miller and Pagano created the first-ever Global Exchange Markets (GEM) Index.

Basic Data

The Miller and Pagano analysis is based on daily US dollar stock returns including dividends for publicly traded financial exchanges in North America, Europe, Asia, and Australia. The complete sample contains data for seventeen companies from eleven different countries, covering the period July 3, 2001 to October 5, 2006. Given that exchanges only recently have been publicly traded enterprises, many exchanges do not have data for the full time range assigned. Therefore, two sets of firms are analyzed as indicated:

1 period December 2002–October 2006 (eleven exchanges);
2 period August 2004–October 2006 (thirteen exchanges).

Over both subperiods, shares of financial exchanges have significantly outperformed their respective stock market indices. Also, many of the exchanges display lower risk as measured by the respective coefficients of variation. For example, in the second subsample (August 2004–October 2006) mean daily returns range three to seven times larger than the average return on the MSCI Index, and three to eight times greater than the average return on the S&P 500. Also, nine of the thirteen exchanges in the subsample report coefficients of variation superior to those of the MSCI World Index.

The potential diversification benefits of exchange consolidation can be observed in the correlation matrices generated in the Miller and Pagano analysis. With only two exceptions, all the firm-to-firm correlation pairs are less than 0.31, with a majority less than 0.1. In particular, the exchanges from the Asia Pacific region tend to have very low correlations with the non-Asia exchanges.

Measuring Potential Merger Performance

Miller and Pagano generate seventy-eight possible merger pairs of the exchanges analyzed. They employ three well-recognized measures to rank mergers with the greatest return per unit of risk: the coefficient of variation, the Sharpe ratio (mean return divided by standard deviation), and the Treynor index (mean return divided by beta). The analysis and rankings result in "top ten combinations" and "bottom ten combinations." Results covering top ten combinations indicate that Asia Pacific exchanges, the Toronto Stock Exchange, and the Chicago Mercantile Exchange represent the strongest combinations of risk and return. The Toronto Stock Exchange has the potential for generating some of the better combinations, particularly when paired with Asia Pacific markets such as those based in

Singapore, Australia, and Hong Kong. The three North American exchanges (NYSE, CME, and Toronto Stock Exchange) appear to benefit most from pairing up with exchanges outside their region. In Table 5.2, we present the top ten and bottom ten combinations as reflected by their respective coefficients of variation. The median coefficient of variation for the top ten is 6.659, much lower than for the bottom ten combinations.

Results among the bottom ten combinations indicate that many of the hypothetical pairings with the NASDAQ stock market possess some of the lower returns relative to risk, with more than half of these pairs including NASDAQ. Interestingly, Miller and Pagano find that pairing the OMX Group with NASDAQ ranks in the bottom ten for nearly all return to risk measures.[4] Further, the hypothetical merger of the NASDAQ and the London Stock Exchange represents one of the lower return to risk combinations. The NYSE–Euronext merger offers a better return to risk ratio than NASDAQ–LSE, "but is still not one of the highest performers."

Table 5.2 Return to Risk Ratio Rankings, Hypothetical Mergers of Paired Exchanges (December 2002–October 2006)

Paired exchanges		*Coefficient of variation*	
Panel A: top ten combinations			
Sydney Futures	TSX Group	5.713	
Australian Stock Exchange	TSX Group	6.107	
Singapore Stock Exchange	TSX Group	6.285	
NYSE	Deutsche Börse	6.535	
Singapore Stock Exchange	Sydney Futures	6.620	6.659 median
Hong Kong Stock Exchange	CME Group	6.690	
Hong Kong Stock Exchange	TSX Group	6.698	
Osaka Stock Exchange	Hong Kong Stock Exchange	6.828	
TSX Group	CME Group	6.842	
Singapore Stock Exchange	Australian Stock Exchange	6.852	
Panel B: bottom ten combinations			
Singapore Stock Exchange	NASDAQ	10.155	
Deutsche Börse	NASDAQ	10.315	
Osaka Stock Exchange	Australia Stock Exchange	10.354	
Osaka Stock Exchange	Sydney Futures	10.624	
Australian Stock Exchange	NASDAQ	10.747	10.778 median
London Stock Exchange	NASDAQ	10.809	
Osaka Stock Exchange	TSX Group	10.989	
Sydney Futures	NASDAQ	11.528	
Osaka Stock Exchange	OM Group	14.879	
OM Group	NASDAQ	14.985	

Source: T.O. Miller and M.S. Pagano, "Who Wants to Dance? Some Possible Exchange Partners, *Journal of Trading*, Spring 2007, p. 70.

Cautionary Note

We should remember that the Miller and Pagano findings are based on return to risk returns estimated from backward-looking (historical) data, covering a particular time period. This period covers the earliest market trading of shares issued by financial exchanges, a period when these shares outperformed general stock market indexes. Also, it is important to remember that specific merger related synergies are excluded from the Miller and Pagano analysis.

The findings summarized above could change in a substantial manner if mergers between exchanges were to be actively managed, to generate synergies. Actions taken by the combined entities' management could result in large cost savings and revenue gains.

Methodologically, the Miller and Pagano analysis represents a "portfolio construction" rather than a merger involving "control" investment. There exists a qualitative distinction between portfolio and control investments. The qualitative difference gives control investment a combination of benefits, containing varying amounts of free synergies, designed alteration of the new entity's business model, and a dynamic integration process that continuously adapts to competitive conditions.

How Far Have We Come?

Mergers between financial exchanges have evolved toward broader geographic coverage as well as trading more diverse instruments. Our perspective covers a two-decade experience, beginning around 1990. We identify six distinct types of merger or acquisition, as described in Table 5.1. These range in complexity from within-nation consolidation, and acquisitions of ECNs, to pan-European and also transatlantic mergers.

Within-Nation Consolidation

Formation of the Toronto Stock Exchange Group (TSX) was a six-year process, bringing at least nine exchanges together. As early as 1999 the Alberta and Vancouver stock exchanges combined. Two years later the Montreal and Toronto stock exchanges merged. By 2004 the Winnipeg Stock Exchange and Canada's Natural Gas Exchange had joined the TSX Group. At that time the TSX Group had listed equities with a market capitalization almost half as large as that of the NASDAQ market. At midyear 2006 the TSX Group was one of eight North American exchanges that had completed an IPO and listing of its own shares.

Exchange Consolidation in Germany

The pattern followed by the TSX Group has been followed in other countries as well. In 1990 Germany suffered from a fragmented and inefficient capital market. Nine regional stock exchanges operated, market capitalization value was low relative to GNP, and the country lacked an equity culture. Over the next several years reform legislation and a reorganization of the exchanges into a single entity headed by the Frankfurt exchange brought a more modern business model and investment in an efficient trading platform. A derivative exchange was established, initially called Deutsche Termin Börse, later renamed Eurex and partly (20 percent) owned by the Swiss exchange.

Rationale for Merger in Singapore

In December 1999 two of Singapore's most reputable institutions, the Stock Exchange of Singapore (SES) and the Singapore International Monetary Exchange (SIMEX), merged to form the Singapore Stock Exchange (SGX). SGX is the first demutualized and incorporated securities and derivatives exchange in the Asia Pacific region. SIMEX was established in 1983, from an alliance between the Gold Exchange of Singapore and the International Monetary Market (IMM) in Chicago. At inception it became Asia's first eurodollar futures exchange, offering a broad range of futures and options contracts for interest rates, currencies, stock indices, energy, and other commodities. The SES traded in stocks. It was launched in 1973. By 1998 SES had grown to a market capitalization of $26.3 billion and 307 company equity listings, not including corporate bonds which also traded on the exchange. It has become East Asia's largest and most advanced stock exchange.

We can point to five motivations underlying the restructuring and merger of SES and SIMEX, to create SGX as a new and modern entity. These are:

1 Innovation and new product development. Creation of more and more securities and derivatives products has blurred former sharp distinctions between underlying securities and related derivatives. A combined market facilitates better alignment of investment, risk taking, hedging, and arbitrage strategies, minimizes operating costs, and allows more flexible positioning.
2 Globalization. Investors and issuers of securities migrate from one market to another more than before. They seek markets offering enhanced liquidity, better pricing, and improved execution. Exchanges compete with one another more directly than ever before, even while located remotely from one another. In the modern electronic world, exchanges find former relationship advantages eroding, as faster and cheaper communications gives market participants readier access to actual and virtual marketplaces.
3 Technology. Development of new technology allows more players to compete, but technology platforms are expensive, and it is becoming necessary to raise scale and scope of trading on a given exchange to offset technology costs and average down unit trading expenses.
4 Competition. Brokers placing orders for customers now trade in a variety of markets on different continents. This makes brokers highly sensitive to cost differences and the level of service efficiency at competing exchanges. In this aggressive operating environment, exchanges need to reposition themselves to compete more effectively. Over the past two decades the Singapore

exchanges has experienced increased foreign participation. Over the past five years foreign companies have contributed over one-third of market capitalization on the SGX main board.

5 Sophisticated clientele. An increasing number of companies listing their shares are footloose and seek to raise capital at lower cost on market venues that attract a large investor base and high liquidity. Similarly, investors seek more innovative markets, with a wide range of securities and derivatives. SGX has responded by listing foreign companies, and equity indices representing major world benchmarks. As a result, SIMEX ranks among the largest futures and options exchange in the world.

Cross-Border Regional

In Table 5.1 an example is provided of cross-border regional mergers. This is the highly successful formation of OMX Group. This group took shape in the period 1998–2006. Its success was reinforced by the strong technology and system engineering capacity it enjoys, and the need of many small Scandinavian exchange markets to achieve larger scale and scope. The merger process began in 1998 when the Stockholm Stock Exchange merged with a financial service technology provider, OM Group. A little over a year later this group merged with the Helsinki and subsequently Copenhagen exchanges. Following this, the Iceland Stock Exchange was added to the Nordic Exchange component of OMX, and the Latvian, Lithuanian, and Estonian exchanges formed the Baltic Exchange component of OMX.

OMX Group's business model contained three cornerstones: the Nordic Exchange, exchange technology, and a global customer base.[5] Its two main customer offerings include the Nordic Exchange and global technology operations. The Nordic Market includes seven country based exchange operations plus First North. First North is an alternative market with a more simple set of regulations than the main market. It is targeted toward smaller growth companies, such as those listed on LSE's Alternative Investment Market (AIM).

The Nordic Exchange trades equities, bonds, and derivatives. The information services and new markets component is well developed, and includes basic information services and broker services. OMX Group is a world leader in market technology, servicing exchanges, banks, broker-dealers, and financial institutions. In 2007 it counted more than sixty customers in more than fifty nations. In 2007 it introduced its GENIUM Market Info service, provided services to the Saudi Stock Exchange, gained its first technology customer in Spain, and entered the South American service market. Currently OMX has important customers including over twenty clearing organizations and securities depositories in Abu Dhabi, Hong Kong, and Vienna.

At yearend 2007 the CEO, Magnus Böcker, noted that "the lessons we have learned from the creation of the Nordic Exchange convince me that similar mergers can be made in other parts of the world."[6] Early in 2008 OMX Group merged with NASDAQ. We discuss this merger in detail in Chapter 6.

Acquiring ECNs

The success of OMX Group was already apparent across the Atlantic. In 2006 both the NYSE and NASDAQ initiated restructuring of their respective market systems. However, in each case they acquired existing operational technology and business models that were proven successes.

In the case of NYSE, demutualization was accompanied by acquisition of Archipelago. On March 7, 2006 the NYSE Group took ownership of Archipelago as a for-profit entity. In May 2006 the NYSE Group filed a prospectus, offering 25 million shares of its stock, owned by NYSE members and officers, and underwriters.[7]

Prior to its merger with NYSE, Archipelago undertook and completed an alliance and merger with the Pacific Exchange and several other ECNs. As the operator of the trading facility PCX Equities, Archipelago earned revenue from market data fees and listing fees. Also, it was able to reduce clearing costs. Based on its ownership of PCX Holdings (Pacific Exchange), Archipelago conducted trading in equity options. In 2002 Archipelago merged with REDIBook ECN LLC, and acquired GlobeNet Securities. REDIBook was a competing ECN, and its acquisition significantly increased Archipelago's trading volume in NASDAQ listed securities. In the GlobeNet acquisition Archipelago gained technology, including a matching engine platform used to develop an alternative trading system for bulletin board stocks.[8] By yearend 2005 Archipelago handled 23.0 percent, 3.6 percent, and 30.0 percent respectively of trading volume in NASDAQ, NYSE, and AMEX listed equities.

NYSE's merger with Archipelago transformed the NYSE Group into an exchange operator with considerable electronic system trading capacity in equities and equity options, as well as a leading provider of market data in these sectors.

By yearend 2003 it could be observed that ECNs had taken more trading business from the NASDAQ market than from NYSE.[9] In the case of Instinet, part of its success was utilizing its crossing networks. Crossing prices were based on the closing price for exchange listed stocks (on NYSE, AMEX), and the average of the closing bid and ask for NASDAQ stocks. The NASDAQ acquisition of its biggest ECN rival, Instinet, in 2006 was a logical competitive reaction.

Acquiring Stakeholdings and Alliances

Outright merger is one approach to restructuring exchanges. It is complete, generally irreversible, and not flexible as to timing. By contrast, stakeholdings are flexible as to timing and relative pricing (both set at a future date), and usually reversible.

Given the large number of financial exchanges around the world, the vastly differing operating conditions and circumstances, and varied pace of restructuring in each country and at each exchange, it is no surprise that in many cases financial exchanges have opted to take or sell equity stakes in one another. Further, the failure to achieve full agreement on merger terms in so many cases since 1999 adds to the relative attractiveness of the stakeholdings approach.

At midyear 2007 the Tokyo Stock Exchange acquired a 5 percent stake in SGX for $303 million.[10] The SGX already had a fifty-fifty joint venture with the CBOT to list commodity futures on a Singapore platform called Jade. Jade aims at tapping into a growing market for derivatives in the region, and in the year ending June 2007 the market value of SGX tripled. The Tokyo Stock Exchange stake in SGX represents the first capital tie-up between Asian exchanges, and evidences the spread of global consolidation to the region. The deal gives evidence of the astute leadership of Taizo Nishimuro, at the time chief executive of the Tokyo exchange. In 2007 the Tokyo Stock Exchange was planning an initial public offering of its own shares, to take place in 2008 or later.[11] The Tokyo and Singapore exchanges were exploring the establishment of a trading and clearing link for derivatives, Japanese government bonds, and TOPIX products.

Meanwhile, the NYSE Group and Tokyo exchange have been discussing a possible alliance which could involve taking stakes in each other. One obstacle to a share exchange by the two is that the Tokyo exchange has not taken its shares public.[12] The NYSE Group was moving forward to acquire a 5 percent stake in the National Stock Exchange of India, for $115 million. Three other investors, and Goldman Sachs, also indicated they were purchasing similar stakes in the Indian exchange.

Four basic motives lie behind these stakeholdings. First, they are likely to become highly profitable investments. This is due to the high revenue growth combined with then currently low valuations. Second, such stakeholdings may forestall other entities (exchanges or banks) from jumping in ahead. Third, future business ties and development often represent the objective of stakeholdings. Finally, real options theory tells us that a small stakeholding may become an exercisable option sometime in the future, when opportunities become more readable.

In 2008 SGX and OMX signed an agreement to implement a new clearing system, using OMX technology. This aimed at enhancing SGX derivatives and securities clearing capabilities. The OMX clearing technology would improve SGX's ability to clear a wider range of products and offer a new set of clearing services to members. An open interface feature of the clearing system would enable straight-through processing and boost operational efficiency at SGX. The new system was launched in 2009, and led to discussions of possible merger with other exchanges based in Asia.

Joint Ventures

Joint ventures are a highly important method for company restructuring and developing business ties in other regions. Joint ventures possess several advantages, including flexibility, more definite lines of management control, and clear ownership status.

The Tokyo Stock Exchange and the London Stock Exchange launched a joint venture, to develop a second tier market for share trading in Tokyo. This operates similarly to LSE's Alternative Investment Market and builds on the London exchange's success in creating and developing a market designed for small growth companies. Tokyo AIM, as it is called, provides a new funding option for growing companies in Japan and Asia, providing access to capital in a market tailored to the needs of smaller enterprises. Tokyo AIM services an investor base seeking new investment opportunities.

London's Alternative Investment Market has become a world leader, ahead of all other international markets in number of new listings from 2006 onward. Tokyo AIM will enjoy certain advantages over the traditional first time markets in Japan. It usually takes close to a year to prepare an IPO in Japan, but it can be done in as short a period as four months on Tokyo AIM. AIM offers a more flexible regulatory framework, designed for growing companies and aimed at professional investors only. Like London's AIM, Tokyo AIM will require nominated advisers (Nomads), corporate finance advisers approved by Tokyo AIM. As experts in admission and regulatory procedures required, and to satisfy minimum corporate governance standards for the needs of both companies and investors, Nomads will be able to certify the readiness of companies for trading on Tokyo AIM. This certification can apply to requests submitted in English or Japanese, and can require accounting methods conform to International Accounting Standards, to US GAAP, or to Japanese GAAP.

Tokyo AIM commenced operations in 2009, but approval of new listings requires several months' processing. It was reported that the Tokyo AIM joint venture would have an ownership of 51 percent TSE and 49 percent LSE.

Pan-European Mergers

The idea of establishing a pan-European stock market extends back to 1990, when the German stock exchanges began plans to integrate nine regional exchanges in that country. In this section we analyze three mergers that moved Europe closer to achieving a pan-European capital market. These are the formation of Euronext in 2000, the merger of Euronext and LIFFE, and the merger of LSE and Borsa Italiana.

Formation of Euronext

Euronext was created in 2000 with the merger of the Paris, Amsterdam, and Brussels bourses. While we portray the merger as "pan-European," it represents only an initial step in the direction of creating a pan-European market. At midyear 2001 the United States had only three national exchanges and five regional exchanges, while Western Europe boasted close to thirty separate stock exchanges.[13]

With introduction of the single currency, *The Economist* predicted that most European exchanges would not survive the next ten years.[14] Formation of Euronext is one illustration of the race for the top spot in European equities trading. In carrying out the merger, Euronext was able to move ahead of rival Deutsche Börse, as measured by annual equity turnover (Table 5.3). Following the merger which created Euronext, London still accounted for more than two times the turnover of the Paris based entity.

Table 5.3 Turnover on European Stock Markets, Year Ending June 2001 (Percentage of Total)

London Stock Exchange	43.2
Euronext	19.1
Deutsche Börse	14.6
Swiss Stock Exchange	5.1
Other	18.0
	100.0%

Source: *The Economist.*

The merger creating Euronext gave the new exchange four key advantages. These are: the ability to control and lower trading costs; a more liquid market with narrower dealing spreads; access to cheaper technology and alternative trading platforms; and larger size and scale, which could foster future alliances with other exchanges.

Liquidity is a key determinant of who will win and lose in the ongoing battle of the bourses, but liquidity is by no means abundant. Cross-border equity flows can dry up. Growth in the size and number of institutional investors can lead to an increased demand for tradable securities not always matched by supply.

By 2004 the Lisbon Stock Exchange had joined Euronext. The stock exchanges that entered into the Euronext group were willing to sacrifice autonomy for competitive advantage. But many bourses in Europe appear determined to defend their turf and carry on as independent companies. In 2004 Euronext represented a small beginning in the quest for a pan-European stock market. But the year 2004 was to witness another big merger, with the London based LIFFE as the principal target.

LIFFE joins Euronext

LIFFE is the second largest derivative exchange on a global basis. It provides market facilities to hedge and trade across a wide range of derivative products, offering futures and option contracts in the following products: currency futures, interest rate futures, futures and options on equity indexes, and commodities. LIFFE enables participants to hedge risks, and also take exposures for possible profit.

LIFFE was established in 1982, combining the London Commodity Exchange (LCE), where "soft" commodities, agricultural commodities and BIFFEX (the shipping freight rate index) were traded via futures and options, and newly created financial futures and options. Since its inception LIFFE's business has grown at a rate of 40 percent a year, and it is now one of the world's largest financial exchanges. LIFFE shifted from open outcry to electronic trading in the late 1990s, as it suffered an erosion of its market share to electronic markets. LIFFE introduced a new electronic system—LIFFE CONNECT—resulting in a shift from quote driven to order driven trading. LIFFE customers, based in over sixty cities around the world, can trade from their own offices wherever located.

Make an Offer

In 2001 the chairman of LIFFE indicated the exchange might consider any serious offer to acquire the exchange. In summer 2001 LIFFE's shares traded on an unlisted market on a matched bargain basis through Cazenove, a London investment bank. Its shares were appreciating at this time, with market capitalization of £355 million sterling.[15] At this time derivatives exchanges were reporting huge increases in trading volume. By early October 2001 the London Stock Exchange was the only party to have made an offer.[16] LSE was planning to build a new electronic trading system to allow investors to trade shares and futures contracts together. To proceed with this big investment LSE would need to acquire LIFFE.[17]

Rival Bidders

At this time Deutsche Börse entered the bidding battle to acquire LIFFE. Shortly prior to the German exchange entering the bidding Euronext made an indicative offer. LIFFE's minimum price of £14 sterling a share valued the London derivative exchange at £555 million sterling (US$708 million).[18] By October's end Euronext had topped its two rival bidders with a £555 million sterling agreed takeover bid for LIFFE. This ended an intense battle between Europe's three leading exchanges, and represented a bitter blow to the London Stock Exchange. Following this merger with Euronext, London became the hub for Euronext derivatives business, combining the pan-European exchange's equity options business with the fixed income and short term interest rate business in which LIFFE specializes.[19]

According to London's *Financial Times*, "the victory of Euronext in the battle to acquire the London International Financial Futures Exchange marks an important step in the slow-moving but much-needed consolidation of Europe's stock exchanges." However, for the London Stock Exchange and Deutsche Börse, Euronext's victory must mean some soul-searching.[20]

LSE and Borsa Italiana

In June 2007 Borsa Italiana and the London Stock Exchange announced they had entered into an agreement to merge. The merger created the leading diversified exchange group in Europe. This merger brings together two highly efficient and complementary businesses. Borsa Italiana's strengths are in Italian cash and derivatives instruments, plus its post-trade processing services and leading European fixed income trading platform. This is combined with LSE's deep equity market, and strategic advantages from its London location.

The combined group occupies a unique position in Europe as the leading pool of exchange market liquidity, and internationally as the premier listings venue. Reasons for the merger are numerous. They include: reinforcing a unique global position, maintaining the largest European equities trading pool, operating as a primary European and global listings venue, operating Europe's leading fixed income trading platform, strengthening its position as a world leader in exchange trading technology, and operating as the most efficient provider of post-trade services in Europe. We discuss broader reasons and ramifications of this merger, and the competitive status of the merged entity in Chapter 7.

Regional Tie-Up in Asia

In the final quarter of 2010, the Singapore Stock Exchange offered $8.3 billion to acquire and merge with the Australian Stock Exchange (ASX). This was described as the only merger deal in Asia that could be done today.[21] The proposal came two years after completion of a long series of mergers affecting exchanges in the Americas and Europe. Below we analyze the factors inhibiting mergers between exchanges across the Asia Pacific region, and the prospects for success in the SGX–ASX case.

Barriers to Consolidation in Asia

Asia's stock exchanges have not participated in the consolidation of exchanges that has taken place across Europe and North America. Many reasons explain this. They range from political to economic. The communist system in China fails to match up easily with more democratic systems elsewhere. Many Southeast Asian countries have relatively small financial systems and stock markets, as yet uninteresting to acquirers. Size can play a negative role. The Tokyo Stock Exchange is too large a target for potential acquirers in the region. Cultural factors suggest that integration of operations post-merger might present some difficulties.

Disparities in growth also tend to rule out potential pairings. Hong Kong is too busy digesting new listings and IPO offerings to be bothered with growth via merger. In the first three quarters of 2010 Hong Kong Exchanges and Clearing (HKEx) added $44.2 billion of new listings, covering sixty-one companies (Table 5.4). This is close to 40 percent of the value of new listings on the six Asian exchanges included in Table 5.4.

Table 5.4 New Share Listing Volume and Valuation on Asia Pacific Exchanges (Excluding Tokyo Stock Exchange)

	Value of new listings[1]	*No. of listings*
HKEx	44.2	61
Shenzhen	34.6	253
Shanghai	24.8	19
Korea	6.1	17
Singapore	4.9	20
ASX	1.3	41
Total	115.9	411

Source: A. Critchlow and M. Hadi, "SGX Bid for Australia Exchange Misses Mark," *Wall Street Journal*, October 26, 2010, p. C12.

Note
1 Amounts in billions of US dollars.

The SGX bid for ASX had a number of motivations. First, it would give SGX better access to Australia's one-trillion-dollar pool of pension funds, and over 2,000 listed stocks including the world's largest mining companies. Second, the Singapore exchange would be in a better position to grow via new listings. Table 5.4 tells us that the ASX has gained twice as many new listings (by number) as SGX, in the first three quarters of 2010.

Third, SGX would have access to a much larger part of capital in Australia, an economy ten times as large as the Singapore crossroads. Fourth, ASX daily trading is three times that of SGX.

The SGX offer for ASX is priced at 48 Australian dollars (US$47.11) for each ASX share. Of this, A$22 will be in cash and A$26 in SGX shares. The offer came at a 37 percent premium to the last traded price of ASX shares in late October 2010. The primary listing will be in Singapore. The merger would create a US$1.9 trillion market, posing a serious competitive challenge and threat to other Asian exchanges.[22]

The SGX bid marks a possible new trajectory for Asian financial exchanges. The combination of SGX and the Australian exchange would produce the fifth largest exchange entity measured by market capitalization, with more company listings than any other Asian exchange, except Mumbai in India. The deal could trigger other combinations. Atsushi Saito, head of the Tokyo Stock Exchange, has stated that, if the SGX bid goes forward, it would not be good for Tokyo. Other exchanges would have to consider teaming up, and the TSE would be required to strengthen alliances with regional exchanges to better deal with rising competition.[23] TSE is the second largest shareholder of SGX, with a 4.5 percent stake.

Specific Deal Hurdles

As noted in Table 5.2, a combination of SGX and Sydney Futures Exchange (now merged into ASX) ranks fifth among the top ten in the Miller and Pagano study. A combination of SGX and the Australian Stock Exchange ranks tenth among the top ten. The 2010 merger proposal between SGX and ASX would create Asia's second largest exchange group behind HKEx, and the fifth largest in the world. According to Niki Beattie, managing director of the Market Structure Practice, a London consultancy, "strategically long-term, in terms of surviving in the Asian market, they have both got to do a deal. And they are probably the least contentious partners for each other."[24]

During the twelve months preceding its offer for ASX, the Singapore exchange had been making tie-ups with other exchanges in a strategy to be "the Asian gateway." ASX had been upgrading its trading systems to deal with competition from alternative platforms, and to attract high frequency traders (HFTs). Such competition has been pressuring exchanges in large centers in North America and Europe. Both SGX and ASX share the same trading platforms provided by NASDAQ OMX.

Magnus Böcker, chief executive at SGX, formerly held a similar position at OMX when it merged with NASDAQ. He and Robert Elstone, his counterpart at ASX, stated that informal soundings with regulators in Australia suggested the deal would be allowed.

Approval from the Australian government in Canberra appeared to present the single key hurdle. The Australian government owns a 23.5 percent stake in ASX, which would be diluted to approximately 15 percent if the merger deal goes forward.[25] A spokesman for Wayne Swan, Australia's deputy prime minister, who has the power to veto foreign deals, stated it was too early to comment on the takeover before it was evaluated by regulators.

6 Transatlantic Mergers

This chapter focuses on two transatlantic mergers that set the stage for consolidation of financial exchanges on a global basis. These mergers pre-empted other tie-ups for the four exchanges participating in the transatlantic deals. Also, we analyze post-merger integration, shifts in competition such as fee levels and structure, and the changing landscape of exchange trading in North America and Europe. We then evaluate the changing structure and performance of equity trading in New York, as illustrated by the May 2010 flash crash.

Nine Candidates

Chapter 5 describes an early phase of mergers among financial exchanges. In this phase within-country mergers consolidated the financial exchange sector, combining stock exchanges, commodity exchanges, and also derivative exchanges into cohesive national market systems. Also, regional groups of exchanges were developed in Scandinavia, Continental Europe, and elsewhere. These processes took place in Canada, Australia, and Singapore as well. By early 2006 the stage was set for broader based mergers that would create a truly transatlantic exchange. The question was: Which exchanges would move forward to take part in creating the first transatlantic exchange?

The Candidates

We describe nine leading exchanges which play a role as potential participants in mergers that could create a transatlantic exchange or (in the case of Tokyo Stock Exchange) deflect such a merger by itself partnering with a North American or European exchange. Table 6.1 describes nine exchanges, eight publicly owned, which had a combined market value of over $67 billion, making this new stock market and derivatives market sector large and attractive for equity investors.

The New York Stock Exchange demonstrates close to three times the financial muscle of its New York rival NASDAQ, as measured by market capitalization value (Table 6.1). At the time of this comparison NASDAQ had acquired close to a 15 percent stake in London Stock Exchange (LSE), making it the largest investor in the London exchange. Meanwhile, the NYSE was very tight-lipped over

Table 6.1 Nine Main Candidates for Participation in Transatlantic or Other Mergers (2006)

Financial exchange	*Comments on recent initiatives*	*Market capitalization value of exchange*[1]
1 NYSE	Merged with Archipelago	$11.3 billion
2 NASDAQ	Buying LSE shares	$3.8 billion
3 London Stock Exchange	In process of warning off suitors	$4.65 billion
4 Tokyo Stock Exchange	Plans IPO	Not public
5 Euronext	Appears interested in merger with LSE	$9.04 billion
6 Deutsche Börse	Previously sought merger with LSE	$13.7 billion
7 OMX	Swedish-based, high tech platforms; once pursued LSE	$2.3 billion
8 Chicago Board of Trade	Rumored as merger candidate with NYSE	$16.8 billion
9 Chicago Mercantile Exchange	Executed very successful IPO	$6.15 billion

Source: A. Lucchetti, "NYSE Considers Its Next Move," *Wall Street Journal*, April 13, 2006, pp. C1, C3.

Note
1 These represent values as of April 2006.

any designs it might have in merging with another exchange. The Chicago based exchanges (CBOT and CME) also are described in Table 6.1. As we observe in Chapter 5, these merged in 2008.

In April 2006 it was widely believed that the fragmented financial exchange sector was due for consolidation. But how? The NYSE and NASDAQ were working from two very different vantage points. The Big Board listed mainly the largest blue chip companies and maintained its physical trading floor, whereas most other exchanges had shifted to electronic trading. Meanwhile, NASDAQ had developed as a market of dealers connected by phones and computers, listing smaller growth and technology companies.[1]

Euronext operated from four constituent exchanges, and also owned the London derivatives exchange LIFFE. This made it appear likely that an LSE–Euronext tie-up could develop, since the London exchange lacked a derivatives market of any size. Also, this tie-up would present the world with a massive pan-European market entity.

A NYSE–Deutsche Börse tie-up also looked like a strong possibility. The Frankfurt exchange operated Eurex, the third largest derivative exchange in the world, something that NYSE valued highly. However, Deutsche Börse had its sights on Euronext, a preferred partner.

Two Decisions Set the Stage

NYSE–Euronext

In June 2006 the NYSE Group and Euronext agreed to merge to create a transatlantic exchange with an aggregate market capitalization value of $21 billion.[2] This merger created a diversified group with a dominant position in: a) North American equities trading, b) European equities trading in four countries (France, the Netherlands, Belgium, and Portugal), and c) the largest derivatives exchange outside North America and based in London.

This merger left several other exchanges in a more difficult competitive position. The NASDAQ initiated merger with LSE was working through a series of waiting periods, under the UK Takeover Panel rules applicable to this transaction. Deutsche Börse was able to execute a merger with a small American based options exchange, the International Securities Exchange (ISE). ISE was established as a totally electronic platform, and focused on the high growth options trading sector. It quickly became a dominant market in the United States. ISE completed an initial public offering in 2005, and Eurex (a subsidiary of Deutsche Börse) acquired ISE in April 2007 for a reported $2.8 billion. By 2008 it could be asserted that the Eurex–ISE group was playing a dominant role in world equity derivatives and equity index derivatives.

NASDAQ–LSE

At a later point in this chapter we detail the restructuring of NASDAQ, and its successful efforts to remake itself into a transatlantic financial exchange. Here we continue the short story of what events ensued in 2006 that set the stage for mergers in the period 2006–07.

Early in 2006 NASDAQ had made an offer to acquire LSE for $4.1 billion, which was rejected by the London exchange. In subsequent months NASDAQ acquired close to 30 percent of LSE shares, hoping to pressure LSE executives into agreeing to the tie-up. In January 2007 NASDAQ raised its bid price to $5.7 billion. At the time Clara Furse, LSE chief executive, issued a letter to shareholders, suggesting they reject the New York exchange's offer. In August 2007 NASDAQ indicated it would no longer pursue an LSE tie-up. In the following chapter we analyze the NASDAQ bid for LSE from the perspective of the London exchange. As we note below, NASDAQ turned its focus to OMX Group, merging with the Stockholm-based exchange later in 2007.

Meanwhile, LSE executed a merger with Borsa Italiana, giving the London exchange a claim on developing a pan-European exchange. This merger is discussed in detail in Chapter 7.

First Transatlantic Merger

The following describes and analyzes the first major transatlantic merger between NYSE and Euronext. This merger was transformative in at least five respects. It gave strong impetus to consolidation among exchanges. A number of large mergers followed closely, involving leading exchanges. Second, it reinforced NYSE's position as the pace-setter and largest exchange in the world, as measured by market capitalization value of listed equities and by other measures as well. Third, it altered NYSE's business model. For example, based on 2005 average daily value,

Euronext/LIFFE ranked second only to CME in global derivatives trading. The combined business model enjoyed more diverse revenue sources. Also, revenue growth of the combined entity would be higher than NYSE growth prior to merger. This is due to much higher product innovation and growth in derivatives trading. Finally, the NYSE Euronext Group was the first that had any valid claim on the title "First Multi-Market Global Exchange Group."[3]

Transition at NYSE

Early in 2004 John Reed, the interim CEO and chairman of the NYSE, was given the findings of the Webb Report. The Report attacked the compensation package awarded to Richard Grasso, former head of the NYSE in the period 1995–2003. The Webb Report found the process by which Grasso's $140 million pay package was approved to be faulty and subject to question. The 130-page Report was critical of Grasso, and accused him of running an organization rife with conflicts of interest.

As a "good faith" dollar-a-year chief executive, John Reed had encountered similar cases of mischief in his final months at Citigroup, where he had been ousted by Sandy Weill, who wanted to run Citi in his own image. Reed did not hesitate to implement change and reform at the NYSE. Under Grasso a needed and overdue shift to electronic trading had been delayed, protecting floor traders, brokers, and specialists who made their living on the exchange floor. Reed replaced a number of NYSE executives, and hired a former federal prosecutor, Dan Webb, to investigate the Grasso compensation issue.[4]

New Management

In December the NYSE announced an important management change. John Thain, president at Goldman Sachs, was selected by a search committee to become the CEO of NYSE. At this time another Goldman veteran had joined NYSE. Duncan Niederauer, a trading market expert, was an advocate of shifting from floor trading based on labor intensive methods to electronic trading where investment in technology systems would produce faster and more anonymous execution.

Thain's plan was to transform the exchange, by adopting a modern electronic trading platform. Electronic trading had proven its value. The clients that mattered were the institutional investors such as Fidelity that wanted their orders executed quickly, efficiently, and anonymously through a computer system. Thain moved carefully and methodically in bringing about the biggest structural change in NYSE history.[5]

Plans were being formed to purchase an existing system, Archipelago, but Thain would retain a role for the specialist, through a hybrid system of equity trading. Specialists would provide best price in cases where the computer could not.

There was opposition, and Thain needed approval of these changes from a two-thirds super-majority of the 1,366 seat holders at NYSE. Many of these seats were held by specialists, brokers, and market makers. By February 2005 Goldman Sachs had been appointed as investment banker, to carry through the negotiations and arrangements for restructuring. In only a few months the NYSE was demutualized and converted from a not-for-profit entity into a for-profit when it merged with Archipelago in March 2006 and became a wholly owned subsidiary of NYSE Group.[6]

Hybrid Market

Thain effected a smart compromise, to satisfy the pro-electronic trading members and owners of NYSE Group, as well as those wanting to retain traditional floor trading. He implemented the NYSE hybrid market to combine the advantages of existing agency auction trading, and electronic trading. The hybrid market enhanced NYSE's ability to meet the diverse needs of customers. Market participants can use the traditional auction market, where specialists maintain fair and orderly trading markets. Alternately, order execution also occurs through NYSE's electronic trading platform. The hybrid market offers the speed, certainty, and anonymity of electronic trading, as well as the opportunity for negotiation and price improvement provided by the auction market.[7]

An analysis by Boni and Rosen published in 2007 reports on the extent of price improvement on NYSE related to the hybrid market. Implementation of the hybrid market required specialists develop their own proprietary algorithms to carry out the market making function. Boni and Rosen analyzed whether specialist firms provide as much price improvement under the Hybrid as in the prior auction market. Their test was fairly straightforward. "We say that the order received price improvement if the order bought at a price that was lower than the national best offer, or sold at a price that was higher than the national best bid."[8] They report low probability of price improvement in the NYSE hybrid market in the final four months of 2006. However, they report higher amounts of price improvement for NYSE Hybrid traded stocks than for ECN traded or NYSE non-Hybrid traded stocks.[9]

Decade of Electronic Brokerage

Reluctantly the NYSE followed brokers and dealers that adopted electronic order execution and trading, but this was only after it had become quite clear that computerized order execution would be the way of the present and future.

Electronic Brokerage

We noted that under John Thain the NYSE adopted a so-called hybrid market in which the traditional auction system and floor trading operated parallel with a newly adopted electronic trading system. The New York Stock Exchange was the last of the world's leading exchanges to go electronic. Europe had shifted to electronic trading from 1986 onward, when the LSE adopted its SEAQ platform, and most Continental exchanges quickly followed. Derivatives trading also was becoming dominated by electronic trading platforms.

In the United States electronic stock exchanges multiplied in the 1990s. Brokerage houses accepted buy and sell orders over the internet, with most of the transactions executed without the need to speak with another person. As a result, brokers such as Ameritrade, Archipelago, Island, Etrade, REDIBook, Tradebook, and Waterhouse Securities became household words. The growth of internet trading tended to enhance transparency. More aggressive electronic brokerages such as Archipelago and REDIBook were affiliated to or owned by large investment banks such as Merrill Lynch, Goldman Sachs, and Paine Webber. Investment banks were betting on specific trading technologies, and several banks had multiple investments to diversify their technology risk.

Archipelago

Archipelago operated the first all electronic trading system, an electronic communications network (ECN) that facilitated direct trading without need for a trading floor or market makers. Archipelago carried out its IPO in 2004, to become a publicly owned company, operating an electronic securities exchange. In the same year Archipelago purchased the Pacific Stock Exchange, a regional stock exchange founded in 1882 and based in San Francisco. The corporation resulting from this purchase was named ArcaEx.

ArcaEx adopted a modern electronic platform, and initiated trading in NASDAQ listed stocks, NYSE listed stocks, and AMEX listed stocks. This large leap forward brought trading of all exchange listed stocks into a single electronic platform. This platform also traded related equity options.

In the second half of 2005 rumors spread about the anticipated restructuring and reorganization of NYSE, and the possible merger of NYSE with an existing publicly owned company. In March 2006 the NYSE and ArcaEx announced completion of a merger.

Following the merger of NYSE into the ArcaEx corporate unit, the latter's technology platform operated in parallel with NYSE's specialist trading system. Also, the NYSE's product line was enlarged to include options trading. Within a half-year NYSE was enjoying a fully capable electronic trading system, and it continued to utilize several floor trading rooms, as hundreds of floor trading related jobs were phased out.

John Thain and his associates at NYSE saw several key advantages in the merger with ArcaEx. First, NYSE gained ready access to the Archipelago electronic trading system. This facilitated lower cost and speedier trading for NYSE clients. This had been a long overdue and necessary change to defend market share. Second, a one-off cost reduction was achieved. Finally, it became possible to bring equity options trading and cash equity trading onto a relatively efficient and low cost single platform. This provided an initial diversification of traded products that NYSE had been seeking.

Restructuring Initiatives

In the following sections we analyze the key motivations behind NYSE's restructuring in the period 2006–09, following its becoming a for-profit listed and traded company. These include the mergers with Euronext and AMEX, the acquisitions of large minority stakes in the Qatar and other exchanges, and discussions with Deutsche Börse toward affiliation.

The Euronext Merger

In June 2006 the NYSE Group and Euronext agreed to a merger, to create a transatlantic financial exchange whose market value exceeded $21 billion. The merger was approved by the US regulator, the SEC, early in 2007. The portfolio components of the combined businesses are described in Table 6.2. The combined entity listed eighty of the hundred largest blue chip companies in North America and Europe, would create the world's largest liquidity pool with $100 billion daily turnover, and offered investors access to seven exchanges located in six countries.

The NYSE–Euronext merger was the largest to take place between stock exchanges. Here we analyze this merger, with the following objectives. First, we consider the main motivations of both parties. Second, we evaluate the likely synergy benefits. Third, we consider the valuation, the business model, and other competitive implications.

NYSE motivations include strategic, financial, and business. Strategic motivations are based on achieving scale and scope that would position the combined group in a number one leadership role that could not be challenged. The combined entity would enjoy scale and scope advantages allowing large future investments in technology and alliances with other exchanges. Finally, the NYSE Euronext competitive position would be virtually unassailable. Business motives extend from achieving greater diversification to revising the business model. Financial motives include the powerful synergies expected. According to John Thain, synergy cost savings would aggregate $275 million within three years, of which $250 million would be technology linked.[10]

Jean-François Théodore, chief executive of Euronext at the time of the merger, already held the unofficial title of "consummate deal maker in the European

Table 6.2 Main Portfolio Components at Time of NYSE–Euronext Merger

A	Euronext components:
	1 Paris Stock Exchange
	2 Stock exchanges in Amsterdam, Brussels, Lisbon
	3 London International Financial Futures Exchange (LIFFE)
	4 European business hours (time zone) operating capacity
B	NYSE Group components:
	5 NYSE equity exchange including Archipelago
	6 ArcaEx equity and options exchange
	7 Largest (scale factor) equity trading market in the world
	8 North American business hours (time zone) operating capacity

exchange industry."[11] Théodore had overseen the making of Euronext and the tie-up with LIFFE. He is described as a determined but non-confrontational executive. Also, he is described as a patient operator, shrewd, and sophisticated. In 2006 Théodore was negotiating with the German exchange but was faced with a takeover by Deutsche Börse. By contrast, NYSE was offering a "merger of equals."[12] A combination with NYSE would elevate Paris's stature in global financial markets. Further, Thain was planning a merger structure that would keep the Euronext components apart from Sarbanes–Oxley (SOX) jurisdiction and SEC direct oversight.[13] Finally, a merger with NYSE would leave Euronext "wholly in charge of European operations in a combined company."[14]

Many motivations have been attributed to mergers between exchanges. The merger of NYSE with ArcaEx was based on the need to implement electronic trading quickly, constituting a dramatic revision of the business model. Also, that merger produced a more diversified revenue mix, including options trading. Finally, NYSE's competitive position was vastly improved.

Motivations for the NYSE–Euronext merger included the above, plus others. The following motivations appear to cover the most significant:

1 improve the competitive position;
2 revise the business model;
3 achieve better scale and scope;
4 diversification;
5 create synergies.

This merger creates many diversification benefits, from geographic to client base and products traded. The merger of the number one and number four ranked stock exchanges (by market capitalization value) solidifies first rank status. Scope advantages include bringing together North American and European equities and derivatives trading.

The much revised business model provides a unique starting point for further competitive gains, including greater flexibility of investment in better technology.

The AMEX Acquisition

In June 2008 NYSE Euronext announced its intended merger with the American Stock Exchange. AMEX has long been the third ranking exchange in the United States. Closely owned by its member firms, AMEX lists mainly smaller cap company equities, but also trades equity options. It is one of five main options markets in the US, behind CBOE and ISE in trading volume.[15]

Since 1993 AMEX has enjoyed flourishing business listing and trading exchange traded funds (ETFs). This has been a profitable revenue generator and in part explains NYSE's interest in the merger. ETFs replicate the market returns on the index components they are structured to resemble. The shift toward indexation investment has bolstered expansion of investment and trading in ETFs, making them an attractive listing product for exchanges. In a statement made on

January 17, 2008 NYSE said it would achieve an annual savings of $100 million from sharing technology and staff.[16] AMEX planned to relocate its traders to NYSE premises.

A main attraction of AMEX to NYSE is in its exchange traded funds (Table 6.3). The deal solidifies the Big Board's position as pre-eminent market venue in exchange traded funds. NYSE, with 240 ETFs listed and traded prior to the AMEX merger, gained another 380 ETFs (with $256 billion in assets).[17] AMEX was a pioneer in ETFs, and enjoys a strong experience in product development. NYSE Euronext paid $260 million in stock plus the proceeds from sale of AMEX's headquarters in Manhattan to acquire AMEX.[18]

Stakeholdings

In the two-year period 2007–08 the NYSE Group turned to alliances and stakeholdings as a means of preparing for further initiatives in expanding and diversifying its business. For example, in January 2007 NYSE Group and several other investors cooperated in purchasing stakes in the National Stock Exchange of India, located in Mumbai. NYSE paid $15 million for its 5 percent stake, its first investment in Asia.[19] The Mumbai exchange trades equities and equity related futures, and owns stakes in the Indian National Commodity Exchange.

Earlier the NYSE established an alliance with the Tokyo Stock Exchange, second ranking exchange in the world by market capitalization value of listed securities. The alliance has the objective of aligning electronic platforms, which in future could lead to a merger of the exchanges. Other alliances include the Singapore Stock Exchange, where in 2007 NYSE acquired a 4.9 percent stake, and the Tel Aviv Stock Exchange, where an agreement was made in June 2008 to develop cross-listing of shares.

At about the same time as the alliance was made with the Tel Aviv exchange, NYSE Euronext purchased a 25 percent stake in the Qatar Stock Exchange. NYSE Euronext paid $250 million for this stake, and it is understood that the

Table 6.3 Comparison of NYSE Euronext and AMEX

	NYSE Euronext	*AMEX*
1 Name and origins	NYSE Euronext; NYSE was established in 1792	American Stock Exchange was established in 1911 (formerly Curb Market)
2 Ownership	Since April 2007 a merged entity owned by shareholders	Owned by member firms until merger with NYSE Euronext
3 Main business	Equities and derivatives trading in North America and Europe	Since 1993 trading venue for ETFs; one of several equity options markets in US
4 Trading status	Dominant global exchange, with $30 trillion in market cap early in 2008	Trades 90,000 option contracts daily

Source: *Wall Street Journal*, January 10, 2008, p. C3.

transaction is only part of a complex strategic alliance in which the small natural gas rich state's exchange will evolve into an integrated cash equities and derivatives market, possessing global links, and plans to grow regionally.[20]

The stake in the Qatar exchange is the largest single investment by the NYSE Euronext Group in any single exchange. It won in a competitive tender, ahead of LSE and Deutsche Börse. This investment and alliance gives NYSE Euronext a competitive edge in future developments in this region. Nevertheless, Börse Dubai holds a 20 percent stake in LSE, which could lead to a keen rivalry for exchange market leadership in the Gulf region in the future.

Whither Deutsche Börse?

The preceding sections describe NYSE Euronext moving forward, and in several instances trumping both LSE and Deutsche Börse in partnering with other exchange operators. In the following chapter we consider LSE's status in close detail. Here we examine the status of the Frankfurt based German exchange operator.

In April 2009 the *Wall Street Journal* reported that Deutsche Börse and NYSE Euronext were in discussions on a possible deal.[21] While it appeared unlikely the two would agree to combine in the near future, it is highly probable they will continue to study their respective options. One analyst, Diego Perfumo, observed that a joint venture limited to the derivatives and/or clearing business might be feasible as an initial step.[22] Some doubt that significant synergistic cost savings could be gained from a merger of the two. Others argue that the size and complexity of both parties would create difficult integration issues. Valuation disparities pose an even more difficult hurdle. In April 2009 NYSE Euronext shares were valued at slightly over $6 billion, half of Deutsche Börse's $13 billion value.

By the first half of 2009, previously achieved merger consolidations had narrowed the field, reducing the number of combinations considered possible. *The Economist* previously made an analogy of mergers among exchanges as a three-dimensional chess game. This was in summer 2005, prior to the large scale mergers that set off a consolidation trend in 2006–08. *The Economist* pointed out that differences over post-trade arrangements (clearing and settlement) could hamper formation of a pan-European solution. In this regard Deutsche Börse stood as an almost solitary figure, enjoying a profitable and large clearing facility, which tended to isolate it from the potential for merger with other leading exchanges. At that time other exchanges preferred to utilize arm's-length clearing services, such as LCH. Clearnet in the case of the London exchange.

Market Microstructure and Product Initiatives

Floor trading and electronic trading are difficult to integrate. Generally, when a financial exchange shifts from floor trading to electronic, the process is complete and spans a relatively short time period. In the case of NYSE, its adoption of electronic trading was gradual, and took place almost simultaneously with organizational restructuring. Within the three-month period March 2006 to May 2006 the NYSE had: 1) merged with ArcaEx, 2) adopted a shareholder owned in place of mutual structure, 3) carried out an initial public offering, and 4) implemented a dual or hybrid market trading system (Table 6.4).

The Millisecond Market

In its November 20, 2006 issue, *Barron's* welcomed the NYSE Group to the millisecond market. This market serves large and highly active investment funds that require super-fast, ultra-cheap, and anonymous trading. Electronic markets, including that operated by NYSE, have revamped the way they handle share transactions. In this new approach, we witnessed a shrinkage of the Big Board trading floor.

Specialists on the NYSE, who manage trading in individual stocks assigned to them, have depended on an in-person auction market model. For institutional and individual investors the shift toward electronics is good news. Trading costs fall, and there is increased opportunity to get best execution and price. The lower trading costs come from a hybrid market, which facilitates faster trading and order processing, but without reducing transparency. A leading specialist firm observed that, "when stocks are in a routine mode, we'll handle them electronically. When there's news or a dislocation, the crowd will trade them."[23]

The first several months of the hybrid market (the second half of 2006) saw NYSE's market share of trading its listed stocks rise slightly. The test came in 2007 when SEC rules mandated that orders be routed in the market offering best price. Over the period 2004–06 there was a moderate trend where off-floor trading of NYSE listed shares was expanding slowly, whereas floor trading was virtually flat in amount.

The first half of 2007 witnessed a distinct uptrend in the share of off-floor trading of NYSE listed shares, and by yearend there was a near closing of the gap. Two changes took place in 2007 regarding the trading of NYSE listed shares. First,

Table 6.4 Major Steps in Restructuring and Attaining For-Profit Status of NYSE Group

December 1996	Archipelago electronic communications network founded.
July 2000	Archipelago partnered with the Pacific Exchange to develop ArcaEx.
November 2002	Archipelago completed rollout of exchange listed securities on ArcaEx.
April 2003	Archipelago fully integrated its trading platforms and completed the migration of NASDAQ listed securities to ArcaEx.
September 2005	Archipelago acquired PCX Holdings, including the Pacific Exchange.
March 2006	Completion of merger of NYSE and Archipelago, in which the NYSE was demutualized and converted into a for-profit entity. These became wholly owned subsidiaries of NYSE.
May 2006	NYSE Group completes IPO with sale of 25 million shares to the public.

Source: Author's compilation.

automatic trade execution rose to nearly equal floor trading. Second, the NYSE's market share in its own listed stocks trended lower, from 70 percent when the hybrid market system was implemented, to approximately 50 percent (at midyear 2007).[24]

Looking ahead at midyear 2007, a *Barron's* analyst suggested that the NYSE should find a way to preserve elements of a human informed auction market as the general trading environment becomes more fragmented.[25] In the following section we describe how NYSE responded to the challenges of fragmentation and preserving liquidity.

Rebates for Liquidity

In February 2009 NYSE Euronext announced it would adjust its fee structure and boost execution speeds to attract more high frequency traders to the Big Board and its Arca electronic market. The changes offer larger trading fee rebates for market participants that send orders to the exchange, and higher transaction fees for traders that are net takers of that liquidity.[26]

On stock markets we distinguish between liquidity providers and liquidity takers (Table 6.5). The table reflects the typical designation in this regard. The above described fee changes by NYSE simply rewards liquidity suppliers and charges liquidity takers.

For several years NYSE Euronext and other exchanges have followed this fee and rebate model. Stock exchanges have been grappling with a declining share of equity trading as new electronic rivals absorb trading volume.

The new rates, effective early in 2009, include a rebate of 0.1 cent per share for adding liquidity in displayed and non-displayed orders, and a transaction fee of 0.18 cent per share for removing liquidity. The charges were designed to make NYSE's rates the highest for liquidity providing rebates and the lowest for taking liquidity.

This NYSE initiative is in competition with a maker–taker fee and rebate structure employed by electronic marketplaces and other exchanges. For example, two months following the NYSE initiative described above, several exchanges introduced a maker–taker platform. In this case the exchange pays rebates to

Table 6.5 Typical Liquidity Providers and Takers on Leading Stock Markets

Sell-side liquidity providers	*Buy-side liquidity takers*
1 Specialists and other market makers	1 Momentum traders
2 Pseudo liquidity providers (patient traders from money funds)	2 Basket traders
3 Sell-side brokerage firms	3 Value traders
4 Special purpose intermediaries: Instinet, Brut, Pipeline Algorithmic Switching	

Source: S. Chakrvarty, F.H.deB. Harris, and K. Wind, "The Emerging State of the NYSE Market," *Journal of Trading*, Winter 2009, p. 76.

market makers to encourage them to post orders on their platforms. The exchange charges other traders for coming in and matching those orders. In such cases the exchange (or platform) generates revenue by charging the taker more than it pays the maker.

Striking the correct or optimal balance between charges (to the taker) and rebates (to the maker) may not be as easy as may appear at first glance. At midyear 2009 the platform owned by NASDAQ OMX was trailing behind in volume vis-à-vis the three leading multilateral trading facilities (MTFs): Chi-X, Turquoise, and BATS Europe.[27]

Diversifying Products

Over the three-year period 2007–09 financial exchanges have undertaken initiatives aimed at: 1) retaining market share, 2) expanding the scope and product range of markets, and 3) invading what formerly was considered the home turf of rival exchanges. As a result, we can observe a greatly enlarged and diversified series of microstructure and product related initiatives.

NYSE Euronext product initiatives result from merger and de novo launching of new products. The merger with AMEX brought existing equity options and a wider range of ETFs to NYSE. The merger with Euronext produced an even more significant broadening of products offered. In March 2009 NYSE Euronext announced plans to launch a range of stock index products, evidencing the goal of expanding into the fast growing derivatives business. The new index futures began trading in the third quarter of 2009 and are linked to MSCI indices. These MSCI products should compete with CME stock index futures that are based on Standard & Poor's and Dow Jones indexes.[28]

Thomas Callahan, who is in charge of US futures at NYSE Euronext, admitted that the battle for market share in this profitable line will not be quick and easy. Nevertheless, NYSE Euronext's distribution network and client relationships make it well positioned to be a strong competitor. Global derivatives trading grew by 14 percent in 2008, based on Futures Industry Association data. At NYSE Euronext derivatives trading contributed 24 percent of total revenues in first quarter 2009, up from an earlier level of 22 percent.

Microstructure related initiatives include measures taken by exchanges to achieve any or all of the three broad objectives outlined previously. Here we provide useful examples of these initiatives, taken over the period 2007–09.

Exchanges have adopted more complex pricing and fees. The fee plus rebate, and maker–taker examples above outline this. In June 2008 NYSE Euronext unveiled trading fee reductions up to 30 percent to attract high frequency traders. Named Pack Epsilon, the new fee structure came into effect the following month.

According to Roland Dellegarde, head of European execution at NYSE Euronext, growth in trading comes from participants wanting volatility and requiring "speed and connectivity." Buy and sell orders come onto exchanges, and fees are charged on partial execution. Euronext indicated it would charge eligible clients for the first partial order execution only. High frequency traders are estimated to account for 5–10 percent of Euronext volume. Euronext rivals (NASDAQ, BATS, Turquoise) also plan to launch similar multilateral trading facilities. Clearly, the battle for market share is intense in Europe and North America.

Exchanges are discovering that not only must they re-aggregate liquidity, but they must also provide opportunities for anonymous and zero impact trading. Exchanges are fending off competition in a growing number of dark pools. These pools allow clients to trade stocks without the risk of moving the public price on exchanges. In response, exchanges are entering partnerships with technology firms to provide complex event processing (CEF) capabilities for algorithmic trading.[29] A partnership between NYSE Euronext and Advanced Trading Solutions moves in this direction. The partnership extends into risk management and order routing. This technology enables traders to monitor, analyze, and actionably trade on events (price changes) within milliseconds.

In October 2008 the Big Board hit a low point when trades handled by its floor fell to 24 percent of the listed share market volume. This compares with a market share of 80 percent three years earlier. The expansion of high speed and automated electronic trading, coupled with technology employed by rivals, has reduced NYSE's share of trading its own listed stocks. In January 2009 the floor market share was 26 percent. Overall, the NYSE Group handles approximately 42 percent of trading its own listed shares. This includes floor trading and electronic execution combined.[30]

Block Trades

In an effort to regain trading in large transactions or block trades, NYSE Euronext formed a joint venture with BIDS Holdings, a company owned by several large banks. The venture, called NYEX, lets brokers, hedge funds, and other money managers trade large volumes of shares anonymously and without showing their orders to other market participants. Electronic orders can be matched on the NYSE, including so-called reserve orders. These are orders that may display only a small amount of stock for sale or purchase.[31]

Block trades are defined as transactions involving at least 10,000 shares or that have a value of $200,000 or more. Until the early 1980s block trades in NYSE shares took place primarily on the exchange floor. With the increase in electronic trading and computerized programs, a rising proportion of block trades could be broken into smaller trades and processed across a range of venues. Between early 2004 and late 2008 the average trade size on NYSE went from 770 shares to 242 shares, reflecting the effects of large transactions migrating away from NYSE.

Exchanges have been fighting back to recapture trading of large blocks, as well as that of high frequency traders and those concerned with lowering trading costs. As noted in this and previous sections, to recapture trading exchanges have revised their trading platforms and systems, added new platforms, and also created their own alternative trading systems (ATSs), or multilateral trading facilities (MTFs). In the section of this chapter "Exchange Landscape in Europe, 2008–09" we examine the results of these efforts as measured by the share of European trading held by exchanges and alternative venues as of late 2008 and early 2009.

Second Transatlantic Merger

NASDAQ is an acronym for National Association of Securities Dealers Automated Quotations, a system created by the National Association of Securities Dealers (NASD). The NASD was created in 1939 to bring order to over the counter (OTC) stock trading. In the 1960s, at the urging of the SEC, NASD explored setting up an automated trading system. A system of high speed transmission lines linking brokerage firms in major cities became operational in February 1971. Known as NASDAQ, the system displayed quotes for over 2,500 OTC stocks.[32]

Over the years NASDAQ evolved from a computer bulletin board service into an electronic stock market. NASDAQ introduced its National Market System in 1982, later renamed NASDAQ National Market (NNM). The next decade saw accelerating changes in the financial markets and their regulation. In 2000 NASDAQ was separated from NASD, becoming an independent public company. In second quarter 2000 the stock market crash badly damaged values of technology stocks, a sector in which NASDAQ was specialized. The bursting of the internet bubble was a serious setback.

In 2000 NASDAQ found itself in a difficult position. NASDAQ was hardly an automated ECN, but also not quite a fully fledged stock exchange. In late 2000 NASDAQ undertook the process of becoming a stock exchange. In 2002 NASDAQ completed a public stock offering, and initiated a listing of its own stock on the new NASDAQ Exchange. Some of the money NASDAQ raised was used to acquire Instinet, which helped improve NASDAQ's technology. Based in New York City, the NASDAQ Stock Market has 3,200 companies listed.

What Is NASDAQ?

Since NASDAQ became a publicly owned company as well as a stock exchange, it has played an increasingly important role. Formerly, it served as the electronic portion of the over the counter market. Now it is the second largest stock exchange in the United States.

With its electronic orientation, one could state that "the NASDAQ market exists anywhere . . . and is an entire trading floor crammed into a suitcase size computer."[33] For decades NASDAQ has been where most exchanges are headed—all electronic and flawless. NASDAQ accounts for roughly one-third of US equities volume, and is pushing into derivatives. According to its CEO Robert Greifeld, NASDAQ's low cost servers allow it to add scale and simultaneity at declining cost.

Greifeld became chief executive at NASDAQ in 2003. He has followed a highly aggressive program of competitive change, including technology upgrades, acquisitions, and product innovation. In 2009 *Forbes* included NASDAQ as one of the Best Big Companies in America. This was despite the highly volatile stock market and at times chaotic trading in 2008–09. However, volatility can be beneficial to stock exchanges. Early in 2009 trading volume on all US exchanges averaged 10.6 billion shares a day, compared with 4.2 billion two years earlier, and 1.5 billion a decade ago.

Greifeld relies on low cost technology to gain and hold business. In 2005 he paid $935 million for Instinet Group, described in the following section. Also, he has purchased other exchange companies in the US, and OMX in Europe. In January 2009 the market value of NASDAQ was $5.3 billion, but this was down 50 percent from its value a year earlier.

Instinet Origins

When NASDAQ acquired Instinet in 2005 the target company operated as an ECN in the so-called third market. The third market is a name designating off-exchange trading in exchange listed shares. However, Instinet had evolved well beyond serving as a third market trading facilitator. Instinet's origins extend back to the earliest phase of electronic trading. More important, we must observe that Instinet was a catalytic ingredient in the evolution of equity trading in the United States and overseas.

Five years prior to NASDAQ's acquisition, Instinet was the largest privately owned ECN. At that time it was officially only a broker-dealer. Instinet was established as a for-profit business in 1967 to compete with the NYSE, by offering computer linkages between institutional investors. It became operative in 1970 as an ECN and also as a provider of securities market information. It generated commission revenues on equity trades served by Instinet terminals. Several years later it became a member broker-dealer of regional exchanges in the US and NASD.

In 1984 Instinet was servicing bid and ask offers on 3,500 stocks, covering all US exchanges. Its broker-dealer clients numbered 500, including virtually all specialists operating at that time. Instinet's service allowed clients to call up a stock on a video terminal screen, obtain price quotes in several different markets, and select the market in which to complete the trade.

In 1985–86 Reuters, the British producer of financial market data and news, made several investments in Instinet, and by 1987 held a 49 percent stake. In 1987 Instinet introduced Crossing Network, an after-hours trading system that matched trades using end-of-day closing prices. This successful venture was "the most important crossing network" trading US equities. Other important crossing networks include ITG's POSIT and the New York Stock Exchange's After Hours Trading Session.[34] By 1990 Instinet's operations were extending into Europe. Instinet was a member of the London Stock Exchange, served an expanding group of British clients, and included a number of actively traded European stocks in its network.

By the mid-1990s Instinet accounted for 20 percent of NASDAQ trading volume and 60 percent of trading in NASDAQ's 100 largest stocks. Instinet was one of the lowest cost trading venues, facilitating its conquest of NASDAQ trading. By 1995 Instinet revenues exceeded $327 million.

Market Innovator

Throughout its existence Instinet has played the role of stock market innovator. It was launched as an alternative and rival trading network vis-à-vis existing exchange and OTC equity markets. Over time it gained considerable market share in NASDAQ and NYSE shares, and expanded into European share trading. In 1999 Instinet purchased minority stakes in Archipelago and W.R. Hambrecht. The latter, a San Francisco investment bank, was specialized in venture capital financing and IPOs.

The purchase of Instinet by NASDAQ in 2005 was viewed as an aggressive move, to bring into the NASDAQ Group a successful, market gaining rival. However, this aspect of the tie-up never reached fruition, and the merger was unwound. What NASDAQ did gain was a temporary relief from Instinet's absorption of NASDAQ volume in US equity markets. By early 2006 NASDAQ was looking in other directions to change the business mix and achieve restructuring.

Merger Initiatives

In 2006 NASDAQ launched a merger effort with the London Stock Exchange. The New York based exchange operator had very good reasons to seek this connection:

1 LSE was the world's third largest stock market, with close to 10 percent of global equity market capitalization.
2 LSE enjoyed a long-standing lead position in listing and trading blue chip securities from around the world on its main platform.
3 Through its Alternative Investment Market the LSE had supplanted New York (including NASDAQ) as the premier early stage–growth company IPO launch pad.
4 LSE had spent large sums developing a high speed trading system named Infolect, which became operative in 2009.
5 LSE already had been a merger target of Deutsche Börse and OMX on several occasions, and success by NASDAQ in this respect could result in considerable "real option" value.
6 LSE enjoys a location advantage. London is one of two premier global financial centers. A merger with LSE would position NASDAQ in both New York and London, an advantage that would become unavailable to others should NASDAQ succeed in its quest to link itself with the London exchange.

NASDAQ offered close to $4 billion to acquire the LSE in March 2006. This offer was rejected. Subsequently, NASDAQ acquired close to 30 percent of LSE shares, and by January 2007 NASDAQ's offering price was valued at $5.7 billion. This also was rejected. By summer 2007 NASDAQ was preparing to liquidate its holding of LSE shares.

Need to Sell

NASDAQ's failed bid for the LSE was not a riskless exercise. In the early weeks of 2007 NASDAQ faced considerable costs in this respect. These could include: 1) interest cost on funds borrowed to acquire LSE shares, 2) possible losses in the ultimate disposal of LSE shares at lower prices than paid for these shares, and 3) potential sell-off of NASDAQ shares following the failed bid. NASDAQ's first quarter 2007 profit increased by a mere 1.7 percent, impacted by costs related to the failed merger. NASDAQ's operating results included a pretax charge of $24.9 million from costs related to the LSE offer.

In April 2007 it was reported that NASDAQ was considering the sale of its near 30 percent stake in LSE.[35] Several hedge funds reportedly held big stakes (or short positions) in exchanges expected to participate in sector changing consolidations. While the LSE was considered a trophy property, with a number of acquirers interested in a tie-up, the basic question remained: Would the LSE be comfortable merging with another exchange?[36] By the middle of 2007 NASDAQ had turned its focus to merging with OMX, a Scandinavian based exchange operator. NASDAQ needed money to fund its deal with OMX. In August 2007 a rival bidder, Börse Dubai, came onto the scene.

Börse Dubai and NASDAQ entered discussions concerning their respective bids for the Swedish based exchange. Börse Dubai had bid $4 billion for OMX, and this placed both OMX and NASDAQ in a difficult position. OMX directors were obliged to get the best value for shareholders, even while a tie-up with NASDAQ could, in the long run, bring significant value creating benefits. Meanwhile, NASDAQ was desperately seeking to find a buyer for the large stake in LSE. Börse Dubai had accumulated a 28.4 percent stake in OMX within a very short time period. Any bid needed approval by the Swedish regulator (Financial Service Authority—FSA). Investor, a Swedish fund, was OMX's largest domestic investor, with a 10.7 percent stake. Investor noted: "it was not obvious that a cash bid at the level pitched by Dubai was more attractive than NASDAQ's bid."[37]

The move by government owned Börse Dubai demonstrated how Dubai might wish to use linkages with European trading centers to boost itself as a global financial center. The Dubai initiative put added pressure on NASDAQ. After being spurned by LSE, NASDAQ agreed to purchase OMX in a cash and share deal valued at $3.7 billion. In August 2007 the *Wall Street Journal* reported that Börse Dubai could decide to retain a stake in a combined NASDAQ–OMX.[38] Two days later the same publication ran a story explaining "Börse Dubai's Vision" behind the bid for OMX.[39] Börse Dubai hoped to use OMX to consolidate exchanges in the Middle East and develop an international financial hub in the region. But at mid-August 2007 Dubai had a long way to go before securing ownership of OMX. Large investors in Sweden and the Swedish regulatory body had to sign off on the deal. The Swedish regulator sent a letter to Börse Dubai, requesting it to clarify its plans for OMX should its bid receive approval.

Four-Way Complexity

Over the period August 2007 to February 2008 a four-way transaction developed, in which a number of ownership and structural changes took place. First, NASDAQ divested its large stake in LSE. Second, Börse Dubai raised the offer price for OMX, but then surrendered its large stake in OMX. Third, the Qatar Investment Authority acquired a large stake in OMX but then exchanged it for a stake in LSE held by Börse Dubai. Finally, NASDAQ offloaded its stake in LSE, formed an investment partnership with Börse Dubai, and merged with OMX. Börse Dubai became a large (19.9 percent) stakeholder in the combined NASDAQ–OMX.

It was in May 2007 that NASDAQ announced its $3.7 billion offer for OMX. As could be expected, NASDAQ shares fell 3.4 percent and OMX shares rose nearly 11 percent on the announcement.[40] OMX's largest shareholder, the Wallenberg family controlled Investor AB, declined to comment on the deal. Within three months a rival bidder, Börse Dubai, made an offer of $4 billion for OMX.

At the time when Börse Dubai made a higher offer for OMX, the Qatar Investment Authority (QIA) was considering purchase of NASDAQ's stake in LSE. This would facilitate NASDAQ's bid for OMX. QIA's interest in the LSE stake was based on the objective of using the London exchange as a model for developing securities trading in the Gulf region. QIA possesses deep financial pockets, one of the several Middle East sovereign wealth funds developing a diversified portfolio of properties around the world.[41]

By late September 2007 NASDAQ and Börse Dubai asserted they had received commitments from large Swedish investors to tender 18.5 percent of OMX shares. This came in spite of the possibility that QIA with a 9.9 percent ownership of OMX could enter the bidding. Both NASDAQ and Börse Dubai pledged to work toward a "Finansplats Stockholm," and bolster the city's role as a financial center.

Early in 2008 a four-way deal was completed, to the apparent satisfaction of all interested in the merger. The NASDAQ–OMX combination was carried out, with Börse Dubai owning 19.9 percent of the transatlantic exchange. QIA gained a large stake in LSE formerly owned by NASDAQ. This followed QIA's purchase of 14.9 percent of LSE shares in 2007 (Table 6.6).

Table 6.6 Outline of Essential Elements in the Four-Way Deal Leading to Consolidation of NASDAQ and OMX

1	May 2007	NASDAQ announced $3.7 billion bid for OMX.
2	August 2007	Börse Dubai launches $4 billion bid for OMX.
3	August 2007	QIA considers buying NASDAQ's LSE stake.
4	September 2007	Swedish investors (Investor AB and Nordea Bank) commit to tender their 18.5 percent stake in OMX.
5	October 2007	QIA applies for permission to raise its 9.98 percent stake in OMX.
6	October 2007 to February 2008	Negotiations between four interested parties.
7	February 2008	Agreement among four parties to a complex asset exchange.

Source: Author's compilation.

NASDAQ OMX

NASDAQ enjoyed a big victory in its merger with OMX. The business, financial, and strategic benefits were considerable. The financial benefits consisted of paying an original offer price for OMX, despite the apparently higher valuation that other bidders were willing to pay. Also, NASDAQ was able to divest its large stake in LSE via exchanges of stakeholdings without the need to sell into what could have been an adverse market.

Business benefits include geographic diversification, acquisition of a global technology business, and enhanced scalability. The scalability benefit simply means that scale economies can be realized, while increased trading volume can be handled at near zero cost, and with the further advantage of significant operating leverage. Geographic diversification comes from combining a North American and a European exchange. The OMX operates in Scandinavia, the Baltic nations, and Armenia.

Strategic benefits come from creation of the second largest transatlantic exchange, retention of long term ties with Gulf region nations and their sovereign wealth funds, and an enlarged board of directors representing Scandinavian, Middle Eastern, and North American points of view.[42]

Boston and Philadelphia

In October 2007 NASDAQ indicated it was purchasing the Boston Stock Exchange (BSE) for $61 million. An important aspect of the deal is BSE's clearing capabilities in the dark pools business. The deal makes NASDAQ the first large US equities exchange with the ability to provide post-trade services, essential for domestic derivatives exchanges.[43]

According to Larry Tabb, an exchange consultant, the merger is "all about clearing."[44] There exist only three clearing licenses in the US, that held by BSE, and two held by Philadelphia Stock Exchange (PhilEx) and the Depository Trust and Clearing Corporation, a central clearing house for US equities trading. At the time, NASDAQ was planning its own options exchange, but was waiting for approval from the SEC. According to Robert Greifeld, CEO of NASDAQ, owning a second exchange (in options or equities) provides market structure flexibility.

Prior to its purchase of the Boston exchange, NASDAQ was in discussions with the Philadelphia Stock Exchange. The PhilEx is the oldest US stock trading venue, created in 1790, two years before the NYSE. In 2007 it was the third largest equity options market in the US, with close to 14 percent of trading volume. The Chicago Board Options Exchange (CBOE) and International Securities Exchange (ISE) account for 34 percent and 28 percent respectively of equity options trading volume. At the time the PhilEx was viewed as an attractive target. Options trading was expanding much faster than cash equities and was a more profitable business.

In October 2007 NASDAQ led the contenders seeking to buy the PhilEx. It had been negotiating with owners of the Philadelphia exchange for several months. At the time the Philadelphia exchange had an estimated value of $600 million. Purchase of PhilEx also would give NASDAQ a futures exchange—the Philadelphia Board of Trade—as well as a clearing house that could service options and futures. PhilEx was majority owned by six broker-dealers that had paid $33.8 million for the stake in 2005.[45]

NASDAQ's purchase of PhilEx for a reported $650 million was agreed to in early November 2007. This was NASDAQ's first major step into the US derivatives business. The Philadelphia exchange built a "strong franchise with relatively sophisticated technology for trading options."[46] In addition to single equity options, PhilEx also trades index options, stocks, and currency contracts. Closing the deal on PhilEx left NASDAQ with a massive integration and restructuring assignment.

Integration Post-Merger

The year following the three mergers with OMX, PhilEx, and the Boston Stock Exchange was a long and active period for NASDAQ. The OMX deal was completed in February 2008, closely followed by the Boston and Philadelphia Stock Exchange deals. A main focus for NASDAQ in 2008 was to achieve planned progress in the areas of revenues, technology, and cost reduction.[47] In August 2008 NASDAQ announced it was on target to realize over $100 million in cost savings from the OMX merger. Greifeld had achieved a transformational series of mergers. Big blue chips such as Nokia and Ericsson were taken into NASDAQ's trading platforms, OMX technology became part of the business, and long term strategic partners such as Börse Dubai held big stakes in the transatlantic entity.

Post-merger integration was not the only challenge facing NASDAQ OMX. ECNs initiated competitive threat, requiring appropriate and effective response. An aggressive price war broke out in 2007–08, led by BATS Trading, a successful ECN. BATS took third position behind NYSE and NASDAQ in the US market, and the two lead exchanges responded by cutting prices on their respective trading platforms.

BATS adopted a structure now used by many trading venues. This was the fee and rebate system applied vis-à-vis liquidity providers and takers. BATS quickly went from 2 percent to 10 percent of the North American trading of equities. BATS low pricing is possible because overheads are low. It is difficult to compare pricing as well as trading costs, given the use of a rebate system, and that pricing also includes routing fees. In Table 6.7 we present trading and routing fees on four venues in North America in fourth quarter 2007. As can be observed, BATS charges the lowest trading fees, but indicates higher routing fees. These fees do not indicate other costs of trading for investors, such as "price impact" and "delays in trade."

Despite intensified competition, NASDAQ OMX reported a sixfold jump in net income for first quarter 2008. This is based on a revenue distribution of 24 percent from stock trading, 19 percent from providing market data, 17 percent from derivatives, and 8 percent from selling technology to other exchanges.[48]

Table 6.7 Trading Fees on NYSE and NASDAQ Listed Shares, by Venue (Fourth Quarter 2007)

Trading market/ venue	*Net fee for trading NYSE securities*	*Net fee for trading NASDAQ securities*	*Routing fee*
ARCA	$0.05	$0.05	$0.00
NYSE	0.08	n.a.	0.30
NASDAQ	0.10	0.10	0.075–0.08
BATS	0.00	0.02	0.26

Source: *Financial Times*, October 25, 2007, p. 27.

Note: These fees cover those specifically charged by exchanges and electronic trading enterprises. They do not take into account other costs experienced by traders, such as "delay in time" and "market impact." Reflects charge per 100 shares.

NASDAQ OMX reorganized its European activities early in 2008. A former head of international listings was placed in charge of the Pan-European Exchange, operating from a London office. This new market targeted high volume market participants such as hedge funds employing algorithmic trading.[49]

NASDAQ OMX set pricing for its Pan-European Exchange, a multilateral trading facility similar to that used by Chi-X. But NASDAQ OMX also offers to redirect customer orders to other exchanges or platforms if necessary.[50] This listings venue in London is in direct competition with the London Stock Exchange for initial public offerings. As part of an effort to expand into Europe, the strategy also includes lower pricing than other venues, and a global listings center to handle listings in other jurisdictions.

Exchange Landscape in Europe, 2008–09

Ultimately transatlantic mergers impact pan-European trading. In this discussion we analyze data pertaining to stock market trading positions in Europe, and consider the competitive trends facing European and transatlantic exchanges.

Overall Trading

Early in 2009 two of the largest exchange operators unveiled new plans in competing for share trading. The Deutsche Börse indicated it would launch a pan-European trading platform designed to compete directly with LSE. Meanwhile, LSE indicated it would launch Baikal, a new stock trading venue for large orders in European company shares. The two exchanges follow different approaches. Both have faced fierce competition from MTFs such as Chi-X, and both have lost market share in their respective home markets. Both LSE and Deutsche Börse came to realize that these initiatives confirm or validate the NYSE Euronext strategy of operating a pan-European market through Paris based Euronext. Exchanges in Europe face a bewildering array of competing venues, including MTFs, and a number of dark pool block trading systems.

As European exchanges saw 2008 end and began operations in 2009, most market operators continued to enjoy a dominant position in share trading in their respective home markets. Table 6.8 demonstrates that only two exchanges of the eight in the table held less than 60 percent of trading in their respective home market. These two (Brussels and Sweden) are relatively small markets. Four exchanges held 74–82 percent of home market trading. Both Zurich and Milan enjoyed high percentages of their home market equity trading.

In Table 6.8 we observe that MTFs account for a majority of the inroads against market share formerly held by main European exchanges. Chi-X, the earliest established MTF, represents the main dragon-slayer, with anywhere from 6.6 percent (Brussels) to 14.7 percent (Amsterdam) of trading. More recently established Turquoise accounts for less than one-fourth of Chi-X's market share.

Blue Chip Rivalries

We observed the European exchanges face rising competition for market share from MTFs. Here we examine a more specific segment of share trading in Europe—blue chips. This equity market component in some respects is a key part of a successful equity trading business, since it represents the largest money value of trading and generally the more liquid strata of transactions in equity markets.

According to a *Wall Street Journal* analysis, "London Stock Exchange Group home market has lost more market share to these so-called multilateral trading facilities than any of its rivals but nonetheless remains the busiest trading venue, according to data by Thomson-Reuters."[51] The data in Table 6.9 indicates that over the period January 2008 to May 2009 LSE's share of blue chip equity trading

Table 6.8 Share of Equity Trading Held by Main Domestic Exchange and Alternative Trading Systems (Yearend 2008–Early 2009) (Percentage of Total)

National market domestic exchanges	*Domestic market*	*Chi-X*	*Turquoise*	*NASDAQ*	*BATS*	*Others*
1 Euronext						
France (Paris)	74.8	13.2	2.7	0.1	2.5	6.7
Netherlands (Amsterdam)	74.5	14.7	3.3	0.1	2.4	5.0
Belgium (Brussels)	59.3	6.6	1.4	0.1	1.4	31.2
2 OMX						
Sweden (Stockholm)	56.6	6.7	1.4	0.1	0.2	35.0
3 LSE–Borsa Italiana						
UK (LSE)	75.2	16.7	4.5	0.2	3.4	—
Italy (Milan)	93.4	4.7	0.9	0.03	0.7	—
4 Germany (Frankfurt)						
Deutsche Börse	82.3	12.6	2.3	0.1	2.7	—
5 Switzerland (Zurich)						
SWX	89.8	7.0	2.7	0.1	0.4	—
Median	75.0	12.9	2.7	0.1	2.4	—

Source: J. Grant, "Big Exchanges Come Round to Multilateral Approach," *Financial Times*, April 20, 2009, p. 16.

Table 6.9 Share of Large Cap (Blue Chip) European Share Trading by Exchange (Percentage of Total)

Exchange	*Share in January 2008*	*Share in May 2009*
London Stock Exchange	22.9%	20.7%
Euronext	14.0	9.6
Deutsche Börse	16.8	11.5
Borsa Italiana	8.2	8.0
NASDAQ OMX	4.2	5.0
Subtotal	66.1	54.8
Other*	33.9	45.2

Source: T. Fairless, "New Platforms Nip at Old Guard," *Wall Street Journal*, May 18, 2009, p. C6.

Note

* Other includes Chi-X and similar MTFs, and European stock exchanges not included in the table.

declined from 22.9 percent to 20.7 percent of the European total. Newcomers, primarily MTFs, account for a major part of this erosion. The data in Table 6.9 reflects several day trading samples, and should not be interpreted as a firm basis for forecasting trends. These markets reflect high volatility, especially over the period covered.

Table 6.9 indicates that four of the five exchange markets experienced declines in their share of European blue chip trading. Only NASDAQ OMX experienced an increase, from 4.2 percent to 5.0 percent, of European blue chip trading. The five exchanges in aggregate account for 54.8 percent of European blue chip trading (May 2009 sample period). The remaining 45.2 percent of blue chip trading would be accounted for by MTFs and other exchanges not included in Table 6.9. Borsa Italiana experienced the smallest decline in percentage market share, from 8.2 percent to 8.0 percent.

The London Stock Exchange has been responsive to these competitive pressures, as have other European exchanges. LSE has revised its pricing model, updated its platform, and gained cost synergies from consolidating its Italian and UK trading to a single platform, according to Miranda Mizen of TABB Group, a US based financial markets research firm. High frequency traders arbitraging between LSE and MTFs enjoy greater opportunities for arbitrage in London than in Paris or Frankfurt owing to LSE's faster trading system and lower all-in trading costs. Also, LSE enjoys a very wide range of sectors listed, such as mining and financial stocks, not as well represented elsewhere in Europe.

Euronext Paris and Deutsche Börse experienced even greater slippage in their European blue chip trading, as shown in Table 6.9. MTFs enjoyed 24 percent of the Paris CAC index trading in the sample period compared with Euronext's 9.6 percent. The exchange's new Universal Trading Platform is expected to provide the Paris market with an improved ability to match the speed and capacity of rival MTFs. The German exchange has lured some high frequency traders, but it hasn't been as successful as LSE. In part this is because the overall cost of trading in Frankfurt is considerably higher.

Post-Merger

In the two-year period following the transatlantic mergers the exchange groups faced difficult challenges. In each case, NYSE Euronext and NASDAQ OMX responded aggressively to these challenges, and undertook new initiatives to strengthen their respective positions in the ever changing competitive landscape.

New Directions

In late 2009 a *Wall Street Journal* writer interviewed Duncan Niederauer, CEO of NYSE Euronext, with questions concerning the status of the transatlantic exchange. Shortly prior to this interview Allianz, the large German insurer, had announced it would delist from NYSE. Mary Anastasia O'Grady, the *Wall Street Journal* reporter, asked if this could be a sign of decline in New York's role as a global financial center.[52]

Niederauer's response came in three parts. First, twenty years ago it made sense for companies like Allianz to list in New York, which provided market liquidity and depth, as well as easier access for big institutional investors. These trading advantages were lacking in most markets at that time, even in Germany. Now the Frankfurt and other stock markets are larger and more liquid, and highly accessible. Second, other foreign companies are taking the place of Allianz and similar blue chips in New York. Close to seventy Chinese companies list on NYSE, and more are coming from other emerging markets. Finally, one legitimate reason for Allianz delisting could be adverse regulation, in part via the 2002 Sarbanes–Oxley Act.

Niederauer went on to point out that listing income currently accounts for 17 percent of exchange revenue, about the same proportion as derived from market data services. Derivatives trading is more important, generating 26 percent of revenue that includes trading in AMEX options. AMEX was acquired in 2006. This also includes revenues from LIFFE, which operates in London.

Niederauer expressed concern for what government may be doing to risk takers. In 2008 virtually no companies backed by venture capital came to market via IPOs. But, looking ahead, he noted the IPO pipeline looks stronger.

Renewing the Floor

In 2009 NYSE Euronext committed to an eighteen-month, $5 million facelift for its 100-year-old trading floor. The floor serves as a central backdrop for business-television programs. The redesign is part of a strategic move to attract more electronic traders to floor trading, where the person-to-person "buzz" of live trading is expected to attract increased business. At third quarter 2009, floor trading reportedly accounted for 17 percent of NYSE equity trading.[53]

Technology upgrades will make it easier to electronically trade stocks, futures, and options at multiple exchanges from the NYSE floor. According to NYSE Euronext officials, revamping NYSE's floor has aroused interest from brokerage firms that are not trading on the floor, but see possible value in the new venue. All of NYSE Euronext's competitors in the US markets, including NASDAQ, OMX, BATS, and Direct Edge, operate only electronically. The new floor venue offers a more distinct combination of floor trading atmosphere and ability to access multimarkets electronically.

Technology Investment

NYSE Euronext appointed Dominique Cerutti, an IBM veteran, as its deputy chief executive and global head of technology. This October 2009 appointment signals the increasing importance leading exchanges assign to technology. A month earlier the London Stock Exchange purchased a Sri Lankan trading technology firm, MillenniumIT. More exchanges regard themselves as technology companies, evidenced by their investing large sums in this area.

NYSE Euronext is investing in two large data centers, in New Jersey and the United Kingdom. These will facilitate co-location, as trading clients install their computer servers next to the exchange's matching engines.[54] This and other innovations introduced by the exchange lead us to the question: Can the company find the correct balance between tradition and innovation in a cutthroat industry?

Consolidating computer servers and trading engines into two major data centers, one outside London and another close to New York City, will save $30 million a year in operating costs. Equally important, this move will bring the company's small mountain of computer hardware to the doorstep of the world's high frequency traders.[55]

All About Efficiency

Fragmentation of equity market trading continues to challenge exchange operators. Robert Greifeld, head of NASDAQ OMX, noted early in 2009 that more exchange-like institutions will emerge as long as regulatory bodies allow ECNs and niche players to compete. Despite mergers, fragmentation has been increasing.[56] Greifeld and other exchange executives suggest that in five years the world of stock exchanges will consist of four or five large global players and many smaller trading venues.

Transparency Versus Volume

Early in 2009 NASDAQ OMX Europe announced the launch of a new "dark liquidity pool" to be named Neuro Dark. This low cost matching platform is based on the best bid and offer prices available on public markets. NASDAQ's initiative is in keeping with efforts by the largest exchanges to counter or reverse erosion of market share going to these dark pools. Shortly prior to NASDAQ's announcement of this new platform, William Brodsky, chairman of the World Federation of Exchanges, stated that these pools introduce distortions into equity markets by relying on the pricing mechanisms developed by exchanges without shouldering any of the costs.[57]

Regulators on both sides of the Atlantic have expressed concerns similar to those of Brodsky. They fear that, as the share of trading in given equity securities becomes larger in these dark pools, the reliability and fairness of pricing come more into question. As alternative trading systems increase their market share of trading in listed stocks, the validity of price discovery comes into serious question. Transparency is lost, and pockets of transactions with minimal impact on price become larger and more frequent.

These questions of pricing efficiency in financial markets arise at a point in time when overall efficiency and rationality of financial market pricing are being most seriously questioned. In a review of *The Myth of the Rational Market* by Justin Fox, a highly respected economist, Richard Thaler, summarizes the efficient markets hypothesis (EMH), and juxtaposes the myth with current criticism:[58]

> The bad news for EMH lovers is that the price is right component is in more trouble than ever. Fischer Black (of Black-Scholes fame) once defined a market as efficient if its prices were "within a factor of two of value" and he argued that by this (rather loose) definition almost all markets are efficient almost all of the time.

Thaler continues, noting that the technology bubble of the 1990s and current housing and financial market crisis raise serious questions concerning market rationality and pricing efficiency.

ECNs continue to fragment equity markets, and this heightens questions concerning pricing efficiency. Over their lifetimes stock exchanges have promoted transparency and market efficiency. What is the level of fragmentation beyond which regulatory bodies will no longer consider equity markets able to provide this key service?

Options, Shares, and ETFs

Financial exchanges increasingly trade multi-products. For example, in the US NASDAQ OMX trades shares, options on shares, ETFs, and options on these portfolios. Volume changes in any one of these types of securities are a function of trading in the others, which are relatively close substitutes. In some cases risk management requires investors to trade the related instrument to hedge its existing open position.

NASDAQ has been a leader in developing multi-product trading. The substitutability of trading between these products complicates pricing of trade services.

NASDAQ faces competition in trading equities, ETFs, and their respective options from NYSE, OTC venues, and ETFs from several exchanges (NYSE–AMEX, ISE, and the CBOE). Early in 2009 NASDAQ elected to not charge taker fees to investors who carried out trades on its NASDAQ Options Market Exchange. But at midyear 2009 NASDAQ was planning to assess a 20 cent taker fee for customers who buy and sell options that trade in penny transactions.[59] These are most popular and liquid contracts, and likely to generate revenue. An investor that wanted to buy 100 options contracts, with the right to buy or sell 10,000 shares of stock, could pay a $20 taker fee.

May 6 Flash Crash

On May 6, 2010, financial markets in the United States experienced a severe drop in prices. In a few minutes equity prices fell more than 5 percent, but recovered a short time later. May 6 began with unsettling political and economic news concerning the Eurozone debt crisis, injecting uncertainty which grew during New York trading. This led to a flight to quality by investors, and a spike in premiums for buying protection against possible default by the Greek government. Shortly after 2:30 p.m., Eastern Daylight Time, the decline in equity markets escalated. Morning trading in equities witnessed a slow erosion of prices, reflected in the S&P 500 index closing close to 1154 at noon (Table 6.10). But in the fifteen minutes from 2:30 p.m. to 2:45 p.m., the S&P 500 lost 6 percent of its value, accompanied by related instability in the CBOE and other derivative exchanges (Table 6.10). This

Table 6.10 Performance of the S&P 500 on May 6, 2010

Time (EDT)	*Level of market index*	*Percentage change from previous*	*Market direction*	*Description of market condition*
1 10:05 a.m.	1168		Up	Equities reach high point of day at 10:05 a.m.
		−1.1%		
2 Noon	1154		Down	Losses accumulate, reacting to unsettling news.
		−1.1%		
3 2:08 p.m.	1141		Down	VIX index of volatility climbs to highest level of year.
		−0.9%		
4 2:23 p.m.	1131		Down	Equity sell-off accelerates with S&P 500 down 3 percent.
		0.0%		
5 2:30 p.m.	1133		Up	CBOE announces it will disregard quotes from NYSE electronic Arca.
		−6.0%		
6 2:45 p.m.	1066		Down	In 14 minutes S&P 500 plunges 5.7 percent; NYSE suspends trading. Electronic orders cascade onto other venues.
		+0.7%		
7 2:47 p.m.	1073		Up	Growing chaos in the market; S&P falls over 30 percent.
		+4.5%		
8 2:54 p.m.	1120		Up	In less than 8 minutes, the market bounces back 47 points, with a 3.2 percent day loss.

Source: N. Mehta, L. Thomasson, and P.M. Barrett, "The Machines That Ate the Market," *Bloomberg Business Week*, May 24, 2010, p. 49.

decline was followed by an equal recovery in stock prices. This extreme volatility in the markets suggests a temporary breakdown in the supply of liquidity. This market instability is unprecedented in terms of speed and scope.

Two weeks after the flash crash, regulatory agencies (SEC and the Commodity Futures Trading Commission) issued a preliminary report, noting they had not as yet found a catalyst for the market plunge and rebound. The SEC and CFTC representatives did tell the Senate committee they were focused on the structure of the fragmented equity market, the close interrelationship between futures and cash equities, how trading groups provide prices, and the dominant role played by computer trading.[60] Further, the SEC announced that four public exchanges in the US were ready to introduce circuit breakers on stocks in the S&P 500. The circuit breakers would allow a five-minute pause in trading should the stock price experience a 10 percent change over the preceding five minutes. The pause would give the markets an opportunity to attract additional liquidity.

Preliminary Findings

The SEC–CFTC joint report, dated May 18, 2010, provides valuable insights concerning how equity trading has evolved into a complex of interacting markets and venues, the development of weak spots in trading systems, and the variety of approaches followed by active traders.[61]

The report chronicles events in US markets, and describes several working hypotheses:

1 a possible linkage between decline in stock index prices (ETFs and E-Mini S&P 500 futures) and waves of selling in individual securities;
2 a severe mismatch in liquidity, withdrawal of liquidity by electronic market makers, and use of market orders (stop-loss) that create a cascade of orders;
3 the extent to which the liquidity mismatch was exacerbated by disparate trading conventions among various exchanges;
4 the use of "stub quotes" designed to provide a "two-sided quote" but at prices not intended to be executed;
5 the use of market orders that might have contributed to market instability and temporary breakdown in orderly trading;
6 the impact of ETFs, which suffered a disproportionate number of broken trades relative to other securities.

A key theme to be pursued in the investigation is linkages between trading in equity index products. Attention focuses on trading in the E-Mini S&P 500 futures contract, where one trader reportedly carried out large sell orders. CME data indicates that trading in E-Mini S&P 500 futures was very high, with more orders to sell than buy.

The report noted: "all of these markets are closely linked by a complex set of traders and trading strategies. The precipitous decline in price in one market on May 6 may have influenced a sustained series of selling in other financial markets. The rapid rebound in price in one market could similarly have been linked to a rebound in price in another."[62] But not all securities experienced the sharp declines noted within the twenty-minute period in which the flash crash took place. Approximately 86 percent of securities reached lows for the day that were less than 10 percent away from the price at the commencement of the crash. The other 14 percent of securities suffered greater declines than the broader market, some trading all the way down to one penny.

Several key factors were highlighted in the preliminary report:

1 There were disparate practices among securities exchanges in the US.
2 Some securities were particularly affected by stop-loss orders.
3 Approximately 70 percent of the US securities with declines of 60 percent or more were ETFs. As a class, ETFs were affected more than any other category of securities.
4 There were many more sell orders than buy orders in the period 2:30 p.m. to 2:45 p.m. in E-Mini S&P 500 futures.

Low Frequency Report

Early in October 2010 the SEC–CFTC released a second report, providing more direct details concerning how the flash crash could have taken place. A large order by a traditional investor was the trigger for the wild market swings, and not a high speed trading firm. The SEC–CFTC report explained that the May 6 sell-off was sparked by a rapidly executed $4.1 billion sale of stock index futures by a large institutional investor engaged in hedging.[63]

The order was placed via a computer based program so quickly, in just twenty minutes, that it triggered wild automated trading by other traders, including high frequency traders. Regulators did not explain why the seller, identified as Waddell & Reed, demanded that the trade be executed so quickly. The actions of this plain-vanilla type trader leaves many questions unanswered. This type of automated trading can lead to a surge in volume, driven by high speed computer programs. Approximately a dozen HFTs dominate volume in equity markets. Reinforcing the issue of adequate liquidity, needed to support such high volume, is the continued fragmentation of equity trading. Some fifty venues share the equity trading business in the United States. The NYSE still plays a central role in equity trading, but now shares much of the trading with ECNs, dark pools, and other trading platforms.

The HFT–Algo System

In this and the following section we summarize findings of how the May 6 crash took place. In this section we focus on an early October 2010 report concerning a single trader's impact. In the following section we take a broader perspective, which suggests that, unless structural and behavioral patterns are modified, it could happen again.

The long awaited report of the SEC–CFTC holds that investors engaged in hedging entered their trade orders into an "Algo" computer system, with intentions to complete all trades as quickly as possible, regardless of price. A chief operations officer of a leading money manager, who is well experienced, observed that "using a simplistic manual trading strategy, to input a very large order into an Algo, with no price or time limits, is borderline irresponsible."[64]

According to the official report of the SEC–CFTC, the automatic sale of a large block of futures by a single mutual fund touched off a chain reaction of results. The Dow Jones Industrial Average (DJIA) plunged more than 600 points in only a few minutes. The mutual fund initiated a program at 2:32 p.m. to sell $4.1 billion of futures contracts, utilizing a computer sell algorithm, and over the next twenty minutes dumped 75,000 contracts onto the market, accelerating sales as prices plunged.[65] Apparently, the equity market meltdown began on derivative market trading venues, but spread quickly to cash equities trading.

Financial market regulators note that a large size trade such as the one triggering the May 6 crash could be repeated, since large transactions are becoming commonplace. The algorithm that executed this trade is widely used across markets, and was provided by Barclays Capital. When the mutual fund sold, much of the buying was carried out by HFTs. As these buyers became aware of their excessive "long" positions in a declining market, they began to sell aggressively. This caused the mutual fund's algorithm in turn to accelerate selling. Computers took on "hot potato" behavior, with trades growing at an alarming pace. This selling pressure was transferred from the futures market to the stock market by arbitrageurs, who bought cheap futures and sold higher valued cash equities.

Machines Did It

A May 24, 2010 report in *Bloomberg Business Week* titled "The Machines That Ate the Market" provides a useful narrative of how stock trading has evolved over four decades. Several key points emerge in this analysis that explain how such a meltdown could take place and why it might be repeated. First, the near monopoly in stock trading once enjoyed by the NYSE ensured price discovery and liquidity concentration that fulfilled the needs of market traders. The erosion in NYSE market share which began in the 1970s with mandated flexible commissions and the upgraded status of NASDAQ reflected a pro-competitive stage in stock trading. Accelerated changes came in the period 1998–2007, with decimal pricing of shares, and efforts to further raise the level of competition and transparency. As a result, the NYSE share of equity trading fell from 80 percent in 2005 to 50 percent in 2007 and under 25 percent in 2010. High frequency traders account for as much as 60 percent of equity volume according to the TABB Group, a financial market consultancy.[66] The most active of these include Getco in Chicago, Tradebot Systems in Kansas City, and RGM in Austin.

Second, quantitative trading systems direct much of daily trading employing algorithmic computer models, where trading is initiated without a decision or instructions from humans. However, during the May 6 crash many large traders employing such methods simply shut down their computerized trading systems, given the uncertainty and lack of accurate data feeds.

Third, the composition of trading has shifted away from dedicated and long term investors toward more speculative transactions. HFTs place simultaneous buy and sell orders on different market venues, in an effort to exploit price discrepancies that result from mismatches in the structural and computer systems employed by these venues.

Clearly, the regulatory bodies have much work ahead to further analyze and plan reforms that will prevent flash crashes in the future. The May 6 crash is an important signal. It points to the highly interconnected status of financial markets, where pressures in futures trading can elicit equally strong, or even stronger, reactions in markets for the underlying securities.[67]

7 London Calling

Introduction

The London Stock Exchange stands among the top financial exchanges in the world measured by number of companies listed, market capitalization value of shares, value of equity turnover, foreign share issues listed for trading, and size and role of market for smaller growth companies. LSE undertook a reorganization of its membership and share trading in 1986, not long after the NYSE went through a similar reorganization. Since that date the LSE has been one of the pace-setters in the world of financial exchanges.

This chapter focuses on the London Stock Exchange, one of the pivotal players among exchanges. The financial exchange sector is modernizing at a rapid pace, and LSE is one of the more active participants in this process. In the following sections we describe how the LSE is building a better business, analyze how and why it has chosen to continue as an independent entity, outline how its trading platforms have been modernized in response to new challenges, and evaluate new initiatives.

Not Exactly a Consolidator

In the following sections we describe a race for hegemonic status between two increasingly competitive rivals, why the planned alliance between these rivals did not come to fruition, and how technology failed to produce equity market consolidation in Europe.

Two Hegemonic Forces

The period 1986–2002 witnessed a growing rivalry between two financial exchanges—LSE and Deutsche Börse. Below we chronicle the development of this rivalry (Table 7.1). It begins with the Big Bang restructuring of LSE in 1986, intensifies as the German exchanges modernize, unify, and press forward under a "Finanzplatz Deutschland" banner, and comes to a climax in 2000 as final negotiations are carried out toward strengthening a 1998 alliance between the two exchanges.

Table 7.1 LSE and Deutsche Börse Initiatives, 1986–2002

Year	*Deutsche Börse*	*LSE*
1986		Big Bang restructuring.
1987–89		Continental share trading shifts toward LSE platforms.
1990	German futures and options exchange established.	
1992	German finance minister presents plan for simple, unified stock exchange.	SEATS hybrid trading system introduced by LSE.
1993	Deutsche Börse created as holding company, owning all regional exchanges.	
1995		LSE introduces the Alternative Investment Market (AIM) for small growth companies.
1996	Deutsche Telekom IPO completed, second largest in the world, valued at $13 billion.	
1997	Neuer Markt and Xetra trading systems are introduced.	LSE introduces the SETS trading system for large cap stocks.
1998	German and Swiss derivative exchanges merge to form Eurex.	LSE enters alliance with German exchange. Objective is to develop a common electronic trading platform.
1999	Germany joins new euro single currency group. Eurozone a new challenge with its horizontal equity market.	UK opts out of euro system. LSE launches its techMARK exchange, for new economy and high tech listings.
2000	Merger with LSE is announced, but fails to be realized.	With breakdown of merger talks with German exchange, LSE receives a bid from OM Gruppen, which is rejected.
2001	German exchange launches initial public offering.	
2002	Unsuccessful Neuer Markt is closed for business.	

As the German exchange reorganized into a single entity, from nine separate regional exchanges, LSE introduced new trading systems in response to new rivals, such as electronic communications networks (ECNs). LSE's responses to the new and rapidly changing equity trading environment included adding and improving existing trading platforms, and considering partnership with exchanges based in rival financial centers. Later in this chapter we describe how LSE developed new trading platforms such as AIM, SEATS, and techMARK.

With the arrival of the single currency, the euro, in 1999, European bankers, politicians, and business executives heralded this event as putting the Continent on the path toward developing a pan-European equity market. In 1998–2000 observers could assert that there were too many exchanges in Europe. Consolidation would be the way of the future, but what pattern would it follow? One possible pattern could be a merger of the two largest exchanges (LSE and Deutsche Börse) to yield one of the largest equity trading markets in the world. A second pattern could be for the LSE to act as a consolidator, merging with smaller exchanges, and for Deutsche Börse to follow a similar pattern as a rival exchange group.

By the mid-1990s each of these large exchanges had risen to a threshold of hegemonic power and status in Europe. Table 7.1 outlines the steps taken by the London and Frankfurt based exchanges leading to this hegemonic status, and later sections of this chapter further describe LSE initiatives toward this status.

In 1986 Big Bang in London provided Continental exchanges with an early warning of competition to come. As a result, London attracted European share trading like a magnet, and it took a series of little bangs for Continental stock exchanges to reverse the tide of share trading. In the period 1986–89, Continental exchanges witnessed a shift of share trading from Continental exchanges to LSE. The little bangs across the Continent were the responses of the Paris, Amsterdam, and other Continental exchanges aimed at recapturing share trading volume. In Germany business leaders and bankers expressed a yearning for a "Finanzplatz Deutschland" centered in Frankfurt.

By 1990 eight regional stock exchanges in Germany had agreed to unify as a Frankfurt centered equity market. In the same year the Deutsche Termin Börse was opened, Germany's new futures and options exchange. The Frankfurt based Deutsche Börse moved steadily in the 1990s to create a Neuer Markt for trading smaller growth companies, and introduced its Xetra electronic trading system. A year later (1998) the Swiss and German derivatives exchanges united to establish Eurex, which now is one of the three largest derivatives exchanges in the world.

A casual look at the initiatives of the LSE and German exchange covering the period 1986–2002 (Table 7.1) leads to a simple conclusion. The two exchanges were racing to gain competitive advantage and become a potential core member of a to-be-organized pan-European equity trading group. At this juncture we could ask: Will these two exchanges continue to operate as rivals, or will they consider an alliance or even merger?

In 1998 the LSE entered into an alliance with the Deutsche Börse, with the objective of creating a common electronic trading platform. From 1998 to midyear 2000 the two exchanges held a series of discussions and negotiations on how to implement an alliance, and whether it should take the form of an outright merger. The following section analyzes these negotiations, and explains why they failed to bring about a lasting cooperation between the two parties.

Planning Problems

In 2000 a merger between the Deutsche Börse and London Stock Exchange was considered a good idea, but many analysts saw two important drawbacks. First, the business plan developed by the two parties looked like a failure from the start. Second, the politics of European Union financial market development excluded important constituencies.

The business plan called for creation of two new markets. One, referred to as iX, would include the largest company share issues, cash, and futures options markets.

The second market would be a joint venture with NASDAQ, operating a growth company market. This would replace two existing (and successful) exchanges with two new exchanges. Critical observers noted that this approach failed to cut costs, and probably would lead to higher costs.[1]

On the political side, the location of an exchange is a symbol of the success of a financial center. Changing the location of the merged British and German exchange operations and headquarters would give rise to divergent points of view. With London's position in 2000 as Europe's preeminent financial center, there would be no question that the merged entity should be based anywhere other than in London. This could be said despite the reality that from an economic viewpoint location of the merged exchange's operations is irrelevant. London was and remains the only financial center in Europe with the potential to challenge New York for global leadership.

With the organization of Euronext in 2000, the French had no interest in a successful merger of LSE and Deutsche Börse. At this time the French were more interested in establishing a pan-European regulator of financial markets. As a result, MiFID came into effect in 2008, presenting new problems for traditional exchanges trying to retain their share of equity trading under new and more liberal competition rules.

Difficulties with both the operational and the political aspects of unifying the British and German exchanges led to a breakdown of negotiations, and cancellation of the merger. But there was one lasting effect: the LSE now was in play as a merger and acquisition candidate.

Technology Doesn't Always Win

With negotiations between the management of the German and British exchanges reaching an impasse, those hoping for exchange consolidation in Europe turned to Euronext and a small exchange group in Scandinavia. Earlier we described the mergers leading to creation of Euronext and OM Gruppen. Here we consider OM Gruppen's hostile bid for LSE, which created turmoil among LSE executive ranks and led to the replacement of LSE's chief executive, Gavin Casey, in September 2000. Shortly after breakdown of merger negotiations between the German and British exchanges, OM Gruppen launched a $1.2 billion hostile bid for LSE.

At this time OM Gruppen enjoyed two key advantages in its quest to play a central role in creating a pan-European equity market. First, it was building a Nordic alliance of exchanges. The first stage involved linking the Stockholm and Copenhagen exchanges, the first time two stock exchanges made use of the same trading system. Eventually seven exchanges were committed to join together and use the Saxess electronic trading system (Scandinavian and Baltic exchanges).

Second, technology always held a central position at OM Gruppen. Scandinavia is one of the most active centers of internet banking and broking. The "net culture" translates into investors ready to use technology, and demanding the efficiencies for investors that come from high tech securities trading systems. OM Gruppen is one of the world's leaders in developing and applying advanced computer and internet technology to develop securities trading services.

In 2000 bankers and other observers in Scandinavia believed that OM Gruppen would not lose from its bid for LSE, whatever the outcome. If they won in the bid to merge with LSE, there would be a superb opportunity to become the focal point of European exchange consolidation, but even if they did not win they would gain invaluable publicity and recognition.[2]

By yearend 2000 it was clear that LSE would not merge with its Scandinavian suitor. However, this would not end the story. Each exchange would move forward into other merger dialogues, and each would discover a merger "solution." In the case of LSE, the London exchange would reject a NASDAQ overture, and eventually merge with Borsa Italiana. In the case of OM Gruppen, there would be a complex four-way exchange of ownership in shares of financial exchanges, and a tie-up of the Scandinavian group with NASDAQ.

Building a Better Exchange

The London Stock Exchange has pursued a policy of independence allowing it to focus on building a better exchange, utilizing internal skills and resources. In this section we outline LSE's approach toward this goal. LSE's focus has been on: 1) providing superior technology and trading facilities, and 2) developing a more diversified business mix.

LSE Advantages for International Companies

In 2001 the LSE issued a promotional publication of about eight pages titled "London: The First Choice for International Companies." This publication notes that London is the world's most international financial center, and leader in Eurobond and forex trading, and hosts over two-thirds of all international equity underwriting. The LSE services more international equities trading than any other market.

London enjoys these advantages since it can bring together international companies and global fund managers. The publication further notes that London is the first choice of international companies seeking to raise capital from investors. More international firms choose to list on LSE than any other market in the world. This advantage is enhanced by the LSE's growing family of trading markets, each designed to meet the needs of diverse companies and investors. These include: techMARK, the LSE market for innovative technology companies; and AIM, the market for smaller growth companies.

In its 2001 literature LSE describes eight significant advantages which attract international listings (Table 7.2). One factor underlies the advantages described in Table 7.2. That is the flexibility of the process of LSE listing. This flexibility carries over into other areas as well, especially trading and settlement, and currency of choice in conducting trading and settlement.

Table 7.2 LSE Advantages Attract International Listings

Type of advantage	*Explanation*
1 Capital	London is the world's largest equity fund management center. Institutions account for 80 percent of all trades on the LSE.
2 Liquidity	The value of trading in international shares in London is consistently higher than in any other market.
3 Visibility	The size, people, and reach of the London markets allow international companies listed and traded to gain global attention and coverage. LSE trading and information systems are accessed by more than 100,000 international investors worldwide.
4 International outlook	The European investment community is highly receptive to international companies. European institutions invest much more than their North American counterparts in international equities.
5 Knowledge and expertise	UK institutions have the deepest knowledge and expertise in international companies. This has been built up over many decades.
6 Respected regulation	Standards of regulation in London are respected worldwide. International companies find that London imparts greater prestige from its listings in the eyes of the global investment community.
7 Flexibility and anonymity	LSE makes the burden of joining its markets flexible and straightforward.
8 Currencies	International companies can list in London in any currency they choose. LSE trading technology can support trading in all major currencies, and its systems ensure that processes of listing, trading, and settlement are identical in every case.

Source: London Stock Exchange, "London: The First Choice for International Companies," 2001.

Implementing a Better Exchange

Over the eight-year period following LSE's rejection of the Deutsche Börse and OM Gruppen bids, the London exchange has worked to build a better exchange. Central to this is the strengthening of its global reach and trading systems for all clientele. This operates both in trading system technology and in providing more refined infrastructure and software that support data and information services to global users. In LSE's 2006 annual report, Clara Furse, chief executive officer of LSE, stated that the exchange's "market data is received in terminals in more than 100 countries as numbers [of terminals] increased from 95,000 to 104,000." In the same report LSE projected a doubling of SETS trading volume in the period 2006–08.[3]

Expanded trading volume depends on increased listings. Furse noted that LSE enjoys an "exceptional customer franchise," supported by its premier status for attracting foreign flotations. At yearend 2007 LSE reported it had attracted eighty-six IPOs from twenty-two countries, raising $28 billion. This was double the amount raised in offerings by non-US companies conducted on NYSE and NASDAQ combined.[4]

LSE's second market, AIM, gained competitive advantage over NASDAQ in 2000–01, and continued to make inroads in smaller growth company issuance and listing in the period 2002–07. AIM seems attractive to smaller US health care and tech companies. AIM views itself as a more attractive destination for companies seeking a broad investor base. An AIM listing gives the company an international focus. Also, the London market provides a way for listing at an earlier stage and with less onerous regulations.

A slowdown in AIM listings in 2008 mirrored a similar decline on NASDAQ. Nevertheless, the LSE is continuing to take its message around the world in AIM road shows across Europe.[5]

One of the competitive strengths enjoyed by the London Stock Exchange is the "light touch" regulatory approach followed by the UK Financial Services Authority (FSA). This contrasts with much more "heavy-handed" and poorly organized regulation of financial services in the United States.

In keeping with this advantage, LSE in 2007 announced plans to launch a regulation light market for private equity, property, and hedge funds. The market will apply only minimum standards of regulation. Hedge funds and other asset managers have been looking forward to the opportunity to float closed end funds that consist of stakes in other funds. These "funds of funds" now can trade on the AIM market. London hosts 80 percent of the European hedge fund industry. Retail investors will not be prevented from buying funds in the new market, but its description as a "professional" market should cause them to take a careful second look before investing.[6]

A discussion of LSE's efforts to build a better exchange must include a growing emphasis on speed of trading. In June 2007 the London exchange unveiled its new TradElect system. One of the fastest in the world, TradElect cuts the time for placing an order to its final confirmation to an average of 10 milliseconds, or one-tenth of a thousandth of a second, from 140 milliseconds. The system can handle 3,000 trades a second, up from 600 under LSE's older system. Similar speed and capacity upgrades are being undertaken by Deutsche Börse and NASDAQ.[7]

In the following sections we chronicle LSE's evolution of trading systems, and examine its changing business model. Also, we analyze mergers completed and not completed, and finally consider how a theory of oligopolistic reaction might apply to LSE in the future.

Evolution of LSE Trading Systems

Prior to the Big Bang the LSE operated a single capacity system. Stockbrokers functioned as an agent of the buyer or seller. Alternately, market makers were called "jobbers." Their main function was to make a market in the shares they inventoried. Brokers routed orders to buy and sell shares through jobbers, and could not take positions in shares. Brokers earned a commission for their service, which was on a fixed schedule until Big Bang.

Jobbers were required to quote prices on shares to the brokers. Prices were expected to be competitive, since in many cases several jobbers were making a market in a given share issue. Trading was located on the floor of the LSE. Big Bang changed these arrangements, introducing a more flexible and competitive environment.

Single and Dual Capacity

Big Bang introduced dual capacity, where brokers could opt to be simply agents, or dual capacity agency brokers. The latter can act as market makers, functioning as broker-dealers. Broker-dealers take a position in shares, buying and selling at bid and ask prices. As a market maker, the broker commits to quoting firm bid and ask prices on shares during trading hours.[8]

Prices quoted by market makers on LSE are entered into a computer system, known as Stock Exchange Automated Quotations (SEAQ), and displayed on a computer screen, the Teletext Output of Price Information by Computer (TOPIC) screen. TOPIC screens may display share prices for several market makers dealing in a given stock. The screen displays bid and ask prices, and the number of shares that can be (firm-)traded at that price.

The SEAQ system was introduced in 1986 with Big Bang, and based on the NASDAQ system, which operates on computer screens. LSE chose to model its trading system on NASDAQ for several reasons. First, London's culture has been one oriented toward market making. Therefore, institutional traders contact stock exchange members asking if they wish to buy or sell, and assume the related risk. Patterns of doing business persist, and it was understood that an order routing system focused on the role of market makers would be easier to work with.[9] Second, the NASDAQ system was perceived to be more up to date than its alternatives. The NASDAQ system is quote driven. The alternative order driven system utilized by the NYSE continued to rely on floor trading and required large staffing.

Allowing brokers to act as market makers, and also permitting market makers to organize as limited liability companies rather than partnerships, the LSE was successful in increasing the number of competing market makers. Larger brokers wanted to become dealers, since they could match buyers and sellers from their own clients, and earn the bid–ask spread enjoyed by the jobber. To protect buyers and sellers, the exchange requires market makers to match with the best price on the TOPIC screen.

LSE Introduces SETS

In 1997 the London Stock Exchange introduced the Stock Exchange Electronic Trading System (SETS). SETS is used for FTSE 100 stocks, shares traded in the Eurotop Index, and stocks with traded options on LIFFE. SETS is an order matching system. Orders are placed as a limit order, or for best price available. Continental exchanges for the most part are order driven, and introduction of SETS gave LSE an ability to re-establish its close connectivity with clients who might be tempted to wander across the Channel and use the French, Belgian, German, Italian, or Swiss order driven trading systems. Also, SETS strengthened LSE's ability to retain institutional trading clientele.

Large orders can be a challenge. They are vulnerable to difficult-to-mimic impact and timing costs. One solution is for brokers to match block trades between institutions. LSE's strong liquidity advantage attracts this business from the Continent. London traders are well prepared to take risks.

In a quote driven system (SEAQ on LSE and NASDAQ) a market maker quotes continuously bid and ask prices at which it will buy and sell shares. The difference is the spread, defining the gross profit margin. These systems tend to be driven by quotations. Whereas the top 100 shares in London are traded on the SETS system, other shares are handled by the SEAQ system.

Too Small or Too Large?

Over the past few decades several trends have operated to make life difficult for brokers and dealers. First, large institutional clients are less in need of the services of a traditional broker. They are more likely to go directly to a market maker. As institutions have taken a larger share of trading, it has become necessary for dealers to assume greater risks, including those related to block trades. As Golding notes, the equity capital markets business is lumpy, giving investors and traders a rollercoaster ride.[10]

While large trades create problems for order driven systems, market makers often are reluctant to service trading in small company shares where market liquidity is low. In such cases spreads may be wide, discouraging traders.

To summarize, order driven markets experience difficulty in servicing large trades that strain available liquidity. At the same time, quote driven markets may not be able to create sufficient liquidity for small company shares. The LSE sought to deal with these two problems, in 1992 launching a new trading system called Stock Exchange Alternative Trading System (SEATS). This hybrid system appoints a market maker for stocks with low liquidity. The market maker is obligated to make continuous two-way prices. Market makers must execute orders according to time priority if they are at the same price as or a better price than a proposed trade. Also, any orders to be matched by brokers must be offered to the official market maker, who in turn can trade at a better price on own account or by matching against posted orders.

Hybrid systems like SEATS contain both order driven and quote driven features. Market orders can be routed to an assigned dealer, who is obliged to execute at best price or match against limit orders. The NYSE launched its own hybrid system in 2006, as a refinement of its specialist order driven system.

Taking AIM

Companies that do not meet the listing requirements for a stock exchanges main trading platform require a "second market." In the United States this takes the form of NASDAQ, by tradition the place where small or early stage growth companies go public. In the period 1985–99 the links between Silicon Valley and NASDAQ intensified, as more and more venture capital financed enterprises launched IPOs.

The European financial community saw the benefits of facilitating growth company securities issuance. During the 1990s several European countries launched second tier markets for early stage company shares. Companies that could not meet the strict listing requirements of the main equity market could go public on an alternative market. This includes the UK Alternative Investment Market (AIM) in 1995, and several EuroNM markets created within the Eurozone in 1999.[11] As early as 1996 a group of European and American banks formed a market (EASDAQ) intended to operate as a pan-European trading place for equities, including early stage enterprises.

AIM has been the most successful of these second markets (Table 7.3). AIM utilizes an informal screening of company share issues, with nominated advisers (Nomads) sponsoring new issues. Nomads (investment banks specializing in small company advisory and listing) certify to the "readiness" of the company for listing and trading on AIM. This allows for a less costly due diligence and certification process than that which operates in the United States or on the LSE main market.

London's Alternative Investment Market has attracted overseas companies at a rate challenging NASDAQ's former position as first choice for listing growth companies.

LSE Business Model

Previous sections of this chapter describe how the business model of the London Stock Exchange has been evolving, at times at a rapid pace. In the following we describe the LSE business model, and focus on business segments and revenue mix as methods of identifying the specific nature of this model.

Current Status

In 2007 Clara Furse, then chief executive of LSE, pointed out five strengths in the position of the London equity market. First, the strategy followed is delivering strong growth. The customer franchise enjoyed by a London based exchange

Table 7.3 LSE Equity Trading Systems

SEAQ	*SEATS*	*SETS*	*AIM*
1986	1992	1997	1995
Automated trading of UK and foreign listed shares, displacing slower floor trading. Flexible commissions provided competitive advantage over rival exchanges.	One of the first hybrid systems. Overcomes liquidity needs for smaller, less traded share issues.	Aids trading in large capitalization share issues. Order driven system.	First successful share trading market for small, growth issues. Lead venue for venture capital type issues outside the United States.

provides exceptional opportunity. London has become the "world's IPO venue of choice."[12] LSE benefits from a "secular shift to derivatives linked ... electronic trading." In 2007 a new technology platform was launched to provide the fastest and most reliable equity trading platform in the world.

Second, London's global reputation, the quality of markets, and access to deep pools of international capital attract companies to a London listing.

Third, the Alternative Investment Market, becoming the world's most vibrant growth equity market, is specifically designed for smaller growing companies. In 2006 AIM quoted 247 foreign companies. AIM targets, among others, European early stage growth companies.[13]

Fourth, LSE is experiencing a structural shift in the way UK equities are traded. SETS, an electronic order book, experiences strong growth. SETS allows tax efficient trading for hedging, and sophisticated algorithmic trading that enables users to capture very short period opportunities. In the period 2001–06 SETS trading was increasing at annual rates of 35 percent. SETSmm has brought similar advantages to midcap equity trading.

Fifth, LSE is committed to developing cutting edge technology. In 2003 LSE launched a Technology Roadmap (TRM). In 2006 two related milestones were achieved: 1) Infolect, LSE's new market data ticker plant, went live, reducing information broadcast latency from 30 to 2 milliseconds; and 2) a trading platform upgrade doubled core trading capacity.

Business Segments

LSE operates four primary business segments, including issuer services, broker services, information services, and derivatives services.

Issuer Services

Issuer services are responsible for attracting companies and supporting them before and after listing. LSE has operated two listing markets (Main Board and Alternative Investment Market). Currently, a third market (Professional Securities Market) has been added. In the year ending March 2007, 108 companies listed on the Main Market and Professional Securities Market, and 395 companies joined AIM (Table 7.4). These companies raised over £29 billion in capital, up 44

Table 7.4 Number of New Company IPOs Listed on LSE (2002–07)

Year	*Main market*	*AIM*
2002	119	170
2003	48	154
2004	43	193
2005	82	432
2006	107	510
2007	108	395

Source: LSE, *Annual Report 2007*, pp. 12–14.

Table 7.5 Total Number of Company Share Issues Listed on LSE (2002–07)

Year	*Main market*	*AIM*	*Total*
2002	2,238	641	2,879
2003	2,072	705	2,777
2004	1,901	792	2,693
2005	1,789	1,127	2,916
2006	1,868	1,473	3,341
2007	1,608	1,637	3,245

Source: LSE, *Annual Report 2007*, pp. 12–14.

percent over the previous year.[14] At March 2007 there were 3,245 company share issues traded on LSE markets (Table 7.5). This includes sixty-seven US companies listed on AIM, Rosneft (the largest Russian company, which raised £3.6 billion on LSE), and numerous Asian companies (Samsung, South Korea). In the fiscal year ending 2007 UK companies' shares worth £3.4 trillion traded on LSE.

In the bond market, London Stock Exchange accounts for 14 percent of all bonds listed in Europe.

LSE benefits from the large professional investor base in London, with over US$13 trillion of assets managed. Also, 75 percent of European hedge fund assets are under management in London. Of the Main Market listings made each fiscal year, key markets targeted include China, Russia, and India. The Asia Pacific office in Hong Kong was opened in October 2004. This office targets large privatization deals, and has attracted major listings.

AIM has become the world's most robust growth market. It celebrated its tenth anniversary in June 2005. The 510 companies listing in 2006 raised over £7.9 billion. In 2006 the combined market capitalization of AIM's 1,473 companies was £71.6 billion. AIM now is a mainstream asset class, over 40 percent owned by institutional investors. Almost every major institution in the UK now invests in AIM listed equities. The LSE actively markets AIM through seminars and a network of nominated advisers.

Through Nomads, AIM outsources much of its policing responsibilities. Nomads often are the same brokerages that take companies public. To list on AIM a company needs a nominated adviser and a broker. The LSE states that the Nomad is a company's most important adviser, who warrants to the Exchange that the company is appropriate for joining AIM.[15] Nomads receive a modest financial reward for lending their expertise, ensuring that the companies they regulate are in compliance with LSE rules. They may pick up lucrative broking business if they also have a broking arm. In 2004, 57 percent of AIM mining sector placings used the same firm as both broker and Nomad. The success of AIM lies in its flexible regime, which works well for growing companies that can deal directly with a Nomad without going through the regulatory listing system.[16] This yields such advantages as no need for a minimum track record, no pre-vetting, and no minimum float in public hands.

Broker Services

LSE broker services is responsible for providing the trading platforms that help customers develop their businesses. An important measure of success in this sector is the growth in trades and secondary trading volume. In 2006 the number of trades expanded 35 percent, and average daily value traded on SETS increased by 33 percent to £4.7 billion.

Program and algorithmic trading continues to evolve rapidly. LSE trading levels break former levels repeatedly, for domestic as well as international business. Trading levels are sensitive to marginal costs. Therefore, new trading activity becomes viable when costs are reduced. LSE introduced a discount scheme in April 2004, and volumes surged. In the period 2002–07 SETS volumes doubled every two to three years. LSE account managers and product managers work closely with customers, and analyze trading and behavior patterns to detect opportunities that will expand volume.

Discussion of broker services would not be complete without mentioning the role of corporate brokers on the LSE. LSE uses a corporate broker system, whereby the broker represents the interests of the company on the stock exchange in matters relating to share ownership, trading patterns, and control stakeholdings. The brokerage firm Cazenove has been a dominant service provider in this area. Cazenove formed a joint venture with JPMorgan Chase to better provide these services in the future. The following section analyzes recent trends in corporate broking.

Corporate Brokers in London

Corporate broking is a uniquely British business that involves a bank acting as the main point of contact between companies and their investors. Fierce competition operates, as banks vie for FTSE 100 clients. This competition appears on the surface foolish and wasteful, since direct profitability is low. The main advantage for the bank serving as corporate broker is the prospect of a more lucrative advisory role.

At yearend 2010 companies were beginning to see light at the end of a difficult recessionary tunnel. The period 2008–10 was one of lower profit, declining share prices, and difficulty in finding a better direction for corporate strategy, but by yearend 2010 companies were developing new strategies. According to Alisdair Gayne, head of corporate broking at Barclays Capital, "some companies are clearly disappointed with the advice given during last year's cash calls and as a result are likely to review their corporate broking relationships."[17]

Corporate broking is one of the hardest businesses to build. Relationships are sticky, and newcomers experience setbacks. Lehman Brothers did not have a leading client until 2006. The business requires long term investment by banks, but in the long run it can be highly rewarding. It leads to business that is less capital intensive and therefore less risky.

The three dominant players—JPMorgan Cazenove, UBS, and Bank of America Merrill Lynch (Table 7.6)—enjoy a large critical mass of broker relationships.

Table 7.6 Leading Corporate Brokers on LSE

Corporate broker	*Number of clients**	
	FTSE 100	*FTSE 250*
JPMorgan Cazenove	37	100
Bank of America Merrill Lynch	32	34
UBS	29	39
Morgan Stanley	19	0
Deutsche Bank	18	18
Citigroup	16	19
RBS Hoare Govett	10	37
Credit Suisse	9	20
Goldman Sachs	8	0
Nomura	3	0

Source: Lina Saigol and Megan Murphy, "Pressures on Banks to Build up Broker Share," *Financial Times*, October 8, 2010, p. 19.

Note
* Includes joint brokerships.

Bulge bracket investment bank Goldman has focused on large cap company ties. Smaller independent brokers in the UK, such as Collins Stewart and Evolution Group, serve smaller companies. All three approaches have paid off in gaining mandates for merger advisory and financing deals.

Information Services

The LSE is the source of some of the most widely followed and analyzed data in the world. Price and volume data from LSE not only affects trading decisions of thousands of equity market professionals, but also is studied closely by private investors, institutional investors, and derivatives traders.

The information services unit at LSE is responsible for broadcasting data from London markets, in real time, to the widest audience. At yearend 2007 LSE real time market data was being received on terminals in over 100 countries. More than 116,000 terminals were in operation, a 12 percent increase over the previous year.

In recent years LSE has increased its focus on "latency" or speed of data transmission, as well as international reach. The success of Infolect has been an important milestone. Infolect carries over 15 million messages a day to customer terminals. Trading desk operations are enhanced by this service. New and novel algorithmic trading strategies are being developed, based on LSE information.

As primary and secondary markets become more international, the potential client base of LSE expands. Real time data from LSE is received in more than 100 countries. Information services works with data vendors globally, finding ways to distribute data and promote trading. Proquote, the Exchange's trading and market data system, continues to enhance its usefulness and grow its terminal subscribers. At yearend 2007 there were 4,000 Proquote terminals in operation.

Derivatives Services

LSE serves a wide range of derivatives clients. Its link with OMX exchanges and Oslo Børs extends these services across the Scandinavian countries. Trading in equity and equity index derivative contracts exhibits high growth. Fixed income and interest rate derivatives have also demonstrated strong growth.

Through EDX, London's innovative Marketplace Service, large and complex orders are facilitated for member firms. By early 2006 sixty-three member firms were being serviced. LSE operates a substantial covered warrant market service. Two distinct products exist, covered warrants and structured products. The structured product market is targeted toward institutional clients.

In fiscal year 2007 derivatives revenue increased 21 percent to £9.3 million. EDX, 76 percent owned by the LSE, successfully introduced Russian derivative products beginning in December 2006.[18]

Completed and Aborted Mergers

Over the past decade LSE has been the recipient of numerous merger proposals. It has successfully repelled all of these overtures (Table 7.7). In the following we analyze LSE's perspective in rejecting the NASDAQ merger proposal in 2006–07. Also, we analyze the LSE merger with Borsa Italiana, which took place in 2007.

Table 7.7 Major Acquisition Bids for LSE (2000–07)

Potential acquirer or merger partner	*Approximate date*	*Offer bid*	*LSE valuation*
1 Deutsche Börse	May–August 2000	50–50 merger	N/A
2 OMX	September 2000	—	\$1.2 billion
3 Deutsche Börse	December 2004 – March 2005	£5.30	£1.4 billion
4 Macquarie Bank	December 2005 – February 2006	£5.80	£1.5 billion
5 Euronext	December 2004 – March 2006	Discussions, no announced offer	
6 NASDAQ	March 2006	£9.50[1]	\$4.2 billion initial indicative offer
7 NASDAQ	April 2006	NASDAQ initiated purchases of LSE stock and became subject to UK Takeover Panel Rules	

Sources: Various press releases; author's compilation.

Note

1 Eventually, NASDAQ made a higher offer, discussed in the text.

Repelling NASDAQ

In the previous chapter we discussed the rationale for NASDAQ's attempt to merge with LSE. Here we consider the LSE perspective, and why a tie-up with the New York based exchange failed to attract LSE's interest. We consider LSE's rejection of the NASDAQ merger initiative from several viewpoints. These are:

1 NASDAQ and LSE were a bad fit.
2 LSE was undervalued in the stock market, and to "sell" would be detrimental to the interests of LSE shareholders.
3 LSE had a strategy to follow, which would unlock substantial value for shareholders. A considerable "hidden option value" could be lost by a merger with NASDAQ. At the time of the bid LSE was in the process of new initiatives that could create substantial added value. These necessarily would be aborted should a merger be entered into.

In March 2006, shortly after NASDAQ indicated its intention to merge with LSE, a Wall Street report called the $4.17 billion offer by NASDAQ an opportunity to further consolidate and give more global scope to the financial exchange business.[19] The NASDAQ initiative came only a few days after NYSE agreed to merge with Archipelago Holdings. According to the *Wall Street Journal* analysis, a NASDAQ–LSE tie-up would unite the premier market for technology companies in the United States with one of the oldest venues for share trading in Europe. Together this would be the world's second largest exchange, with more than 6,000 companies listed, and aggregate market capitalization exceeding $7 trillion.

A Bad Fit

The LSE considered a merger with NASDAQ a bad fit for several reasons. First, LSE has achieved a global stature with its prominent position as the one-and-only equity trading market in London, the main international financial center outside New York. Second, LSE listings far outshine NASDAQ listings, which are heavily weighted with smaller technology companies.

The success of the London exchange in promoting AIM as an alternative to NASDAQ for "growth" companies also highlights the "bad fit." AIM has moved ahead of New York for launching IPOs, and for listing public companies in need of a less localized trading market. Over the period 2003–07 non-UK companies had chosen to list on London's AIM in increasing numbers. In 2005 EBT Mobile China listed on AIM even while a more neutral home would have been NASDAQ. EBT's chief executive noted that the company needed: 1) an international market where small companies without a track record could raise money, and 2) a liquid market offering good valuation and access to knowledgeable investors willing to take on a small company. While initially EBT might have gotten a higher valuation on NASDAQ, AIM scored higher on all other counts.[20]

In 2005 when EBT listed, AIM was half the size of NASDAQ, with over 1,260 stocks on the London index, with average size about £25 million. Even US companies are listing on AIM. Much of its success relates to cost. The LSE estimates that the cost of floating on AIM is 4–5 percent of funds raised, but in the United States it is 6–8 percent.

With a competitive edge over NASDAQ in a vital area such as listing growth companies, it appears that LSE had good reason to spurn the New York exchange's offer to merge.

LSE Was Undervalued

What is a company worth? Does the stock market fairly value the shares of all publicly owned companies? Are the shares of companies that are "in play" valued differently from those not involved in merger talks? These questions are widely discussed in textbooks focused on investments and corporate finance. In the specific case of NASDAQ's efforts to merge with LSE, we can observe several important points suggesting that the final offer for LSE seriously undervalued the London institution.

First, considerable cost savings or synergies were believed to exist. Technology is the key to cost savings in the case of mergers between exchanges. NASDAQ stated in early 2006 that its past success with technology integration constituted a key advantage of its bid.[21] Did NASDAQ's offer of £12.43 a share give LSE shareholders little or none of the synergy benefits? According to several stock analysts, NASDAQ could have bid up to £16.50 without diluting earnings.

Second, control ownership often is cited as worth more than portfolio (diversified) ownership. Therefore, a target company may contain considerable hidden value, related to how the acquirer manages the new integrated exchange. It was believed that rival bidders would have made bids considerably higher than that of NASDAQ. However, the most eligible parties (NYSE and Deutsche Börse) were unable to enter the bidding, owing to alternative commitments.

Third, the UK Takeover Panel imposes a highly restrictive time frame on actual and potential bidders. When NASDAQ made its "final offer" of £12.43, and extended the closing date for LSE investors to tender their shares (to February 10, 2007), the clock started ticking. If the LSE board had agreed to a new bid, under UK takeover rules NASDAQ could no longer have increased its offer, unless a rival bidder appeared or the board recommended a higher price.[22]

Finally, there can exist hidden real options value. This depends on the ability of existing management to take initiatives in the future that will create value that is not clearly visible at the present time. This is supported by the fact that discerning stakeholders, such as Heyman Investment Associates, were increasing their shareholdings in LSE at the time that the London Exchange was putting off the New York bidder's offer. Heyman reportedly paid in excess of NASDAQ's final offer price to increase its stake in LSE.[23]

LSE Strategy at the Time of the Bid

Between March 2006, when the NASDAQ bid emerged, and February 2007, almost a year after, the share prices of LSE and NASDAQ diverged by a considerable amount. LSE's share price expanded threefold, whereas that of the New York acquirer languished.[24] In that period the LSE unveiled a series of shareholder friendly measures. These included share repurchases, launching cost controls, and the introduction of a high speed share trading platform. Concerned with new competition from multilateral trading platforms (MTPs), LSE indicated it was preparing its own innovative platform.

Perhaps the most important LSE initiative was its TradElect trading platform, aimed at serving users who employ high speed algorithmic trading. This system displays prices within 2 milliseconds of receipt. In short, during the period when LSE was holding NASDAQ at bay, it was 1) improving its own internal trading and information services and 2) searching for potential merger and alliance partners.

Clara Furse, LSE's chief executive, held preliminary discussions with exchange operator Borsa Italiana concerning the potential for a deal. These early stage talks were interrupted by rival approaches from Australia's Macquarie Bank and from NASDAQ, but at this early stage Borsa Italiana indicated it considered the LSE a potentially interesting partner.[25]

Between Merger Deals

Simultaneously to the LSE repelling the unwanted advances of NASDAQ, the London exchange was engaged in serious operational skirmishes. Competition was squeezing revenues and profits, while improvements in platform efficiency were elevating costs. The LSE is located at one of two financial centers where liquidity concentration attracts more and more rival trading systems. New York and London have become the main battlegrounds, much like the Battle of the Bulge in Europe in 1944. Rival ECNs and share cross-listing pull trading from the LSE, compressing its profitability and sources of revenue.

These points are reflected in Table 7.8, which shows the status of eleven leading financial exchanges on the eve of LSE initiating a merger with Borsa Italiana. At this point LSE ranked fifth in revenues and profit, and seventh in profit margin (Table 7.8). LSE revenues were being squeezed by competitive pressures, but LSE also lacked diversification in its revenue base that other exchanges enjoyed.

For example, Deutsche Börse, second in revenues and first in net profit, operated its own clearing house, which generated substantial revenue and profit. By yearend 2008 NASDAQ OMX was operating eight clearing businesses.[26] Most leading exchanges in Table 7.8 enjoyed the benefit of sizeable derivatives businesses, with the exception of LSE. The London exchange had lost in its bid for LIFFE several years earlier. Two Asian exchanges (Hong Kong and Singapore), BME, and Deutsche Börse enjoyed much higher profit margins than LSE, in large part owing to their clearing and derivative businesses. Even the much smaller SWX had a profit margin of 46 percent, larger than that of LSE.

The preceding tells an interesting and revealing story. While LSE did not see advantage in a merger with NASDAQ, it was in need of initiatives that could improve its business model and competitive status.

Table 7.8 Revenues and Profit Margins at Leading Exchanges, 2007

Exchange	*Total revenues*[1]	*Net profit*[2]	*Percentage profit margin*[3]	*Rank for net profit*	*Rank for profit margin*
1 NYSE Euronext	4.20	630	15	3	11
2 Deutsche Börse	3.40	1,290	38	1	5
3 NASDAQ	2.45	515	21	4	10
4 Hong Kong Exchange	1.10	814	74	2	1
5 London Stock Exchange (LSE)	0.95	314	33	5	7
6 Tokyo Stock Exchange	0.75	173	23	9	8.5
7 OMX (Nordic)	0.65	150	23	11	8.5
8 BME (Madrid)	0.55	292	53	6	3
9 SWX Swiss	0.51	230	46	7	4
10 Toronto (TSX)	0.45	158	35	10	6
11 Singapore (SGX)	0.40	216	54	8	2

Source: Jeremy Grant, "Case for Change Loud and Clear," *Financial Times*, February 9, 2009, p. 16.

Notes
1 Billions of US dollars.
2 Millions of US dollars.
3 Net profit as percentage of revenues.

The data in Table 7.8 reflects the need for LSE to strengthen its competitive and financial status. LSE needed a more diversified revenue base, in which a higher level of profitability could become possible.

The answer to this need would come from a merger with a Milan based exchange. The marriage would be one of complementarities, yielding a more diverse revenue mix. Immediate gains would be derived from a marriage of LSE and Borsa Italiana. But several real options also would lie in the future, including the prospect for vitalizing the vast number of small family companies and boutiques that could shift from private ownership to public company status.

Marriage Italian Style

Any discussion of a given merger transaction almost immediately requires consideration of the specific details. This applies most especially in the case of LSE's proposed merger with Borsa Italiana. In the following we consider general factors leading to merger plans between these two exchanges, and the business plan aspects. Following this, we consider several strategic aspects of this transaction, notably the importance of the MTS bond trading platform as one of the key prizes.

Merger Impulses

The London Stock Exchange has been a merger target since 1999, when the single currency came into being. Elsewhere in this chapter we document efforts by other exchanges to merge with LSE. LSE is an attractive merger partner given its size, leading role in trading foreign equities, time zone proximity to other operating exchanges, and location—situated in one of the major global financial centers.

At midyear 2007 LSE announced plans to merge with Borsa Italiana. Given the former independent attitude of the London exchange, it is necessary to look carefully to gain an understanding of how the LSE executives and directors would have come to a point where merger would be given a positive signal.

According to Clara Furse, LSE chief executive in 2007, the merger deal with Borsa Italiana worked well at three central levels: financial, industrial, and strategic. The financial aspect relates to the impact on profit and earnings. The merger was immediately earnings enhancing. The industrial aspect relates to the merger's impact on the central business activities of the merger partners. In this case the merger would accelerate stock listing and share trading in the Italian market. Finally, the strategic aspect relates to the attractiveness of LSE as a partner in the exchange industry. Furse asserted that LSE's status would be elevated from this strategic level.[27]

Prior to merger with the Italian exchange it could be stated that the LSE business plan was lacking in important respects. These are absence of a serious derivative trading operation and absence of a competitive bond trading platform. These deficiencies could be corrected by a merger with an exchange in possession of a complete bond trading business and derivative trading business, and hence the interest of LSE in merging with Borsa Italiana.

Borsa Italiana had enjoyed considerable success in building an effective and competitive exchange business. At June 2007 Borsa Italiana was Europe's seventh largest stock market by value of companies listed (Table 7.9). A merger of the Italian exchange and LSE would propel them to first rank among Europe's stock exchanges.[28] It is understood that NYSE Euronext also was interested in a tie-up with the Italian exchange. This would have linked the Borsa Italiana with a more diversified business than LSE.[29]

An LSE–Borsa Italiana merger would give the London exchange operator greater power in any efforts by NASDAQ or other suitors that might attempt to take over the United Kingdom exchange. NASDAQ owned close to 30 percent of LSE shares. Exchanges around the globe were under pressure to merge, cut costs, and offer a broader range of products and services.

Table 7.9 Europe's Largest Stock Exchange Operators by Value of Domestic Companies Listed (May 2007)

Exchange	*Trillions of euros*	*Trillions of US dollars*
Euronext	3.13	4.19
London Stock Exchange	3.00	4.01
Deutsche Börse	1.47	1.97
Madrid (BME)	1.13	1.51
SWX Swiss Exchange	0.98	1.32
OMX	0.97	1.29
Borsa Italiana	0.84	1.12

Source: *Wall Street Journal*, June 22, 2007, p. C2.

While there existed many reasons favoring a go-ahead between LSE and the Milan based exchange, there were many hurdles. One was the reaction of NASDAQ against such a deal. Another was the attitude of hedge funds that had acquired LSE shares in expectation that the London exchange would be taken over at a high premium price, and might be opposed to any high cost acquisition by LSE which could dilute the value of their stake.[30]

Complementary Business Models

One of the expected benefits of an LSE–Borsa Italiana merger was the complementary business models of the two exchanges. LSE brings size, a large base of diversified foreign share listings, and the AIM platform housing small, entrepreneurial companies. Borsa Italiana brings added heft (seventh ranked exchange in Europe by market capitalization), a significant derivatives business, and the MTS bond platform.

The LSE initiative gave it an opportunity to claim the MTS bond trading platform, jointly owned by Euronext and Borsa Italiana. Originally MTS was created by Bank of Italy to trade Italian government debt, and was owned through a holding company, MBE Holdings (Figure 7.1). In turn MBE is owned 51 percent by Euronext and 49 percent by Borsa Italiana. MBE owns 60.37 percent of MTS, with the remaining 39.63 percent owned by bank customers of MTS, many of which actively trade on the bond platform.[31] Bank shareholders expressed concern over possible changes in trading costs on MTS should the ownership structure be modified.

Some describe the LSE initiative to merge with the Milan exchange as in part defensive. In 2007 LSE's largest shareholder was NASDAQ, which had made a hostile bid for the London exchange in 2006. In 2007 it was expected that NASDAQ might renew this bid when the takeover rules in the UK allowed such action. Some have termed the LSE–Borsa Italiana merger as akin to a poison

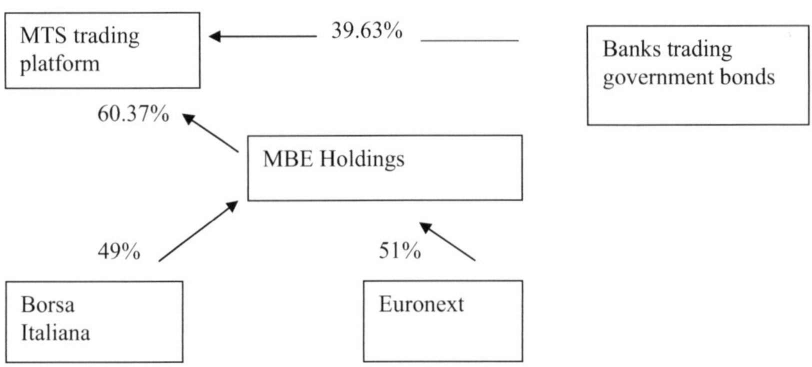

Figure 7.1 Ownership Structure of MTS Bond Platform (Midyear 2007)

Source: *Wall Street Journal*, June 22, 2007, p. C2.

pill, diluting NASDAQ's holding to about 20 percent of the combined group.[32] Analysts describe the deal as largely defensive based on the five directors the Milan partner would elect to the combined entity's board of directors.

New Stock Offerings

One important factor that explains LSE's interest in the Milan exchange is the prospect of gaining a pipeline of new stock offerings. Italy's economy is heavily based on small and medium size family owned companies. Potentially, these companies could provide a stream of new stock offerings on the stock exchange. To activate this channel, it would be necessary to overcome skepticism among Italian investors. Borsa Italiana has recorded several failed efforts to develop a market for small and midsize companies. Also, it would be necessary to persuade these companies that equity market financing provides clear benefits over traditional local bank financing. Borsa Italiana has failed on several occasions to establish a popular trading venue for small and medium size businesses.[33] The cost of listing and lack of analyst research coverage have been tough obstacles.

LSE has enjoyed broad success in making its Alternative Investment Market (AIM) a success. New admissions have climbed, as has trading volume. The key question is whether the LSE can operate within the Italian financial system and improve the brand image of the Italian market. The Borsa history reflects serious struggle in raising the level of new listings. The Parmalat scandal and delisting in 2003 is well remembered. The bottom line is that the LSE has enjoyed success with its light touch regulatory approach, and this has enabled AIM to prosper in attracting listings of small international companies. Italian bankers view the prospect of smaller Italian companies gaining the interest of large institutional money flowing from London as a real possibility.

More Diversified Business

The combined LSE–Borsa Italiana enjoys a more diversified revenue base than either of the two exchanges entering the merger. The Borsa itself is a sprawling group of businesses, including equities, derivatives trading, clearing, settlement, and custody. Also, it owns a large share of MTS and is exercising an option to purchase the other part from Euronext. Given the increasingly competitive market for cash equities in Europe, any exchange that diversifies its revenue sources is bound to look more appealing to shareholders.

Prior to the merger with LSE the Borsa had the lowest tariffs for trading, clearing, and settlement of any European exchange, based on a study completed in 2006 by the European Commission. Nevertheless, profit margins on earnings before interest and tax were 38 percent. This is impressive, given the low level of tariffs.

By the end of June 2007 it appeared highly likely that the LSE–Borsa Italiana merger would move to the point where shareholder approval would be obtained. Clara Furse, LSE chief executive, informed a press briefing that its largest shareholder (NASDAQ) did not have the right to veto or block the transaction. Mamoun Tazi, an analyst at Man Securities, stated: "the deal is value enhancing for shareholders . . . reduces the probability of a takeover by NASDAQ."[34] The value of the combined company would be so huge it would stretch beyond NASDAQ's borrowing limits if the US based exchange should attempt a debt financed bid. Furse further stated that LSE was confident enough to not insist on a break fee.

Going Forward

The merger of Borsa Italiana and the London Stock Exchange creates the leading diversified exchange group in Europe, and a platform on which to build a European based exchange capable of global scale. After merger, the combined entity accounted for 48 percent of the FTSE Eurofirst 100 by market capitalization, and the most liquid order book by value as well as volume traded. Also, the combined entity became Europe's first ranked fixed income market through its ownership in the MTS platform.

Outcome From Merger

The merger of LSE and Borsa Italiana brings together two highly efficient and complementary businesses. It creates a leading force in a broad range of businesses and establishes strong foundations for future strategic positioning in several areas. These include:

1 Unique global position. The group occupies a unique position in Europe as the leading market liquidity pool and premier international listing venue.
2 Largest European equities pool. The combined entity offers extensive coverage of the European markets as measured by market capitalization. Also it holds a strong lead in average daily value of equities traded.
3 Primary European and global listing venue. The merger consolidates LSE's lead position as the primary center for international companies, by number of listed companies, and increases the visibility and access to European and global capital for issuers.
4 Lead European fixed income trading platform. With Borsa Italiana's exercise of its call option to acquire full control of MBE Holdings, the combined group controls the MTS fixed income trading system, with unparalleled liquidity, transparency, and efficiency.
5 Leader in trading technology. LSE has built one of the world's most advanced exchange trading infrastructures, establishing high standards for speed and execution certainty following its successful launch of TradElect in April 2007 in Johannesburg, and two months later in London.
6 Most efficient provider of post-trade services. Borsa Italiana is acknowledged as the lowest cost provider of central counterparty (CCP) clearing and central securities depository (CSD) services in Europe. Therefore, the combined group is uniquely positioned to take advantage of market opportunities

presented by the future implementation of the Code of Conduct, to facilitate customer choice in securities clearing and settlement.

The group holding company remains incorporated in the UK, and in addition to its listing in London is listed on Borsa Italiana. It will continue to operate from offices in London, Hong Kong, Milan, and Rome. Also, it will maintain the Borsa Italiana and London Stock Exchange brands.

New Managerial Impetus

In May 2009 Xavier Rolet became the new chief executive of the London Stock Exchange Group plc. Two months later Rolet presided over the Group annual general meeting (AGM), where he put forward a broad outline of the new management goals and trajectory. When Rolet took over the executive position formerly occupied by Clara Furse, he noted in an interview with the press that "the exchange is considering whether to provide services that would allow investors to trade British and European corporate bonds."[35] The LSE has an existing bond trading business, focused largely on Italian and other sovereign bonds.

The UK corporate bond market is a difficult trading place for many investors, as is the corporate bond market in many parts of the European Continent. According to Rolet, LSE is considering rolling out trading services to markets based on apparent demand.

The 2009 AGM at which Rolet made these comments was one in which the LSE reported a sharp decline in revenue from a year earlier. This could be attributed to the economic downturn, new stock trading platforms that compete against LSE, and a fall-off and diminished trading in new stock listings. At midyear 2009 Rolet was under pressure from shareholders and analysts to come up with a strong blueprint for expansion. According to Thomson-Reuters, the data provider, LSE accounted for 67 percent of share trading in the top 100 UK stocks, whereas its new rival Chi-X Europe accounted for 20 percent.

Rolet has cut operating costs at LSE, with reduced staffing. Further, he has expressed interest in buying a stake in a Dutch clearing house—the European Multilateral Clearing Facility. At midyear 2008 the London Stock Exchange unveiled plans for a new type of share trading facility—a dark pool given the name Baikal. For the past decade dark pools have been expanding market share in North American stock markets. Now they are repeating their act across Europe, in some cases with disastrous results for traditional stock exchanges. However, exchanges are getting in on the act. For example, Deutsche Börse launched its own dark pool, Xetra Midpoint, in November 2008.

The entry of numerous dark pools gives recognition to a huge change in the way equities are traded. The growth in algorithmic trading, slicing orders into smaller packages, influences share trading in a fundamental way. More trades are required, with faster execution to keep ahead of information-seeking traders. High speed and high frequency electronic systems are needed to service this trading, calling for investment in technology and systems.

Operators of dark pools believe these venues provide a useful service, at a time when rapid changes are taking place in how equities are traded. However, these pools have attracted the scrutiny of regulators, focused on maintaining transparency.

LSE's response in the form of Baikal recognizes that exchanges cannot afford to miss out in attracting order flow. Large investors, such as pension funds and insurances, post big orders. These "buy-side" orders require special handling. In an interview with John Wilson, Baikal's chief executive, the following description of Baikal's operation was outlined. Baikal offers trading in most blue chips across Europe, with clearing handled by Borsa Italiana. Originally, Baikal was designed to access buy-side orders directly, but John Wilson intends to pick a relatively small number of co-investors from sell-side banks, which will be liquidity-contributing to the dark pool. Buy-side traders will access through them, preserving the banks' traditional role as brokers to the buy-side.

In April 2009 Baikal selected Fidessa, a trading technology and market data company, and BNP Paribas as technology partners. With over a dozen existing dark pools in Europe (at June 2009), LSE faces a significant challenge to ensure success in launching Baikal. According to John Wilson, of the $57 billion in daily equity trading across Europe, some $12 billion goes to dark pools. Baikal will offer a differentiating service, an order routing platform that can send orders or parts of orders to other dark pools for matching. This is common practice among exchanges and alternative trading systems.[36]

To further add to its technology weapons, the LSE bought MillenniumIT for $30 million. MillenniumIT is a Sri Lankan vendor of trading systems. The deal is significant, giving evidence that the London exchange is engaged in a hot technological arms race. Until July 2009 LSE held to an earlier strategy of sharing better in a "bigger pie." This implied that faster technology would spur more quality trading, and allow LSE and others to share in an expanding market of high frequency and algorithmic trading. However, in late 2009 intensified competition suggests exchanges like LSE and NYSE will be required to become leaders in trading technology.

In August 2009 NYSE's market share in its own listed stocks was 34 percent, and in September 2009 LSE hosted close to 60 percent trading in FTSE 100 equities (Table 7.10).[37]

Table 7.10 Daily Market Share of FTSE 100 Index (September 2009) (Percentage of Turnover)

LSE	59.3%
Chi-X	20.7
BATS Europe	8.6
Turquoise	6.0
Euronext	2.9
Others	2.5
	100.0%

Source: *Financial Times*, September 17, 2009, p. 14.

Xavier Rolet has moved away from a complex system of variable rebates for order flow, applying bigger discounts for larger orders. The TradElect platform launched in June 2007 is being replaced with MillenniumIT. The technology cycle may be getting shorter for financial exchanges like LSE. The expectation and hope of exchanges is that a negative correlation operates between that cycle and financial exchange valuation.

8 Derivatives Dominate

This chapter provides a clear explanation of the financial revolution that is taking place, threatening traditional stock exchanges, causing these exchanges to carry out dramatic restructuring. This financial revolution has several components, namely: 1) ascendance of derivatives as financial trading instruments of choice by investors, arbitrageurs, and asset managers; 2) increasing importance of cross-border financial flows and investment; and 3) rising financial power of emerging market centers and their respective instrumentalities in world finance, both as users and as providers of capital.

Why Derivatives are Dominant

Derivative Types and Markets

Derivatives are claims on related, underlying financial assets. They take several forms, the most common including options, futures, and swaps. Options give the holder the right to exercise the optional claim, to buy (call option) or sell (put option) the underlying financial asset. For example, a put option in Microsoft stock gives the holder the right to sell (or put) Microsoft stock to the option writer at a designated strike (exercise) price within a specific time period. Alternately, a call option gives the holder the right to buy (or call) Microsoft stock from the writer at a designated strike price within a set time period. Since the 1970s trading in single stock options has grown rapidly, and continues to outpace the growth of trading cash equities. Stock options and other types of option contracts are actively traded on financial exchanges.

Futures contracts originally were used to facilitate trading in staple commodities, such as corn and wheat, but in the 1970s several financial exchanges created futures contracts for foreign currencies, short and long interest rates, stock indices, and other types of financial claims. These became very popular, and trading in these futures contracts continues to grow.

Swaps appeared shortly after interest rate futures were launched. Generally swaps are traded over the counter, with large banks functioning as counterparties. The first major swaps were interest rate oriented. They allowed bond market borrowers and investors to swap fixed interest rate (coupons) for floating rate cash flows. The market for interest rate swaps has become the largest derivative market sector, by notional value of obligation. More recently, credit default swaps have become an important component, in this case allowing investors and others to swap away from or into credit default exposures. By buying or selling credit default swaps, bond market investors, intermediaries, arbitrageurs, and others can increase or diminish their exposure to credit risks in the corporate and sovereign debt market.

Advantages of Derivatives

The advantages of trading derivatives over the underlying securities are widely documented. Here we provide a very brief overview of these advantages. Then we analyze these advantages in greater detail.

First, derivative markets provide important price discovery, often in futures markets that open for trading shortly before the related stock exchanges. Second, derivative trading can be low cost. For example, financial futures markets are highly efficient with respect to transaction costs, the main component of expense taking the form of interest on deposited fractional margins. Third, substantial leverage is built in, and the degree of gearing is substantial. Fourth, exchange traded derivatives require initial and maintenance margin, removing counterparty credit risk. Finally, exchange traded futures and options provide participants with anonymity. In many cases this is a highly important advantage to institutional investors with large positions to unwind or hedge.

Equally important, derivatives reinforce the flexibility of investors and market traders. Futures and options multiply the number and variety of hedges that are available vis-à-vis a given security holding position. Similarly, they expand the channels through which arbitrage pairs trading can move.

Also, derivatives expand the ability of investors to deal with shifts in volatility. In this regard, holders of positions in securities can convert the exposure into a hedged or neutral position quickly and at low cost, reversing this when the volatility change has abated. Finally, derivatives allow investors to create synthetic securities.

Derivatives trading has been growing at a much faster rate than trading in the underlying securities. This is due to the creation of new derivative instruments, and to the advantages that we have outlined relative to cost, leverage, flexibility, and other factors. Below we analyze these advantages in greater detail.

Low Trading Cost and Leverage

Low trading cost is characteristic across most components of the derivative markets. This, combined with a substantial leverage position, explains the popularity and high growth of all derivative market sectors. For example, in futures trading the notional value of securities (fixed income or equities) underlying the contract is a considerable multiple of the margin required by the futures exchange. This allows traders to position with expenses equal to the cost of capital deposited as margin, rather than the opportunity cost of the full amount of capital when investing in the cash market.

In options trading the premium paid is subject to control by the trader, who can use out-of-the-money options, where the cost is reduced to the time value of the option. In swaps trading the market is enormously large, competitive, and relatively cost efficient. Participants buy and sell protection against interest rate and credit default risk for notional amounts, paying a "premium" for this coverage. Again this imputes a high leverage and consequently low cost to the market. That can be said despite the fact that until yearend 2008 the market was non-transparent and subject to counterparty clearing and settlement risk.

Efficient Hedging

Derivative markets accommodate high volumes of trading, with anonymity and speed of execution. Market participants can hedge large outstanding positions without transacting in the underlying cash markets. Banks and other financial institutions can divest their positions vis-à-vis regular clients in a manner that is not apparent to their clients or counterparties, facilitating continued relationship activities.

Securities issuers can hedge against changes in cost of funds in the period leading up to the date at which these securities are actually issued in the primary market.

Market Signals

Derivatives markets may provide early warning signals in how the underlying market may perform in the near term future. Studies have examined the joint time series relationship between derivatives and underlying spot assets. In some cases the causal relationship between the two markets is somewhat controversial. Nevertheless, a number of studies demonstrate that derivative markets can provide advance signals concerning the direction or return behavior of selected spot markets.

Several studies document the structure of futures markets and their relation with stock markets. Chan shows that the futures lead the cash index, and that this lead–lag holds between futures and all index component stocks, suggesting that the futures market may be the major source of market-wide information.[1] Rationales for any linkage between derivative and cash markets include: 1) trading mechanisms, and 2) behavior of informed traders. Informed traders tend to trade in the markets with lowest costs, therefore influencing prices and returns first in derivative markets.

In a study that examines the interrelationships between options, futures, and stock markets in Taiwan's emerging derivatives markets, Fung and Tsai find that there are co-integrating relationships between options, stock, and futures markets, with option prices as the adjustment mechanism. Their findings are consistent with the information causality hypothesis, where information flows from option to stock and futures markets. Option prices Granger-cause stock market and futures market prices and volatility. In Taiwan, institutional traders account for over 60 percent of index options volume, while individuals account for over 70 percent of stock market volume and over 60 percent of futures market volume. Institutional traders may possess superior information and provide a material role in price discovery and information flow between the stock and derivatives markets.[2]

Flexibility

Derivatives markets provide flexibility to a wide range of participants. This flexibility relates to capital required, type of instrument available, and time-of-day trading. With respect to time-of-day trading, derivatives related to US Treasury notes and bonds can be traded almost 24 hours a day, from non-US as well as US marketplaces. Similarly, interest rate futures, options, and swaps can be traded in all major currencies virtually round the clock. This same flexibility applies to a wide range of stock index futures and options, covering all main market indices.

Capital required for derivatives trades relates to margin requirements. If a certain futures contract calls for an initial margin of 5 percent, the trader can take an initial position on that asset that is twenty times as large as the funds available for margin deposit.

Finally, derivatives come in different forms, including options, futures, swaps, and many other types. This gives the trader the ability to be discriminating concerning what form of hedge or other position to select.

Exchange Traded and OTC Derivatives

The Industry

Prior to the 1970s derivatives trading was confined largely to over the counter activities, and carried out by specialized brokers and dealers. In part, derivatives trading finds its roots in the centuries-old commodities trading business. Derivatives markets entered a high growth phase in the 1970s, when several Chicago based exchanges introduced interest rate, currency, and index futures contracts. Around this time period equity option contracts were introduced on financial exchanges. Following the mid-1970s, financial exchanges and broker-dealer firms expanded trading by introducing new products, creating novel hedging and speculative strategies, and expanding the geographic scope of the business.

At present derivatives and underlying cash products are traded in two distinct market venues: 1) regulated securities exchanges, and 2) OTC markets. Exchanges offer trading in instruments with standardized contracts, and also provide central counterparty clearing and settlement with little or no risk. OTC markets facilitate transactions involving bilateral contracts. Often these OTC contracts are privately negotiated. OTC markets generally do not provide a central clearinghouse, although some clearinghouses are seeking to develop such services for OTC trades. This issue is discussed in a later section of this chapter.

On a global basis derivatives have experienced rapid growth in volume, exceeding the growth in stock and bond trading. This growth is driven by several factors. These include development of new products and markets, greater profit focus by financial exchanges and investment banks, growing demand for risk management tools, development of more scalable and fully electronic markets and trading platforms, deregulation, and market convergence.

Types of Derivatives

A derivative is a contract between a buyer and a seller, the value of which is determined by the performance of underlying financial or physical assets (interest rates, equity securities, energy products, metals, and other commodities, and indices based on these assets). Most derivatives are financially settled, through cash payments based on the value of the underlying asset.

The most common types of exchange traded derivatives are futures and options on futures. Additional types traded on OTC markets include swaps, forwards, and options. Derivatives exchanges are regulated entities, with over 100 operating in at least forty countries. Basically, these markets are restricted to standardized contracts. By contrast, OTC trading does not take place on a regulated exchange, and participants enter into privately negotiated and non-standardized contracts. In recent years participants have begun to clear OTC contracts which resemble exchange traded contracts and which are in part standardized and cleared through a central clearinghouse.[3]

Market Participants

Derivative industry participants include at least five distinct entities. They are clients, futures and options brokers, introducing brokers, regulated exchanges, and clearinghouses.

Clients include financial institutions, manufacturers, and professional traders. Clients buy and sell derivative contracts for risk management, asset allocation, speculation and arbitrage, and other purposes. Futures and options brokers execute trades, and some act as clearing members of clearinghouses. As a clearing member of an exchange, a broker is subject to regulatory agreements regarding client margin position and minimum capital.

Introducing brokers have relationships with market participants and provide the typical function of a broker. The exception is that they do not accept the money, securities, or property of a client. Introducing brokers direct the orders made by their clients to brokers for execution and clearing.

Regulated derivatives exchanges number over 100, located in over forty different countries. In Table 8.1 we identify a number of the largest exchanges operating around the world.

Finally, clearinghouses are centralized service providers. They may be associated with a single exchange or may support a number of exchanges. Historically, OTC trades have not made use of clearinghouse facilities, but in recent years certain clearinghouses have initiated settling OTC trades. For example, the New York Mercantile Exchange ClearPort Clearing provides for clearing of trades in OTC derivatives executed off exchange.[4]

Table 8.1 Leading Derivative Exchanges and Markets

A Exchange traded and over the counter markets
- 1 Exchange traded—approximately 20 percent of business
  - Trading in currency, interest rate, and stock index futures
  - Trading in equity and other options
  - Trading in energy, metals, and other commodities futures and options
- 2 Over the counter—approximately 80 percent of business
  - Trading in interest rate swaps
  - Trading in credit default swaps

B Main derivative exchanges
- 1 Three largest exchanges
  - a) Chicago Mercantile Exchange (CME)[1]
  - b) London International Financial Futures and Options Exchange (LIFFE)[2]
  - c) Eurex (owned by Deutsche Börse and Swiss Exchange)
- 2 Three large specialized exchanges
  - a) London Metal Exchange (LME)
  - b) New York Mercantile Exchange (NYMEX)[3]
  - c) Intercontinental Exchange (ICE)
- 3 Five equity options exchanges in the US
  - a) Chicago Board Options Exchange (CBOE)
  - b) American Stock Exchange (AMEX)
  - c) Philadelphia Stock Exchange (PhilEx)
  - d) Pacific Stock Exchange (PCX)
  - e) International Securities Exchange (ISE)[4]

C Derivative exchanges located outside North America and Europe
- 1 Sydney Futures Exchange
- 2 Singapore Exchange Ltd
- 3 Tokyo and Osaka Futures Exchanges
- 4 Hong Kong Exchanges Ltd
- 5 Bolsa Mercadorias e Futuros, BM&F (San Paulo)[5]

Source: Compiled by author.

Notes
1 CME acquired Chicago Board of Trade (CBOT) in 2007.
2 LIFFE became part of Euronext in 2002.
3 NYMEX was acquired by CME in 2008.
4 ISE was acquired by Deutsche Börse in 2008.
5 Merged with Sao Paulo Stock Exchange in 2009.

Growth

Over the period 2001–07 both exchange traded and OTC derivatives demonstrated spectacular growth. In this period exchange traded contracts expanded to over three times their 2001 level, while OTC trades increased to over four times the initial year level. Overall, exchange traded contracts enjoyed a cumulative average growth rate (CAGR) of 22 percent, whereas OTC notional value enjoyed a CAGR of 32 percent (Table 8.2). The fastest growth in exchange traded contracts was for commodity (27 percent), currencies (26 percent), and equity index (25

Table 8.2 Growth of Exchange Traded and OTC Derivatives, 2001–07

A Exchange traded derivatives	
1 By market (billions of contracts)	
Interest rate	19%
Currency	26
Equity index	25
Commodity	27
Single equity	*20*
Total	22%
2 By region—CAGR(1)	
North America	26%
Europe	16
Asia Pacific	23
Other	*22*
22%	
3 Year end total (billion contracts)	
2001	4.5
2002	6.7
2003	8.1
2004	8.6
2005	10.1
2006	12.0
2007	15.5
B Global OTC derivatives, outstanding contracts, notional amounts ($ billions)	
1 By market	CAGR[1]
Foreign currency	21%
Fixed income	
interest rate swaps	31%
Equity linked	33%
Commodity	59%
Credit default swaps	NM[2]
Other	*30%*
Total	32%
2 Year end total ($ trillions)	
2001	111.2
2002	141.7
2003	197.2
2004	259.9
2005	297.7
2006	415.2
2007	516.4

Source: MF Global, *Annual Report 2008*, pp. 12–13.

Notes
1 CAGR denotes compound annual growth rate.
2 NM indicates that a percentage for this category would not be meaningful. At this point in time, growth of this category was very high.

percent) contracts. By region, the highest growth in exchange traded contracts was North America (26 percent) and Asia Pacific (23 percent).

The two highest growth categories in OTC derivatives were commodity (59 percent) and equity linked (33 percent), but the largest growth components of

OTC derivatives notional amounts were fixed income (interest rate swaps) and credit default swaps. According to the Bank for International Settlements data, at yearend 2007 interest rate contracts (swaps) had a notional value of $393 trillion, while credit default swaps had a notional value of over $62 trillion.[5]

Main Exchange Groups

At yearend 2008 we can point to sixteen derivatives exchanges that play a dominant role in the exchange traded derivatives sector (Table 8.1). They include the three largest derivatives exchanges (CME, LIFFE, and Eurex), additional exchanges that play a more specialized role in trading, and several exchanges outside the North American and European regions that are dominant markets in their respective countries.

The Chicago Mercantile Exchange offers trading in a wide range of foreign currency, interest rate, and commodity products. Mergers with the CBOT and NYMEX (2007–08) have broadened CME's product range, to include energy futures, metals, and other equity index products. As a result, CME has become by far the world's largest financial exchange by volume of business and market value of its outstanding shares.

Since 2002 LIFFE has been a component of the Euronext Group, which in turn merged with NYSE to form the transatlantic exchange NYSE Euronext. LIFFE operates the largest derivative trading business in Europe, and its lead position has improved by the merger between Euronext and NYSE. Its London base of operations gives LIFFE a competitive edge in retaining this lead position.

Eurex had early success when Deutsche Börse launched the derivatives exchanges. Also, Eurex benefits from its co-ownership, which includes the Swiss stock exchange (20 percent owner). In more recent years Eurex has faced growth barriers. Its main parent, Deutsche Börse, has not been able to bring about closer alliances or partnerships with other exchanges that would promote greater flow of business to Eurex. Nevertheless, Eurex makes an important contribution to Deutsche Börse's revenue flow, as indicated in our discussion in Chapter 3.

Three Specialized Exchanges

Three financial exchanges play an important role in worldwide trading of energy products and industrial metals. NYMEX and Intercontinental Exchange tend to dominate world trading in derivatives related to energy. As we observe below, their rivalry has intensified with respect to introducing new products and in connection with their efforts to participate in mergers with other exchanges. The third of these specialized exchanges, London Metal Exchange, plays a unique role in global trading in industrial metals.

London Metal Exchange

The London Metal Exchange (LME) operates daily trading markets for over ten commodities (metals and plastics). The LME operates traditional floor trading sessions (morning and afternoon) for each of the products. Prices established become benchmarks for trading on a global basis.

LME also operates its own electronic trading platform, LMEselect. This provides an alternative to floor trading. Traders are obliged to deliver or take the physical commodity, based on the contract. Physical delivery is effected using warrants at LME registered warehouses around the globe (the UK, Europe, Singapore, the USA, and Japan). Following this, all contracts are cleared through LCH.Clearnet.[6]

LME continues to operate as the dominant venue for trading non-ferrous metals (Table 8.3). In 2007 over 90 percent of trading, measured by tons traded, took place on LME markets.

Commodity exchanges such as LME render important economic benefits to market participants, traders, and consumers of the staple products covered by the contracts traded. Market transactions, prices, and sources of demand and supply become more visible and transparent. Development of larger and more liquid markets adds to their stability. Futures markets provide necessary and low cost hedging opportunities for buyers and sellers for commodities that often exhibit wide price swings. Finally, small players are less at the mercy of large sources of supply. Further, post-trade clearing and settlement become risk free, since buyers and sellers trade standard contracts, with the exchange providing a central counterparty.

Given the upswing in commodity prices and increased pace of trading in the period 2004–07, the LME made it possible for new membership. In 2007 LME members approved issuance of one million new B-shares, which give holders the right to trade and clear on the exchange. The B-share issue was intended to make it easier for new members to join the exchange. The B-shares were issued in June 2007. B-shares have traded in the past through the JPMorgan Cazenove "matched bargain facility." B-share prices increased sharply when they began to trade.[7]

Record prices for metals (lead, copper, aluminum) in 2006–08 attracted trading houses, investment banks, and metals users to what was formerly considered a niche market. New members must buy between 2,500 and 25,000 B-shares, depending on their level of membership in LME.

Early in 2008 the LME indicated it was launching a steel futures contract that would facilitate hedging against price volatility. This brought opposition from some in the steel industry, including the world's largest steelmaker, ArcelorMittal. Arcelor produces three to four times the steel tonnage of second ranked Nippon

Table 8.3 Percentage Share of Non-Ferrous Metals Traded on LME and Rival Exchange Markets (Tons Traded)

LME	90.9
Shanghai	5.5
COMEX	2.1
MCX, Tokyo, NCD, CJCX	1.5
	100.0%

Source: LME, *Ringsider*, Second half 2008, p. 13.

Note: Data for 2007.

Steel, and as much tonnage as the four producers ranked second through fifth in production (Table 8.4).[8]

The steel contract is in response to fundamental changes in the structure and competitive position of the world market for steel products. First, a high growth in demand has operated as large emerging nations seek to modernize. Second, mergers among the largest steel companies have brought a more concentrated group of steel companies (Table 8.4). Finally, several countries now play a key role on the buying (China) and selling (Russia) side, increasing the importance of market structure and transparency.

In 2008 aluminum was the most heavily traded commodity on the LME, but acceptance of aluminum futures trading took at least a decade following the launch of the futures contract in the late 1970s. The new steel futures contract rejects the shadowy world of steel price negotiations, and likely will shift pricing power from large producers to traders and financial investors. According to leading bankers, the steel contract is rapidly gaining support among physical traders, medium size producers, and asset managers eager to obtain exposure to a booming sector. The LME steel futures contract will be traded as long as fifteen months ahead, and based on billet, a semi-finished steel product. Two contracts, one for the Mediterranean region and one for the Far East, were formally launched in April 2008.[9]

Steel is the second largest commodity by value traded in the world, after oil. Emerging market nations, whose trade is expanding rapidly, lead as buyers and sellers of steel in international trade. Despite its opposition to the launch of steel futures trading, ArcelorMittal has upgraded its membership in LME, especially as a protection against volatile zinc, nickel, and tin prices.

More on LME Members

LME trading is highly structured. This assures market participants of an orderly market, providing protection to traders via specified roles and obligations of those

Table 8.4 Twelve Largest Steel Producers (2006)

Company	*Headquarters country*	*Production**
ArcelorMittal	Luxembourg	117.2
Nippon Steel	Japan	32.7
JFE	Japan	32.0
Posco	South Korea	30.1
Tata/Corus	India/UK, The Netherlands	24.7
Baosteel	China	22.5
US Steel	USA	21.2
Nucor	USA	20.3
Tangshan	China	19.1
Riva	Italy	18.2
Severstal	Russia	17.5
Thyssen/Krupp	Germany	16.8

Source: *Financial Times.*

Note: * Million tons.

admitted to the process. Five types of members and trading participants operate on the trading platform or Ring floor (Table 8.5). These include: Ring dealing members, associate broker clearing members, associate trade clearing members, associate broker members, and associate trade members.

We describe the manner in which the five categories of participants function in Table 8.5. The first category, Ring dealing members, enjoy full trading privileges, including the exclusive right to trade in the Ring, to issue client contracts, and to operate as members of the London Clearing House. Only the ten Ring dealing members enjoy all these rights. In this capacity they may act as principal or agent for clients. Included among these ten members are MF Global, Newbridge Group, and Societe Generale.

The second category, associate broker clearing members, enjoy most of the privileges of Ring dealing members, except they cannot trade in the Ring. The twenty-nine associate brokers function through the 24-hour Inter-Office Market, and are members of the London Clearing House. A number of well-known

Table 8.5 Market Participants on London Metal Exchange, Category, Number of Participants, and Role Played

Participant category	*Number of members in category*	*Description of member activities*
Category 1: Ring dealing member	10	Can trade in the Ring during Ring trading sessions. Also may operate 24-hour market by trading Inter-Office. Ring dealing members are members of the London Clearing House, and authorized under the Financial Services Authority Act. Can issue client contracts, and enjoy exclusive right to trade in the Ring.
Category 2: Associate broker clearing member	29	Enjoy advantages of Ring clearing members, except may not trade in the Ring. Operate through Inter-Office market. Members of London Clearing House.
Category 3: Associate trade clearing member	2	May not trade client products or trade in the Ring. Are entitled to clear their own business.
Category 4: Associate broker members	6	May issue LME contracts, but not members of the clearing house. Not permitted to trade in the Ring. Operate through the 24-hour Inter-Office market. Are members of the FSA.
Category 5: Associate trade members	42	Have no trading rights, except as clients.

Source: London Metal Exchange.

companies and institutions are among the associate brokers, including Bank of America Securities, Citigroup Global Markets, Goldman Sachs, Dresdner Bank, Deutsche Bank, Credit Suisse, Koch Metals, and Toyota Tsusho Metals.

The third category, associate trade clearing members, includes only two firms. These firms cannot service clients, nor can they trade in the Ring. Their main activity is to clear trades for their own business.

The fourth category, associate broker members, has only six firms. These companies can issue LME contracts, but are not members of the clearinghouse. They do not trade in the Ring. These broker members include Bank of London and the Middle East, Fortis Bank, RBS Sempra Metals, and Standard Chartered Bank.

The fifth category, associate trade members, has the largest number of firms—forty-two in total. These members enjoy no trading rights, except as clients. This category includes a wide range of company types, covering all metals sectors which trade on LME. Typical firms include Alcan Trading, Ashton Commodities, BHP Billiton Marketing, Britannia Refined Metals, Chile Copper, Freeport McMoran, Glencore (UK), Inco Ltd, and Rio Tinto (London) Ltd.

Fewer than ninety member firms constitute the core trading community and membership on London Metal Exchange. Through their trading, market making, clearing, brokerage, and other activities, these firms provide transparent, liquid, and efficient markets for the commodities traded on the several market venues serviced by LME.

Ring and LMEselect Trading

Here we describe and contrast Ring and electronic trading on LME. This is the only exchange in London on which face-to-face open-outcry trading takes place. On the LME Ring, trading is governed by precise five-minute trading sessions, in a circle only 6 meters in diameter. Nevertheless, this relatively small Ring holds an unrivalled position as the world's premier non-ferrous metals market, discovering prices referenced by approximately 98 percent of the global physical trading in these commodities.[10]

Table 8.6 outlines the schedule for each five-minute trading segment in Ring trading. The first session operates from 11:40 to 14:55 London time. The second session operates from 14:55 to 17:00. Table 8.6 also outlines trading times for the Inter-Office (telephone) Market, and the LMEselect screen trading.

The three distinct transaction venues described in Table 8.6 reflect the high level of flexibility available through LME trading. This flexibility includes timing of positions taken (long term and short), financing, and transparency. The Ring accounts for about one-third of the exchange's trading volume. A typical day for Ring members starts at 07:00, checking overnight trading in the Far East. Preparation for Ring trading can be detailed and intricate, given the short (five-minute) sessions assigned to each commodity.

Ring dealing members are required to sit down on the circular red benches in the Ring for the entire length of the trading sessions. At these sessions members declare their buying or selling prices, and the dates in which they are interested.

Table 8.6 LME Market Venues and Trading Times

	Trading venue	*Description*	*Trading times*	
I	Inter-Office Market	Telephone market,	24 hours a day connects brokers and clients	
II	LMEselect screen	Screen trading on electronic platform	From 01:00 to 19:00, London time	
III	Ring trading	Open-outcry trading	From 11:40 to 17:00 London time Ring trading times as follows:	
			First session	
			Steel FF and FM	11:40 to 11:45
			Aluminum alloy and NASAAC	11:45 to 11:50
			Tin	11:50 to 11:55
			Primary aluminum	11:55 to 12:00
			Copper	12:00 to 12:05
			Lead	12:05 to 12:10
			Zinc	12:10 to 12:15
			Nickel	12:15 to 12:20
			LL, LA, LE, LN	12:20 to 12:22
			Interval	12:22 to 12:23
			PP, PA, PE, PN	12:23 to 12:25
			Interval	12:25 to 12:30
			Copper	12:30 to 12:35
			Aluminum alloy and NASAAC	12:35 to 12:40
			Tin	12:40 to 12:45
			Lead	12:45 to 12:50
			Zinc	12:50 to 12:55
			Primary aluminum	12:55 to 13:00
			Nickel	13:00 to 13:05
			Steel FF and FM	13:05 to 13:10
			Interval	13:10 to 13:20
			Kerb trading	13:20 to 14:45
			Interval	14:45 to 14:55
Second session				
			Aluminum alloy and NASAAC	14:55 to 15:00
			Lead	15:00 to 15:05
			Zinc	15:05 to 15:10
			Copper	15:10 to 15:15
			Primary aluminum	15:15 to 15:20
			Tin	15:20 to 15:25
			Nickel	15:25 to 15:30
			Steel FF and FM	15:30 to 15:35
			LL, LA, LE, LN	15:35 to 15:37
			Interval	15:37 to 15:38
			PP, PA, PE, PN	15:38 to 15:40
			Lead	15:40 to 15:45
			Zinc	15:45 to 15:50
			Copper	15:50 to 15:55
			Primary aluminum	15:55 to 16:00

Tin	16:00 to 16:05
Nickel	16:05 to 16:10
Aluminum alloy and NASAAC	16:10 to 16:15
Kerb trading	16:15 to 17:00*

Source: London Metal Exchange, *Ringsider*, 2008, p. 173.

Note: * At 16:35 tin, PP, and LL cease trading; at 16:40 lead and steel cease trading; at 16:45 nickel ceases trading; at 16:50 zinc ceases trading; at 16:55 copper ceases trading; at 17: 00 primary aluminum, aluminum alloy, and NASAAC cease trading.

Hand signals are used to indicate prices, bids, and offers. Actual verbal outcry makes for a noisy market. Ring traders have a back-up team, often employing the phones to take orders.

The LME has developed a sophisticated electronic trading system. LMEselect is an efficient way of conducting outright business. Introduced in 2003, the system is highly versatile, making it possible to replicate all the dates and spreads that are traded in the open-outcry market.[11] LME makes its Select trading easily available to users outside its European hub. In 2005 Select trading hours were extended, to capture growing Asian trading.

Electronic trading increasingly services investment funds, and many of LME's Ring dealing members and associate broker clearers now connect their clients directly to Select.

LMEselect and Ring trading coexist harmoniously for several important reasons. First, Select trading of standard three-month contracts is supplemented by myriad Ring (face-to-face) deals, including multi-month spreads tradable out to ten years. These are difficult to handle on LMEselect. Ring trading accounts for 80 percent of this specialized activity. Second, global reference prices are recorded on the floor shortly after 12:30 London time. There is little expectation that this vital price discovery will migrate from the floor. The floor is critical because it establishes the reference price.

The LME is continuously improving its electronic trading on the Select platform, but electronic trading is far from sounding the end of open-outcry trading on LME. Floor and electronic trading remain necessary complements of each other.

Two Energy Exchanges

The New York Mercantile Exchange and the Intercontinental Exchange (ICE) have developed into intense rivals. Both aim at becoming dominant in a wide range of energy trading products. ICE may be considered an upstart when compared with NYMEX. ICE was incorporated as recently as 2001, and is the result of a fertile and entrepreneurial mindset by its chief executive, Jeffrey Sprecher.

By comparison, NYMEX is a venerable institution, founded in the late nineteenth century. Prior to its agreed merger with CME early in 2008 (Table 8.7), the New York Mercantile Exchange was the world's largest physical commodity futures exchange, specializing in energy and precious metals. Commodities

Table 8.7 Exchange Consolidation—Derivatives and Stock Exchanges (2006–08)

Date	*Target*	*Acquirer*	*Deal value ($ billion)*
October 2006	CBOT (US)	Chicago Mercantile Exchange (US)	11.6
May 2006	Euronext (Netherlands)	NYSE (US)	10.2
February 2008	OMX (Sweden)	NASDAQ (US)	4.7
August 2007	International Securities Exchange (ISE) (US)	Deutsche Börse–Eurex (Germany)	2.7
June 2007	Borsa Italiana (Italy)	London Stock Exchange (UK)	2.6
September 2007	London Stock Exchange (UK)	Borsa Dubai (UAE)	1.6
September 2007	London Stock Exchange (UK)	Qatar Investment Authority (Qatar)	1.3
September 2008	New York Board of Trade (NYBOT) (US)	Intercontinental Exchange (US)	1.1
	NYMEX (US)	Chicago Mercantile Exchange (US)	9.4
June 2008	American Stock Exchange (US)	NYSE (US)	1
November 2007	Philadelphia Stock Exchange (PhilEx) (US)	NASDAQ (US)	2

Source: *Financial Times*; financial exchange reports.

Notes

1 AMEX members received $260 million plus proceeds from sale of the AMEX headquarters building.

2 This transaction reportedly was valued at $650 million. Since PhilEx was closely held, there was no requirement for publishing or disclosing the price paid.

traded include aluminum, coal, copper, crude oil, electricity, gasoline, gold, heating oil, natural gas, platinum, propane, silver, and uranium. Trading is conducted through two divisions: the NYMEX division (home to energy and platinum) and the COMEX division (in which all other metals trade).[12]

ICE and NYMEX have become more direct rivals as a result of several competitive initiatives at each exchange, aimed at increasing market share at the expense of the other. For example, in February 2006 ICE introduced a successful cash settled copy of NYMEX's US light sweet crude contract. ICE forced NYMEX to open its screen energy trading to all and to offer it around the clock. Similarly, NYMEX introduced copies of New York Board of Trade contracts for sugar, cocoa, coffee, cotton, and frozen orange juice on CME's electronic Globex platform. This was an attempt to beat ICE to screen trading.[13]

Intercontinental Exchange Inc. is an Atlanta based online commodity and financial products marketplace. ICE shares are listed on the NYSE, and it operates a business with three major segments. These are ICE Markets, ICE Services, and ICE Data. Under ICE Markets the company runs three regulated securities exchanges located in the US, Europe, and Canada. These exchanges trade energy commodities, agriculture and soft commodities, stock market indices, and US dollar and foreign currency futures and options. ICE Services provides clearing services and electronic confirmation. ICE Data covers real time and historical commodity prices, indices, and end-of-day settlements.

ICE origins trace back to when Jeffrey Sprecher, ICE chief executive, acquired a controlling interest in Continental Power. This firm operated a market network in which sixty-two member utility companies could buy and sell small amounts of surplus electricity. In 1999 Enron launched the first online power exchange soon after Sprecher lined up seven partner investors.[14] In May 2000 Intercontinental Exchange was organized with the partners pledging $20 million in development money. A consortium of electricity suppliers also joined as members of ICE. Trading began in the second half of 2000 in precious metals, energy, crude oil, and natural gas. ICE added a clearing facility early in 2001 when it acquired London based International Petroleum Exchange (IPE), which held an established clearing arrangement with London Clearing House (LCH).

The acquisition of IPE expanded ICE capabilities in several directions. These included the clearing arrangement, and trading North Sea Brent crude oil contracts. The addition of IPE futures brought together in one market operator for the first time ever an over the counter and futures market. In 2002 ICE announced plans to replace the IPE traditional floor trading with an all-electronic platform.

Steady revenue and profit growth in the period 2000–05 led to ICE launching a successful IPO in November 2005. First-day trading on the NYSE produced a 67 percent return. In 2006 revenues doubled, while net income tripled in amount. The following year ICE agreed to purchase the New York Board of Trade (NYBOT) in a cash and stock deal valued at $1.1 billion (Table 8.7). The addition of NYBOT was important for several reasons. First, it diversified revenues and profits beyond energy. NYBOT's business was mostly in soft commodities (cocoa, coffee, cotton, sugar). Second, ICE quickly brought electronic trading to NYBOT, gaining scale ability advantages from its technology base. Traders enjoyed the flexibility of a high speed and efficient electronic marketplace or, alternatively, floor trading.

In March 2007 ICE entered the competition to acquire Chicago based CBOT, offering in excess of $9.9 billion, substantially above CME's bid. A CBOT–CME merger would create a juggernaut that would control 85 percent of the market for US futures and other derivatives. Futures traders saw the ICE bid as a "bold move" by an increasingly key player and its Wall Street backers.[15] ICE has held close ties with Wall Street firms, and many investors believed that an intense bidding war for CBOT would take place. While CME raised its bid and completed the merger with CBOT (Table 8.7), the ICE bid forced up equity valuations, and CME paid much more. Meanwhile, ICE generated favorable publicity for itself.[16]

Three months following the ICE bid for the Chicago exchange, the Atlanta based group acquired ChemConnect, a commodity trading firm. ChemConnect operated the leading electronic marketplace for US natural gas liquids (NGLs), including propane, ethane, and chemical products (ethylene, propylene, and benzene). ChemConnect was a good complement to ICE, and its trading was shifted to the ICE electronic platforms. Shortly after the ChemConnect acquisition ICE paid close to $50 million for the Winnipeg Commodity Exchange. The exchange, which trades wheat, barley, and canola, was renamed ICE Futures Canada.

In its brief history ICE has developed a favorable track record for integrating exchanges. It has completed two merger deals over the decade and, according to its chief executive, the NYBOT merger gave the company the ability to pursue even bigger deals. At the time ICE was bidding for CBOT it ranked sixth globally in number of contracts traded (Table 8.8).

OTC Issues

The financial crisis of 2008–09 focused attention on several issues related to trading and post-trade clearing and settlement of derivatives. These issues are summarized as follows:

1 What is the status quo in derivatives trading, and does this satisfy the basic requirements of financial markets?
2 What factors are causing the high growth in commodities trading, and what type of market structure best suits trading in commodities?
3 How can swaps trading be made more transparent, and given more certainty and stability in clearing and settlement?
4 What regulatory changes are necessary to bring OTC derivatives markets to qualitative parity with exchange traded derivatives markets?

We address these questions below.

Status Quo in OTC Derivatives

Before we consider proposals to reform trading in OTC derivatives, let us take a grand tour of the sector. In this way we can better understand the several distinct perspectives of: a) dealer banks, b) clientele who utilize these instruments, and c) regulators concerned with proper market functioning. At midyear 2008 the total notional amount of global OTC derivatives outstanding was $693 trillion, a herculean sum.

Table 8.8 Leading Futures Exchanges: Number of Futures and Options Contracts Traded (2006) (Billions of Contracts)

Eurex	1.53
CME	1.40
CBOT	0.81
Euronext–LIFFE	0.73
NYMEX	0.28
ICE	
NYBOT in US	0.04
ICE Futures UK	0.09

Source: *Wall Street Journal.*

OTC derivatives fit well into the FICC categorization,[17] understood to dominate investment bank strategies that generate large proprietary trading profits for many large banks. Well over 80 percent of global derivatives business takes place over the counter, where there is little transparency and, until recently, little expectation of assured centralized clearing. In contrast with exchange trading of derivatives, where the exchange is a central counterparty (CCP) to market participants. OTC trading has relied on dealer banks to arrange post-trade services.

As can be observed in Table 8.9, OTC derivatives are dominated by interest rate swaps, foreign exchange contracts, and credit default swaps. Bank dealers generally earn narrow profits on this trading, which has become commoditized. Nevertheless, in first quarter 2009, a period in which volatility and dealer profits soared, FICC revenues accounted for half to one-fifth of revenues for large bank dealers (Table 8.9).

These OTC derivatives serve a vital purpose in the global economy, helping institutions and companies manage balance sheet risk and reduce the cost of capital. However, bilateral OTC derivatives are seen as a "dangerous web of obligations between financial institutions."[18] The demise of Lehman and the unsteadiness of AIG attest to the risky position faced by intermediaries and dealers of OTC derivatives.

Merchants of the status quo would like to protect their profitable trading business. The five biggest bank derivative dealers in the United States in second quarter 2009 held 97 percent of the aggregate value of OTC derivatives. This concentration of risk in US banks deemed "too big to fail" suggests that taxpayers could be asked again to bail out these institutions, unless markets are reformed and better

Table 8.9 Overview of Global OTC Derivatives Markets (Midyear 2008)

A	OTC derivatives outstanding (amounts in trillions of US dollars)	
	1 Interest rate swaps	$458
	2 Foreign exchange	63
	3 Credit default swaps	57
	4 Commodity forwards	13
	5 Equity linked	10
	6 Other	82
	7 FICC aggregate*	$683
B	Contribution of fixed income, currencies, and commodities (FICC) as percentage of group revenues (first quarter 2009)	
	Goldman Sachs	70%
	Deutsche Bank	50
	BNP Paribas	36
	Societe Generale	34
	Barclay	28
	JPMorgan Chase	20
	Morgan Stanley	15
	UBS	10

Source: Lex Column, "OTC Change," *Financial Times*, June 5, 2009, p. 12.
Note: * Denotes fixed income, currency, and commodity OTC derivatives.

structured. Proposals to reform markets include: 1) standardize swap contracts (already initiated), 2) clear these derivatives through regulated clearinghouses (also in part taking place), and 3) establish margin requirements for standardized derivatives.

Transparency and Clearing Problems

During the crisis period 2008–09, credit default swaps took a center stage role in discussions over: 1) the nature of the problem, and 2) what remedies could be implemented. Credit default swaps (CDSs) are analogous to an insurance contract. CDSs insure the holder of the contract against a corporate or sovereign default. In return the writer of the CDS contract receives a "premium" payment. The credit event insured against is a default by the debtor who issued the instrument.

In a typical transaction the seller of protection takes on credit risk associated with a reference entity in return for a quarterly premium paid by the buyer. The premium or spread is quoted as the total payment divided by the face amount of the reference entity debt protected. CDS premiums are quoted as basis points. In a standard contract protecting $10 million, and a contract life of five years, the investor (protection buyer) holding the corporate debt might pay 120 basis points (1.20 percent), costing $120,000 a year to protect itself against default on the bonds.[19]

Credit default swaps cover only the losses from debt default, the amount determined in one of two ways. The holder of the CDS can surrender the defaulted bond and be paid its face value (physical settlement). Alternately, the bond holder can be paid the difference between face value and market value in a cash settlement. Physical settlement requires the underlying asset be presented, but often the market value of the debt following default can be difficult to determine. The underlying debt may no longer be traded.

Owning a CDS is a bet against the financial prospect of a corporation or sovereign, and selling a CDS is a bet for them. These contracts provide speculators with a way of gaining exposure vis-à-vis a corporate or sovereign credit. To reduce counterparty credit risk, many CDS contracts contain provisions for collateral posting, the collateral required changing as CDS prices fluctuate. The security gained from collateral posting is contingent upon the transparency of CDS pricing. Generally, the CDS market lacks the transparency and enforcement mechanisms common to futures clearinghouses and exchange traded securities markets. Trading is not transparent, leading to questionable pricing. OTC derivatives markets have lacked a centralized clearing. Without clear pricing the market value and collateral needs of a given CDS instrument are difficult and expensive to determine.

More important, the OTC markets lack a centralized clearing system, which hampers attempts to determine the size and location of credit risk exposure of a particular reference entity. As a result the holder of a CDS seeking to provide credit protection must write a new contract protecting a new counterparty. The original CDS buyer must hold two contracts that cancel each other out. As a result, part of the large CDS market is redundant. This double counting goes even further. In 2008–09 CDS exposure held by commercial banks in the United States was $14.6

trillion, above US gross domestic product. On a case-by-case basis, CDS contracts outstanding for a given reference entity often exceed the actual debt outstanding. This means that, if physical settlement is called for, investors may be unable to obtain the underlying securities, given the absolute scarcity relative to the volume of CDS contracts outstanding.

The location or distribution of CDS exposure also is of great concern. The near meltdown of the US financial system in September 2008 was in part caused by AIG's excessive exposure to OTC derivatives. This big insurance–reinsurance company had sold CDS contracts to commercial and investment banks around the globe. Growing collateral calls from counterparties threatened AIG's solvency, resulting in a substantial loan from the Federal Reserve. Failure by AIG to meet collateral calls would have led to a massive counterparty default, dangerously decapitalizing dozens of large financial institutions.

Market opaqueness made it impossible for participants to know where AIG counterparty default could occur. This uncertainty contributed to a massive effort to gain liquidity. Writing in July 2009, the Federal Reserve was compelled to admit that the financial system still did not have a clear picture of these exposures.[20]

Regulatory Reform

In the heated financial markets of 2008, repeated outcry could be heard in the US and Europe for reform of OTC derivatives markets. In a set of recommendations related to OTC securities trading, Burton Malkiel, noted financial economist, observed that the causes of crisis could be traced to faulty practices in the CDS and mortgage backed debt markets. While a proponent of efficient markets, Malkiel cautioned against regulatory change that would impair the ability of CDSs and other instruments to play their positive role in risk reduction. He proposed "a shift from the current over the counter bilateral CDS market to an exchange traded market." He noted that OTC contracts should be made standard or plain vanilla. They should be fully collateralized and traded on central exchanges. Contracts would be guaranteed by capital contributions from clearing members of a central clearinghouse. Contracts would be marked to market daily. Transparent pricing and volume information would be provided by the exchange on a timely basis. The resulting advantages of greater liquidity, transparency, and safety would help make the entire financial system stronger, less opaque, and more trustworthy.

Shortly after Malkiel's proposal to shift OTC derivatives trading to exchanges, congressional hearings produced strong endorsements of this approach by top executives at Deutsche Börse, NYSE, and CME Group. The general counsel at ICE noted: "clearing should be mandated for most credit default [swaps] instruments."[21]

In May 2009 the Obama administration put forward a comprehensive plan to regulate OTC derivatives. The plan, issued by Tim Geithner, US Treasury secretary, contained three main provisions.[22] First, a distinction is made between standard and non-standard swap instruments. Standard OTC derivatives would be traded on exchange markets. Second, standard OTC derivatives would be cleared through central clearinghouses, to reduce the risk of investors being exposed to a single counterparty. Finally, market transparency would be provided, as central clearers have the obligation to provide data on trading, prices, market liquidity, and market participants. While the US Treasury plan would not require that customized derivative instruments be traded on an exchange, it would subject these transactions to record keeping and reporting requirements.[23]

Proposals to regulate OTC derivatives in the US have been echoed in Europe. In Brussels, European Union officials welcomed the Obama administration initiatives. Europe has utilized somewhat different approaches to derivatives clearing. As noted earlier in Table 4.13, four basic models operate for securities clearing in North America and Europe. Mayes describes the different paths taken by Europe and North America in evolving their respective securities clearing systems, noting that the "European market has historically been strongly divided along national lines."[24] Many of the European systems are relatively small scale and inefficient. By contrast, the US system "is already largely integrated at the exchange, clearing, and settlement levels," providing integration and servicing a wider range of products.

The financial markets were not taken by surprise when Geithner proposed regulatory reforms for OTC derivatives. In the two decades prior to onset of the 2008 crisis, financial exchanges had invested several billion dollars in trading and post-trade technology systems, software, and platforms. As Gorham and Singh describe, this has resulted in "a new, more complex electronic trading model that relies on other vendors and even other exchanges to complete the trade cycle."[25] To compete effectively in this rapidly evolving and technology driven sector, exchanges outsource to vendors, lease services (especially in clearing trades), and develop partnerships with other exchanges to share specific technology or platforms.

As of 2008 a number of central clearinghouses were being used by multiple exchanges. These included the Options Clearing Corporation (OCC) and CME Group in the United States, LCH.Clearnet in Europe, and JCCH, which is a common clearing platform used by Japanese commodity exchanges (Table 8.10).

ICE is no stranger to the concept of providing central clearinghouse services for other exchanges. In 2008 ICE was providing such services for its own trading, NYBOT, the International Petroleum Exchange (London), and the Winnipeg Exchange. Early in 2009 ICE introduced clearing of CDSs with the approval of

Table 8.10 Illustrations of Central Clearinghouses Utilized by Financial Exchanges

Central clearinghouse	*Exchanges serviced by clearinghouse*
1 CME Clearing	CME, CBOT, NYMEX
2 Depository Trust and Clearing Corporation (DTCC)	NYSE, NASDAQ, AMEX
3 LCH.Clearnet	Euronext LIFFE, LME
4 ICE Clear	ICE, NYBOT, IPE, Winnipeg
5 Options Clearing Corporation (OCC)	AMEX, CBOE, ISE, PCX, PHLX

Source: Adapted from M. Gorham and N. Singh, *Electronic Exchanges*, Elsevier, 2009; and David G. Mayes (editor), *The Future of Financial Markets*, Palgrave Macmillan, 2006.

the Securities Exchange Commission and Federal Reserve.[26] At that time other exchanges were planning to introduce clearing services for derivatives, including CME Group. By November 2009 ICE had announced that "nearly all new credit default swaps contracts would be cleared centrally by the end of the month," meeting a key demand of the regulators. ICE collaboration with the main CDS dealers allowed it to clear more than 43,000 individual trades in Europe and the US with a notional value of over $3.5 trillion.[27] The chief executive of ICE noted that some 95 percent of new index trades would be cleared via ICE's central clearing.

Clearing Opaque Markets

By yearend 2009 several important changes had taken place in the derivatives markets. First, as described in the previous section, ICE had gained a lead role as central clearing counterparty in the large credit derivatives sector. Second, this change provided a high degree of clarity in formerly opaque markets. Third, concerns over risks were shifting their focus to other OTC market sectors, including sovereign debt and currencies. Finally, several important lessons were learned, the subject of this section.

As early as June 2009 the Bank for International Settlements (BIS) reported that the total notional amount of OTC derivative contracts outstanding had risen 10 percent to over $604 trillion. This increase, together with the rapid shifting of credit derivatives clearing onto exchanges during 2009, was welcomed by analysts and regulators, but market participants, including many corporate users of credit default and commodity option instruments, were complaining that capital tied up in margin requirements potentially could make it too costly to use these risk hedging tools.

Terry Duffy, chairman of the CME Group, stated he had little sympathy for those who wanted to escape the requirement to post collateral. Any cost of failed trades would likely be imposed on the taxpayer. E.ON, Europe's biggest public utility, stated it might have to raise 7.5 billion euros in new credit lines or cash reserves if EU proposals for margin requirements were enacted.[28] Many large nonfinancial companies do not have to post margin on trades when they deal directly through banks. However, according to Duffy, "the crisis would have been less severe if all derivatives had been cleared by a central counterparty."

Several exchanges other than ICE had formulated plans to establish clearing services for OTC derivatives. According to Gerry Jones, global head of derivatives at NYSE LIFFE, OTC clearing is a utility business. Nobody will make a lot of money out of it.[29] NYSE LIFFE withdrew from OTC clearing after launching a facility to clear CDSs that attracted few clients. The NYSE LIFFE initiative did not attract the biggest dealer banks, many of which had been using the ICE facility. ICE enjoyed a "first-mover" status.

NYSE LIFFE was not the only rival of ICE to be outdistanced. Eurex Credit Clear also launched a CDS clearing initiative, followed by CME Group. The industry still expects regulatory rules to be put in place, covering trading (pre-clearing), but at yearend 2009 there was continued uncertainty regarding how these trading rules would be formulated, if at all.

Even the OCC, the large equity options clearer in the US that services all such clearing, was not able to clarify its own plans for clearing OTC derivatives, waiting for federal legislation and guidelines. Meanwhile, NASDAQ OMX was moving ahead with International Derivatives Clearing Group, a new OTC interest rate swaps clearing business. According to Robert Greifeld, the NASDAQ chief executive, this would be a "nine figure revenue opportunity."

Shifting Systemic Risk

In the United States the Federal Reserve Bank of New York has taken a lead role in reviewing and pushing for better organization of the swaps over the counter markets, and has urged lead trading banks to adopt acceptable clearing procedures. On almost a monthly basis ten large derivatives dealer banks that operate in New York, London, and other financial centers have met at the Federal Reserve Bank of New York to discuss and plan for a more comprehensive and fail-safe method to clear and settle OTC derivative trades. At January 2010 we could identify at least fifteen separate clearinghouses operating in North America and Europe, with responsibility to clear various types of derivatives and underlying securities (Table 8.11). Weakness in this infrastructure supporting these markets did exacerbate the financial crisis of 2008–09, as problems in clearing and settlement of swaps contracts reflected failures in risk management. Several large institutional participants in the financial markets took excessive risks, relying on swap and other instruments to provide hedges against outstanding risk positions.[30]

The specific issues uncovered in the analysis of swaps trading include the following. First, lack of a central clearing facility led one or more institutions (including a large insurance company) to trade in the swaps market as if it could function as a central counterparty, leading to near insolvency. Second, the issuance of credit default swap contracts vis-à-vis corporate debt grew to many times the value of the underlying debt paper, threatening a scarcity of real paper should it become needed for physical settlement. Third, the opaque nature of trading left most parties in the dark concerning the status of the market in general, and for specific debt issues in particular. Finally, there existed no organizational base for clearing on a centralized basis.

Both in North America and Europe regulatory bodies have been calling for centralized and faster clearing of derivatives traded over the counter. This can be accomplished either by a) forcing derivative trading and clearing onto exchange platforms, or b) requiring that at minimum certain types of swaps and other OTC contracts be cleared through a clearinghouse where a central counterparty becomes the responsible settlement agent to each contract.

However, requiring that OTC derivatives clearing be carried out in clearinghouses may shift risk into a different form. The shift may remove systemic risk from one area of the financial system, but at the same time concentrate new risks in the clearinghouses themselves.[31] Many of these OTC products never have been handled by clearinghouses. Clearers themselves need to be robust enough to sustain a default by any member. Clearinghouses utilize funds in the form of margin,

Table 8.11 Existing Clearinghouse Facilities for Derivatives and Related Underlying Securities, North America and Europe (January 2010)

	Clearing unit	*Clearing functions*
I North America		
A Chicago	1 CME Group	Most US exchange traded futures.
	2 The Clearing Corporation	Clears for Chicago Climate Exchange.
	3 Options Clearing Corporation (OCC)	All US exchange traded options.
B New York	4 Depository Trust and Clearing Corporation (DTCC)	Clears for all US exchanges' cash equities trades.
	5 ICE Clear US	Unit of Atlanta based Intercontinental Exchange. A number of commodity and derivative contracts.
	6 ICE Trust US	Clears credit default swaps.
C Winnipeg	7 ICE Clear Canada	Clears commodity futures.
II Europe		
D London	8 LCH Clearnet	Clears for London Stock Exchange, Euronext, and London Metal Exchange.
	9 EMCF	Jointly owned by NASDAQ MD and Fortis Bank (Netherlands). Clears for BATS Chi-X, Europe, and Quote MTF.
	10 EuroCCP	Owned by DTCC; clears for Turquoise, NYSE Arca Europe, SmartPool, and Pipeline.
	11 ICE Clear Europe	Clears energy futures and swaps and credit default swaps.
E Frankfurt	12 Eurex Clearing	Owned by Deutsche Börse, clears German cash equities and derivatives.
F Zurich	13 X-Clear	Owned by SWX Group; clears Swiss stocks and some UK stocks.
G Milan	14 CC&G	Clears for Borsa Italiana.
H Madrid	15 Iberclear	Clears for BME (Spanish exchange).

Source: Aline Van Duyn and Jeremy Grant, "Use of Clearers to Rein in OTC Derivatives Poses Fresh Dilemma," *Financial Times*, January 15, 2010, p. 21.

deposited by market participants, to guarantee trades can be completed with full cash settlement.

In January 2010 the New York Federal Reserve Bank issued a policy paper which noted the need for CCPs to successfully clear a large quantity of derivative trades. It went further, stating that failure of a CCP could suddenly expose many major market participants to losses. European financial regulators are equally concerned with the risk of imposing concentrated clearing risks upon CCPs. Clearing concerns have been magnified by reforms pushed by the European Commission that were introduced to encourage competition between clearers and reduce post-trade costs. In a discussion paper sent by the Brussels based regulatory commission, the staff recommended tough new regulation governing clearing, including "robust" regulatory requirements for CCPs.

In Europe clearinghouses are regulated by the national securities regulators in each country. Xavier Rolet, chief executive of the London Stock Exchange, warned that it could be dangerous for clearinghouse capital bases and risk models to differ from country to country. He called for more unified central bank oversight over clearers across Europe, and preferably on a global basis.

Equity Options: Market Microstructure

Option prices provide information about the underlying security not readily available from its primary trading market. The price quote of a given security is a mean valuation. The prices of the related options, including strike prices and maturities, present a more complete picture. The price discovery process in the options market is not limited to simply finding the appropriate price of the underlying stock. It includes a broad picture of the conditional distribution of value at different possible realizations and conditioning horizons.

Market making in options is distinct from markets of the underlying stock in at least two respects. First, counterparty risk is separate from the underlying company. In the United States exchange listed options are cleared by the Options Clearing Corporation. All options exchanges are members of the OCC. Second, related to the underlying stock are dozens (hundreds) of options with different strike prices and maturities. Prices and quotes for a single equity security and its related options become an equilibrium, no-arbitrage system.

These unique characteristics of the options market require that options market makers possess detailed knowledge of a range of no-arbitrage conditions, and the technology to update quotes rapidly across all relevant market sectors.[32]

Two Models

As of 2008 two models were operative for trading options on traditional exchanges. The AMEX, PCX, CBOE, and PHLX use the floor-based model. Here brokers and market makers interact face to face to execute orders for different options. AMEX and PHLX employ a specialist structure, resembling the trading on stock markets. Alternately, the CBOE trades options under a designated primary market maker (DPMM), which is a modification of open outcry used in futures pits. The PCX also follows a modified outcry structure and trades options under a lead market maker (LMM). Under the DPMM and LMM methods, market makers disseminate quotes, provide liquidity via own account trading, and represent public limit orders. Options traded under a DPMM may also be traded by other market makers.

Contrasting with the four floor based exchanges, market making on the International Securities Exchange (ISE) is fully electronic. Quotes are consolidated with a centralized system. A variety of interfaces are available to allow broker-dealers to link order delivery systems to ISE's order management system.

ISE is not an alternative trading system (ATS) or an electronic communications network (ECN), where customers trade against one another via electronic limit and market orders. Also, ISE is not a dealer market like NASDAQ in which broker-dealers trade vis-à-vis their own customers. The ISE is a registered exchange, trading listed options via auction. Customers direct orders to broker-dealers, who in turn route these to any of the five options exchanges.

Market makers at the five competing exchanges provide bid and ask quotes. At all five exchanges transactions are subject to a formal clearing procedure. The structural difference between the ISE and the four floor based exchanges is that transactions on ISE are centralized and cleared electronically, without the need for broker-dealers and market makers to gather at a physical location and face one another.

ISE Market Making

All five options exchanges share the principle of operating an auction market, but the ISE differs based on technology and trading procedures. Three classes of members operate on ISE, all registered broker-dealers.

ISE divides stock issues into several bins. Each bin is administered or served by one primary market maker (PMM) and several competitive market makers (CMMs). These entities are operated by large, global financial institutions with a sizeable capital base and trading experience. In each bin one PMM and several CMMs submit quotes on the same set of options (Table 8.12). The quote consolidating mechanism consolidates quotes and posts best available bids and offers in each options series. Market makers and customers observe only the consolidated quote screen, not the sources of quotes (anonymity).

Table 8.12 Classification of Members in International Securities Exchange (ISE)*

1	Primary market maker (PMM)	Significant market making duties. Determines opening price based on limit order book.
2	Competitive market maker (CMM)	Market makers who quote independently add liquidity. Required to provide continuous quotations for at least 60 percent of options in its assigned group.
3	Electronic access member (EAM)	Broker-dealers who represent agents or proprietary orders on the exchange. Cannot enter quotations. Enter the market by providing market or limit orders.

Source: Y.E. Simaan and L. Wu, "Price Discovery in the US Stock Options Market," *Journal of Trading*, Winter 2008, pp. 70–71.

Note: * Floor brokers are not needed because orders are input by broker-dealers directly at the point of sale in the electronic order book.

The PMM in each bin is a market maker, with the responsibility to oversee opening, provide continuous quotations in all assigned stock options, and ensure that customer orders are not executed at prices inferior to those available at other options exchanges. At the commencement of trading each day the PMM determines the opening price based on the limit orders outstanding. During the day the PMM must provide continuous quotations and guarantee best execution. In return, the PMM receives preferential treatment for order flow allocation. If a CMM and the PMM are at the best quote when an order arrives, the PMM receives 60 percent of the order and the CMM receives 40 percent.

CMMs are market makers that quote on an independent basis. They contribute liquidity and depth. A CMM must provide continuous quotes for 60 percent or more of stock options in its assigned group. Electronic access members (EAMs) are broker-dealers who represent agency or proprietary orders on the exchange. They do not enter quotations or engage in market making. They enter the market by providing market or limit orders.

All customers that want to trade in listed options must go through a registered broker-dealer. The customer posts margin with the broker-dealer. In turn, the broker-dealer posts margin with the OCC.

The ISE differs from traditional options exchanges in the number of market makers who can give quotes. On traditional exchanges only one market maker gives quotes. Market makers rarely compete against one another on the same floor within the same exchange. On the ISE one PMM and several CMMs send in independent and competitive two-sided quotes for each option series. These are submitted anonymously, which provides a competitive condition among market makers.

Recent Trading Developments

Early in 2004 the Boston Options Exchange (BOX) started trading options. The BOX and ISE are similar, since both are fully electronic and without a trading floor. They share the concept of electronically aggregating quotes from many market makers to stimulate competition.

In 2005 the Archipelago Exchange (ArcaEx) acquired the PCX to leverage its technology and expertise for application in the options market. In 2006 the New York Stock Exchange (NYSE) merged with ArcaEx to form the NYSE Group. In October 2006 the NYSE Group launched its options trading platform. In April 2007 the NYSE Group merged with Euronext to form NYSE Euronext. In the same month the ISE undertook a merger agreement with Eurex, owned by Deutsche Börse and the Swiss Exchange. Further, the ISE has expanded its business into stock trading through a new stock exchange platform.

The preceding reflects two trends for derivatives. First, global consolidation moves the financial markets closer to 24-hour-a-day trading. Second, the integration of derivatives market making with market making in the underlying security appears to be the trend of the future. This will allow more flexible hedging of positions by market makers and other market participants.

Mergers Affecting Derivatives Exchanges

Restructuring is an important dynamic among derivatives exchanges, as well as stock exchanges. In the following we describe mergers taking place affecting several types of exchanges. These mergers are taking several forms. In some cases stock exchanges have acquired derivatives exchanges. In other cases, mergers have taken place between derivatives exchanges. In the following sections we analyze mergers affecting derivatives exchanges. First we examine several cases where stock exchanges acquired options exchanges. Then we analyze the cases of the CME merging with the CBOT and NYMEX.

In the previous sections of this chapter we examined the equity options market, primarily from the perspective of five American based exchanges competing for trading business. Here we describe and evaluate mergers that have taken place in quick succession, creating stronger links between cash equities trading and equity options trading.

Stock Exchanges Acquire Options Exchanges

According to Steven M. Sears, writing for *Barron's*, "the options market is a curious place. As other market exchanges rush to consolidate worldwide, the number of options exchanges keeps increasing."[33] The NASDAQ exchange is active in this respect. In addition to its stock exchange, NASDAQ operates two options exchanges addressing a different clientele. Its "maker–taker" model exchange launched in April 2008 pays market makers for providing liquidity. This new model appeals to professional traders. By contrast, the more traditional model, the Philadelphia Stock Exchange, which NASDAQ purchased in late 2007, allows some brokerage firms to be compensated for sending orders. The Philadelphia Exchange appeals to discount brokerage firms. Each of these models services a different clientele.

In this regard the options market is not different from the equity markets of the 1990s, with multiple execution venues on given exchanges designed to carry out specific trading services. Meanwhile, Deutsche Börse acquired the ISE shortly prior to the above-mentioned mergers (Table 8.7). The German exchange seeks to expand its capacity to service options trading in North America.

Key differences separate options from stock trading. While companies issue their own shares, the Options Clearing Corporation in Chicago issues options. OCC clears only exchange traded options, but could change these rules. However, the exchanges operate OCC, and possess the power to approve or not any rule changes. Until now, no party has requested the OCC undertake clearing non-exchange option trades.

CME and CBOT Merge

In July 2007 some 95 percent of CBOT shareholders voted to accept the CME offer to merge the two Chicago based exchanges. The merged entity became the largest merger by value in the financial exchange sector, and created the largest market capitalization exchange in the world. In the following we analyze why this merger took place, and its implications and importance within the financial exchange sector.

Chicago Mercantile Exchange

The Chicago Mercantile Exchange (the Merc) has its origins in the nineteenth century. Following construction of the Erie Canal in New York State, Chicago grew rapidly as an urban and business center, but more significantly as a financing and transshipment link between the Midwest agricultural regions and New York City. Chicago emerged as the country's largest market for corn, wheat, lumber, and meat. Growth of the grain market in Chicago led to the futures markets becoming a basic component of Chicago's financial system. Chicago's grain traders began using forward contracting in the early 1830s. In 1848 the Chicago Board of Trade was formed, and the Chicago Produce Exchange was launched in 1874. The latter focused on butter and egg trading. In 1895 merchants organized the Produce Exchange Butter and Egg Board to improve on price setting. In 1919 the Chicago Mercantile Exchange was organized to trade a wider range of commodities than its predecessor entities, including potatoes, onions, and cheese. Since that date the CME has traded futures on over fifty products, from frozen pork bellies and live cattle to eurodollar interest rate and index futures.

In 1967 a group of younger traders not satisfied with the direction and management of CME organized as the Broker's Club. This group forced the board of directors to act more closely relative to the needs and desires of the membership. In 1968 a new chairman was selected, and the Chicago exchange began to examine prospects for new types of futures trading.

In 1969 Leo Melamed became the chairman of CME. Within a few short years he introduced currency futures and the International Monetary Market (IMM).[34] The Merc quickly added new financial futures contracts to its trading business, covering long and short maturity interest rates, and stock index futures.

In the 1980s the CME continued to operate as a clubby fraternity where commodities and financial futures traded via an archaic system of open outcry. But in 1987 Leo Melamed faced the question of how to deal with a growing globalization of financial markets. A year earlier the London Stock Exchange had gone through a restructuring, and the CBOT had created an after-hours trading session.

The CME gave its strategic planning committee the task of determining how to prepare for rising competition. The committee recommended extending CME's trading day, not by use of extending floor trading but with screen based trading. Now Melamed had to assure exchange members, the ownership group, that a new electronic system was essential to the success of the exchange and posed no real threat to the floor trading operation. The CME chose Reuters Holdings as its partner. Reuters was a UK based company that leased thousands of computer terminals to securities traders around the globe. Reuters had acquired Instinet, an electronic equities market that served large institutions. Together Reuters and CME were to bring a new electronic trading system into operation.

The final product of the CME-Reuters partnership was Globex. In late 1987 CME members approved the development of Globex, and in 1992 the electronic system began operating as an after-hours market. Five years later the CME began a transformation of its trading systems, in which Globex became a regular-hours trading market for most of its products. Subsequently, CME made Globex available to other exchanges. This included NYMEX for its crude oil and natural gas futures (2002) and for NYMEX gold and silver contracts a few years later. When the CBOT and CME merged (2007), CBOT trading was moved onto the Globex platforms.

As the decade of the 1990s came to an end, the Chicago exchange unveiled a new strategic plan. This included more electronic order routing on the trading floor, side-by-side electronic and open-outcry trading in eurodollar contracts, and demutualization. With demutualization CME was the first US financial exchange to become a public company, listing its shares on the NYSE (2002). The IPO raised $130 million, needed to put in place modern electronic systems.

Soon after its IPO the Merc faced a serious threat. At that time the Merc's biggest contract was eurodollar futures and options. With 1.5 million contracts traded daily, this business still operated on the floor via open outcry. At this time Paris based Euronext owned the London based LIFFE exchange. Euronext LIFFE launched an electronic contract for 90-day eurodollars. Trading this new contract would be cheaper as well as faster. If sufficient banks and others migrated to the LIFFE platform, CME might never recover this business. The Merc board met without delay, decided it needed to promote electronic trading, and scheduled a meeting with members that traded eurodollar contracts. At the end of a tumultuous meeting it was agreed that eurodollar futures would have to be traded electronically. By this action the CME board and executives saved the business, and CME still dominates trading in the contract.

Such threats indicated that the competitive landscape facing derivatives exchanges was changing. In a few years large scale mergers would present the Merc with the prospect of competing against giant financial exchanges able to launch competing products with ease. The New York Stock Exchange merger with Euronext LIFFE would force the Merc to reconsider its options and prepare for tougher competition.

Chicago Board of Trade

Organized in 1848 primarily to facilitate grain trading, the CBOT expanded steadily. In the 1970s CBOT launched trading in Treasury bond futures and Government National Mortgage Association (GNMA) mortgage rate futures. In the 1980s it introduced options on several futures contracts, including Treasury bonds and soybeans.

In 2005, a year before the CME made its initial bid for the CBOT, one could observe that the CBOT was one of the busiest commodities exchanges in the world. With over 3,600 members trading in several dozen different contracts, including Treasury bonds, silver, soybeans, wheat, and futures in the Dow Jones Averages, its annual trading volume exceeded 200 million contracts.

CBOT operated as a not-for-profit company, utilizing open-outcry trading. Traders met face to face on the CBOT trading floor. Facing competitive pressures, in the late 1990s CBOT adopted computer trading for several of its products. Competition from European exchanges was becoming particularly problematic. In particular, Eurex (in commodities) and LIFFE (in financial futures) challenged the CBOT for market share.

In 2003 CME and CBOT came to an agreement in which the Merc completed CBOT trades utilizing its computerized trading and settlement systems. Fees collected by CME helped control costs facing CBOT, and represented additional revenue flow for CME. CBOT's technology alliance with CME set the stage for subsequent negotiations between the two Chicago exchanges, moving them closer to an eventual merger bid by CME.

CME and CBOT Negotiate

The Chicago Board of Trade conducts a business that is a complement to the product lines offered by the CME. Unlike the Merc, CBOT did not operate its own electronic trading system. It cleared trades through a separate service provider. Top executives at the CME wanted to get CBOT's clearing business, but Eurex had similar plans. At the time Eurex was the largest derivatives exchanges, and had set up an American unit in Chicago. Also, Eurex was angling to gain the Chicago Board of Trade's clearing business.

In April 2003 CBOT and CME signed a deal where the Merc would clear CBOT trades. To strengthen the arrangement and further freeze Eurex out of US business, the CBOT temporarily dropped some trading fees to zero. In response, Eurex filed an antitrust suit, which never gained any traction. In October 2006 a discouraged Eurex sold a large piece of its American venture to Man Group, a London based futures broker.

Underlying the successful economics of futures trading are three variables: innovation, technology, and scale economies. Both CBOT and the CME had been successful in creating new products, some of which commanded a huge worldwide clientele. A strong position in technology by CME led to the 2003 deal by which CBOT would use CME services. Scale economies called for continued close cooperation between these two large exchanges.

Leaders at the CME estimated it would cut overhead costs by tens of millions of dollars by offering all (CME and CBOT) futures products on a single electronic system. Further, this could lead to expanding into over the counter derivatives trading, which accounted for a major share of the total by notional value. In 2005 the CBOT was planning to go public. CME made an unsolicited offer to buy the CBOT, hoping to achieve the above-described merger benefits, but the CBOT board rejected the offer and the exchange went public in October 2005. Investors placed a $6 billion valuation on CBOT, probably somewhat less than the exchange's executives had hoped for. Early in 2006 CBOT and the CME resumed merger discussions. In October 2006, a year after CBOT went public, an $8 billion deal was announced that would join the two Chicago exchanges into the world's largest by market value. The deal would create an exchange with dominant positions in futures and options contracts in interest rates, stock index futures, currencies, and numerous commodities.[35]

Critics quickly voiced protestations that the enlarged CME Group would wield too much power. Others expressed fear that competition would be reduced. Simultaneously, the Intercontinental Exchange, led by Jeffrey Sprecher, raised its offer for CBOT to $10 billion. In 2001 ICE had purchased the London based International Petroleum Exchange and converted it to an electronic trading market. The ICE offer for CBOT appeared to have won the battle, but Merc leaders reviewed their position.

Originally the Merc offer was 0.3 shares of CME stock for each CBOT share. The Merc raised that to 0.35 Merc shares. On the Friday before the July 2007 vote, CME made a final offer of 0.37 shares, worth close to $11 billion. When the CBOT shareholder vote was tallied, 95 percent supported acceptance of the offer. At the time the merger was approved by CBOT shareholders, it was estimated the combined CME group would have a market value of $32 billion.[36]

Economics of the CME–CBOT Group

The CME success in merging with CBOT is a restatement of why and how derivatives dominate. This applies in two areas—new product development in derivatives, and per unit revenue generation.

Trading derivatives is impressively profitable. American exchanges on average collect 60 cents for each derivative contract traded. In 2006 close to 8 billion contracts were traded worldwide. By contrast, NYSE Group collects one-tenth of a penny for each share traded. In 2006, 18 trillion shares traded worldwide.[37] As we can observe in Table 8.13, the revenue from derivatives trading in 2006 was one-fourth the revenue from equity trading, but it is important to note that derivatives trading is growing faster than cash equities trading. Revenues per trade are stable for derivatives, but continuing to fall from stiff competition in equities trading. Therefore, the logic of the CME–CBOT merger is indisputable. The CME–CBOT merger concentrates much of the worldwide trading in the most profitable instruments onto a single exchange operator.

Finally we should note that derivatives exchanges make more profit per dollar of revenue than stock exchanges. ICE pockets 40 percent of revenues as profits, while NYSE pockets less than half that percentage. The CME, CBOT, and ICE focus growth on developing new products, unlike the NYSE, NASDAQ, and

Table 8.13 Economics of Derivatives Versus Cash Equities Trading (2006)

	Revenue per contract	*Number of contracts traded*	*Gross revenues*
Derivatives	60 cents	8 billion	$4.8 billion
Cash equities	0.1 cents	18 trillion	$18 billion

Source: *Wall Street Journal*, March 20, 2007, pp. C1, C2.

LSE, which devote much of their resources to courting companies for new stock listings and investment in more speedy trading platforms.

CME–NYMEX Merger

The first half of 2007 saw the completion of trend-setting mergers among financial exchanges. The NYSE merger with Euronext was completed at this time. Deutsche Börse's surprise acquisition of the International Securities Exchange reportedly angered its shareholders.[38] The Chicago Mercantile Exchange made an agreed deal with CBOT that thwarted a hostile bid by rival Intercontinental Exchange.

Each financial exchange entering into discussions with another exchange has its own very specific needs and considerations leading it to sit at the merger table. However, several "generalized" factors play a role as well, and underlie the rationale for most mergers of exchanges. These include scale economies and scalability of operations, expanding and diversifying the product base and business model, and moving closer to achieving 24-hour-a-day trading capability.

At midyear 2007 it was believed there might be intensive bidding for NYMEX by three entities: 1) NYSE Euronext, 2) Deutsche Börse, and 3) the Chicago Mercantile Exchange. At this time the CME was in the final stages of a bidding war for the CBOT. CME already had developed a partnership with NYMEX, in which the New York based marketplace utilized CME technology and electronic trading systems. Shared technology has been a factor in bringing together pairs of exchanges, one needing and the other providing this service, but NYMEX had other reasons for considering a tie-up with another exchange.

NYMEX was seen by many as too limited in its product and geographic reach to remain an isolated island in the sea of exchange consolidation. Consultants viewing the exchange sector considered a NYMEX merger inevitable. Second, NYMEX's chief rival, ICE, was moving forward at a fast pace, making acquisitions with other exchanges, and developing its own new products. For example, ICE overtly had its sights on several of NYMEX's high volume energy contracts.

From the CME perspective a merger with NYMEX would diversify the Chicago exchange into energy trading, a part of the business that was growing at a strong rate. Probably more important, closing the deal with NYMEX would give CME control of close to 98 percent of the US futures business.[39]

The CME worked diligently in negotiating and bringing the deal to a close. The Chicago exchange did not raise the stock portion of its cash and stock offer, but dissident members of NYMEX won several concessions. This included raising the per seat bid to $750,000, and providing that members could continue to own their seats and sell them whenever they wished.[40]

The CME–NYMEX merger was agreed in late August 2008. This came at the end of a five-year period in which a number of mergers took place involving one or more derivatives exchanges (Table 8.7). The exchange landscape was vastly different at yearend 2008 as compared with 2000. If anything, one could state that fewer, larger, more diversified derivatives exchanges had become a dominant aspect of the terrain within the financial markets.

CBOE Goes Public

In June 2010 CBOE Holdings Inc. became a publicly owned for-profit corporation. In the IPO, with shares priced at $29.00, the investment banks that underwrote the issue earned a discount of $1.9575, or 6.75 percent. The stock offering generated $339.3 million of gross proceeds before payment of the $22.9 million underwriting fee. Close to 20 percent of the proceeds was distributed to selling stockholders (CBOE members), and the remainder to CBOE Holdings.

Established in 1973, CBOE was the first organized marketplace for trading standardized listed options on equities. It is one of the largest options exchanges in the world. According to the CBOE prospectus, US options trading has enjoyed a 25 percent growth rate since the mid-1970s. CBOE is a global leader in this trading.[41] While the options business has demonstrated high growth, several competition questions pose hurdles for options exchanges like CBOE. Institutional interest in options trading is increasing the customer base, but these traders are highly sophisticated and demand improved services, including risk management techniques. Development of electronic order routing and matching systems requires investment in technology. Consolidation has intruded itself into the options sector, with most of the exchanges in this sector merging with large stock exchanges. For example, Deutsche Börse has acquired ISE, and NYSE has acquired AMEX. Payment for order flow has become an important part of business practice.[42]

The CBOE has been a leader in developing its own proprietary indexes and index methodologies for options trading. These include volatility indexes, and broad based market indexes such as the S&P 500, the DJIA, and the Russell 2000. Also, the CBOE generates revenue from the calculation and dissemination of over thirty real-time index values for third party licensors.

In addition to its activities in options, the CBOE owns several companies in related businesses. These include a 20 percent equity interest in the Options Clearing Corporation. Each of the five options exchanges in the US owns similar stakes in the OCC. Also, CBOE holds a 49.96 percent equity stake in CBOE Stock Exchange (CBSX), which was established in 2006 to trade equity securities listed on NYSE, NASDAQ, and AMEX. Several broker-dealers (LaBranche & Co., Susquehanna International, and others) own stakes in this exchange. At yearend 2009 there were sixty-two CBSX trading permit holders and ninety-seven CBOE members with trading access to CBSX.[43]

Other trading venue companies and related enterprises owned by CBOE Holdings are described in detail in the CBOE offering prospectus. They include: OneChicago LLC (23.7 percent interest); NSX Holdings Inc. (4.6 percent interest); Signal Trading Systems (50 percent interest); CBOE Futures Exchange LLC (wholly owned subsidiary); C2 Options Exchange Inc. (wholly owned subsidiary); and CBOE Execution Services LLC (wholly owned subsidiary).[44] These businesses are closely related to CBOE Holdings' activity in options trading, but they also extend further into areas in which existing operations provide a "head start" advantage.

9 Asia Pacific Exchanges

This chapter and Chapter 10 describe and analyze exchanges and financial systems in five countries and territories. In this chapter we consider three country financial systems and their respective exchanges: Japan and the Tokyo Stock Exchange, Singapore and the exchanges operating there, and Australia and the Sydney based exchange. The chapter examines the Asia Pacific region, which is fast growing in importance, and analyzes the underlying economic factors that facilitate successful development of the financial markets and exchanges.

Chapter 10 focuses on two financial systems and their respective financial exchanges: Hong Kong and Mainland China. These two financial systems are quite different in their structure, level of development, and regulatory approaches. However, they are important complements to each other.

Region of High Growth

The Asia Pacific region has enjoyed above-average economic expansion for at least two decades. In fact, Japan's period of high growth (1955–85) precedes that of China and India, which is of more recent vintage. Currently, high growth translates into rapid modernization in the financial sector, especially in the city states of Singapore and Hong Kong.

Comparative Economies

A comparison of the five Asian countries and territories with the United States and United Kingdom provides valuable insights concerning how high growth is facilitated, and the strategies required to perpetuate high growth rates. For this purpose we observe in Table 9.1 the wide disparities in size and structure of the Asian economies. Mainland China's population is more than double that of the other six countries combined, but China has a relatively low population density, especially when compared with Singapore and Hong Kong. Like Australia and the United States, China possesses a huge land area.

Comparisons of GNP must be used with caution, given the hidden forces that lie beneath the surface of income and product valuations. Nevertheless, we can observe dramatic differences in Columns 3 and 4 in Table 9.1. US gross national

Table 9.1 Economic Structure of Five Asian Markets

	1. Population	*2. Population density*	*3. GNP*	*4. GNP per capita*	*Value added per sector as percentage of GDP*		
					5. Agriculture	*6. Industry*	*7. Service*
Japan	128	351	4,813	37,670	2	30	68
Singapore	5	6,660	149	32,470	0	31	69
Australia	21	3	755	35,960	3	28	69
Mainland China	1,320	142	3,120	2,360	12	48	40
Hong Kong	7	6,647	218	31,610	0	9	91
United States	302	33	11,886	46,040	1	23	76
United Kingdom	61	252	2,608	42,740	1	24	75

Source: World Bank, *World Development Report*, 2008.

Notes: Data for calendar 2007. Column 1 in millions; Column 2, persons per square kilometer; Column 3 in billions of US dollars; Column 4 in US dollars; Columns 5, 6, and 7, percentage of GDP.

product (GNP) is three times that of Japan and four times that of China. Per capita income figures reflect similar disparities. China stands out with an extremely low per capita income, attributable to: a) an undervalued currency, b) a policy of maintaining low wages to facilitate higher product and export growth, and c) data bias and problems with capturing the "real value" of services (housing) provided at Chinese government subsidized prices.

Table 9.1 provides information on the sources of GDP, the value added by agriculture, industry, and services. Mainland China stands out as the only country in which agriculture provides any meaningful part of value added. With respect to the contribution of industry, high industry value added countries include China, Japan, Singapore, and Australia. Moderate industry value added countries include the UK and the US. One country finds itself in the low industry value added category, Hong Kong. Before and since 1997 when Hong Kong reverted to Mainland China political administration, firms manufacturing in the former Crown colony have shifted manufacturing operations into the Mainland China region, where labor and land cost levels are much lower. Consequently, Hong Kong has become a services oriented economy, with 91 percent of GDP value added derived from this sector. Among these are financial and other services, where on a regional and global basis Hong Kong has become a highly competitive financial services provider.

In fact, Hong Kong is approaching the status of the UK and the US, as an economic entity in which services account for a very high proportion of economic value added. As can be observed in Table 9.1, Mainland China ranks lowest among the seven countries in the percentage of value added derived from services. China needs Hong Kong, as a major provider of services, especially financial services.

Financial Balance

In this section we analyze the financial balance within Asian countries, as well as in the UK and US. Financial balance reflects how each main sector contributes to the expenditures flow, which we refer to as domestic absorption. This is the percentage of GDP accounted for by household consumers, general government, and gross capital expenditures. Domestic absorption provides a ready handle to measure: 1) whether domestic entities are spending more or less than is produced at home, and 2) which type of entities are performing differently from their counterparts in other countries.

Overall, the United States reflects the highest domestic absorption (106 percent), while Singapore demonstrates the lowest level of domestic absorption (71 percent) (Table 9.2). Hong Kong and Mainland China occupy a middle range of domestic absorption.

Domestic absorption's mirror reflection, or counterpart, is found in Column 5 in Table 9.2. The external balance for the US and Singapore is −6 percent of GDP and +29 percent of GDP respectively. While the US annually spends 6 percent more than it produces, Singapore annually spends 29 percent less than it produces. How is this possible? The answer to this question is simple. Countries with a positive number in Column 5 enjoy a high savings rate and experience low consumption. Countries with a negative number (high domestic absorption) have low savings, and experience high consumption relative to income. The UK and US have a negative external balance, which can be financed from foreign investment income or borrowing from abroad.

Singapore and Hong Kong earn large amounts as financial entrepots. They render financial, foreign trade, and other services for other parts of the world. Both are trade entrepots, importing goods from neighboring countries and re-exporting for profit. Again, this is in part reflected in Column 5 of Table 9.2, where we observe that Singapore (+29 percent) and Hong Kong (+11 percent) enjoy sub-

Table 9.2 Financial Balance of Five Asian Markets

	1. Consumer household expenditure	*2. General government expenditure*	*3. Gross capital formation*	*4. Domestic absorption*	*5. External balance*	*6. Domestic credit provided by bank sector*
Japan	57	18	23	98	1	294
Singapore	38	10	23	71	29	81
Australia	57	18	27	102	−1	142
Mainland China	34	14	44	92	8	136
Hong Kong	60	8	21	89	11	128
United States	71	16	19	106	−6	240
United Kingdom	64	22	18	104	−4	194

Source: World Bank, *World Development Report*, 2008.

Note: Data for calendar 2007, as percentage of GDP.

stantial positive external balances. Mainland China's external balance (+8 percent) reflects enormous trade (export) surpluses.

Finally, Column 6 of Table 9.2 indicates the level of domestic credit provided by the banking sector as a percentage of GDP. Both the United States and the United Kingdom exhibit high ratios, reflecting very active bank lending in each country. Similarly, Japan exhibits a high ratio. Singapore exhibits a low ratio, reflecting the tendency of households to save a high proportion of income and therefore not require extensive bank credit.

Asian Contrast

In the preceding discussion we observe vast differences between countries and territories in the Asia Pacific region. These include population, density, per capita GNP, and industrial origin of value added, as described in Table 9.1. Also, these differences extend to the composition of domestic demand and its level relative to total GDP (absorption), and financial balance (Table 9.2). Here we continue our analysis of the Asia Pacific region, examining how these countries compare with North America and Europe with respect to the role and operation of financial markets.

Until the global financial crisis of 2008–09, Asian policymakers and intellectuals believed that Western views on the theory and practice of economic development were largely correct. Western economies had grown and prospered following Adam Smith's theories of free markets. However, sharp reversals in 2008–09 elevated questions concerning how economic management should be practiced. Most especially, Asian observers became bewildered when Alan Greenspan proclaimed "that derivative traders did not need any regulation . . . and . . . the vast increase in the size of the over the counter derivatives markets is the result of . . . finding them a very useful vehicle."[1]

Whereas Asian policymakers and business executives follow Western free market approaches, they remain loyal to traditions such as: 1) hard work and personal savings, 2) the need for government to intervene when markets fail, 3) the validity of government initiatives to promote exports, and 4) effective corporate governance as a necessity, as taught at the Lee Kuan Yew School of Public Policy in Singapore. The accepted importance of government initiatives is demonstrated by the rise in the number of free trade areas (FTAs) across Southeast and other parts of Asia.

Thomas Schiller has pinpointed the financial conundrum facing Asia. Until recently, economic success has led to high export growth, rising foreign exchange reserves, and currency strength. At present Asia needs to translate these gains into the growth of more vibrant capital markets.[2] Asian nations find that creditworthiness in world capital markets can be limited by a nation's ability to respond to inflation. In turn, current account surpluses and capital inflows complicate monetary policy execution and efforts to control inflation.

Some countries (e.g., Thailand) have introduced capital controls and, as we discuss in detail in Chapter 10, China employs exchange controls that limit resident and foreign entity cross-border investment and currency flows. These restrictions retard the development of capital markets in Asia. In turn, underdeveloped capital markets "impede the efficient use of domestic savings."[3]

The five Asian financial systems and exchanges we analyze in this and the following chapter reflect widely different stages and intensities of capital market expansion. In Table 9.3 we focus on the stock markets of these five countries. Here we observe that Japan's stock market has developed to a point where market capitalization value is 74 percent of GDP. Also, Japan accounts for 9 percent of world stock market value (Column 4), larger than the other Asian stock markets. Nevertheless, Japan's stock market has and continues to experience little growth and weak dynamics.

The Hong Kong stock market exhibits a high (226 percent) market capitalization relative to GDP. This reflects success in Hong Kong expanding as a regional financial hub, attracting stock listings from the wider region of Mainland China and Southeast Asia, and high valuations of companies listed on that market. We should also observe that the turnover ratio on the Hong Kong market is the lowest of all countries in Table 9.3. Comparing Hong Kong and China directly, we find that China enjoys much higher valuations, a result of exchange controls that channel domestic savings directly into the stock market. By contrast, Hong Kong valuations are more in line with other open and competitive markets such as the US, the UK, and Singapore.

Australia's stock market is well developed, despite the relatively small population. The country enjoys a large land area that is well endowed with natural resources and agricultural areas. Its highly developed industrial sector coupled with resources based industries provides a powerful base on which the stock market has grown. Australia's market capitalization relative to GDP is below that of Hong Kong and Singapore, but in line with the other countries described in Table 9.3.

Singapore has a much smaller stock market than the other countries described in Table 9.3. Nevertheless, its stock market is highly competitive, with over 450 company listings. Average company size (US$ 395 million) generally is lower than its counterparts in the region, but includes a large number of foreign listings. Singapore's ratio of market capital value to GDP is 112 percent, ranking it second only to Hong Kong.

Tokyo Stock Market

Analysis of the Tokyo Stock Exchange (TSE) and Japan's financial markets overall would be incomplete without considering the economic and political background. Japan has experienced almost two decades of economic and political malaise. A faltering stock market is one manifestation of this. In this section on Japan and TSE we consider the adverse economic background, related financial imbalances, and weak system of allocating capital. Further, we analyze financial asset ownership, and finally examine the operations of the TSE in close detail. The Tokyo Stock Exchange has great potential, representing one of the largest economies and stock markets in the world.

Table 9.3 Comparison of Five Asian Stock Markets with the USA and the UK (2008)

	1. Market capitalization value (US$ bn)	*2. Market capitalization as percentage of GDP*	*3. Turnover ratio*	*4. Market capitalization as percentage of world total*	*5. Number of listed companies*	*6. Average company size (US$ m)*	*7. Concentration ratio (capitalization of 10 largest companies as percentage of total)*
Japan	3,220	74%	153%	9.0%	3,299	976	18%
Singapore	180	112	102	0.5	455	395	59
Australia	675	82	103	1.9	1,924	351	43
China Mainland	2,793	87	121	7.8	1,604	1,741	*
Hong Kong	468	226	82	1.3	1,017	460	35
United Kingdom	1,851	67	228	5.1	2,415	766	43
United States	11,737	87	232	32.8	5,603	2,094	18

Source: Standard & Poor's, *World Stock Markets Factbook*, 2009.

Note

* It is difficult to provide a reliable measure of concentration for the Chinese stock market. Shares in circulation are designated as floatable or non-floatable, and also as tradable or non-tradable. The Mainland Chinese market has a high proportion of non-tradable shares owned by government entities. Four types of tradable shares exist: A shares, B shares, H shares, and N shares, all described in Chapter 10. The floatable and non-floatable share distinction is a remnant of the planned economy in China. Non-floatable shares are worth less than floatable shares owing to lack of liquidity. According to Kam C. Chan (*China's Capital Markets*, Edward Elgar, 2007, pp. 26, 161), non-floatable shares are typically exchanged at their book value.

Economic Background

In the decades following World War II, Japan's economy was a world beater. High growth raised the country's per capita GDP from under one-fifth of the US level to near parity fifty years later. Japan became the second largest economy in the world and a dominant exporter of industrial products. Japan was portrayed as a model for successful development, but this economic miracle turned to malaise. In 1989 Japan's economy went into a deep recession, and a lost decade ensued (1989–99). By 2004 Japan's per capita GDP had fallen to 75 percent of the US level.

Japan's labor market also suffered, with unemployment rising from below 3 percent (1975–90) to over 5 percent (2003–05). Similarly, industrial production suffered.

Japan experienced economic stagnation in the two decades following 1989. How was it possible for a country that had enjoyed superior performance for so many decades suddenly to experience a prolonged stagnation? More important, how has this lost decade and continued slow growth affected Japan's financial system and stock market?

Malaise Theories

Explanations of Japan's economic malaise range across economics, culture, and politics. Three sets of theories tend to dominate: 1) bad politics, 2) unchanging culture, and 3) the zombie hypothesis. The so-called zombie hypothesis holds that Japan's banks issued bad credit to large firms, subsequently rolling over these loans at cheap interest rates that did not reflect business and financial risks. This made capital funds scarce in the more deserving sectors, and the overall economy suffered. A Federal Reserve Bank of Dallas report holds that Japan failed to allow a Schumpeterian process of "creative destruction" to operate. The Federal Reserve report also noted that Japan's new business startup rate was only one-third to one-half the level in the United States.[4]

As in other countries, banks in Japan are subject to government regulation. Also, banks reflect cultural factors that can be interpreted as drivers of economic change. Until 1995 Japan's large banks operated within tight groups referred to as *keiretsu*. These groups 1) included financial and industrial companies, 2) enjoyed share cross-holdings with one another, often accounting for one-fourth or more of outstanding shares, and 3) cooperated in formulating business plans and strategies. With the Japanese asset value collapse in 1989 and ensuing stock market downturn, Japanese banks were under severe pressure to restructure and reform. This resulted in a number of mergers of large banks, and a virtual dissolution of former *keiretsu* groups. Nevertheless, cultural and political factors continue to reign as control factors vis-à-vis Japanese banking.

The Economist has noted "Japan's amazing ability to disappoint."[5] In this analysis politicians are to be blamed for the failure of Japan's economy. However, the two-decade episode of economic failure appeared to be in the past after Junichiro Koizumi became prime minister in 2001. Koizumi forced banks and companies to clear up an overhang of bad debts. The economy resumed moderate growth. Koizumi declared war on special interest groups in Japan whose alliance with the long ruling Liberal Democratic Party (LDP) had stalemated economic reform. Koizumi's reforms and moderate success led many to believe that Japan was headed along a modern economic path, but with his departure from the political scene in 2006 economic problems appear to have intensified.

While Japanese companies appear to be much sounder than a decade ago, with lower debt and more focused operations, productivity is low. Also, in the Japanese system managers are scarcely accountable to shareholders. This cultural aspect relates to weak standards of corporate governance. Institutional investors around the world have pushed Japanese companies to improve their governance in several respects. First, many listed companies are operated as if management, not shareholders, are the owners. Second, companies have been allowed to hoard cash, adopt poison pills that entrench management, form cross-shareholder pacts, and issue shares to third parties at a huge discount, which dilutes shareholdings. Also, institutional investors have recommended that Japanese companies appoint independent directors, implement financial methods to raise shareholder value, and adopt globally recognized best practices.[6]

In partial response to these criticisms, the Tokyo Stock Exchange in May 2008 indicated it would draw up corporate takeover defense guidelines that would make it more difficult for Japanese companies to thwart unsolicited bids. The Council on Economic and Fiscal Policy chaired by prime minister Yasuo Fukuda requested the president of the TSE, Atsushi Saito, to consider adopting takeover defense guidelines for listed companies.

As noted, culture can negatively impact relationships between company managers and shareholders, but culture can play an even more internalized role in Japan's ability to modernize its business and financial system. Japanese workers have long been regarded as unwilling to criticize or challenge management. To a certain extent this is understandable. But as foreign managers and executives join Japanese companies they face a cultural divide, and must exert great effort to persuade staff to open up and express themselves more freely.

Cultural inhibitions make it difficult for Japanese staff to express their views directly. Carlos Ghosn, chief executive at Nissan, made one of his top priorities to bring issues into the open to better acknowledge and deal with Nissan's problems.[7]

Long Term Problems

Here we analyze issues facing Japan of a long term nature. These include: a) an aging population and provision of public pensions, b) the central government fiscal position and debt burden, and c) measures that could alleviate the problems in the future. Government stimulus programs "have generated huge structural budget deficits" rather than economic growth.[8] Japan's gross national debt in 2009 was 217 percent of GDP, compared with 81 percent for the United States and 76 percent for Germany (Table 9.4). This debt burden is expected to grow to a

Table 9.4 Government Debt as a Percentage of GDP: Japan Compared with Other Countries (2006–24)

					Projected	
Country	*2006*	*2007*	*2008*	*2009*	*2010*	*2024*
Japan	195	195	202	217	225	222
Germany	66	65	68	76	80	77
Italy	107	104	106	109	112	118
Brazil	64	68	65	65	63	54
United States	62	63	69	81	90	99
G20 countries	63	64	66	73	77	77

Source: J.R. Laing, "Is the Sun Setting on Japan?" *Barron's*, September 28, 2009, p. 26.

crushing level by 2024, as Japan's population becomes older and the number of working age Japanese shrinks. Some analysts suggest that Japan's government debt problems are highly exaggerated, given that, unlike the United States, which owes much money to foreign government holders of debt (China and Japan), much of Japan's government debt is owned by domestic financial institutions including the central government pension fund. Also, interest rates in Japan are very low, and the Japanese government pays about one-third of the interest paid by other governments on their debt (the USA, the UK, Australia, and Germany).

However, Japan's government debt is increasing owing to two fundamentals that should not be overlooked. First, the central government incurs annual deficits that are quite large compared with other nations. Second, the population is aging steadily, which in the long run means a declining population of working age. The latest United Nations data forecasts that Japan's population will fall from 127 million (2009) to 102 million (2050). This translates into a growing burden of government debt, to be supported by relatively fewer working persons. Projections indicate that between 1990 and 2050 the number of Japanese of working age per person aged 65 or above will decline from 10.0 (1990) to 1.2 (2050).[9] Recognizing this problem, the government in Japan is expanding its budget on family friendly programs such as day care services for working parents and parental leave from work.[10]

Central government budget deficits have been a regular happening since 1992, and increased through the 1990s. They reached a peak level of 8 percent of GDP in 2000, and remained at that level for five years. Since 2003 these deficits have been falling, and in 2009 were 4 percent of GDP, still a high and unsustainable level. They are unsustainable given that the deficit as a percentage of GDP far exceeds the economic growth rate. In 2008 the OECD recommended that Japan raise taxes, to reduce the deficit and prevent it from reaching levels that are unmanageable.[11]

Structural reforms could have altered Japan's economic trajectory in a favorable way, but did not occur. Vested interests in banking, agriculture, and heavy industry sit at the center of Japan's political malaise. Some critics go so far as to state that "the government has morphed from promoting [industrial] business to protecting losers."[12] Small and medium business enterprises could become a part of Japan's solution to the economic issues. SMEs represent over 99 percent of companies in Japan, and employ 70 percent of the work force. They account for half of manufacturing by value, and tend to specialize in electronics, precision engineering, and fine chemicals. As is the case in Germany's Mittelstand, many of these companies are family operated, and boast world class technology that supports the competitive position of the big firms they supply.

Densho is one of the more successful in Japan's Mittelstand. Densho was founded two decades ago, and was reportedly considering a public listing, not to raise funds but because a listing often is seen in Japan as a symbol of a firm's maturity.[13] There is a huge spectrum of small and medium firms in Japan like Densho. Some like Densho are prospering; others are being squeezed by the large firms they supply, and suffer low profit margins. In 2008 the government implemented measures to assist these firms, in the form of compensation for rising energy costs. Many of these small firms face the problems of management–ownership succession. Unfortunately, in Japan corporate governance rules and the stock market have not been flexible or responsive to facilitate mergers and restructuring that would allow the most efficient of these firms to expand and spur economic growth. Some believe that a change of government would bring needed reforms.[14]

Fortunately, the TSE is working to implement changes such as Tokyo AIM, a joint venture with the London Stock Exchange to build a second level listing and trading market for small company equities.

The Pension Pot

Michael Connors of Hermes, a leading British pension fund manager, has mockingly compared Japan's shareholder democracy to that of Zimbabwe. He finds corporate governance opaque, company ownership largely off limits to foreign investors, and the Japanese stock market undervalued with share prices below book value.[15] Foreign investors have called for change and in May 2008 the Council on Economic and Fiscal Policy, appointed by prime minister Yasuo Fukuda, put forward a set of proposals so bold that they represented a rebuke to the insularity of company managers. The proposed reforms would make it easier for foreign investors to take stakes in domestic firms, and would have the TSE implement new rules discouraging anti-takeover defenses, and restructure the nation's $1.44 trillion public pension scheme, the world's largest.

Previous efforts to reform the pension fund have been stopped by vested interests. This has resulted in poor investment performance, threatening the reliability of the pensions system into the future. Inadequate investment management has led to sub-optimal capital allocation. Large companies in Japan have been earning a low return on equities compared with North American and European firms.

Two-thirds of the government pension fund is invested in Japanese government bonds (JGBs), whose ten-year yield (midyear 2008) was a modest 1.6 percent. Overall returns of the fund are a low 3.5 percent annually, compared with

7 percent for public pension funds in Norway and Sweden, and 10 percent in Canada and France.[16]

Reform proposals published in May 2008 include:

1 Replace the officials who control state pension funds with professional investors, who could allocate funds to outside managers and monitor performance.
2 Allocate funds to a wider variety of assets, to boost returns and diversify risk.
3 Expand the range and proportion of funds invested beyond domestic, and beyond traditional bonds and equities. The current asset mix (Table 9.5) hampers performance.
4 Expand into alternative asset classes, such as real estate, commodities, and private equity.
5 Separate funds into a number of smaller baby funds, to enhance performance.

Reform of Japan's public pension fund has important implications for capital allocation and mobility, economic efficiency, and renewed development of the equities market. TSE could become one of the most affected beneficiaries of pension fund reform.[17]

Japan Post Bank

In 2007 Japan's government initiated the privatization of Post Bank, further crowding the banking sector. With assets that were in excess of 212.1 trillion yen, the Post Bank is a giant, operating close to 24,000 post office branches and employing 250,000 workers.[18] This is the world's largest financial institution, and accounts for one-quarter of all deposits in Japan.

Despite its size, Post Bank is not aggressive or profitable, investing heavily in low yielding government bonds. Traditionally, Japan Post has been a big lender to government. Japan Post sells investment trust shares, as an alternative to savers simply depositing money in low yielding deposit accounts. In the past Japan Post has earned up to 3 percent sales commission by selling investment trusts, and also another 50 or more basis points a year in fees. According to Fidelity Investments, a mutual fund rival of Japan Post locally, Japan Post is becoming a catalyst in moving new funds into more diversified investment products.

Table 9.5 Asset Allocation of Japan's Public Pension Fund (2008)

Domestic bonds	67%
Domestic equities	11
Foreign bonds	8
Foreign equities	14
	100%

Source: *Financial Times*, May 23, 2008, p. 25.

A member of the Upper House of Japan's government has questioned whether the Post Bank has a viable business model. Post Bank's funding is short term (deposits), while its investments (JGBs) are long term. This could lead to a worst case scenario where deposit withdrawals force Post Bank to sell government bonds in large volumes, depressing prices and leading to a liquidity confrontation.[19] Another concern is that, before full privatization and public listing of shares can take place, Post Bank must become profitable and fully privatized.

Post Bank needs to further diversify its assets. This requires diversification from JGBs into alternate assets and foreign securities. One proposal to accelerate this process would be to allow Post Bank to swap its JGB holdings for US Treasury securities held by Japan's government in foreign exchange reserves. Currently these reserves exceed US$1 trillion.

Political trends in Japan in 2009 turned somewhat against the privatization of Post Bank. With an economic slump, Japanese politicians became more sensitive to fears of rural voters facing losses in postal services and jobs. Second thoughts over privatization and reform of Post Bank were echoed in other countries. Postal financial institutions worldwide are attracting renewed interest as the global financial crisis reveals the "vulnerability" of commercial banks. Alternatively, many economists see a "finance trap," where channeling savings to the government (via Japan Post) reduces incentives to bring government deficit spending under control.[20] Postal banks in Switzerland, France, and Germany have witnessed sharp increases in deposits and the number of new accounts, according to Universal Postal Union, a United Nations affiliate institution based in Switzerland.

The Japanese government plan to privatize Post Bank, launched in 2006–07 under prime minister Junichiro Koizumi, calls for Japan Post to be broken up, and privatized in a decade-long process. Any change in the status of so large a holder of financial assets will exert important side-effects on the Japanese securities markets, and especially the stock market. We discuss this and the profile of financial asset holdings of individuals in the following section.

Financial Asset Ownership

The financial markets of Japan, as a mature industrial economy, contain a diversified range of institutions, market practices, and instruments. However, the ownership distribution of financial assets is specific to Japan. We already have observed that financial asset holdings are more concentrated in "safe" or liquid type assets. This is true of the government operated pension fund, which holds primarily low yielding JGBs. Also, it is characteristic of the Post Bank, which in the past has invested largely in government bonds, but in recent years has marketed investment trusts to households as a means of diversifying its asset base and generate fee income for itself.

In the following section we examine financial asset ownership of Japanese households. Again, we will observe a highly risk averse pattern, but with some limited movement away from the most safe and low yielding asset categories.

Financial Assets of Households

At yearend 2007 the financial assets of individuals in Japan were concentrated into three categories: currency and deposits, insurance and pension reserves, and securities (Table 9.6). This distribution reflects a highly risk averse set of choices, the first two categories affording holders a wide distance away from capital market volatility.

Over the period 2004–07 there were moderate shifts in these holdings, away from currency and deposits, toward securities. Holdings of shares increased moderately, but holdings of investment trusts nearly doubled. Investment trusts hold diversified portfolios of shares and bonds. If we consider investment trusts and share holdings as "moderately risky," taken together Japanese investors increased their holdings in this category from 8.0 percent (2.5 plus 5.5) to 10.6 percent (4.7 plus 5.9). More recent data on household asset holdings suggests further shifts in domestic asset holdings toward "moderately risky" categories.[21]

Share Ownership

Share ownership is fairly diversified in Japan. Financial institutions account for 31 percent of the total (Table 9.7). This is much lower than in the United States and United Kingdom, where institutions are dominant factors in the equity market. Foreign ownership of Japanese equities is quite close to institutional holdings, reflecting the lack of an equity focus among Japanese investors, whether individuals or institutions. Trust banks and investment trusts are the largest equity holders among institutions in Japan.

Business corporations play an important role as shareholders, accounting for over one-fifth of ownership. These corporate cross-shareholdings reflect past *keiretsu* affiliations among groups of companies. With the economic difficulties and reforms in the period 1990–2000, banks merged and *keiretsu* groupings tended to be altered and often to diminish.

Table 9.6 Holdings of Financial Assets of Individuals (Percentage of Total)

	2004	*2007*
1 Currency and deposits	55.3	50.8
Currency and cash	17.6	21.7
Time deposits	37.6	29.0
2 Insurance and pension		
Reserves	26.3	26.2
3 Securities	13.3	18.6
Shares	5.5	5.9
Investment trusts	2.5	4.7
Other securities	5.1	8.0
4 Other	5.0	4.5
	100.0	100.0

Source: Tokyo Stock Exchange, *FactBook*, 2008, p. 64.

Table 9.7 Share Ownership by Type of Investor, Yearend 2007 (Percentage of Total)

1 Financial institutions	31.1%
City and regional banks	4.6
Trust banks	17.9
Investment and annuity trusts	8.2
Life insurance	5.4
Non-life insurance	2.2
Other	1.0
2 Business organizations	20.7
3 Securities companies	1.8
4 Individuals	18.1
5 Foreign	28.0
6 Government	0.3
7 Total	100.0%

Source: Tokyo Stock Exchange, *FactBook*, 2008, p. 61.

Note: Overlap in financial institution categories results in higher numbers than the total indicated for financial institutions.

A significant part of the 28 percent foreign ownership reflects efforts by non-Japanese asset managers to gain exposure to the Japanese stock market via partially indexed portfolios. Indexed or passive management by investors in global equities has become an important and widely applied approach. Japan's stock market is the second largest in the world as measured by market capitalization. Therefore, asset managers would be remiss if they did not include a certain proportion of Japanese equities in their globally diversified equity funds.

Individual ownership reflects a widening number of Japanese becoming shareholders. Between 1960 and 2006 the number of Japanese individuals who were shareholders increased from 5 million to 40 million. This increase reflects an expansion in the activities of securities companies in Japan, and development of a broader-based equity culture in the country.

Tokyo Stock Exchange

Originally established in 1878, the TSE has functioned as the nation's central securities market, playing an important role in the growth and expansion of the economy. In 2007 the market capitalization value of shares listed exceeded $US4.7 trillion (589 trillion yen), representing 2,413 companies. The value of domestic company shares traded in 2007 was $US5.7 trillion (678 trillion yen).[22]

TSE provides a wide range of exchange services, including: trading equities, bonds, derivatives, and investment companies; data and information services; and clearing and settlement. TSE became a for-profit corporation in November 2001, and established a holding company group in 2007 under the title Tokyo Stock Exchange Group Inc.

Global Direction

According to Atsushi Saito, president and CEO of the Group, at present ten financial exchanges around the world are competing to become the leading global marketplaces. Three or four of these groups will emerge as winners in this process. The TSE intends to win in this competition and "secure its place as a core exchange of Asia."[23]

The TSE has identified several policy themes to promote its markets. First, TSE is strengthening system infrastructure. This includes a next generation trading system. Second, TSE is improving market reliability, strengthening its self-liquidity function. This requires comprehensive review of the trading system. Third, TSE is improving the diversity of its market products. As Asia's biggest market, TSE is working to establish a unique market for foreign stocks, focusing on promoting listing of foreign companies.[24]

In the period 2008–09 the Tokyo Stock Exchange appeared to be trailing behind other Asian exchanges in trading volume and new listings. It has delayed going public. Saito, in an interview, noted that there are things the TSE cannot do, such as lower corporate taxes and further ease the regulatory burden on investors.[25] According to Saito, other initiatives are needed, including an increase in the number of independent company directors, and more flexible operating hours to meet the needs of traders located in Asian financial centers outside Japan.

The TSE is revising its corporate structure, to strengthen independence and ensure the effectiveness of its self-regulatory function. Steps in this process include: 1) a holding company organization, and 2) a self-regulatory unit. With this new structure TSE is made up of three distinct components: a) a holding company subject to public shareholder governance standards, b) a trading company unit (TSE) that is operational across a range of markets and services, and c) a self-regulatory unit (Tokyo Stock Exchange Regulation) that operates with its own distinct governance structure.

Alliance Strategies

The Tokyo Stock Exchange has focused on developing and strengthening cooperation with exchanges abroad. This is closely related to the TSE's role as a core market in Asia. Since summer 2006 TSE has strengthened its alliance with the Korea Exchange, the Shanghai Exchange, the Shenzhen Stock Exchange, the Taiwan Stock Exchange, the National Stock Exchange of India, and the Singapore Exchange (SGX).[26]

Specific objectives of these alliances include promoting cross-border trading with Korea and Taiwan, holding joint investment seminars, and joint efforts to list ETFs based on the stock indices of each respective market.

Following a series of discussions between TSE and NYSE Euronext, these exchanges agreed (in January 2007) to form a strategic alliance. This alliance covers trading systems and technology, investor services, investment products, and governance regulation. As a result, NYSE Euronext provides the TSE Group with internal consultation concerning network management and operation, as well as exchange system capacity, performance, and operation. The two exchanges will cooperate in developing and listing new products, and will study market frameworks such as trading infrastructure in response to the expansion of off-exchange transactions (Table 9.8).

The TSE also has developed an alliance with the London Stock Exchange (LSE). The two exchanges signed a cooperation agreement in February 2007. Areas of cooperation include management and regulation of the markets for emerging companies, mutual listing of new products, and the enhancement of mutual access to both markets.

In June 2007 TSE acquired 4.99 percent of Singapore Exchange (SGX) shares. Prior to this, TSE and SGX had entered into a basic agreement to grant SGX access to trade derivatives products and ETF products based on TOPIX related indexes. TOPIX related products now are trading on SGX. Further cooperation between these two exchanges is planned in the derivatives markets. TSE has been promoting the overseas listing of TOPIX based ETFs on Euronext Paris, Borsa Italiana, Deutsche Börse, the Swiss Exchange, and LSE.

Tokyo AIM

In 2009 a joint venture of the Tokyo Stock Exchange and London Stock Exchange, Tokyo AIM, was launched. Based on the LSE's AIM market created fifteen years earlier, it is TSE's answer to skeptics who doubt the ability of Tokyo to adopt an innovative business style. TSE hopes to encourage more risk capital, and make Tokyo a more competitive financial center through foreign company listings.

Atsushi Saito, TSE chief executive, has observed that the list of names of top Japanese companies has not changed over the past several decades, unlike the case in Europe and North America, where the top company list is forever changing. LSE's participation in this venture reflects ambitions to participate fully in the Asian growth phenomenon.[27]

This is not Japan's first effort to create a "second market," but the approach is unique. According to Tetsutaro Muraki, chief executive of Tokyo AIM, the new

Table 9.8 Alliance Strategies of the TSE Group

1	NYSE Euronext	Agreement for strategic alliance and technical consultation.
2	Singapore Exchange	Cooperation agreement on derivatives and ETF products.
3	London Stock Exchange	Cooperation agreement to enhance international presence.
4	Shanghai and Shenzhen Stock Exchanges	Memorandum of understanding to initiate feasibility studies for business alliances.
5	Korean Exchange	Memorandum of understanding to develop market alliances.
6	Taiwan Stock Exchange	Memorandum of understanding to advance cooperation products.
7	Chicago Mercantile Exchange	Discussions on cooperation for JGB futures.

Source: Tokyo Stock Exchange Group, *Annual Report 2008*, pp. 13–14.

market targets subsidiaries of large cap companies, overseas companies, fund raising for project finance, and large unlisted companies that want to raise funds through preference shares. Muraki expects to develop this market at a slow pace, focusing on the quality of companies rather than immediate profitability.

Tokyo AIM is restricted to professionals and overseas investors. It is geared more to patient investors. Disclosure on Tokyo AIM can be in English, and the market allows use of international reporting standards to encourage overseas companies. The market is expected to attract companies with business operations or customers in Japan, and companies that see the large pool of capital in Japan as an attractive component.

Next Generation Trading

Tokyo Stock Exchange developed a plan for a next generation trading system in 2006. TSE chose a system provided by Fujitsu. The TSE ranks among the top three exchanges in trading volume, as well as diversity of products listed and traded. Around the world, exchanges are investing large sums in more flexible operating systems.

Each stock exchange enjoys or suffers from its own market specific determinants of turnover and trading intensity. We describe this interaction in Table 9.9. At the top of the table are cost and speed of execution factors. Trading volume and intensity expand as cost and effectiveness of trading improve. In recent years TSE has achieved considerable improvement in this area. In the three-year period 2005–08 TSE jumped ahead of London, Paris, and Frankfurt to become the second lowest cost equity trading center. This is based on Elkins/McSherry global universe data. Only the New York exchanges (NYSE and NASDAQ) indicate lower overall equity trading costs than TSE (Table 9.10).

This picture reverses when we examine factors related to demand for trading. These include information flow, openness to corporate restructuring, and frequency of corporate reporting and new initiatives. We can view the equity market as a trading process in which the frequency of trading becomes a function of information events that bombard the trading surface. Japan's equity market may be positioned far below many others when we count or measure frequency of

Table 9.9 Market Specific Determinants of Turnover and Trading Intensity

I Factors related to cost (supply) of trading
- A Trading fees and commissions
- B Bid–ask spread
- C Market impact cost
- D Speed of trade execution

II Factors related to demand for trading
- A Information flow
- B Openness to corporate restructuring activities
- C Frequency of corporate reporting and new initiatives

Table 9.10 Stock Trading Costs in Japan, Other Asian Centers, and New York

	Commissions	*Fees*	*Market impact*	*Total*
Japan	15.04	0.10	7.41	22.56
Singapore	19.88	2.64	11.19	33.69
Australia	25.29	0.82	34.42	60.53
China	18.92	9.30	17.06	45.28
Hong Kong	17.85	10.30	11.87	40.02
United States				
NYSE	9.86	0.07	4.89	14.82
NASDAQ	12.47	0.04	6.06	18.57

Source: Standard & Poor's, *Stock Exchange Factbook 2009*, pp. 346–347.

Note: Costs are stated in basis points.

events that cause more intensified trading. Until very recently, Japan discouraged corporate initiatives for restructuring, and other events that lead to arbitrage or related forms of trading activity.

A more hospitable environment for corporate "events" in Japan should elicit a higher level of trading. Possibly the next generation of trading will witness this.

In early January 2010 the Tokyo Stock Exchange launched its new trading platform, aimed at boosting trade volume. In part, the new trading system aims to accommodate high frequency trading, which accounts for an increasing proportion of volume on large exchanges such as NYSE Euronext, Deutsche Börse, and the London Stock Exchange. Trades on Tokyo's new Arrowhead trading platform will require only 5 milliseconds to complete. High frequency traders make large numbers of trades in very short bursts. They seek to profit from tiny differences between prices and trading speeds on various exchange platforms.

The Arrowhead system includes co-location facilities for brokers and other high speed traders. Co-location has become increasingly important for investors who want to beat rivals to best price and execution. The Tokyo exchange expects a sharp rise in trading volume as the faster Arrowhead system demonstrates its advantages and as investors take advantage of high speed services. There appears to be strong demand for co-location services. With the combination of the new Arrowhead platform, co-location services, and planned reduction in tick size, the TSE will be able to offer a more competitive service.[28]

With the new trading system, TSE still will be a bit behind other exchanges. For example, NASDAQ OMX trades require under 1 millisecond, LSE trades take 2.7 milliseconds, and NYSE Euronext requires 2–3 milliseconds. But the TSE also is introducing a co-location service, where trade systems are placed closely adjacent to the stock exchange's matching engine. This cuts the time required for executing trades, as the "electronic highway" over which order flow travels is reduced to a near zero length. All of TSE's co-location space has been taken up by market participants, but the exchange will provide additional spaces within a short time span. Introduction of Arrowhead and related technology improvements are expected to advance trading volumes and place the Tokyo Stock Exchange on a par with other leading exchanges.[29]

Singapore Exchange

In its 2007 annual report Singapore Exchange labels itself as "Your Asian Gateway." Geographically the city state is a small dot on the map of Asia, but its economic and financial footprint has expanded steadily and impressively. As a regional business and financial hub Singapore has become a major destination and gateway for regional and global investment. Similarly, the Singapore Exchange is growing at a fast pace, attracting international investors and company listings.

Singapore Exchange Limited was the first to demutualize in Asia proper. In late 1999 following the merger of the Stock Exchange of Singapore and the Singapore International Monetary Exchange (SIMEX), plans were developing for SGX to be the first exchange in the Asia Pacific region to be listed as a publicly owned company. In 2000 a public offering of shares took place, parallel with a private placement, therefore including the Exchange as a component of the MSCI Singapore benchmark and the Straits Times Index.

Organizational and technical milestones followed quickly. In 2002 the first local exchange traded fund, the Straits Times Index Fund, was listed. The following year, SGX's Quotation and Execution System for Trading (SGX QUEST), the world's first integrated trading engine for securities and derivatives, became operational. In 2005 SGX completed a partnership with the Chicago Board of Trade (CBOT) to establish the Joint Asian Derivatives Exchange (JADE), an electronic commodity derivatives market. Around this time the FTSE/ASEAN Indices were launched in partnership with the FTSE Group and other regional exchanges. Following this, SGX took a 5 percent stake in the Bombay Stock Exchange, and also launched SGX AsiaClear, the over the counter clearing facility for oil and freight derivatives.

In the following we provide further details, analyzing the SGX, its accomplishments, and its special role both regionally and around the globe.

Main Features of SGX

The SGX has enjoyed considerable success owing to several advantages it enjoys. These advantages relate to: 1) location in a viable and well-managed financial center, 2) provision of a broad range of services, 3) high level and quality of corporate governance, 4) favorable business growth, and 5) openness and outreach of Singapore overall. This fifth point is reflected by a large number of international listings, and many initiatives toward building alliances and partnership with other financial exchanges.

The SGX offers a diverse mix of securities and derivatives products to a global network of broking members. Securities products traded on the SGX electronic system include: bonds and debentures, equities, exchange traded funds, global depository receipts (GDRs), infrastructure funds, real estate investment trusts (REITs), and warrants. A wide range of derivatives products, traded electronically, include interest rate futures and options, equity index futures and options, and structured warrants. SGX provides a wide range of data and information services.

Partnerships and Alliances

SGX has achieved high growth in revenues. In fiscal year 2007 return on equity exceeded 37 percent, profit on tradable equity products advanced by 125 percent, revenue growth exceeded 41 percent, and the cost to income ratio was a low 36 percent. This robust performance can be attributed to excellence in governance and management, both discussed below. Further, SGX has maintained effective outreach, and implemented a flexible business plan.

SGX has maximized outreach via securing international listings and by emphasizing alliances with other exchanges. Over the past several years SGX has actively developed new alliances, as described in Table 9.11. These initiatives aim at achieving shared use of trading, clearing, and information systems, and therefore enhancing scalability. Also, these partnerships develop new products through which both partners can develop, diversify, and grow their respective businesses. Finally, these partnerships create cross-shareholdings, which in future provide opportunities that cannot be fully anticipated when the partnership is begun.

International Listings

Singapore is a regional fund management center enjoying flows of investment money managed by large institutions across Asia. This assists SGX in attracting foreign company listings. In fiscal year 2007 new foreign listings accounted for 70 percent of the total growth in listings.

Foreign based companies from over twenty countries are listed on SGX. Over one-third of all companies listed on SGX are from overseas, making SGX a truly international exchange and listing hub. The SGX effort to diversify is bearing fruit as more non-regional companies from Australia, Europe, Malaysia, and the United States undertake an SGX listing.

Early in 2010 it was reported that several large multinational companies based in Europe and North America were considering listing on SGX. The UK insurer Prudential was a prominent member of this group. One rationale for such cross-

Table 9.11 SGX Alliances and Partnerships

1 October 2006	Renewed mutual offset system agreement with Chicago Mercantile Exchange.
2 November 2006	Signed memorandum of understanding with Korea Exchange.
3 December 2006	Closer collaboration with Tokyo Stock Exchange.
4 January 2007	Signed agreement with OMX to develop new data feed system.
5 January 2007	Signed memorandum of understanding with Abu Dhabi Securities Market.
6 February 2007	Signed memorandum of understanding with Ho Chi Minh City Securities Trading Center.
7 March 2007	Agreement to invest in a 5 percent stake in Bombay Stock Exchange.
8 April 2007	Signed memorandum of understanding with Hanoi Securities Trading Center.
9 June 2007	Tokyo Stock Exchange acquired a 4.99 percent stake in SGX.

Source: Singapore Exchange Limited, *Annual Report 2007*, pp. 4–5.

listing is to be included in a to-be-created pan-Asian index. Prudential books one-third of its global sales in Asia, and is listed in Hong Kong as well as London. GIC, the Singapore based sovereign wealth fund, is understood to have a strong interest in enlarging its stake in insurances such as Prudential.[30]

SGX is one of only a half-dozen exchanges around the world that account for the bulk of cross-listings. Its main rivals in this regard include the NYSE, LSE, Luxembourg Exchange, and Swiss Exchange.

Rank—Divide by Three

The Singapore Exchange seems determined to punch above its weight. Chairman of the exchange J.Y. Pilling, at midyear 2008, stated that his exchange was prepared for the widest range of possible unknowns. More than most other exchanges, SGX must consider carefully how to stay in the game, as exchanges battle for trading liquidity. SGX is relatively small in size, and its global ranking as measured by market capitalization is a low 22, below Taiwan, South Korea, and Bombay (Table 9.12).[31]

Nevertheless, SGX has demonstrated an ability to punch over its weight. It is the sole exchange whose initial public offerings come largely from outside the home market. Half its revenues come from trading financial instruments it developed on its own market. SGX has pursued a program of continuous innovation in products and services. SGX has collaborated with SingTel, the local telecoms provider, to launch an ultra-fast electronic trading system.

Singapore is building on the 143 Mainland Chinese companies already listed on SGX, and in 2008 opened a representative office in Beijing to attract further listings and other businesses. These initiatives suggest SGX's ranking might be more correctly depicted if we divide its ranking in Table 9.12 by three.

New Initiatives

SGX is a leader among exchanges in launching new products and innovative services. Here we focus on two such initiatives: AsiaClear and Catalist. AsiaClear

Table 9.12 Largest Stock Exchanges by Domestic Company Capitalization, Midyear 2008

Exchange rank	*Exchange*	*Market capitalization*
1	NYSE	$14.6
2	Tokyo Stock Exchange	4.2
3	Euronext	3.9
4	LSE	3.5
5	NASDAQ	3.3
6	Shanghai	2.8
8	Deutsche Börse	1.9
22	Singapore Exchange	0.5

Source: J. Grant and S. Tucker, "SGX Is Determined to Punch Above Its Weight," *Financial Times*, June 12, 2008, p. 14.

Note: Amounts in trillions of US dollars.

is a clearing house for over the counter trades in oil and freight derivatives. The expansion in use of OTC derivatives for major commodities indicates that SGX is on the mark in responding to provide financial services offering high value and added types of hedging instruments. The benefits take the form of greater commercial opportunities, as well as a larger range of market sectors in which to trade and practice risk management.

With the onset of a global financial crisis in 2008–09, clearing of OTC traded instruments has become a major issue. At midyear 2009 SGX and OMX announced the signing of an agreement to implement a new clearing system using OMX technology. The clearing technology enhances derivatives and securities clearing. The open interface feature of the system will enable straight-through processing and boost the operational efficiency of SGX. The partnership with OMX includes the QUEST-DT engine, a new data feed system launched in early 2008, and the new securities trading engine QUEST-ST.

SGX has indicated an interest in clearing other OTC derivatives, such as options on indices, Asian currencies, and interest rate swaps. In connection with this, SGX was working in mid-2009 to link up with a commodities trading platform, which would allow SGX members to trade commodity futures products, with clearing provided by SGX.[32]

Magnus Böcker, SGX chief executive, noted early in 2010 that creation of clearing links for commodities with exchanges in Asia and beyond would make SGX a "global gateway" for trading equities, commodities, and derivatives on a variety of platforms.[33] SGX is expanding rapidly in OTC commodities, with more than 98,000 contracts cleared in 2009 compared with barely 1,000 in 2006. Böcker stated that SGX would probably seek to establish a range of different agreements with exchanges and clearing parties that could include areas such as London, New York, and Hong Kong. In late 2010 SGX launched Asia's first central clearing platform for over the counter financial derivatives. SGX noted it would offer central clearing in US and Singapore dollar interest rate swaps, with other products added later.

These initiatives by SGX come at a time when competition is heating up in Asia for derivatives and commodities trading and clearing. The recently created Singapore Mercantile Exchange (SMX) in second half 2010 introduced new futures contracts in gold, crude oil, and the euro exchange rate vis-à-vis the US dollar. Also, it plans to introduce currency futures contracts covering the Australian dollar and Japanese yen. Meanwhile, Singapore Exchange Ltd revealed its plans to introduce futures contracts for base metals, as part of an agreement with the London Metal Exchange (LME).[34]

The above outlines a "first phase" set of product launches related to the growing appetite in Asia for commodity trading and hedging. This will be followed by multiple product launches by SMX and others (CME, LME). Traders tend to choose the most liquid platform for their activities. This tends to place new exchanges like SMX at a possible disadvantage. One advantage enjoyed by SMX is its ability to settle contracts locally, or in Asia, rather than at a more remote location in North America (CME).[35]

Catalist is the successor of SESDAQ, which was established in 1987 as the Stock Exchange of Singapore Dealing and Automated Quotations. The purpose is to meet the fund raising needs of SMEs. In 2007 SESDAQ was replaced by Catalist, at which time there were 160 companies listed on SESDAQ. With market capitalization of 10 billion Singapore dollars, Catalist is the first sponsor supervised listing platform in Asia. Sponsors include qualified professional companies that are experienced in corporate finance and compliance advisory work. They determine the eligibility of a company to list on Catalist. Sponsors supervise listed company compliance. In turn, sponsors are authorized and regulated by SGX through strict admission and continuing obligation rules.

Collins Stewart, a UK investment bank, opened a Singapore office in January 2008 to take advantage of opportunities available through Catalist. Catalist is the Asian rival to LSE's Alternative Investment Market. Collins Stewart intends to strengthen its international business in high growth economies, conducting services in Singapore on the Catalist platform, as it does on London's AIM market.[36]

Unlike NASDAQ, but like AIM, Catalist will require companies to have an adviser, a bank or accounting firm that carries much of the policing and regulatory responsibility. This differs from the traditional exchange supervised market, where the exchange reviews IPO documents and approves the listing of the company. Also, the supervisory role for companies on Catalist is undertaken by sponsors, who must be formally authorized and regulated by SGX. Several issues arise in the case of sponsor authorized admission to exchange trading. First, the regulation of sponsors becomes a critical factor. Will sponsors impose necessary and adequate procedures to regulate Catalist listed companies? Second, is it possible for sponsors to manipulate the market and encourage rent-seeking behavior? How is conflict of interest within sponsors avoided? Finally, the credibility of a sponsor supervised market is unclear. The companies listed in Catalist are directly supervised by sponsors rather than exchanges. The past success of London's AIM suggests strongly that proper adherence to rules of enforcement and supervision by sponsors can yield very good outcomes. London investment banks have placed their reputations on the line as sponsors in the AIM market. A parallel success seems possible on SGX.

Governance and Ownership

The past two decades have witnessed an upheaval in ownership and governance of financial exchanges. SGX has participated fully in this dual transformation of exchanges. Ownership and governance follow a new paradigm. The following sections analyze this in detail.

Governance

Annual reports issued by the SGX are reminiscent of reports issued by UK listed companies. A great part of the material in the report is focused on governance and the board of directors. For example, in the 2007 report of SGX, the central part (pages 16–21) contains a description of the board of directors' membership and their affiliations. Details abound concerning the makeup of committees, a summary directors' report, and directors' interests in shares and share plans.

The SGX board consists mainly of independent directors. Of the twelve directors, only one is not an independent director, the chief executive of SGX. The audit, nominating, and remuneration committees contain only independent directors. Corporate governance in SGX appears to conform closely to Cadbury Code principles.

The summary directors' report (pp. 22–30) informs us that the "principal activities of the Company are those of investment holding, treasury management, provision of management and administrative services to listed corporations, provision of securities related processing services and sale of software, and other corporation services."[37] Subsidiaries of the holding company include operating securities and derivatives exchanges, providing clearing and related services, providing computer services, providing corporate share registration and trading related services, and providing facilities for the registration of options, and maintenance margin for options. A seven-page section describes arrangements that enable directors to acquire shares, director interests in shares or debentures, and actual share plans.

Ownership of SGX Shares

In 2007 the share capital of Singapore Exchange Limited (the company) consisted of 1.81 billion shares. At August 2007, 99.62 percent of issued ordinary shares were held by the public. The ownership distribution of SGX shares is fairly concentrated. Over 82 percent are in holdings of 1 million or more shares, and another 9.8 percent are in holdings of 10,000 to 1 million shares.

SGX identifies the twenty largest shareholders in its annual report. In 2007 these were seven securities firms, six nominees, five individuals, one bank, and one institutional investor. The largest eight are identified in Table 9.13. In 2007 the top twenty owners accounted for over 86 percent of outstanding shares, or 919.4 million shares.[38]

Table 9.13 Eight Largest Shareholders in SGX Group

Rank	*Shareholder*	*No. of shares*	*Percentage*
1	SEL Holdings Pte Ltd	241,991	23.53%
2	DBS Nominees Pte Ltd	183,822	17.31
3	Citibank Nominees Singapore Pte	119,807	11.28
4	HSBC (Singapore) Nominees Pte Ltd	81,067	7.63
5	Raffles Nominees Pte Ltd	76,811	7.23
6	DB Nominees Pte Ltd	66,126	6.23
7	DBSN Services Pte Ltd	63,888	6.01
8	Morgan Stanley Securities Pte Ltd	23,127	2.18

Source: SGX Group, *Annual Report 2007*, p. 48.

Revenue Mix

Innovation Diversifies Revenues

SGX enjoys a diversified income base. We can analyze this from the perspective of the many new initiatives launched in recent years, as well as from the pivotal location of Singapore as a national crossroads of Southeast and greater Asia.

For example, in 2006 new trading products on SGX trading platforms included a China "A share" index futures contract. Later in that year SGX AsiaClear introduced clearing of over the counter balance of month fuel oil swaps. Also in 2006 SGX launched the world's first ASEAN exchange traded fund, the FTSE/ASEAN 40 ETF. In 2007 SGX listed the first global depository receipts, Uttam Galva Steels Ltd.

To enhance its competitive position, SGX has lowered securities transaction costs, also increasing its market liquidity. In this connection, SGX signed an agreement with OMX in January 2007 to develop a new data feed system.

Revenue Mix of SGX

The revenue mix of SGX is one of the most diversified of the leading financial exchanges. This is due to: 1) the broad base of trading including derivatives and equities, 2) the growing role of Singapore as a post-trade processing hub, 3) the status of Singapore as a trading and transshipment center for commodities, and 4) managerial innovation leading to the continuing growth in new products and listings.

In Table 9.14, we analyze the revenue mix of SGX. It is clear from the table that Singapore Exchange's ability to attract an ever widening base of participant trading gives the exchange a pivotal role for securities clearing, which accounted for 38 percent of revenues in 2007. This is the largest component of revenues. Second in importance are revenues from derivatives clearings. Singapore's role as a risk management center explains the importance of this revenue source. SGX has

Table 9.14 Revenue Mix of SGX Group (2007)

Securities clearing fees	38.3%
Securities related processing fees	8.3
Access fees	10.2
Net derivatives clearing revenues	20.3
Account maintenance and corporate action fees	6.1
Terminal and connection fees	3.0
Listing fees	5.4
Membership fees	1.2
Price information fees	4.0
Sale of software and other computer services	1.7
Other	1.5
	100.0%

Source: Singapore Exchange Limited, *Annual Report 2007*, p. 34.

developed a diversified range of index futures and options, required for portfolio hedging and related purposes.

Five of the ten specified revenue sources in Table 9.14 account for 6 percent or less of total revenues. This includes services such as price information fees, listing fees, sale of software, membership fees, and terminal and connection fees. The broadly diversified revenues reinforce SGX's assertion that it is a truly international exchange.

Australian Stock Exchange

At present Australia enjoys one of the world's most innovative and successful financial sectors. The Australian Stock Exchange has benefited from sweeping financial reforms, and the domestic economy has enjoyed rising profit and growth. In this section we analyze the favorable financial environment, describe the factors underpinning expansion of Australia's saving-investment pool, and describe the development of the stock market.

Favorable Environment

Australia traditionally has been described as a commodity based economy, given its huge land area and natural resources, and relatively small population of 20 million. Australia more than holds its own in global financial services. With the world focus shifting progressively more toward the Asia Pacific region in the twenty-first century, Australia and its financial sector are well positioned to enjoy increasing global importance.

Australia, which ranks eleventh in level of national GDP, domiciles the world's fourth largest pool of savings. This is due in part to a compulsory employee retirement savings system given the distinct name of "superannuation scheme." The country recently passed the 1 trillion Australian dollar mark in contestable assets that fund managers compete to manage. Official estimates indicate this amount will grow to A$2.5 trillion by 2015.

Australia's pension funds increasingly look to invest overseas, as reflected by diversification of portfolios into other country capital markets. The domestic stock market necessarily offers a limited investment pool, and fund managers indicate they plan to increase their exposure to large emerging economies such as China and India. In the banking sector the big four Australian banks regularly rank among the world's best creators of shareholder value. They have benefited from consistent economic growth at home and limited competition. In recent years the dramatic success of investment firms such as Macquarie Bank and others places Australia on the map of worldwide interest. Macquarie has enjoyed huge success in establishing and managing infrastructure funds, and in 2005 made a bid to acquire the London Stock Exchange.

The country has enjoyed success in attracting global and regional companies to base their back office operations, with UBS, Fidelity, and others locating global information technology support and sales and marketing in Australia. In this regard, Australia has overtaken Singapore and Hong Kong in number of employees working in financial services.

The insurance and hedge fund sectors also are operating competitive and expanding businesses. In 2006 Australia was host to hedge funds whose assets exceeded those of all other such institutions across Asia. Private banking in Australia is supported by the large number of high net worth individuals, exceeding the number in Singapore and Hong Kong combined.[39]

Despite these successes, Australia faces challenges in further developing its financial sector and stock market. Regional rivals such as Hong Kong enjoy lower taxation. Also, Australia geographically lies in a more remote part of the globe, distancing it from countries that otherwise constitute favorable complements to its ascending financial markets.

Saving-Investment Pool

As noted above, Australia enjoys the fourth largest pool of investment funds, aggregating A$10 trillion. In Asia, Japan's pool is only two-thirds the size, while its economy is six times as large.[40] The driving force behind the growth of Australia's fund management sector is the compulsory pension, or superannuation scheme.

The decision by the Hawke–Keating Labor government in the 1980s to introduce a compulsory national pension savings system proved to be one of the most visionary reforms. It has given Australia a retirement system that is the envy of many developed countries. It has fostered the creation of a larger and more internationally competitive domestic investment industry than a population of 20 million could otherwise support. When the scheme began in the mid-1980s, only 40 percent of Australians had pension plans. Today 90 percent of Australians enjoy pension savings. Further, the country enjoys a higher ratio of pension fund assets to gross domestic product as compared with other OECD countries.

The compulsory scheme was extended to all employees in 1992 when Paul Keating introduced a set of revisions. The 3 percent minimum payment was lifted gradually to 9 percent in 2002. Employees now can make their choice of the fund into which contributions are paid.

The legislated growth built into the private pension sector has attracted the world's largest private pension managers, including AXA, UBS, Deutsche Bank, ING, and Barclays. Also, it has fostered a large support industry, made up of asset consultants, ratings agencies, research firms, personal financial planners, and asset custodians. Local banks have bulked up, to service growing needs in asset management and related back office servicing. Many banks have recast their image as wealth managers. Success creates problems, and these include a rising competition for skilled personnel, including fund managers and analysts.

In 2005 the introduction of Super-Choice, the right of employees to choose the fund into which their compulsory pension is paid, placed corporate and pension funds at a severe disadvantage. The compulsory savings system utilizes a three tiered structure, in which manufacturing, administration, and distribution of investment products are increasingly operated by different specialist providers.

With this, a high level of sophistication spawns product diversification and a range of boutique fund managers. Growth fuels diversification, and diversification begets increased use of offshore assets. Beneficiaries of diversification include the large listed property trust management, and pioneers in specialized infrastructure funds like Macquarie and Babcock & Brown.

Stock Market

In July 2006 the Australian Stock Exchange (ASX) completed its A$2.3 billion takeover of the Sydney Futures Exchange (SFE). This merger created the world's ninth largest bourse, taking the exchange into the twenty-first century model combining equity and derivatives trading.[41] ASX was the first exchange to demutualize and list itself, in 1998. The merged ASX/SFE combines the fast-growing derivatives market with the stock exchange's profitable franchise. Over the past five years gross profits have grown at a compound rate of 18 percent annually.

According to Maurice Newman, chairman of the ASX at the time of the merger, the merged entity possesses both scale and a broad based product range. Since merger, ASX has unveiled changes in its pricing structure. The net results of pricing changes make the exchange one of the lowest cost providers in the world. A Citigroup analyst holds that ASX is cheaper than Hong Kong and Singapore in most of its big ticket trades. By contrast, some large institutional investors see the new price structure adding to fees. As can be observed in Table 9.10, Australia is highly competitive on the fee component of overall trading costs, but less so in market impact costs.

Future prospects can be considered favorable for ASX. The superannuation fund, forecast to reach A$2.5 trillion by 2015, provides an almost unending flow of liquidity into the Australian capital markets. While the Australian market is worth a mere 2 percent of global financial markets, its importance far exceeds that number.

Also, Australia possesses Asia's most active mergers and acquisitions markets. In 2005 there were a record 227 initial public offerings on the ASX, worth around A$23 billion, while secondary listings raised A$28.3 billion (Table 9.15). M&A announcements exceeded US$100 billion in 2004–05. In the first eight months of 2006 M&A announcements exceeded US$80 billion. The Australian Stock Exchange has a large number of listed companies, reflecting a vibrant business formation and entrepreneurial sector. Over the period 1999–2008 the number of listed companies increased from 1,217 to 1,974 (Table 9.16).

Table 9.15 Australian Stock Market Activity in Peak Years (2005–06)

1 No. of initial public offerings	227
2 IPO funds raised	A$23 billion
3 Secondary equity offerings	A$28.3 billion
4 Annual inflow of funds to superannuation schemes	A$35 billion

Source: *Financial Times*, Australia Finance Supplement, September 6, 2006, pp. 1–3.

Table 9.16 Australian Stock Exchange Development (1999–2008)

		1999	*2005*	*2006*	*2007*	*2008*
1	No. of listed companies	1,217	1,643	1,751	1,973	1,974
2	Market capitalization	427	804	1,095	1,298	675
3	Trading value	194	616	826	1,322	1,013
4	Turnover ratio	51.4	78.0	84.3	109.0	102.7
5	GDP		406	674	724	820

Source: Standard & Poor's, *Stock Exchange Factbook 2009*, p. 93.

Note: Amounts on lines 2, 3, and 5 in billions of US dollars.

Early Rivalry

The Australian Stock Exchange dates back to 1861 with the creation of stock exchanges based in six of the regional states (Sydney, Melbourne, Adelaide, Brisbane, Hobart, and Perth). Melbourne and Sydney gained leadership in securities market activities, with the largest stock exchanges. In 1937 the six regional exchanges organized an industry association, the Australian Associated Stock Exchanges. More uniform listing standards, brokerage rules, and commission rates were introduced.

Melbourne evolved into the dominant center and stock exchange in the period surrounding World War II. Sydney's highly conservative views on business allowed Melbourne to retain its lead in underwriting and share trading. In 1953 an oil discovery by a company listed and traded on the Sydney Stock Exchange led to surging prices and turnover. High turnover caused delays on the stock exchange, and the morning call and afternoon call were extended. This heralded the end of the call system.

Following extended call hours, oil stocks were transferred to a new "trading post," open for continuous trading. In 1954 all shares were shifted to the apparently more efficient trading posts for specialist handling. The Melbourne Stock Exchange shifted to this trading post system in 1961.

The 1960s and 1970s enjoyed a domestic oil and minerals boom, which lifted trading on the Sydney Stock Exchange above that of the Melbourne market. Over the period 1974–77 the Sydney and Melbourne Stock Exchanges developed and implemented a plan to cooperate closely and to align their trading systems. In 1976 the Sydney Stock Exchange launched the Australian Options Market, with the Options Clearing House established as a subsidiary of the exchange. In 1985 the Melbourne Stock Exchange launched the Australian Financial Futures Market.[42]

Sydney's Lead—Formation of ASX

By the 1980s the Sydney Stock Exchange enjoyed several advantages over its rival in Melbourne:

1 computerized broker-to-broker trading;
2 a strong research capability, providing data useful to investors and brokers;
3 a lead in introducing computerized trading.

With computerized trading unifying equity markets in the six regional exchanges, and a national clearing and settlement system in place, the next logical step was to combine administration of the exchanges into a single and more efficient operation. In 1987 all of the exchanges came together to form the Australian Stock Exchange (ASX), which would use the all-electronic trading platform SEATS (Stock Exchange Automated Trading System). The ASX was demutualized in October 1998, and listing of its shares followed, with 606 individual and corporate shareholders each allocated 166,000 shares (Table 9.17).

First-day trading of ASX shares valued them at A$4.25.[43] Each membership had a value of A$705,500, and the aggregate value of the ASX was A$427,533,000 (Table 9.17). Eight years later ASX shares were valued at A$32.58, giving ASX an aggregate value of A$3,297 million.

The Australian Stock Exchange was a profitable company, and fast growing. It has enjoyed a high level of new listings and initial public offerings. New product listings and trading platforms facilitate high growth. In 2006 ASX launched a new trading platform, Click XT. Developed by the OMX, this platform integrates trading of equities and derivatives.

Merger with Sydney Futures Exchange

Futures trading in Australia has had a slow and difficult start. In the nineteenth century commodity futures (wool) experienced a difficult beginning.[44] Not until the 1970s was futures trading extended to gold and short term interest rates.

At yearend 1986 the Sydney Futures Exchange was the tenth largest futures exchange globally. During the 1980s high growth in derivatives trading strained the capacity of floor trading. A shift to electronic trading was accompanied by SFE becoming a shareholder owned entity. In the period 2004–06 rumors grew of a possible merger between the Sydney Futures Exchange and ASX. Those opposed to the merger claimed that the monopoly power of the combined entity would be excessive. Those favoring the merger noted that the global competition was grow-

Table 9.17 Initial Valuation of ASX Compared with Valuation Eight Years Later

	October 1998	*June 2006*
Number of members	606	606
Shares per member	166,000	166,000
Price per share	A$4.25	A$32.58
Total valuation of exchange	427,533,000	3,297,417,680
Value per holding	A$705,500	A$5,408,280

Source: Jim Bain, *A Financial Tale of Two Cities*, University of New South Wales Press, 2007, pp. 102–103.

Note: Values in Australian dollars.

ing rapidly and that a combined entity would be necessary if Australia was to retain its own financial exchange. The merger proposal gained wider acceptance as it became clear that the dynamic factors of a global nature in technology, regulation, and securities innovations were causing an accelerated upheaval in the competitive balance. In 2006 the merger of SFE and ASX went forward.

Benefits perceived from the merger include those accruing to shareholders of both exchanges. Specific benefits to ASX and SFE shareholders allow participation in a larger entity, achieving a critical mass on which to expand equity and other business, better positioning for the combined group to participate in global and regional exchange consolidation, access to synergies, combination of two complementary businesses with minimal product duplication, a better platform for product innovation, and the ability to continue a favorable dividend paying policy.

Existing ASX shareholders gain entry into the interest rate derivatives market and a new revenue stream; they access a team of proven leaders in derivatives exchange management, and the expectation of continued positive earnings performance. Existing SFE shareholders gain a strong premium price to recent share price performance, favorable earnings performance, an increased dividend payout ratio, and scale entry into the cash equities business.

The merger of these two exchanges further attests to the trend of consolidation as a key to survival for exchanges. Synergies and other benefits appear to make the SFE and ASX an attractive match.

Eighth Rank in the World

In 2009 the Australian Stock Exchange was the eighth largest exchange in the world, listing over 2 percent of equity market capitalization and over 1,900 companies. ASX operates from 10 a.m. to 4 p.m. Australian Standard Time, with a pre-market session in the three hours prior to regular opening. Daily trading has a value of A$1.1 trillion.

Worldwide recession in 2008–09 required the ASX to introduce several changes in trading to increase investor confidence and enhance services. In 2008, short selling was halted. Nevertheless, investors have access to numerous alternative hedging mechanisms in the highly developed derivatives trading on the futures and options markets.

In 2008 the ASX established the AQUA trading platform for investment products and managed funds. This market provides access to financial products that do not fit neatly into the main ASX equity listing rules. The AQUA market essentially can be considered a derivative market where the value of a product is tied to the price of an underlying asset. A similar market exists in the London Stock Exchange for exchange traded funds. However, AQUA possesses several of its own unique features. AQUA is divided into a trading market and a quotation market. The AQUA trading market facilitates buying and selling products listed on AQUA, which is consistent with other existing markets. The AQUA quotation market offers an innovative feature to traders, providing a price discovery option for off market trading. An issuer can post an action price that can be viewed by all other market participants. If a market participant wants to trade at this action price, then that participant can contact the issuer directly and the trade is completed.

All products traded on AQUA are required to have a daily redemption facility and transparent pricing for the underlying asset. AQUA also allows a platform for foreign products to be listed. The AQUA facility is expected to increase the liquidity of managed funds and off market trades.

10 Hong Kong–Shanghai Nexus

In this chapter we make a bold assertion—that the Hong Kong–Shanghai nexus is under control. But what is this nexus, and how can one reasonably expect two such disparate financial systems and their respective stock markets to blend together?

To answer these questions we provide a brief outline of the Mainland financial system, and discuss goals and means to accomplish such goals in a formerly communist economic system in transition. We consider how a "one nation, two systems" philosophy of economic management may pose serious challenges and obstacles.

Following this, we describe in more detail how the Hong Kong stock market has developed. We turn to the Mainland stock market and compare the two financial systems and stock markets. There exist vast differences between the Hong Kong and Mainland stock markets, in terms of their purposes, and their role in servicing geographic regions, and in many other respects.

Finally, this chapter takes a brief look ahead. We raise questions concerning which countries and exchanges are likely to become predominant in commodities trading in the region?

Controlled Transition

This section describes and analyzes probably the most complicated and difficult to understand financial exchanges covered in this book. The complexity and difficulty stem from the following. First, developing a financial market system in a formerly communist based economy poses unusual challenges and questions. Adding a formerly ultra-free market city state financial system (Hong Kong) to the broad national financial complex is tantamount to mixing oil and water. Any future melding together of two such disparate systems is likely to be accompanied by numerous bumps and setbacks. To China's credit, a cautious approach has produced only a few reasonably controlled bumps and setbacks.

Nexus Under Control

"Nexus" is defined in *Webster's* as "the link" or, alternately, "a connected series." Our use of the term in this discussion is to focus attention on the efforts of China's leaders to bring about a successful development and integration of the Hong Kong and Mainland financial systems. But how do we measure success? Do we use People's Republic stated objectives, and measure the degree to which these have been attained? Or do we utilize more general criteria followed around the globe?

As we describe in this chapter, Mainland financial markets and institutions are evolving, growing as rapidly as the fast-paced real economy of China. Most especially, the stock market has gained in market capitalization and trading volume at a pace not easily matched in other emerging market countries. At the same time, Hong Kong markets are evolving in a more sophisticated and advanced way. Hong Kong can be considered the third ranking world financial center. Only two financial centers hold advantages, New York and London.

Given that Mainland financial markets and institutions are developing at a favorable pace, while Hong Kong has attained third rank among world financial centers, it would appear that the nexus is succeeding. Moreover, the penultimate test, a blending of the two systems, remains an open question. We can state honestly that the nexus is developing. It is under control.

To put it simply, Hong Kong and Mainland financial markets are moving in tandem, although the evolution is very slow. But what other outcome could prevail?

While the nexus, or blending, remains under control, we must raise certain questions regarding organization, structure, and operation of the Hong Kong and Mainland financial markets. These questions are addressed in the following sections.

Brief Outline of Mainland Financial System

China's capital market has developed in an impressive way since the opening of the Shanghai Stock Exchange in 1990. Nevertheless, the capital market continues to be a bank oriented system. Bank credit plays a lead role in capital allocation in China. The opposite is true in the United States, where stock and bond issuance exceeds bank credit.

Until 2005 Chinese investors put their money primarily in bank deposits, but since that year these investors have demonstrated greater interest in the stock market. This shift in saving and investment patterns drove up share valuations, causing the government to take measures to cool off the stock market. Reforms are needed to improve transparency and ensure a more steady flow of liquidity between stock market and bank deposit channels.

Stock Exchanges

The Shanghai and Shenzhen Stock Exchanges are the major equity markets in China. At yearend 2007 over 1,400 companies were listed on the two exchanges. Both A shares and B shares are listed and traded on China's stock exchanges. Domestic investors trade Chinese company A shares in local currency. B shares are issued by Chinese companies to foreign investors or to Chinese investors who have foreign currencies, Hong Kong or US dollars. Some companies issue both A shares and B shares, but must satisfy the exchanges' listing standards. H shares are issued by Chinese companies, traded on the Hong Kong Stock Exchange, and in conformity with that exchange's listing requirements. H shares are traded in Hong Kong dollars. Finally, N shares are listed and traded on the US stock exchanges (NYSE and NASDAQ).

Initially the Chinese government created the A and B share markets to achieve better control of the flow of money. This organization of the stock market allows foreign investors to participate in the stock market, largely segmented from the capital market via currency controls. In this way an artificial segmentation of the stock market is accomplished. The government relaxed restrictions on domestic investors in 2001, permitting them to participate in the B share market. At yearend 2002 China launched the qualified foreign institutional investor (QFII) program, which allows foreign institutional investors to invest in the A share market. This program has been expanded in the amounts of funds QFIIs can invest in Chinese shares. Custodian banks play a central role in this program. Custodian banks must possess a fund custody department, have paid-in capital of RMB8 billion, have the ability to manage financial assets in a professional manner, be qualified to conduct foreign exchange transactions, and have a clean record of market operations over the previous three-year period.[1] Close to three dozen foreign financial institutions operate QFII programs in China, each investing in sectors (energy, machines and equipment, food and beverages) in which they require portfolio exposure.

In 2000 a proposal by the government to establish a Growth Enterprise Board (GEB) was put forward. This second market was visualized as operating somewhat like the US NASDAQ over the counter market. This would facilitate growth and high tech company financing. However, not until four years later was real progress made in initiating a second market when the China Securities Regulatory Commission (CSRC) issued an implementation proposal with the Shenzhen Stock Exchange serving as the operating center for this market. Within a year fifty companies had been approved to go public and floated on the second board. In 2003 China established a new equity exchange, the China Technology and Equity Exchange, in Zhongguancun, Beijing. The market is mainly for high tech firms. In 2009 the ChiNext second tier market was created, based in Shenzhen.

Bond Market

China's bond market is not highly developed. There are three main components: an interbank market, an over the counter market, and a stock exchange type market. The interbank market involves trades between banks, institutions, enterprises, and financial investors. Banks use the market to adjust liquidity and asset allocation. The central bank (People's Bank of China) carries out open market operations in this market. Spot and repurchase operations are carried out on the interbank market. Corporate bonds including convertibles are generally traded on the stock exchange markets. The corporate bond component remains quite small relative to government bonds and bonds issued by financial institutions.

If we compare the bond markets of China with those of South Korea, Singapore, and Thailand, China's market reflects less development as measured by the percentage of outstanding bond value to GDP. This reflects lack of development in the corporate bond market sector, a poor legal and regulatory framework, diverse and at times chaotic bond issuing prices, and weak transparency. A bond futures scandal in 1995 has been a long lasting setback. However, forward bond trading began in 2005, representing a step toward development of financial derivatives in fixed income securities.

Financial Institutions

China's capital markets rely on three main types of financial institutions: banks, insurance firms, and securities firms. China's banking structure includes four large state banks, China's policy banks, shareholder banks, and city and rural banks. A small number of foreign banks operate in China. The banking sector has been plagued by monopolistic practices, poor management, and the need to shift bad loans to asset management companies for workout and collection.

Chinese banks have been able to overcome the bad loan problem, and periodically issue bonds to finance their ongoing loan and investment activities. A high domestic savings rate provides a large volume of relatively low cost deposit funds to banking institutions.

Most large banks in China have been privatized, with their shares listed on the stock exchange, but even with a public listing these institutions are not completely driven by considerations of cost of capital or return on investment. Instead, these banks are instrumentalities of the state. Central government concerns ultimately dictate bank loan policies and practices. As of 2010 these include: 1) disparities in economic development between coastal and inland provinces, 2) low cost financing of infrastructure in export sectors and high tech demonstration projects, and 3) disparity between rural and urban housing standards. Boards of directors of large banks are window dressing, covering the fact that the party remains the ultimate overseer.[2]

The insurance industry has been an important component of China's capital market. As a World Trade Organization (WTO) member, China is obliged to open the insurance sector to foreign competitors. The insurance business has been growing rapidly, along with high economic growth across the nation.

China's securities industry is served by a relatively small number of firms. This reflects tight control over the industry and the monopolistic status of the sector. Close to three dozen fund management companies service the professionally managed funds sector.

According to Douglas and Huang, growth of China's securities industry can be broken into three distinct periods.[3] These are the strong period (1987–90), the rapid growth period (1991–99), and an adjustment period (1999–2008). The first period witnessed the growth of some fifty securities firms. These firms operated in an extremely immature legal and regulatory environment. The number of companies listed on the stock exchanges grew from 14 (1991) to 720 (1997). In the second growth period, the CSRC was established to regulate the industry. This led to enactment of key laws such as the Company Law. The third period began in 1999, when China enacted the Securities Law. This period saw China's accession to WTO (2001). At this time there was widespread consolidation of securities firms.

The securities industry is heavily concentrated, with most big firms headquartered in three major cities: Beijing, Shanghai, and Shenzhen. A small number of top investment banks dominate the field, with heavy reliance on brokerage commissions for revenues. Government policies play an important role in company financing activities. China's capital markets tend to be policy driven, and central government needs and policies are ubiquitous. Previous tight controls on IPO approval and current questions of non-floatable company shares point to the uncertainties that prevail in a communist economy in transition.

Foreign Exchange Market

Since China's opening and reforms in 1978, the foreign exchange market has made significant progress and enjoyed high growth. However, the country operates a complicated exchange control system that calls for careful analysis and understanding of policy needs and goals. Here we outline how the system is structured and operates as a financial market. We then describe how policy objectives mandate the way government administers and operates foreign exchange controls.

Greater China effectively possesses three currencies:

1. the yuan for domestic trade and investment;
2. the renminbi for foreign exchange purposes, including onshore and offshore trading; and
3. the Hong Kong dollar, mainly used in Hong Kong as a domestic currency and also as a basis for foreign exchange trading in Hong Kong.

With inconvertibility of the renminbi (RMB) under capital account, China's foreign exchange market remains largely insulated and disconnected from movements in global foreign exchange markets.[4] This structure helps insulate China from external stocks and speculative movements of funds. Policymakers in government can better control the channels of fund flows through the capital market. However, this control comes at a high cost. China's foreign exchange market lacks depth and liquidity, and suffers from a restricted range of participants.

Markets operating with exchange controls are subject to compulsory surrender (sale) of foreign exchange, and strict limits on capital transfers. Also, such markets stimulate black market activity. China has experienced several episodes of a flourishing black market, with wide disparity between the official and black market rates of exchange. In the period 1984–93 a widening gap developed between the official and black market RMB/US dollar rate, which was closed in 1994 in the second unification. From 1994 on, China's trade surplus expanded rapidly, and its foreign exchange reserves grew, from $100 billion in 1997, to $400 billion in 2003, and to $700 billion in 2005.

The onshore foreign exchange market is an electronic system with high transparency and several hundred banks and institutions authorized to trade directly. An electronic broker automatically matches buy and sell orders. Offshore RMB markets have expanded to facilitate hedging risk and taking speculative positions. The expansion of this market reflects restrictions on non-resident access to domestic forward markets. This offshore market enjoys a growing investor base, including multinational corporations, portfolio investors, hedge funds, and proprietary foreign exchange accounts of large banks.

Under pressure from its trading partners, in 2005 China reformed the exchange rate regime, moving into a floating exchange rate vis-à-vis a basket of four currencies: US dollar, euro, Japanese yen, and South Korean won. The RMB exchange rate against the US dollar was set at RMB8.11, an appreciation of 2.1 percent. Over the period 2005–08 the renminbi appreciated against the US dollar, reaching a level of close to RMB6.8/US$. In December 2008, when US Treasury Secretary Henry Paulson was making his periodic visit to Beijing to discuss exchange rate and related issues with his Chinese counterparts, he was greeted by headlines in local newspapers stating that the renminbi had reversed course and depreciated against the dollar. This was the biggest one-day fall in the RMB/US dollar rate allowed by the central bank in its management of the floating rate system.[5] During 2008 the Beijing government allowed the renminbi to appreciate steadily on the US dollar in efforts to reduce inflationary pressures.[6] Controls on inflows of speculative money were put in place. Chinese companies and investors were given greater freedom to hold foreign currencies, and access to domestic financial markets was tightened.[7] In 2010 offshore trading of Chinese currency was introduced.

Goals and Means

Previous sections outline how the capital markets are structured and operate in China. We observe in the previous discussion that foreign exchange controls continue to play an important role. Similarly, operation of the stock exchanges is strategically important to achieving China's ambitious economic goals.

China's central goal is to maintain high growth in output and exports. The operation of China's capital markets and foreign exchange system is governed by this imperative. China's high household saving rate plays a necessary but not sufficient condition for high growth. Three additional elements are necessary, all under control of government policymakers. These are: 1) a system of foreign exchange controls that limit inflows and outflows of funds by amount and type, which has the secondary effect of "guiding" the exchange rate and trade balance; 2) control over bank lending, to ensure that business sectors with high growth and export potential obtain low cost financing and that industrial development proceeds at targeted levels; and 3) monitoring a flow of new equity issues (IPOs) that channel capital to companies enjoying high growth and to state enterprises. Sale of shares in state enterprises absorbs domestic capital market funds which the government can recycle to finance investment in infrastructure. Also, IPOs through Hong Kong and other offshore stock markets provide foreign exchange that companies can use for international mergers and acquisitions. Hong Kong IPOs elevate that exchange's status and prestige in world rankings, giving Greater China equity markets a more elevated status in global comparisons.

From the preceding, we should note that China's capital markets, stock exchanges, and foreign exchange market can be viewed as means to an end. In this regard, we find it difficult to evaluate their status and performance in the same manner as financial exchanges based in other countries.

One Nation, Two Systems

Since 1997 when Hong Kong administrative control reverted to China, the Beijing government has described Greater China, Mainland China plus Hong Kong, as one nation operating under two systems. Prior to 1997 observers depicted Hong Kong as Adam Smith's legacy to Asia, and the city state operated as a competitive, free market entity. Competition was encouraged, new businesses and investment were invited, and regulation and taxation were kept to a minimum. By contrast, Mainland China operates a former communist economy, still in transition. Deregulation and privatization continue to change the balance between competitive markets and regulated trading. In the following sections, we provide brief descriptions of how these two disparate components are cooperating as parts of a complex regional partnership.

Hong Kong

When Mainland China regained political control of the British administered Crown colony in 1997, the Basic Law (or new constitution as it was called) obliged China to maintain the city state's status as an international financial center. From that date forward Hong Kong and China would operate as one nation with two systems. The Mainland economy would continue its transition toward a capitalist type business system under communist governance, and the Hong Kong city state would continue to enjoy relative freedom to operate as a competitive marketplace following the economic traditions inspired by Adam Smith.

Hong Kong enjoys several of the hallmarks of quasi-autonomy, including regularly scheduled democratic elections, a separate currency (the Hong Kong dollar), and a banking and financial sector of its own denominated in the local currency and managed as a separate and distinct monetary system.

Since 1997, Hong Kong along with Tokyo and Singapore has continued to function as one of only a few key financial centers in the Asia Pacific region. It operates one of the leading offshore banking centers, trading Asian dollars against local currency, and its foreign exchange market is one of the five largest in the world. Hong Kong is a center for bank loan syndications and other debt financing as well. Finally, Hong Kong has emerged as one of the top choices of companies launching initial public offerings, challenging New York and London based stock markets for this business.

The city plays an important role in financing regional and global trade between Southeast Asian nations, China, and the United States. It also serves as a headquarters location for international banks and multinational companies operating in the region.

The Hong Kong dollar is highly regarded as a hard currency, and has been useful to Mainland China exporters as a means of invoicing trade and as a financing currency. Availability of the Hong Kong currency facilitates Mainland China transactions with the rest of the world, given that the Hong Kong dollar enjoys a fixed rate of exchange with the US dollar.

But the relationship between the Hong Kong, Mainland China, and US currencies in the forex market has been evolving. We can observe this evolution in Table 10.1, covering a period of over twenty-five years. In that period the Hong Kong dollar has been pegged at a fixed rate with the US dollar, at HK$7.8 per US dollar. China's currency was pegged at RMB8.3 to the US dollar for a twelve-year period until mid-2005, when it was revalued and a somewhat more flexible system was put in place. In the period 2005–07 the renminbi appreciated against the US dollar. In January 2007 it broke through the significant RMB7.8 barrier, placing it on an equal value basis vis-à-vis the Hong Kong dollar.

From mid-2009 to late 2010 pressure was mounting in Hong Kong to revalue its currency, which was estimated to be undervalued by 10–15 percent. Several arguments were used at that time to support revaluation. First, Hong Kong's economy was becoming more tied to Mainland China, demonstrating high growth. The US economy was in the midst of a prolonged and deep recession. Second, interest rates in the US were kept at very low levels by the Federal Reserve. Meanwhile, Hong Kong feared the development of an asset price bubble, requiring higher

Table 10.1 Relative Status of Hong Kong Dollar, Mainland China Renminbi, and US Dollar (1983–2010)

1	1983	Hong Kong dollar pegged to US dollar.	Midpoint rate HK$7.8. Band of 7.75–7.85.
2	1994	China's renminbi pegged to US dollar.	RMB8.3/US dollar.
3	July 2005	Revaluation of renminbi.	Renminbi in guided float and appreciating vis-à-vis US dollar.
4	July 2005 – January 2007	Renminbi appreciates on US dollar.	Early 2007 RMB7.8/US dollar, on par with HK dollar.
5	January 2007 – mid-2009	Renminbi continues to appreciate vis-à-vis US dollar.	Renminbi rate moves from RMB7.8/US dollar to RMB 6.4/US dollar.
6	Mid-2009 – November 2010	Hong Kong dollar appreciates strongly vis-à-vis US dollar.	Hong Kong dollar interest rates much higher than US dollar rates.
7	June 2010	Introduction of offshore trading in yuan, via Hong Kong based yuan deposits.	In first six months' trading, daily level of $400 million reached.

Source: Gaiyan Zhang, "China's Foreign Exchange Market," in K.C. Chan, H.-g. Fung and Q.W. Liu (editors), *China's Capital Markets*, Edward Elgar, 2007, pp. 182–212; various news accounts of exchange rate movements and trends.

interest rates. Finally, the conditions in financial markets invited speculative trading, calling for careful monitoring by the Hong Kong Monetary Authority.

The Basic Law, promulgated in 1997 when Hong Kong administrative control reverted to Mainland China, positions the Hong Kong dollar as the only currency until 2047. It seems inescapable that Hong Kong is on a path to becoming a dual currency center. It has not been in the best interest of Hong Kong to tamper with its currency system. Hong Kong has prospered under a stable currency arrangement, and may prefer stability for at least a few more years.[8]

Hong Kong authorities state that they remain committed to the stable US dollar peg, which has carried the territory through several political and financial maelstroms since it was adopted in 1983.[9]

Early in 2007 the Beijing government decided to allow Chinese financial institutions to issue renminbi bonds in the Hong Kong territory. This provides an outlet for deposit funds that previously could only be held passively in Hong Kong deposit accounts or be repatriated to China. This gives Hong Kong banks and securities houses the opportunity to participate in a new component of the financial markets, and strengthens the status of the city as China's leading financial center. The opening for renminbi debt issuance by Chinese financial institutions in Hong Kong is an important first step for the Chinese currency, stated Joseph Yam, chief executive of the Hong Kong Monetary Authority, and could lead to development of a secondary trading market for renminbi denominated debt. In effect, Hong Kong is serving as the testing ground for full convertibility of the renminbi.[10]

While this is an important step forward, it should be remembered that only a few designated parties (individuals and specified merchants such as retailers and restaurants) can hold Chinese currency in Hong Kong. At yearend 2006 Hong Kong banks held only the equivalent of US$3 billion of renminbi accounts. In 2007 China's domestic financial market was being equipped with a tidal wave of liquidity. Increasingly each year Chinese companies are raising a greater share of funds from capital markets as opposed to direct bank loans. By 2006 Chinese companies had raised over one-fifth of external funds from capital markets.

At mid-June 2010 Chinese authorities launched offshore trading of yuan. Between June and December 2010 daily trading of offshore yuan grew to $400 million. This trading allows business firms to buy and sell yuan to finance trade and investment. This limited freeing of yuan trading still leaves the currency value under the control of the Chinese government.

Foreign exchange trading banks have set up new trading systems, and back offices to conduct what is expected to be a high growth market. Norman Chan, head of the Hong Kong central bank authority, noted "this is the beginning of a new era," the first step toward convertibility of China's currency.[11] Given that daily trading on the global forex market exceeds $400 trillion, the level of yuan trading appears minuscule. Nevertheless, trading has reached a level of critical mass, and companies are placing yuan into accounts in Hong Kong where offshore trading is allowed. At mid-December 2010 the yuan was trading at 6.6670 per dollar. This is a 2.4 percent gain in value vis-à-vis the US dollar since mid-June 2010 when trading commenced.

The introduction of offshore yuan trading represents another phase in the evolution of the foreign exchange system of Hong Kong and Mainland China (Table 10.1). Banks and individuals are free to trade yuan outside of Mainland China. This is a first step toward allowing the Chinese currency to float freely and allow markets to set the valuation. However, at present China will hold a tight rein on the value of the yuan. In early December 2010 the Chinese authorities broadened the scope of this new system, expanding the number of exporters that can use yuan to trade, from a few hundred to close to 70,000.

To trade yuan offshore, one needs an account in Hong Kong. Chinese companies may move money to offshore accounts only for business purposes (export and import). Banks such as HSBC are offering investors yuan-priced options and interest rate derivatives. Corporations (Caterpillar in the US) have issued debt priced in yuan; this market is referred to as the "Dim Sum" bond market.

The Asian Development Bank (ADB) has supported development of Hong Kong's yuan denominated bond market. In October 2010 ADB issued a US dollar 180 million landmark bond denominated in the currency of Mainland China. ADB enjoys a triple A rating, and this bond provides a benchmark recognized internationally.[12]

Mainland Finance

China initiated economic reforms in 1979 and, from that date to 2008, gross domestic product (GDP) reportedly grew at an average annual rate of 9.5 percent. Foreign trade has been a cornerstone of China's growing economy, and a combination of widening trade surpluses and inflow of foreign investment has resulted in vast accumulations of foreign exchange reserves.

Mainland China is fast developing its internal financial system. This includes stock exchanges, more modern bank operations, financial institutions, and more active capital markets. This system remains largely segmented from the outside world, with Hong Kong serving as a necessary window through which limited and controlled capital flows take place. Massive savings in China are directed into infrastructure and industrial investment. A slow to moderate privatization liberates the central government from the burden of administering state enterprises, and financial reforms move along at a careful pace.

While Hong Kong continues to operate as a free market city state, benefiting from Mainland high growth, important residual questions are unanswered. Will these two important systems blend into one? In the process of blending, will Mainland financial markets and stock exchanges become more capitalistic and competitive? Or will Hong Kong markets drift toward a more regulated pattern, to become consonant with conditions prevailing in Shanghai and Shenzhen? Will continued foreign exchange controls in Mainland China offer Hong Kong opportunities to service arbitrageurs, investors, and borrowers seeking to profit from parallel currency systems in the city state? When will China accelerate privatization?

The question of privatization is raised by a Yale School of Management finance professor who enjoys specialized and in-depth understanding of Mainland China's business and financial system. According to Zhiwu Chen, China has a large, untapped source of growth in its vast, state owned companies, land, and other productive assets. Privatizing these assets would transform China's growth model to include a greater mix of consumer spending.[13]

Today the Chinese government still owns 70 percent of productive wealth. To China's credit, past practices and policies have led to high growth and industrial development, but, according to Chen's analysis, the high growth and export oriented model has run its course. Rising protectionism, growing export orientation in other emerging countries, and commodity price inflation tell us that now is the time for a change in Chinese policy. Consumption has grown at a laggard pace in China, partly owing to the government enjoying a disproportionately large share of the income pie. The government share of income has been rising, at the expense of private citizens. From 1995 to 2007 the government share of revenues grew at 16 percent yearly, compared with 8 percent and 6.2 percent respectively for urban and rural households. The private household share of China's income is shrinking, leading to slow growth in consumption.

Any favorable wealth effects from the high economic growth, and rise in asset values (equity markets and housing) have gone to the government, which owns all property and 70 percent of the stock of productive (company) assets. A wealth effect on private consumption is not possible unless consumers own more wealth. It is true that in state owned businesses (China and Russia) growth is driven by investment, not consumption.[14]

Chen asserts that China should distribute ownership of the remaining state assets among the citizens. This would restore the missing wealth effect to millions of families. Significant to financial market development, distribution of government held shares in large state enterprises would increase the equity ownership base and enhance development of an equity culture in China. This would exert manifold effects on stock exchange and financial market development.

In the following sections we describe and analyze operations of the Hong Kong and Mainland stock exchanges. They each fulfill similar but also different purposes and objectives. Hong Kong continues as a regional stock market for Southeast Asian and Mainland China needs. Shanghai and Shenzhen pursue more localized tasks, privatizing state enterprises, mobilizing part of the vast savings generated within China, and acceding to the plans of a Politburo that does not as yet fully appreciate the importance and role of transparency in its financial system.

Hong Kong Stock Exchange

Regional and Global Hub

Hong Kong ranks among the top five international financial centers around the globe. Its importance is growing owing to the rising share of world trade and production stemming from the Asia Pacific region, its link with China, and its ability to juxtapose itself effectively between China in transition and hard currency

Table 10.2 Hong Kong Basic Data (2007–08)

		2007	*2008*
1	Gross domestic product*	206.7	221.6
2	Real GDP growth	6.3%	4.6%
3	GDP per capita (US dollars)	$41,935	$44,863
4	Inflation rate	3.8%	4.7%
5	Unemployment rate	3.5%	3.0%
6	Foreign exchange reserves*	152.7	163.5
7	Government budget balance (percentage of GDP)	7.2%	2.9%
8	Net public debt (percentage of GDP)	7.0%	6.0%
9	Current account balance*	$27.4	$20.2
10	Sovereign credit rating:		
	Moody's	Aa3	
	Standard & Poor's	AA	
	Fitch	AA	

Source: *Financial Times*, June 30, 2008.

Note
* Lines 1, 6, and 9 in billions of US dollars.

regions (Europe, North America, Japan) with relative ease. A cornerstone of Hong Kong success is management of the foreign exchange and domestic monetary system (Table 10.2, Lines 3, 4, 5). Hong Kong can be viewed as Adam Smith's ideal city state economy, with minimal regulation, low taxes, and encouragement of entrepreneurial initiative.

Foreign Exchange Management

Hong Kong has maintained a fixed exchange rate vis-à-vis the US dollar for over a quarter-century. The Monetary Authority operates in the forex market to keep the exchange rate within a narrow range (HK$7.75–HK$7.85 per US dollar). Designed to reduce exchange rate volatility, the currency peg assures the public that for every 7.8 Hong Kong dollars in circulation there must be one US dollar in reserve. Since October 1983 when the peg was introduced it has served two masters, Queen Elizabeth II and the Chinese communist party.[15] Stability often comes at a price. As the renminbi has appreciated against the US dollar, Hong Kong has found imports (water and energy) from the Mainland rising in cost. However, a rising renminbi also attracts numerous investors and arbitrage funds, bringing securities market trading to Hong Kong institutions and adding to the depth and liquidity of its markets.

In 2008–09 large fund inflows to Hong Kong resulted from investors unwinding arbitrage and other trading positions. These inflows required currency intervention by the Monetary Authority, to keep the HK$/US$ rate within the authorized range. Some analysts see Hong Kong approaching a crossroads, where the slowing American economy and breakneck Chinese one will put pressure on the city state authorities to consider altering the long-standing peg.[16]

Economic Management

Hong Kong can boast exemplary economic management, as evidenced in Table 10.2. Above-average GDP growth has placed per capita income at high levels, measured in US dollar purchasing power (Table 10.2, Line 3). The unemployment rate remains moderate, even with global recession in 2008 (Table 10.2, Line 5). A surplus government budget allows a downtrend in public debt (Table 10.2, Lines 7–8), and a current account surplus reflects the sizeable surplus earned by the former Crown colony from financial, commercial, and other business services provided for domestic and foreign enterprises.[17]

Hong Kong has a long history of attracting capital. In 1949 Chinese tycoons fled the Mainland, settling in Hong Kong. Li Ka-Shing reputedly is the wealthiest of these tycoons, with a $32 billion net worth (Table 10.3). His sons Victor Li and Richard Li hold high positions in family controlled enterprises. Among the eight tycoons described in Table 10.3, Gordon Wu reported the most modest net worth of $1.3 billion.

Wealthy family dynasties can flourish in a business and financial setting such as Hong Kong. Economic expansion has been impressive, income taxation is low,

Table 10.3 Leading Tycoons in Hong Kong

Founder tycoon	*Age*	*Net worth*	*Second generation tycoon*	*Age*	*Company and title*
Li Ka-Shing	79	$32.0	Victor Li	44	Deputy chairman and managing director of Cheung Kong.
			Richard Li	41	Chairman PCCW.
Lee Shau Kee	80	$23.0	Peter Lee	45	Vice chairman of Henderson Land.
Cheng Yu-tung	82	$9.4	Henry Cheng	60	Managing director of New World Development.
Stanley Ho	86	$9.0	Pansy Ho	45	Managing director of Shun Tak.
Peter Woo	62	$5.0	Jennifer Woo	31	President of Lane Crawford.
Henry Fok	Deceased	$4.5	Timothy Fok	62	Hong Kong legislator. President of the Sports Federation and Olympic Committee of Hong Kong.
			Ian Fok	59	Managing director of Henry Y.T. Fok Group.
Lui Che-Woo	78	$2.7	Francis Lui	53	Deputy chairman of Galaxy Entertainment.
Gordon Wu	71	$1.3	Thomas Wu	35	Co-managing director of Hopewell Holdings.

Source: J. Lau, "Tycoons Who Aim to Keep It in the Family," *Financial Times*, Hong Kong Supplement, June 30, 2008, p. 4.

Note: Net worth in billions of US dollars.

and it is possible to benefit from outsourcing production on the Mainland, where cost levels are low. Also, wealth holders are free to move funds into or from the territory without restraint.

The Chinese diaspora also provides an explanation for Hong Kong's rise as a financial hub. Multitudes of Chinese have residence in nearby Southeast Asian countries, where financial systems are not nearly as stable and predictable as in Hong Kong. This diaspora makes use of Hong Kong banks and financial markets for remittances, savings, investment, and other financial needs. Consequently, Hong Kong tends to enjoy a perennial flow of funds, bolstering market liquidity and supporting the Hong Kong dollar exchange rate. Rising interest in using Hong Kong as a relatively safe gateway into Mainland financial investments has accentuated the Hong Kong Monetary Authority's status as a balancing agent in this regional hub.

High Ranking Center

In 2007 the Z/Yen research consultancy launched its Global Financial Centers Index, which ranks forty-six cities around the world.[18] This evaluation includes five areas: people, business environment, market access, infrastructure, and general competitiveness. The index utilizes the results of online surveys with several hundred financial services officers. The report found in 2007 that only two cities (London and New York) can validly be considered "global" financial centers. Hong Kong ranked third overall, and is considered the world's only "international" center. Until 2007 Hong Kong and Shanghai had jointly floated the world's biggest IPO when Industrial and Commercial Bank (China) bypassed London and New York in its $21.9 billion offering of shares. Asia can boast that four of the top ten ranked financial centers of the world include: Hong Kong (ranked third), Singapore (fourth), Sydney (seventh), and Tokyo (ninth). Table 10.4 indicates the point rankings of the three leading centers, with a maximum possible score of 1,000.

Hong Kong boasts the fourth highest number of chartered financial analysts in the world, not far behind the US, Canada and the UK. Can Hong Kong or any other Asian center rise to the top globally? The Z/Yen report reflects some doubts that Hong Kong, Shanghai, or Shenzhen will emerge as a "global" center.

Table 10.4 Three Highest Ranked Financial Centers: Rankings by Great Financial Centers Index (Midyear 2007)

Financial center	*No. of points earned*
London	765
New York	760
Hong Kong	684

Source: *Financial Times*, March 17, 2007, p. 12.

Note: Maximum points possible is 1,000.

Moreover, it may not be possible for any single center to emerge as a third global center, equal to London or New York. Financial centers are where liquidity concentrates. As yet, none of the Asian centers, including Hong Kong, has attained a status where it can gain any monopolistic hold on regional liquidity.

High Ranking Exchange

In 2005–06 Hong Kong Exchanges and Clearing (HKEx) ranked first in profit margin and fourth in total profits among the world's twelve largest stock exchanges (Table 4.6). Since that period the exchange has demonstrated high growth, as a result of: a) above-average economic expansion of Mainland China, b) financial development and deepening in the Greater China region, and c) the increasing role played by Hong Kong as a financial center for the Asia Pacific region. Between 2000 and 2007 average daily turnover on the HKEx increased 160 percent in share trading, 71 percent in derivatives trading, and 150 percent in stock options contract trading. As a result of these increases, profit before taxes expanded 143 percent, and earnings per share 144 percent.[19]

HKEx management has been active in improving its market infrastructure, as well as launching service enhancements. These include introducing a new market maker regime for stock options and futures, upgrading computer trading and information systems, providing information to clientele for assessing services in both the English and the Chinese language, shortened delays in posting market data, expanded ETF listings, and adjusted position limits for futures and options trading of H shares. The exchange enjoys high growth in daily market turnover. In 2007 total turnover in the cash market amounted to HK$21.6 trillion, with average daily turnover of HK$88.1 billion, 2.6 times the level in 2006 (Table 10.5). Total market capitalization of companies listed on the stock exchange increased 55 percent in 2007, to HK$20.7 trillion.[20]

On a global basis, in 2007 HKEx overtook Deutsche Börse to rank first in derivative instruments turnover. Also HKEx passed the Australian Securities Exchange to become the largest stock options market in Asia. As can be observed in Table 10.6, HKEx ranked fifth and seventh globally in capital funds raised and market capitalization. It ranked tenth in share trading value.

Table 10.5 Average Daily Turnover on HKEx (2003–07)

	Value of average daily securities turnover (HK$ billions)
2003	10.4
2004	16.0
2005	18.3
2006	33.9
2007	88.1

Source: Hong Kong Exchanges and Clearing, *Annual Report 2007*, p. 9.

Table 10.6 Hong Kong Exchanges and Clearing: Ranking Position Among World Exchanges in 2007

Type of activity	*Value/volume*	*Ranking*
Securitized derivatives turnover	US$507 million	1
Stock options market	45,982,968 contracts	1 in Asia
ETF market	US$20,592 million	2 in Asia
Capital funds raised	US$70,178 million	5
Market capitalization	US$2,654,416 million	7
Share trading value	US$2,138,699 million	10

Source: Hong Kong Exchanges and Clearing Limited, *Annual Report 2007*, p. 9.

Market Quality and Sustainable Development

The HKEx has focused on growing sustainable financial markets, via maintaining quality and reliability. Initiatives related to these goals include:

- a pilot scheme begun in 2008, requiring a listing applicant to post information on the HKEx website prior to providing this information to institutional investors;
- taking initiatives toward good corporate citizenship. HKEx has been regarded as a Caring Company by the Hong Kong Council of Social Service.

Hong Kong continues to be recognized as a leading international financial center, evidenced by its first place rank by the Heritage Foundation in its Index of Economic Freedom, by the Fraser Institute in its Economic Freedom of the World ranking, and by the Japan Centre for Economic Research for its Political Competitiveness Ranking, and its second place ranking by the United Nations World Investment Report for its status as most preferred destination for foreign investment in Asia.[21]

Complement to Mainland Markets

HKEx's chief executive officer Paul Chow Man-yiu describes the exchange's important and necessary complementary role to the Mainland exchanges. This has promoted overall economic development. The benefits are detailed in HKEx's annual report as follows:

1 Mainland enterprises gain exposure to international standards and best practices, aiding corporate governance and management. This has operated from 1993, when the first Mainland company was listed on HKEx.
2 Competition between exchanges is continuous, as HKEx marketing activities on the Mainland promote Hong Kong as a preferred listing venue.
3 Secondary market improvements are continuously featured, leading to cooperation and coordination with Mainland authorities and intermediaries. Five Mainland brokers were admitted as HKEx participants in 2007.
4 HKEx has broadened its range of products, and expanded the number of options and futures contracts on Mainland related stocks and indices. The

HFI Futures was introduced in April 2007. This provides direct and indirect liquidity accretion to numerous financial products traded on Mainland markets. HKEx has worked to reduce market barriers, separating the Mainland and Hong Kong capital markets. For example, HKEx has been successful in lifting the position limits of H shares Index Futures (March 2007), and relaxing other such limits.

New Products

HKEx seeks to introduce new products. In 2007 the exchange listed its first ETFs linked to global equities, US equities, and sectors already represented among its listings. The ETF market in Hong Kong has grown to become the largest in Asia Pacific, except for Japan, as measured by turnover value.[22]

A key initiative in HKEx's strategic plan is to "open the equity listing regime further to issuers from overseas jurisdictions."[23] This has paid off, and companies from Taiwan, Vietnam, Malaysia, and Australia raised HK$15 billion in 2007 on HKEx's platform. Also, the exchange is working toward easier listing of overseas companies via depository receipts.

HKEx has boosted efficiency with its cash market for equities and its derivative market. In 2007 it invested HK$101 million to upgrade capacity and technology, increasing daily processing capacity more than threefold, from 1.5 million trades to 5 million trades, in January 2008. The migration of all cash and derivatives markets to a single integrated network (SDNet) offers a more reliable network on Optical Ethernet technology. Together with the planning and upgrade of trading/clearing system capacity and technology, HKEx is able to handle peak trading volume seamlessly. This was demonstrated on October 3, 2007 when trading volume was recorded at HK$210.5 billion, from 1.2 million trades involving 110 billion shares.

Market Information

In June 2007 the Hong Kong Cash Market entered a new era of electronic disclosure, with rollout of the EDP. Both Main Board and GEM listed company issuers are required to submit their disclosures to the exchange electronically. This brings issuer information and dissemination in line with standards in other major international financial centers. This infrastructure provides better search, archiving, information storage, and retrieval of information for investors and regulators.

On the market information side, HKEx has made more timely trading information available with respect to the cash and derivatives markets on its website. A new market data package was added to HKEx services for vendors that provide news and commentary.

Listing and IPOs

HKEx has developed an aggressive and flexible listing regime. Recognizing that listings can be the lifeblood of healthy operation, HKEx's listing regime consists of the following components:[24]

1 Retain a leading role as regional financial center and listing venue for Southeast Asia and the greater Asia Pacific region.
2 Continue to develop and share listings from Mainland China, including new enterprises on its Growth Enterprise Market (GEM) Board and privatization issues of state owned enterprises.
3 Develop listings from far-flung locations (North America, Australia, Bermuda) that facilitate round-the-clock trading for institutional investors.
4 Facilitate issuers to list depository receipts on the exchange.

With these objectives, the Hong Kong exchange has undertaken efforts to improve transparency and regulatory efficiency. HKEx operates a Main Board and the GEM Board. Market infrastructure assists development of listings on both boards.

HKEx has enjoyed success in attracting a high volume of IPOs, as can be observed in Table 10.7. In 2007 a total of 125 listing applications were accepted. In that year eighty-two applicants were listed on the Main Board, and two on the GEM. Some forty-two applications were in process at the yearend. Also, in 2007 Main Board listed companies attained a high of 1,048, and an additional 193 were listed on the second (GEM) market. Over the period 2003–07 listings increased on HKEx by over 20 percent.

Business Model

Hong Kong Exchanges and Clearing's business model can be characterized by three striking features: high growth, volatility due to its locational and regional focus, and role as a regional trading center. In part these attributes are reflected in Table 10.8, where HKEx income sources are presented. Approximately 60 percent of income is generated by trading, quite high for financial exchanges.

As a regional hub HKEx experiences the ebb and flow of trading within its broad region. Therefore, regional commodity boom and bust impacts reverberate into the Hong Kong stock market. Similarly, world trade cycles spill over into the Hong Kong market.

We can expect high growth to continue into the future, as the Mainland economy expands rapidly. Organic growth and its financing by Mainland companies, together with pressures to accelerate the pace of privatization, should have valuable spillover benefits for HKEx.

Table 10.7 Hong Kong Exchanges and Clearing: Listings Initiated and Completed in 2007

Applications for listing	125
Listings completed on Main Board	82
Listings completed on GEM	2
Yearend 2007:	
Main Board listings	1,048
GEM listings	193

Source: Hong Kong Exchanges and Clearing, *Annual Report 2007*, p. 38.

Table 10.8 Hong Kong Exchanges and Clearing: Income Sources as Percentage of Total (2006–07)

	2006	*2007*
Market turnover	57.7%	62.9%
Stock exchange listing fees	11.2	8.2
Information and data services	9.4	8.1
Net investment income	14.5	14.8
Other income	7.2	6.0
Total	100.0%	100.0%

Source: Hong Kong Exchanges and Clearing Ltd, *Annual Report 2007*, p. 66.

Investors have found the business model at HKEx attractive. During the global financial crisis of 2008–09 shares of financial exchanges lost considerable market value. By contrast, share valuations for HKEx and BOVESPA (Sao Paulo, Brazil) became higher than those for NYSE Euronext, NASDAQ OMX, and London Stock Exchange. In June 2009 HKEx became the second highest valued financial exchange in the world, second only to the Chicago Mercantile Exchange (CME). Deutsche Börse ranked third in value and BOVESPA fourth, at June 2009. A stock market rally in second quarter 2009 elevated market values of stock exchanges by 27 percent in the month of May 2009, according to Mondo Visione, a developer of global exchange indices.[25]

Mainland China Exchanges

The following sections focus on China's Mainland exchanges. First, we analyze and describe the multi-hub approach, necessary in a large country trying to find answers to appropriate sequencing in the development of financial services. Second, we examine the role played by China's two main stock exchanges. Third, we describe progress in developing futures markets, a necessary component of any modern system. Finally, we describe past practices and implicit strategies utilized in overseas listing of Chinese companies.

Multi-Hub Approach

Glancing at a map of the People's Republic, we observe a very large land area. China ranks among the four largest countries globally in square miles of contiguous territory.

In such a large country regional, linguistic, and business practices vary, leading to development of local markets and exchanges. This is true of China, where local stock trading markets evolved in most major cities. Similarly, in the period 1990–93 close to fifty commodities futures markets sprang up. For a variety of reasons, outlined below, the central government concentrated equity and commodity futures trading into a small number of locations or hubs.

The current status of financial trading hubs in China is outlined in Table 10.9. Four cities host six exchanges, with Shanghai hosting the Shanghai Stock Exchange

Table 10.9 Main Multi-Hubs in China

Financial exchange	*Year established*
A Stock exchanges	
1 Shanghai Stock Exchange	1990
2 Shenzhen Stock Exchange	1990
3 ChiNext	2009
B Futures exchanges	
4 Dalian Commodity Exchange	1993
5 Shanghai Futures Exchange	1999
6 Zhengzhou Commodity Exchange	1990

Source: K.C. Chan, H.-g. Fung and Q.W. Liu (editors), *China's Capital Market*, Edward Elgar, 2007; *Financial Times*, various issues.

and the Shanghai Futures Exchange. The Shanghai Stock Exchange has grown much faster than its counterpart in Shenzhen, but Shenzhen is more proximate to Hong Kong. The three futures markets trade different commodities, related to their specific regions.

The multi-hub works well in Mainland China, and is distinct from the Hong Kong situation. Hong Kong faces external needs and opportunities, whereas Mainland hubs must attend to primarily domestic needs. Also, Hong Kong's stock exchange and financial markets are far more advanced and sophisticated. Mainland financial markets are in a much earlier development stage, responding to problems locked within a largely segmented market system. Hong Kong markets are more innovative, while Mainland markets are emulative.

Finally, as China's economy expands at a high pace, Hong Kong becomes more exposed to Mainland volatility shocks, and caught between conflicting pressures. Its currency and interest rate structure relates to the US dollar and Federal Reserve policy, owing to the peg maintained with the US dollar. But macro-spillovers from the adjacent Mainland are becoming larger as China's economy grows and as Hong Kong's economic ties with Mainland China increase. These ties are reinforced as more and more equity listings come from the Mainland.

China's Stock Market

China undertook capital market reform in the 1980s. A major advance took place in 1990 when the Shanghai and Shenzhen Stock Exchanges were launched. These facilitated listing shares of state owned enterprises. In this section we describe stock exchange operation and development, consider regulation and performance of the stock market, and describe efforts to develop a second tier market.

Shanghai and Shenzhen Stock Exchanges

Chinese publicly traded companies have two classes of shares, tradable and non-tradable. Government units own non-tradable shares, generally accounting for more than half of those outstanding. There are several types of tradable shares, listed for trading on stock markets. A shares and B shares of Chinese companies originally were to be owned and traded by residents and foreign investors respectively. B shares are traded in foreign currency. H shares of Chinese companies are traded on the Hong Kong Stock Exchange. N shares of Chinese companies are traded on North American exchanges. A shares enjoy the largest market. Shares of some companies ultimately owned by Chinese investors, traded in Hong Kong, are given the name "red chips." While legally Hong Kong companies, the ultimate ownership can be traced to Chinese investors.

The Shanghai and Shenzhen exchanges follow listing requirements and standards comparable to other emerging markets. The initial public offering must be approved by the China Securities Regulatory Commission. Public shareholdings must equal 25 percent or more of shares, with a minimum number of total shares, and a good credit record in the most recent three years.

Stock exchanges in China do not use dealers or market makers. Rather, share trading is automated with electronic trading. Both Shanghai and Shenzhen can handle high trading volumes. Trading is order driven, with daily price limits, set at 10 percent in a single trading day. Morning and afternoon trading sessions are held.

China has worked to develop a second tier stock market, but real success in this endeavor did not arrive until 2009. Prior to that time a Small and Medium Enterprise Board (SMEB) was launched (May 2004), but without great success. Early success of the Shanghai exchange, via privatizing state enterprises, was not easily duplicated with small private sector startup enterprises.

In 2009 the government created ChiNext, which operates as part of the Shenzhen exchange. Its purpose is to make equity capital more readily available to "strategically important emerging industries." As of November 2010 ChiNext listed 141 company stock issues. ChiNext maintains easier requirements for companies to be eligible for listing: net assets of 20 million yuan (US$3 million), two consecutive years of profits, and a cumulative profit of 10 million yuan. This compares with requirements on the Shanghai exchange of 30 million yuan in net assets, three consecutive years of profit, and total earnings of 30 million yuan.[26]

ChiNext enjoyed an auspicious first year of operation. In that period (ending October 30, 2010) 134 companies raised close to $15 billion through initial public offerings. In the same period the Shanghai exchange completed twenty-four IPOs.

While ChiNext can provide needed capital to private sector enterprises in their early development stage, bank funding still is required to enable continued growth. State owned companies continue to corner the market for bank loans at the expense of smaller private sector companies. China needs to establish small, private banks that will focus on the capital spending needs of companies that gain equity funds through ChiNext share issuance.

Regulation

The Mainland stock market is heavily regulated, owing to: 1) the former communist economic model with extensive controls, and 2) the desire of the government to manage the financial system in a manner that facilitates high levels of investment and growth. Writing in 2007 Chan, Fung, and Kwok reported eight major laws governing the stock market.[27] The CSRC administers these laws. Regulations cover brokerage firm operations, procedures for initial public offerings, and listing requirements.

Stock exchanges are responsible for maintaining and enforcing regulations, and China follows other countries in operating exchanges as self-regulatory bodies. Stock exchanges monitor listing, share price movements, and securities firms operating on their markets.

Numerous regulatory changes have been implemented as the stock exchanges have expanded, as experience provided a test of new rules, and as problems emerged. Policy and regulatory reversals have been frequent. Poor corporate governance appears to be related to the large volume of non-tradable shares circulating in private markets. The Chinese government has begun a process of converting non-tradable shares into tradable shares. The potential benefits include an accelerated privatization of state owned companies, better governed and managed companies, and healthier expansion of the stock market.

Performance

We now consider performance of China's stock market from the perspective of: 1) financial reporting and transparency, 2) comparative growth of the two main markets, 3) share price movements, absolute and relative, and 4) volatility and riskiness.

Chinese companies listing H shares in Hong Kong must meet stricter and more demanding accounting and disclosure requirements than those listing A shares on Mainland exchanges. Nevertheless, A shares trade at a large premium to B shares and H shares. We discuss this premium in the next section.

Chinese companies are required to follow the People's Republic of China Generally Accepted Accounting Principles (PRC GAAP) when preparing accounting statements. Companies issuing B shares also need to convert their accounting statements to International Accounting Standards (IAS), considered a tougher standard. Since the Chinese stock market is relatively new, it may lack sufficient alternative information sources other than published reports.

During the initial fifteen years of operation (1990–2005) both the Shanghai and the Shenzhen stock market displayed impressive growth in market capitalization, turnover, and number of companies listed. We present summary data as of the end of this fifteen-year period for both exchanges in Table 10.10. The Shanghai Stock Exchange was four times as large as its counterpart in Shenzhen, as measured by market capitalization and annual turnover. Its lead in number of companies listed is somewhat smaller.

An analysis of holding period returns and risk for the Shanghai, Shenzhen, and Hong Kong markets, covering the fifteen-year period to 2005, is reported by Chan, Fung, and Kwok.[28] They find that the Shanghai market performed better than the Hong Kong market, which in turn performed better than the Shenzhen

Table 10.10 Comparison of Shanghai and Shenzhen Stock Exchanges in 2005

	Shanghai	*Shenzhen*
Market capitalization[1]	3,807	933
Annual turnover[1]	4,977	1,242
Number of listed companies[2]	824	544

Source: Adapted from several sources, Standard & Poor's *Stock Market Factbook*, *Financial Times*, and *Wall Street Journal.*

Notes
1 Billion renminbi.
2 At yearend.

market. In terms of risk, measured by standard deviation of annual holding period returns, the Shanghai and Shenzhen markets exhibit higher risk than the Hong Kong market.

In 2006–07 China's A share market assumed a bubble-like performance. The Shanghai Composite Index emerged from a three-year slumber and over a period of two years outperformed virtually all stock markets around the globe. In 2006 it appreciated in value 130 percent. In 2007 it gained close to 100 percent, reaching a market capitalization value of US$3.6 trillion.[29]

The Chinese stock market bubble had several important supporting structures. These included: 1) A shares enjoyed a captive audience, since Mainland markets offered few alternatives for local savers; and 2) real interest rates in the two-year period touched on negative, causing savers to shift to the stock market to protect capital.

The 2006–07 bubble in China's stock market brought attention to disparate pricing of same company shares in the A share, B share, and H share markets. High premiums on A shares vis-à-vis B shares and H shares constitute a puzzle, which is discussed below.

Puzzle of the A Share Premium

Integrationists hoping for a melding together of Mainland and Hong Kong territory stock exchanges are repeatedly disappointed as the A share price premium rises and falls over time. This price premium is measured by comparing the A share and H share prices of same company shares traded in Shanghai and Hong Kong respectively, and adjusted for currency of denomination. In October 2007, when the renminbi valuation was RMB1 = HK$1.03, near parity, the ten largest A share premiums ranged from 143 percent to 231 percent (Table 10.11).

A share price premiums relative to same company H share prices follow the ebb and flow of the broader Shanghai Composite Index and Hang Seng Index (Hong Kong market) over time. In January 2007 there was a premium on all of the thirty-seven dual listed Chinese company shares. This compares with the earlier situation, when in March 2006 a third of the twenty-six dual listed shares traded at higher valuations in Hong Kong than in Shanghai.[30]

Table 10.11 Ten Largest A Share Premiums for Dual Listed Companies (October 2007)

		H share (HK$)	*A share (RMB)*	*A share premium %*
1	Sinopec Yizheng Chemicals	4.08	13.12	221
2	Sinopec Shanghai Petrochemical	6.37	19.65	209
3	Beiren Printing	3.60	9.75	179
4	China Oilfield Services	19.60	51.65	387
5	Northeast Electric Development	2.59	6.79	161
6	Jiangxi Copper Company	29.70	75.19	269
7	Nanjing Panda Electronic	3.44	8.65	151
8	Shandong Xinhua Pharma	2.95	7.32	149
9	China Eastern Airlines	8.00	19.05	138
10	Tianjin Capital Environmental Protection	4.57	10.79	136

Source: Tom Mitchell, "Integration of Bourses Is Not Black and White," *Financial Times*, October 12, 2007, p. 27.

Several theories have been put forward to explain the puzzle of the share price premium, including divergent expectations, no arbitrage, repressed investors, and emerging bubbles. Divergent expectations gives recognition that investors in Hong Kong and Shanghai operate in different types of market, one a regional and international center (Hong Kong) and the other a much less developed market. Also, investor types vary considerably, Hong Kong hosting global and footloose institutions, and Shanghai mostly retail investors.

The no-arbitrage explanation focuses on China's strict capital controls that prevent Mainland residents from moving to offshore markets. High savings being directed to a local stock market results in relatively high valuations. This leads to local investors facing difficult choices—bank deposits or the stock market. When interest rates fall below inflation rates, negative real returns make bank deposits a poor alternative.

Analysts view emerging markets as associated with periodic bubbles. These bubbles produce rising and falling price premiums on A shares as compared to H shares. These premiums may not persist fully through the full market cycle. In October 2007 average A share premiums over H shares were 55 percent, and projected to narrow to 35 percent during the following year.

Hong Kong and Mainland government officials have expressed concern over the premium and its unpredictability. Bankers are even more concerned. In 2007 Joseph Yam, chief executive of the Hong Kong Monetary Authority, stated that it could be feasible to create a channel between the two markets based on certificates of ownership. This arbitrage mechanism would aim at narrowing or removing the price premium. Sir David Tweedie, chairman of the International Accounting Standards Board, asked, "Do I use the Hong Kong or Shanghai price to value a dual listed share?"

The puzzle of premium prices also is of great concern to investment banks launching IPOs. Chinese government authorities also are concerned when large IPOs of state enterprises are planned. In the China Life initial public offering of January 2007 the share price more than doubled in first day of trading in Shanghai.

However, H shares reel in value. We return to the topic of dual listing in overseas markets in a following section.

The Ascent of Shenzhen

Previously we described the Chinese stock market as highly centered in Shanghai, with Shenzhen playing an important supporting role. Here we describe and analyze the ascent of Shenzhen. We also described the growing role of ChiNext, a second tier market headquartered on the Shenzhen exchange. Shanghai's past dominance of the Mainland stock market is in part attributable to the decision of government leaders to conduct privatization of large state enterprises in Shanghai and also Hong Kong.

In 2009–10 the Shenzhen exchange experienced an extraordinary boom in IPOs by smaller private companies. In the first four months of 2010 the Shenzhen exchange witnessed 241 companies raise a record $33.6 billion from new listings, surpassing the $24.1 billion raised in the same period on the Shanghai exchange. New listings in Shanghai in this period were fewer than fifteen. Shanghai issues on average were twelve times larger than the average Shenzhen listing.[31]

According to Peter Fuhrman, chairman of China First Capital, the rise of Shenzhen reflects recognition on the part of policymakers of the central importance of allowing private companies greater access to equity capital. The IPO boom in Shenzhen represents a substantial new source of capital for smaller, more entrepreneurial companies, previously starved for funds. ChiNext accounts for $11 billion of the new equity funds provided in 2010.

Investment banks have found Shenzhen a source of profit. IPO fees in Shenzhen average 4.4. percent of funds raised, compared with 2.4 percent charged in Shanghai. Shenzhen's ascent has been profitable for domestic banks, since foreign investment banks have largely been frozen out of the lucrative small company new issuance. Fraser Howie, co-author of *Privatizing China*, observes that foreign banks have been "elephant hunting" by focusing on big privatization deals.[32] Now they are refocusing on smaller, venture capital type businesses.

Success in launching ChiNext comes at a propitious time. Chinese companies seeking listings on second tier market venues have enjoyed limited success. Only a small number of Chinese companies have listed on the London Stock Exchange AIM. When raising equity is not feasible owing to market conditions, some Mainland companies have issued convertible loan notes. The investor earns a sizeable interest income, and has the option to convert the debt paper into shares when it becomes attractive.[33]

Overseas Listing

We discussed cross-listing in detail in Chapter 4. Here we focus on: 1) an overview of how Chinese companies have cross-listed beyond the Mainland exchanges, and 2) specific advantages derived from cross-listing in Hong Kong, Singapore, New York, and London.

Overview of Cross-Listing

In 1993 Tsingtao Brewery was the first Chinese state owned company to issue shares overseas. Since that time many Chinese state enterprises have launched an IPO or secondary share issue on an overseas market. As in the case of Tsingtao Brewery, the majority of overseas listings are in Hong Kong. Historically, Hong Kong has been a preferred habitat for Chinese cross-listers, so much so that in the future we can expect closer co-movement between the Hong Kong and Mainland stock markets.

By 2005 some 287 Chinese companies had cross-listed on overseas stock exchanges. Table 10.12 provides an overview of the overseas exchanges on which Chinese companies have listed. Hong Kong accounts for 120 Chinese company listings, a third of which are on the Growth Enterprise Market (GEM). The GEM was established in 1999 to provide capital for growth companies that lacked alternate sources of funds. Hong Kong enjoys geographic proximity, similar language, and strong cultural ties. Twelve of the companies listed in Hong Kong also had cross-listings in the United States.

Four Overseas Markets Attract Cross-Listings

As noted in Table 10.12, four stock markets attract overseas listings of Chinese companies. The first overseas listing took place in Hong Kong, which offers two listing venues, the Main Board and the Growth Enterprise Market. The Main Board appeals to established companies with a profitable operating record. The GEM offers an alternative for companies in all industries and all sizes. Listing standards on the Main Board are higher than on the GEM. In April 2004 the Hong Kong exchange lowered its listing standards, exempting Main Board applicants from the need to show profits if they had a market capitalization of HK$4 billion and annual sales of HK$500 million.

Mainland Chinese companies have raised a considerable amount of capital from listing in Hong Kong. Over the period 1995–2005 they raised HK$408,828 million through IPO and post-IPO issuance on the Main Board. In the period 2000–05 they raised HK$5,603 million through IPOs and post-IPO issuance on the GEM.

Table 10.12 Number of Chinese Companies Listed in Four Major Overseas Markets (2005)

Hong Kong*	120
USA	69
Singapore	92
London	6
Total	287

Source: Adapted from C. Wu, "Overseas Listing of Chinese Companies," in K.C. Chan, H.-g. Fung and Q.W. Liu (editors), *China's Capital Market*, Edward Elgar, 2007, p. 253.

Note
* Of this total, 40 companies are listed on the second tier Growth Enterprise Market in Hong Kong.

Listing on the New York Stock Exchange (NYSE) and NASDAQ has been popular for large companies headquartered around the world. An American cross-listing generally takes the form of a depository receipt (DR). We discuss DRs in detail in Chapter 4. Such issuance utilizes the expertise of an underwriter or investment bank, and also requires SEC registration and approval of public offerings. In the period to 2005, when sixty-nine Chinese companies issued and listed in American stock markets, thirty-four listed on NYSE or NASDAQ, twenty-four issued shares on the over the counter market, and eight sold shares in the Rule 144a private placement market. Clearly, the US capital market provides a range of venues which appeal to Chinese companies with distinct and varied funding and listing requirements.

The number of Chinese company listings in the United States declined from 2004 onward, explained by several factors. First, the Sarbanes–Oxley Act has proved a deterrent, especially to state owned companies that find it difficult to modify corporate governance practices in accord with the US legislation. In 2005 two very large IPOs of state owned companies, China Construction Bank and Bank of Communications, cross-listed only in Hong Kong. Second, a class action lawsuit in New York against state owned China Life alleged that officers and directors of the Chinese insurer failed to adequately disclose financial fraud at China Life's parent company. Finally, Hong Kong, Mainland stock markets, and other capital markets are growing rapidly, offering alternatives to New York. Singapore is an example of other regional financial centers and stock exchanges becoming more competitive as they vie for overseas listings.

The Singapore Exchange (SGX) ranks ahead of New York and London in the number of Chinese companies that have listed. SGX has worked strenuously to gain overseas listings, and ranks high on a global basis as a stock exchange for foreign listings. A Singapore listing enables high growth companies to obtain funding on a market recognized for requiring high standards of governance. Singapore is an attractive alternative to Hong Kong, especially at times when the Hong Kong stock market offers less liquidity or softer share pricing. Singapore has attracted many smaller Chinese companies, whose average market capitalization is lower than that of Chinese companies listing in Hong Kong.

Until 2005 only a relatively small number of Chinese companies listed on the London Stock Exchange (LSE). In 2004 LSE opened a regional Asia Pacific office in Hong Kong, which enables the London exchange to communicate more closely and actively with existing Asian customers and attract Asian companies to a London listing. LSE faces tough competition in attracting listings from Chinese and other Asian companies owing to competitive pressures from Hong Kong and New York.

Futures Exchanges

Futures markets began trading in China in the early 1990s. With the revelation of several trading scandals in the early high growth period, the government implemented mandatory reforms in the governance of these markets. These included: 1) standardized futures trading, 2) control over market scope, 3) uniform contracts, and 4) closer regulation and monitoring of exchanges. In 2010 China launched trading of stock index futures in Shanghai.

Overview of Futures Exchanges

Futures exchanges are self-regulated, not-for-profit, legal entities. China operates three commodity exchanges and one financial futures exchange. The latter was established in 2010.

Over the period 1993–2007 commodity futures trading volume, measured by number of contracts traded or value of turnover, has moved through two business cycles. The first cycle lasted from 1993–2000, when contracts traded and turnover reached a low point. From 2000 to 2007 a second cycle manifested itself, reaching considerably higher volume and turnover value than in the previous cycle.

China's futures exchanges use electronic trading systems. Orders enter the system via terminals, and also access brokers' offices. Two trading sessions take place daily. All trades are executed through brokerage firms registered with the CSRC.

Risk control measures include daily price limits, position limits, margin deposits, and maintenance of margin via mark to market valuation.

Three Major Commodity Exchanges

Commodity trading in China is served by three exchanges, described briefly in Table 10.13. The Shanghai Futures Exchange (SFE) operates through over 250 terminals located across China. Over 200 members include brokerage firms and proprietary trading members. Most of the trading on SFE is in copper, aluminum, rubber, and palm oil.

The Dalian Commodity Exchange (DCE) was established in 1993. DCE has close to 200 members, most of which are brokerage firm members. The main con-

Table 10.13 Major Traded Products on China's Futures Exchanges (2005)

	Major commodity traded	*Dominant exchange in 2005*	*China trade as percentage of dominant exchange*
Shanghai	Copper	LME	30.6%
	Aluminum	LME	2.5
	Rubber	TOCOM	131.8
Dalian	Soybeans	CBOT	8.6
	Soybean meal	CBOT	25.5
	Corn	CBOT	1.6
Zhengzhou	Cotton	NYBOT	94.1
	Wheat	CBOT	5.6

Source: Adapted From Jot Yau, "Futures Markets," in K.C. Chan, H.-g. Fung and Q.W. Liu (editors), *China's Capital Market*, Edward Elgar, 2007, p. 74.

Note: LME—London Metal Exchange; TOCOM—Tokyo Commodity Exchange; CBOT—Chicago Board of Trade; NYBOT—New York Board of Trade.

tracts traded cover corn, soybeans, soy oil, and soy meal. DCE is the largest futures exchange in China by number of contracts traded. In 2005 trading in soybean meal was equivalent to over a fourth of trading in the same commodity on CBOT in Chicago, at that time the leading futures market for that commodity. DCE's success is related to soy, a major staple of the diet in China. Corn futures contracts also are an important part of the DCE business. China is the world's second largest corn producer and consumer.

The Zhengzhou Commodity Exchange (ZCE) has over 200 members, mostly brokerage firms. Twenty percent of members are proprietary traders. ZCE trades contracts in wheat, cotton, and mung beans (Table 10.13).

China has emerged as a global driver of commodity trading and price discovery. Prices of commodities such as cotton and copper are increasingly influenced by market conditions in China. However, China's commodity exchanges do not yet play a parallel global role. Their development is limited by laws banning foreign participation, and currency exchange controls. Also, China's commodity exchanges open for trading only four hours a day. Further, legal protection for investors is not as transparent and certain as befits a country seeking global status for its financial markets.

Product innovation has spurred development of China's commodity exchanges. Unique products (Shanghai's rebar steel contract) are driving trade volume up. The Dalian exchange is developing the world's first future contracts for coke, a key input in steel making. In 2009 Dalian introduced a contract for PVC piping.[34]

The China Futures Association is the industry self-regulator, and helps enforce laws and regulations pertaining to the futures market. Members of the China Futures Association include futures exchange firms, futures exchanges, and licensed individual futures traders.

Financial Futures

In April 2010 China launched its new financial futures trading. On the third day of trading the value of stock index futures traded on the China Financial Futures Exchange exceeded the value of trades on the Shanghai Stock Exchange. The new futures contract is based on the CSI 300 Index, which tracks the Shanghai and Shenzhen markets. Each contract is worth RMB300 ($44 at late April 2010).

The high volume on the first days of trading is remarkable because the Beijing government had imposed restrictions aimed at keeping inexperienced investors out of the market. Investors must pass an examination and meet certain criteria for educational background, income, and liquid assets.[35]

The surprise is that institutional investors and hedge funds rank below individual wealthy investors as dominant participants. According to Dean Owen, Shanghai based chief of Newedge, the French futures brokerage, "the market is dominated by retail investors ... something regulators and the exchange want to avoid." Retail investors are not using the futures as a hedging tool against their existing equity portfolios. Short term speculative traders appear to dominate.

This point is verified by the fact that over 90 percent of trades are opened and closed the same day, reflecting rapid-fire trading for quick profit. This is referred to as scalping. In a typical day of trading, 140,000 contracts may be traded for May settlement, but fewer than 7,400 contracts are left open at the end of the day. In mature Western markets the "open interest" typically is higher than daily trading volume.

The introduction of index futures is part of a broader transformation of Mainland China's stock market. Short selling and margin trading also were introduced a month prior to the launch of stock index futures. These tools allow traders to benefit from falling as well as rising markets, and to hedge existing portfolios. China's stock market is extremely volatile, surging 80 percent in 2009 and falling 65 percent in the early months of 2010.[36]

It is hoped that the introduction of stock index futures will have a stabilizing effect on China's equity market. Nevertheless, regulators are keeping most players out of the market to give futures trading a chance to develop at a moderate pace. Trading in bond futures (1995) and commodity futures (1990s) experienced serious problems when introduced to China's capital markets. At present, risk prevention is a top priority. Regulators in China sense that derivatives can be a double-edged sword. To trade index futures, one must pass an examination, make a minimum deposit of RMB500,000 ($73,238) to open a trading account, and prove one has completed at least twenty mock stock index futures trades or executed at least ten commodity futures trades in the past. Also, it is necessary to pay cash deposits (margin) of 15–18 percent of the contract value. In the early weeks of trading only 6,000 index futures trading accounts had been opened, most by commodity traders with some experience in futures trading.

Officials in Beijing appear intent on improving the allocation of capital in China, and the launch of equity index futures is one of the numerous steps required. This development, and other initiatives, will further Beijing's goal of transforming China into a global financial center.

Barring foreign traders is one precaution that regulators will need to reevaluate. Financial markets in China continue to operate largely insulated from the outside world. Some hold that, if markets develop, grow, and become more open to a wider range of traders, they tend to be less volatile. A comparison of stock market volatility in China, Japan, Europe, and the United States indicates that China tops all others in its propensity to exhibit volatile returns, the US is the lowest, and the others are in between.[37]

Futures Trading Competition Across Asia

Asia has become the world's engine of demand for commodities. What is the outlook for development of a commodities trading hub in the region, and which financial centers and exchanges might be more successful in creating this hub? At least seven financial centers and their respective exchanges are possible beneficiaries of rising interest in commodities trading (Table 10.14).

High economic growth in Asia, particularly in China and India, has propelled commodity prices sharply upward in the years following 2000. As a large buyer,

Table 10.14 New and Revitalized Commodities Exchanges in Asia

	Financial center	*New or old exchange*	*New initiative and existing exchange business*
1	Tokyo, Japan	Tokyo Commodity Exchange (TOCOM)	Demutualizing; focus on corporate and financial investors.
2	Singapore	A Singapore Mercantile Exchange	New exchange.
		B Singapore Commodities Exchange	Existing rubber trading, to establish added commodities.
3	Hong Kong	Hong Kong Mercantile Exchange (HKMEx)	Trade fuel oil contracts.
4	Shanghai	A Shanghai Futures Exchange	Copper and gold.
		B Dalian Futures Exchange	Agricultural products.
5	Mumbai, India	Mumbai Multi Commodity Exchange	Developing business plans.
6	Kuala Lumpur, Malaysia	Bursa Malaysia	Trade palm oil, and other derivatives.
7	United Arab Emirates	A Dubai Mercantile Exchange	Oil contracts.
		B Dubai Gold and Commodities Exchange	Precious metals, steel.

Source: J. Blas and L. Whipp, "Asia Accepts the Need for Commodities Exchange Hub," *Financial Times*, October 22, 2008, p. 25.

China has been impacted by rising commodity prices, and government officials have sought remedies to rising prices, and criticized market mechanics. In August 2009 the press reported China had negotiated an iron ore price with Fortescue Metals Group, Australia's third largest iron ore producer. Fortescue agreed to a 3 percent discount on the benchmark price, pending completion of loans from Chinese lenders.[38] The deal with Fortescue would relieve Chinese steelmakers from paying a premium price on the spot market.

A second factor is a shift in investor behavior toward taking larger exposures in commodities. Asset managers in Asia are joining North American and European based investors, more aggressively trading commodity futures and options where liquid markets are available. According to Jim Rogers, the influential commodities investor, with its large population Asia is becoming a more important center for commodities demand.

Third, financial centers like Hong Kong and Singapore view commodities trading as a natural step in the evolution of their financial services business.

Finally, there is a growing need for better risk management facilities in Asia and elsewhere. The global financial crisis of 2008–09 is driving businesses and investors from the opaque, bilateral, and private over the counter markets, to more liquid and transparent markets for hedging and investment. This provides an opportunity and a challenge. Banks and securities dealers are unwilling to give up profitable and privately negotiated hedging business.

Commodities Hubs

In 2008 organizers in Hong Kong announced plans to create the Hong Kong Mercantile Exchange (HKMEx). Opened in the following year, HKMEx trades US dollar denominated contracts for delivery of fuel oil to Mainland China. Additional contracts are traded, including soybeans and iron ore.

Hong Kong's financial services secretary, John Tsang, stated that the new exchange gives Hong Kong a huge opportunity to develop a commodities futures market.[39] To be successful the market must attract investor and corporate interest. HKMEx boosters include Merrill Lynch, Citigroup, and large commodity oriented firms.

Rising incomes and wealth in China are creating a new group of investors, seeking diversification from traditional investment classes. Outstanding commodities contracts in North America have tripled since 2004, but Asia lags behind in developing home grown financial exchanges for commodity trading.

As we can observe in Table 10.14, HKMEx is only one of more than a half-dozen initiatives across Asia. Singapore Mercantile Exchange is a bet that a well-regarded regulatory environment, supported by international banks and traders, will make SMX attractive and a success. Also, Singapore already is a strong hub for over the counter oil trading. Meanwhile, Singapore's old commodities exchange (Table 10.14, Line 2B) is carefully studying the new exchange's maneuvers.

Also, in Tokyo, Shanghai, Mumbai, and Kuala Lumpur, new commodities exchanges are being launched, in some cases parallel to existing exchanges. Bankers and officials in Asia warn that exchanges need to offer unique products to thrive. A Barclays Bank official notes there is potential for niche exchanges with a linkage to large global exchanges. Several bankers have observed that, if exchanges do not offer uniqueness or the ability to attract liquidity, traders will stay with established exchange markets rather than migrate to new venues.

11 Looking Forward

This chapter has three objectives. First, we analyze several new forces operating in global finance that are shaping future opportunities and challenges facing financial exchanges. Second, we analyze how the exchange sector will evolve, considering its competitive structure. We consider how these changes may affect the valuation of financial exchanges as for-profit companies. Finally, we consider challenges facing exchanges in the future.

The financial exchange sector is in an early stage of development. Many industry sectors have evolved through a four-stage evolutionary process, beginning with startup, followed by high growth, consolidation, and finally maturity. It is difficult to apply this simple model to financial exchanges for several reasons. First, most exchanges began as mutual associations, not as for-profit or shareholder owned companies. In that position they had little incentive to grow, gain market share, or even consider profitability. Beginning in the 1990s exchanges undertook a transformation to for-profit status. Second, given the world finance structure, each country has developed its own banking and securities market sector. Until long after World War II, these were kept partly segmented as national entities. But in recent decades there has been a rush to unify national financial systems. As a result, within a two-decade period there has been a magnification of competitive pressures facing exchanges and other banking and financial institutions that formerly operated in a semi-protected national environment. Finally, each country exchange has its own cycle of financial evolution. Clearly the Zimbabwe financial exchange is far behind that of Kenya, which is behind Morocco, which is behind South Africa, which is behind India, which is behind China, which is behind Hong Kong.

For these reasons, it is problematic to place the financial exchange sector in any particular phase of development. As we note, there is little doubt financial exchanges have moved into a consolidation phase, but in many countries the local exchanges are only in an early development stage or entering a high growth phase.

In the following sections we consider sovereign wealth funds, as a new type of financial institution, operating globally and altering the opportunities and challenges faced by exchanges. Next, we analyze a region of rising wealth status, the Gulf Cooperation Council (GCC). This region enjoys huge oil and gas deposits, is increasing its wealth status, and is sponsoring sovereign wealth funds that exhibit a growing appetite for financial investment around the globe. Then we analyze the present and future competitive structure in the financial exchange sector. We follow that with an examination and analysis of trends and shifts in the valuation of exchanges as shareholder owned entities. We conclude with a discussion of challenges for the future.

Sovereign Wealth Funds

Sovereign wealth funds (SWFs) are a growing source of power and influence in world capital markets. According to Robert Kimmitt, SWFs are large pools of capital controlled by a government and invested in private markets abroad.[1] SWFs are growing in size and number, and at yearend 2008 were in control of assets valued at over $2.5 trillion. Kimmitt distinguishes SWFs from other sovereign financial funds, such as official foreign exchange reserves, public pension funds, and state owned enterprises. SWFs have a higher risk tolerance than other sovereign funds, hold more risky assets than foreign exchange reserve funds, and seek higher returns to support future generations.

Two types of SWFs can be distinguished, based on the source of foreign exchange assets: commodity and non-commodity funds. Commodity sovereign wealth funds gain reserves from commodity exports owned or taxed by the government. These funds stabilize fiscal revenues, achieve intergenerational saving, and stabilize foreign exchange inflows. Non-commodity SWFs are established through transfers of assets from official foreign exchange reserves. Large external payments surpluses allow non-commodity exporters to transfer foreign exchange reserves to separate, stand-alone investment funds. Non-commodity funds often arise from exchange rate intervention, absorbing domestic liquidity.

Growing Importance

Sovereign wealth funds play an important role in the shifting tides of financial wealth around the world. SWFs are important wealth holders and accumulators in countries that lack fully developed financial markets or are at an early stage of economic development. As we observe in this chapter, in the Middle East, where several of the largest SWFs are based, the financial market system is only in an early stage of development.

Sovereign wealth funds have made important contributions to the operation and stability of world financial markets. First, they provide relatively efficient engines for recycling surplus foreign exchange earnings. Second, SWFs have proven to be helpful in stabilizing financial markets at times of volatility and crisis. For example, in 2007–08 SWFs made large investments in North American and European banks and financial institutions when these entities were in desperate need to strengthen their capital positions. Finally, SWFs are patient, long term investors. Therefore, they provide an important and necessary source of stable investors at times when others may be unwilling to take on investment risk.

Kuwait established the Kuwait Investment Board (KIB) in 1953, eight years before its independence from the United Kingdom. KIB invested surplus oil revenue. As Kimmitt notes, KIB "perhaps was the first ever sovereign wealth fund."

SWFs have grown rapidly owing to two factors. First, commodity exporters such as Saudi Arabia and Kuwait have enjoyed high prices for their exports, earning huge surplus foreign exchange revenues. The oil price boom in 2003–07 is a striking example. Second, global payments imbalances have expanded since 2000, giving some large exporters the ability to accumulate enormous foreign exchange reserves. Large amounts of these reserves have been placed in SWFs for long term investment.

The Largest SWFs

At yearend 2007 the seven largest sovereign wealth funds held assets worth over $2.4 trillion (Table 11.1). One year later the ten largest held assets in excess of $3 trillion. The largest of these, Abu Dhabi Investment Authority (ADIA), has been operating for more than three decades. In 2007 ADIA made a $7.5 billion investment in Citigroup, apparently part of a trend by SWFs to bolster Western financial institutions. A Morgan Stanley estimate was that these funds injected over $37 billion into financial stocks in the first ten months of 2007. This investment spree was "driven by the rising oil price and growing foreign exchange reserves" which swelled the treasuries of the Middle East and China.[2]

ADIA published its first annual review in first quarter 2010. As can be noted in Table 11.1, ADIA is assigned a low rating of 3 for transparency. Only two of the ten largest SWFs were assigned lower ratings, SAMA Foreign Holdings and SAFE Investment Company. ADIA had never disclosed its overall size or issued reports until early in 2008. The opacity of sovereign wealth funds has been a key focus of Western countries that fear politically driven investment decisions. A debate over this issue led to the International Monetary Fund developing best practices for SWFs. While investment disclosure is improving, few expect SWFs will increase their disclosure and reporting to match that of Norway's Government Pension Fund, which is assigned a high transparency rating of 10 (Table 11.1).

Returning to Table 11.1 we see the Government Pension Fund of Norway ranks second among the largest SWFs. This fund finds itself in an exceptional position, as the least criticized and questioned regarding motives driving its investments. There has long been full transparency of its operations, and its portfolio seems driven by purely financial return objectives. Many other SWFs have been challenged by critics to give assurances that they have no political or other non-financial objectives. Further, SWFs have been warned to refrain from seeking to influence corporate governance and management processes in the companies in which they invest. The Norwegian fund is not an instrument for political positioning or one that makes political investment decisions. According to Norway's minister of finance, the fund was set up to manage Norway's petroleum wealth in a sustainable manner.[3]

Table 11.1 Largest Sovereign Wealth Funds (2008–09)

Country	*Fund name*	*Year begun*	*January 2008*		*January 2009*		*Transparency rating***
			Rank	*Assets*	*Rank*	*Assets*	
UAE	Abu Dhabi Investment Authority	1978	1	$875	1	$627	3
Norway	Government Pension Fund Global	1990	2	343	2	445	10
Saudi Arabia	SAMA Foreign Holdings				3	432	2
China	SAFE Investment Company				4	347	2
China	China Investment Corporation	2007	6	200	5	289	6
Singapore	Government of Singapore Investment Corporation	1981	3	330	6	248	6
Kuwait	Kuwait Investment Authority				7	203	6
Russia	National Welfare Fund				8	168	5
China	National Social Security Fund (NSSF)				9	147	5
Hong Kong	Hong Kong Monetary Authority Investment Portfolio				10	140	8
Saudi Arabia	Various Saudi Arabian funds		4	306			
Kuwait	Reserve Fund for Future Generations*	1960	5	250			
Singapore	Temasek Holdings	1974	7	159			
Totals				$2,463		$3,046	

Source: A. Murray, "Ascent of Sovereign Wealth Funds Illustrates New World Order," *Wall Street Journal*, January 18, 2008, p. A2; R. Wigglesworth, "Sovereign Wealth Funds Start to Open up Their Books," *Financial Times*, March 18, 2010, p. 5.

Notes
Amounts are in billions of US dollars.
* Includes Kuwait Investment Authority, established in 1953.
** A rating of 10 is the highest, indicating high transparency.

In 2008 Singapore had two of the largest SWFs, ranked third and seventh. A year later Singapore accounted for one SWF ranked among the top ten (Singapore Investment Corporation, which ranked sixth). Asian countries accounted for three of the seven largest SWFs in 2008, but five of the top ten a year later (Table 11.1). Asian countries are among the largest holders of official foreign exchange reserves, and have been more aggressively shifting these assets into their respective SWFs.

Temasek, Singapore's second largest SWF, has been increasingly active in large investments valued at $2 billion or more. Its four largest investments include two in the United States and two in Australia, in aggregate valued at close to $35 billion. Temasek's investments in Asian banks reportedly are aimed at supporting Singapore's ambitions to become a strong regional financial rival to Hong Kong. Its purchase of a 9 percent stake in the Swiss bank UBS is viewed as aiming to boost the city state's goal of becoming a global center of wealth management.[4]

The financial crisis of 2008–09 has impacted the investing activities and strategies of SWFs in several ways. A number of these funds have slowed the pace of investing, taking a cautious and conservative stance. This is true of funds in the Middle East and Singapore. By contrast, in 2009 China's sovereign wealth fund was becoming a major backer of natural resource companies worldwide. China Investment Corporation (CIC) purchased a 15 percent stake in Hong Kong based commodities trader Noble Group for $850 million. Two months later (July 2009) it made a $1.5 billion investment in Canadian mining company Teck Resources Ltd. In September 2009 CIC announced a debt investment in Bumi Resources, an Indonesian producer of thermal coal, used to generate electricity.[5] These resource type investments fit in with China's long term strategic interest in securing access to a range of natural resources.

In 2010 sovereign governments focused attention on SWFs as potential investors. In 2009 both the UK and Germany experienced difficulty in attracting sufficient bidders in several of their scheduled bond auctions. As a result, governments now are making special efforts to bring SWFs into the bidding as regularly scheduled bond auctions take place.

Expected increases in government bond issuance following the financial crisis of 2008–09 will result in SWFs playing a more active role in these bond auctions. This will continue as private sector borrowers experience rising business levels and the need to issue greater amounts of debt in global financial markets.[6]

Implications for Financial Exchanges

The ascent of sovereign wealth funds may be one of several signals pointing toward emergence of a new world order. This new regime would consist of larger, more internationally oriented investment funds, owned and ultimately managed by governments. The rising importance of governments seems to parallel other signs of a rise in state capitalism, where the government plays an expanding role in making and executing investment decisions.

Sovereign wealth funds are likely to play a strategic and increasingly important role in world investment. Government holdings of foreign exchange reserves are growing faster than world trade and income, and SWFs play a key role in the ultimate management and disposition of these funds. How will this affect financial exchanges? In part that depends on the mix of investments made by SWFs. Will they opt more for highly diversified portfolios of equities and fixed income assets, traded on exchanges? Alternately, will they prefer large stakes in companies, negotiated privately and off exchange markets? Can financial exchanges develop and maintain trading venues suitable to meet the needs of more sophisticated sovereign wealth funds?

A study by the McKinsey Institute shows that, while one-third of the world's financial assets were held in the United States early in 2008, the share held by emerging market investors was rising, growing twice as fast as in developed countries.[7]

As large investing entities, sovereign wealth funds will add to the demand for financial services provided by exchanges. As traders of large stakes in companies, SWFs will require liquid markets in which to build or sell stakes in the companies in which they invest. Equally important, SWFs will require a high level of price discovery on exchange markets, to ensure fair pricing as they buy and sell. SWFs have a big stake in ensuring they can transact in liquid and transparent markets.

It is clear that a growing number of SWFs will increasingly use financial exchanges in their investment activities. But what type of investor is the SWF? Will SWFs add significantly to stock exchange turnover?

SWFs appear to be patient, conservative, long term investors. Patient investors move slowly and carefully, analyze the range of possibilities, and finally make their investment decisions. As conservative investors, SWFs screen information and fully analyze investment targets. As long term investors, SWFs are unlikely to elevate turnover. They stand at the opposite end of the spectrum to high frequency traders.

Given this characterization, we might expect that, as they grow in importance, SWFs may contribute stability to trading markets. Given the instabilities of the period 2008–09, this should be welcomed. Sovereign wealth funds hopefully will contribute to a more stable trading environment on exchange platforms. Equally important, they should become more vocal in supporting reform of the financial system that will strengthen stability of trading markets.

A Region of Rising Importance

The previous discussion of sovereign wealth funds describes the growing importance of over forty government funds that invest around the globe, to achieve intergenerational prosperity and affluence. Table 11.1 details the size and growth of the largest SWFs. Three of these are based in Gulf Cooperation Council countries, accounting for 60 percent of the $2.5 trillion of resources commanded by the top seven in 2008. In the following we describe the development and growing role of the GCC in world finance, and provide details concerning the role played by their fast-developing stock exchanges.

Gulf Cooperation Council

The Gulf Cooperation Council consists of six separate states: Saudi Arabia, Kuwait, Bahrain, the United Arab Emirates, Qatar, and Oman. According to Rehman, the GCC is one of three groups of countries loosely referred to as the Middle East.[8] Rehman considers three country groups as components of the broader Middle

East, the GCC, the Levant, and North Africa.[9] The GCC was formed in the early 1980s when the six member states adopted a charter for economic cooperation and joint security. The charter is broad and flexible, and represents a gradualist approach. The GCC introduced a customs union for the six states, and has promoted intra-regional movement of capital. Serious discussions of monetary union have taken place, especially at times when currency instability of the dollar and other lead currencies was taking place. In May 2007 Kuwait suspended the practice of pegging its currency to the US dollar.

On average, per capita incomes in the GCC are much higher than in other Middle East countries, four times the level in North Africa, and over five times the per capita income across the Levant. According to Rehman, if we consider the GCC as a collective whole, the economies would be the seventh largest in the developing world, ahead of Turkey and South Africa. In the five-year period ending in 2006, GCC per capita income rose 80 percent. The GCC region aggregate central government fiscal surplus, driven by oil and gas revenues, exceeds 20 percent of regional GDP.

GCC Economy and Finance

The six Persian Gulf states hold 40 percent of known world oil reserves, and 23 percent of global natural gas. Oil and gas income produce huge government fiscal surpluses, and finance local infrastructure and corporate investment.

Capital accumulation tends to magnify the role and importance of the GCC in global financial markets. Further, it stimulates the local economy, promoting private sector investment. Sustained prosperity, high domestic growth averaging over 6 percent per year, and balance of payments surpluses are transforming the GCC into a major global wealth holder and source of capital. GCC countries are extremely careful in their comments on the subject of investment and wealth accumulation. However, as Rehman notes, "on a per capita basis the GCC's public and private savings pool is not far behind legendary Japanese levels."[10]

Macro-Finance

Each of the six GCC states has its own unique characteristics, path of development, and opportunities for the future. By considering each of the six, with their different attributes, we obtain a better insight into the present and future importance of the region, most especially with regard to the prospects for financial wealth accumulation.

We begin with the United Arab Emirates (UAE), described by Rehman as the trailblazer and center of innovation. The UAE, with its capital city Abu Dhabi, is the state that has gained most attention. This is related to an open environment, modern media sector, and aggressive posture. Dubai is the regional economic hub.

The UAE contains seven emirates, federally joined, working together to modernize. Abu Dhabi is the largest and wealthiest emirate, and the capital city. Abu Dhabi is a large exporter of oil and also capital. The Abu Dhabi Investment Authority controls enormous assets invested globally (Table 11.1). The UAE espouses an open-for-business policy, including liberal treatment of business, government investment, protection of foreign business rights, and fast-track investment services. With a population of 4 million and per capita income close to the region's median, the UAE is considered a potential powerhouse economy of the future.

Saudi Arabia is a more complex country than the UAE. To outsiders the country is seen as mysterious and opaque. With a population of 24 million, it is the core market in the GCC. Its stock exchange is the only developed equity market in the GCC (Table 11.2). With a GDP of over $370 billion, Saudi Arabia accounts for over half of the GCC total.

With a vast and arid territory, Saudi Arabia is ruled by a monarchy that enjoys close historical links with the United States and Western Europe. The national oil company, Saudi Aramco, manages the kingdom's large petrochemical sector. The monarchy, religious establishment, and private business sector constitute an intricate web of control and governance in Saudi Arabia.

Qatar is the upstart state in the GCC, pursuing a development strategy aimed at achieving quick results, but avoiding the errors of others. With a small population of 836,000, Qatar enjoys high per capita income and wealth from its abundant natural gas resources.

Qatar's GDP per capita is among the highest in the world, as Qatar enjoys the world's third largest natural gas reserves and is apparently heading for the role of largest liquefied natural gas (LNG) exports. Qatar's two main state gas companies, Qatargas and Rasgas, enjoy a flawless record of supply, with another state owned company, Nakilat, managing fifty-four huge vessels to transport LNG worldwide. Qatar offers an integrated supply chain to countries that sign up for long term purchase agreements. Shell, the Anglo-Dutch energy group, is the largest single foreign investor in Qatar, spending $21 billion on gas liquids projects.[11]

With this wealth, Qatar's public sector investment propels the local economy. The state has pursued an industrial diversification policy. Part of this policy includes development of a world class banking and investment sector, the Qatar Financial

Table 11.2 Stock Markets in the Gulf Cooperation Council, Yearend 2008

	1. No. of listed companies	*2. Market capitalization*	*3. Trading value*	*4. Market designation*
Saudi Arabia	127	246	524	Developed
Kuwait	202	107	122	Frontier
United Arab Emirates	96	97	144	Frontier
Qatar	42	76	48	Frontier
Oman	127	15	8	Frontier
Bahrain	45	21	3	Frontier
Total	639	562	849	

Source: Standard & Poor's, *Stock Market Factbook 2009*.

Note: Columns 2 and 3 are in billions of US dollars.

Centre (QFC). Its diversification strategy also includes the educational system. Qatar has partnered with leading American universities to create an Education City, a complex housing several renowned universities.

In the past Bahrain has been described as the Wall Street of the Persian Gulf. The small state houses hundreds of financial institutions and foreign banks. As an offshore financial center, Bahrain attracts capital and entrepreneurs from Saudi Arabia and other Middle East regions. The economy is diversifying into non-financial activities, including manufacturing and non-financial services.

Bahrain is the first Arab oil state to benefit from large dollar income resulting from hydrocarbon exports. Bahrain will be the first to run out of oil, but decreasing production of petroleum has spurred the government to diversify its economy. As a result, Bahrain has one of the most varied economies in the region, with a mix of manufacturing and service businesses.

Aluminum Bahrain, or Alba, is one of the oldest industries in the kingdom, established in 1968 to produce aluminum. Alba operates the second largest smelter in the Middle East, and employs over 3,000 workers. The company has developed a large downstream business, with half of its production utilized in local manufacturing.[12]

Kuwait enjoys the benefits of a small population (2.6 million) and large oil reserves. Per capita income exceeds $31,000. Following the first Gulf War, Kuwait rebuilt damaged property and undertook political and economic reforms. Its shift toward a more democratic government has been observed and in part followed by its neighbors. Kuwait is an important exporter of oil and dollar valued capital.

Oman ranks fourth in population in the GCC, with 2.6 million people, and enjoys the lowest population density of the GCC states. Its per capita income is one-third that of Kuwait and half that of Bahrain, but its growing middle class supports rising consumer spending, a trend in many emerging countries. Oman enjoys a fairly diversified economy, with services, retail, and tourism adding to the energy sector.

Stock Exchanges

The Gulf region offers prospects for above-average economic growth for several decades into the future. This will be supported by large oil and gas exports, which the governing states have managed in a careful and forward looking way. Their respective stock markets are developing rapidly, given the escalated wealth and income levels, and growing diversification of the economic base.

The basic needs of the GCC states are likely to spur stock market development. These needs include the following:

1 The GCC has become an increasingly more important source of capital, supplying equity and loan funds to all continents.
2 The GCC needs to develop and diversify domestic economies, requiring investment management, and financial institutions capable of allocating capital in a rational framework.

3 Rising wealth and income require that individuals, companies, and government institutions have well-functioning and transparent markets in which to invest and manage financial assets.

In Table 11.2 we observe that the six country stock markets in the GCC 1) vary considerably in size and development, and 2) have an aggregate value that is impressive. At yearend 2008 the total market capitalization value of the GCC stock markets exceeded $560 billion, trading value exceeded $840 billion, and over 630 companies were listed. The Saudi Arabia market is rated a developed market (Table 11.2), whereas the other five are considered frontier markets.

During the decade of 2001–09 the six GCC stock markets experienced a boom, with the Saudi market advancing by over 600 percent and other GCC markets advancing on average at a more modest pace. Rehman notes that the stock market boom in 2001–07 was managed much better than in the previous decade.[13] First, capital was allocated more broadly to local, regional, and Western country markets, as opposed to an earlier focus on investing primarily in Western country markets. Second, local investment was allocated more effectively, to knowledge based industries and infrastructure. Third, the private sector participated more actively in the period 2001–07 both as investors and as decision-makers making capital allocation decisions. Finally, domestic expertise has been developed and better utilized in formulating investment policy and strategy.

Saudi Bourse More Global

Saudi Arabia's Tadawul stock market is the largest in the Persian Gulf region. Until recently it was nearly impossible for international investors to access Tadawul. This changed in August 2008 when the Saudi Capital Markets Authority (CMA) allowed foreign investors to buy equities indirectly, by investment in total return swaps. Through designated brokers non-Saudi parties can gain exposure to specific share issues listed on the Tadawul.

Foreign interest in the Saudi stock market is not hard to comprehend. Saudi Arabia has a large population, a young and energetic workforce, and substantial oil and gas resources.[14]

The country boasts a number of large, well-established industries and companies. The latter include Saudi Basic Industries Corporation (SABIC), one of the world's largest petrochemical producers, with a market capitalization of $68 billion. Al Rajhi Bank is the world's largest Islamic bank, valued on the stock market at $31 billion. Saudi Telecom is the dominant operator in its sector, and Almarai is a major dairy products firm. Kingdom Holding Company is a conglomerate controlled by the Saudi billionaire Prince Alwaleed bin Talal.[15]

Research coverage of Saudi stocks has intensified in recent years. Most of the 120 or more companies listed on the Tadawul market are covered by one or more analysts. In recent global stock market fluctuations the Saudi share market demonstrated resilience. Nevertheless, some fund managers and index providers regard the market as closer to "frontier" status than developed. As a result, a large portion of the non-Saudi investment comes from hedge funds. According to HSBC, which is the largest broker dealing in Saudi swaps, apparently 80 percent of the sixty institutional clients gaining exposure to Saudi equities are hedge funds. Bankers appear confident that Saudi Arabia will become an increasingly important part of the international capital markets.[16]

Similar Trends?

As we move forward in time, will the GCC stock exchanges follow the patterns developed elsewhere as they expand and restructure? The GCC region enjoys unprecedented sources of wealth, but it also faces larger risk, given the region's concentrated dependence on hydrocarbon exports. Current efforts to diversify the real economy in the GCC will play an important role in determining how successful the six-state region will be in developing a more broad based economy and stock market system.

We expect similar trends in stock exchange evolution in the GCC as have taken place in North America, Europe, and Asia. In 2008 aggregate market capitalization of the six exchanges was over 80 percent of regional GDP, and trading value exceeded market capitalization by a wide margin. We can expect some consolidation of stock exchanges in the future, but these restructurings may be a few years ahead.

Evolution of Exchange Sector

Recent estimates of the number of financial exchanges in operation indicate close to 300 separate entities.[17] This includes stock, derivative, and commodity exchanges, as well as mixed exchanges on whose platforms more than one category of securities is traded. In over a dozen countries with leading exchanges, mergers between stock and derivative exchanges have produced mixed (stock plus derivative) markets. This is the pattern in Canada, Hong Kong, Singapore, Taiwan, Australia, and other countries. In several countries with highly developed financial systems, separate and distinct derivative markets have survived. These include several options exchanges in the United States.

In several cases, derivative trading and commodity trading via futures and options operate on exchanges side by side. This is the case in CME, CBOT, CBOE, and ICE. LIFFE and Eurex operate as semi-autonomous derivative and commodity exchanges, under the broad umbrella of parent stock exchange groups. In Japan the Osaka Exchange remains a separate derivative trading venue, while the Tokyo Stock Exchange trades equities, bonds, and derivatives.

At least three distinct patterns can be observed in countries with more advanced financial systems. First, mergers of stock and derivative exchanges are the pattern seen in Australia, Hong Kong, and Singapore. Second, large stand-alone derivative exchanges operate in the United States (CME, ICE). Finally, semi-autonomous derivative exchanges are owned by large stock exchanges (LIFFE and Eurex).

Present Structure

Standard & Poor's publishes an annual *Global Stock Markets Factbook*. This publication provides data on all viable national stock markets, that is, markets in which investors around the globe may gain exposure to some degree. The 2009 edition of this publication contains base data on market capitalization, trading value, and number of listed companies for eighty-six emerging and twenty-nine developed countries. A later section of the S&P *Factbook* provides detailed information on eighty-one country stock markets. These country stock markets are categorized as developed, emerging, or frontier markets. In Table 11.3, we locate these eighty-one country stock markets by region. Only two developed markets (the USA and Canada) are located in the Americas. The majority of emerging stock markets (ten) are located in Asia and the Middle East. Only three African markets (South Africa, Egypt, and Morocco) are among the emerging markets in Table 11.3.

S&P distinguishes frontier markets as a third category. These are smaller, less liquid markets offering only limited opportunities for foreign institutional investors. The median market capitalization of the thirty-three frontier stock markets at yearend 2008 reported by S&P was $10.5 billion. Frontier markets in the Americas include Colombia, Ecuador, Jamaica, Panama, and Trinidad and Tobago. Eight African stock markets are designated as having frontier status, which are Botswana, Ghana, Ivory Coast, Kenya, Mauritius, Namibia, Nigeria, and Tunisia. Of the fifty African nations, only three are labeled emerging stock markets. These are Egypt, Morocco, and South Africa.

Looking Forward to a Paradigm Shift

The most active of the stock markets in Table 11.3 are the developed stock markets in the Americas, Europe, and Asia and the Middle East. We have analyzed and explained the competitive shifts taking place in these regions via mergers, alliances, technology investment, and development of new products. The developed stock markets have taken a lead role in restructuring. We expect that emerging and frontier financial exchanges will extend this paradigm shift over the period 2010–25.

The paradigm shift will embrace stock, derivative, and commodity exchanges. Technology cost factors will encourage mergers: a) between stock exchanges, b) that produce mixed exchanges, and c) between derivative exchanges and also between commodity exchanges. These mergers will reach a pace that reduces the overall

Table 11.3 Present Structure of Stock Markets: Number of Country Markets (2008)

Type of stock market	*Americas*	*Europe*	*Asia and the Middle East*	*Africa*	*Total*
Developed	2	18	5	0	25
Emerging	5	5	10	3	23
Frontier	5	9	11	8	33
Total	12	32	26	11	81

Source: Standard & Poor's, *Global Stock Markets Factbook 2009*.

number of exchanges to far fewer than the 300 exchanges presently operating. The launching of new exchanges will continue, but this will be more than offset by mergers and consolidations. This is due to the basic economics of exchange operation. Scale economies, rising technology costs and challenges, and the need to achieve scalability and effective cost control will exert an overwhelming influence. By 2025 we could witness an exchange landscape with far fewer than 200 exchange entities, many conducting mixed business, trading shares, derivatives, and commodities.

Valuation of Financial Exchanges

The exchange sector is one of the newest tracked by financial analysts. The first publicly owned exchange, Stockholm Stock Exchange, obtained a public listing in 1993. Between 1993 and 2004 another dozen exchanges went public, and at yearend 2004 the thirteen publicly owned exchanges had a combined market value of $29 billion (Table 11.4). In the following we analyze why financial exchanges experience rising and falling market valuations, and the shifting determinants of valuation in this sector.

Table 11.4 Market Capitalization Values of Leading Exchanges at Selected Dates (Amounts in US$ Billions)

	A. November 16, 2004	*B. February 29, 2008*	*C. June 9, 2009*	*D. October 25, 2010*
1 Deutsche Börse	6.2	32.3	17.0	13.7
2 CME Group	6.9	27.8	24.1	18.7
3 BOVESPA BM&F		22.4	12.6	16.7
4 Hong Kong Exchange	2.6	21.2	17.5	25.1
5 NYSE Euronext		17.9	7.6	7.7
6 Intercontinental Exchange		9.3	8.0	—
7 NYMEX		9.2		—
8 LSE	2.1	7.6	3.7	2.8
9 ASX Australia	1.5	6.8		*
10 Euronext	3.6			—
11 Toronto Stock Exchange	1.5			—
12 Stockholm Stock Exchange (OM)	1.5			—
13 Singapore Stock Exchange	1.1			14.0*
14 Athens	0.7			—
15 ArcaEx	0.7			—
16 NASDAQ	0.6		4.1	3.9
17 Oslo Børs	0.2			—
18 Subtotal	29.2	154.5	94.6	102.8

Sources: Compiled by author from various sources, including: *Wall Street Journal*, *Financial Times*, and Mondo Visione. Data for 2004 from Maureen O'Hara, "Searching for a New Center: U.S. Securities Markets in Transition," *Economic Review*, Federal Reserve Bank of Atlanta, 2004, pp. 37–52.

Notes

Data for NASDAQ valuation in 2009 and 2010 refers to the merged NASDAQ OMX combined entity.

* Refers to expected (combined) value of SGX plus ASX should proposed merger go forward.

Early Development of Sector

Close to five years elapsed between the public listing of Stockholm Stock Exchange and the public listing of the Australian Stock Exchange in 1998. These two exchanges probably are not the exchanges a casual observer would guess to have been the first to conduct an IPO and public listing. They appear to be somewhat "off the radar," and certainly not where perceptions of financial innovation are focused. To obtain a complete picture of the creation of the financial exchange sector and determinants of valuation of exchanges, we must examine the broad financial landscape very carefully.

Change and challenges facing individual exchanges are described in detail in Chapters 3 and 4. Changes in technology, clientele, regulation, and competitive issues posed successive challenges requiring exchanges restructure, revise their business models, and go public. In the period 1993–2004 a small but viable exchange sector was created, consisting of thirteen publicly owned exchanges, and many other exchanges still operating as mutual organizations. The thirteen publicly owned exchanges are listed in Table 11.4, Column A. The two largest exchanges (NYSE and Tokyo Stock Exchange) at that time continued to operate under the traditional mutual format. Not until 2006 did the NYSE join the ranks of publicly owned exchanges. At yearend 2010 the TSE had not as yet gone public.

From late 2004 to early 2008 significant changes took place in the valuation of financial exchanges. First, overall valuation of exchanges increased markedly. As we can observe in Table 11.4, Column B, valuations of individual exchanges increased between 270 percent (London Stock Exchange) and 710 percent (Hong Kong Exchange).

Second, several exchanges became publicly owned, including NYSE, CBOT, NYMEX, and ICE. Three of these participated in mergers. This produced high valuations, and shifted the rankings of exchanges according to their relative values. As described in earlier discussions, NYSE and Euronext merged, to produce the fifth ranked exchange by value in 2008. CME merged with CBOT and following that with NYMEX, to produce the first rank exchange group by valuation in 2009 (Table 11.4, Column C).

In the period June 2009 to October 2010, the eight largest exchange groups by market valuation of their respective shares gained 8–9 percent in overall value. This also was a recovery period for global stock markets, with leading indices gaining and turnover expanding. This is shown in Table 11.4, Columns C and D.

The Hong Kong Exchange was a big winner, moving from second rank to first in valuation ($25.1 billion in October 2010). HKEx moved ahead of CME Group, which ranked second in valuation in October 2010. The eight exchanges in Table 11.4, Column D enjoyed an aggregate valuation of $102.8 billion. Deutsche Börse and CME Group lost considerable valuation in the period June 2009 to October 2010, whereas BOVESPA enjoyed a significant gain in valuation. A month earlier (September 2010) BOVESPA hosted a Petrobras share offering, the largest ever.

The Petrobras share offering was a test of the new issuance capabilities of the combined BM&F BOVESPA, the Brazilian financial exchange. The $67 billion

Petrobras offering was over-subscribed by 30 percent. The government raised close to $43 billion by selling part of its stake in Petrobras, and providing it with compensation for extending Petrobras the right to extract national oil reserves. Petrobras is expected to use the remaining $24 billion proceeds as fresh capital to finance its ambitious investment program extending to 2014.[18]

As the largest share offering in history, the Petrobras deal places Brazil and Sao Paulo firmly on the global finance map, but other factors support the ascent of Brazil and BOVESPA toward world class financial status. First, Brazilian companies (Vale, Embraer) are worldwide issuers of debt and equity securities, as well as M&A deal participants. Second, the Petrobras offering opened Brazil to a new brand of investors, those intent on gaining exposure to the now prominent hydrocarbons sector in Brazil. Third, in certain respects Brazil has leaped ahead of other BRICs (China and Russia) that suffer from questionable governance and investor protection with regard to privatized companies.[19] According to Walter and Howie, over the decade 2000–10 China's stock market suffered fundamental problems in defining the status of privatized companies, their ownership rights, and the specific rights of shareholders.[20]

Broad trends operated in the periods 2004–08 and 2008–09, affecting valuations in the exchange sector. Buoyant equity markets (2004–07) elevated valuations in the exchange sector by wide margins, but in 2008–09 these trends reversed, and exchanges overall lost approximately one-third of their value. The FTSE/Mondo Visione Exchanges Index exhibits a similar movement. Between yearend 2007 and October 2008, this index lost slightly more than one-third of its value.[21]

Changing Mix of Entities

Close to 300 exchanges operate on a global basis, but the publicly owned and listed category has never reached twenty. As exchanges grow and go public, at least an equal number merge, to bring the aggregate number of listed entities under the "magic twenty." However, the mix of exchange entities is quite dynamic, bringing about a constant reshuffling and redistribution of sector valuation. Parallel with this, basic valuation determinants are causing the total sector valuation to rise and fall.

Consolidation Pressures

Consolidation has exerted severe pressures on valuations. Mergers create larger entities that can better afford investments required to keep ahead in technology. Also, mergers reduce competitive pressures on pricing of services. As a result, we should expect successful mergers to absorb a greater share of aggregate valuation in the exchange sector. As can be observed in Table 11.4, Column C, CME Group, one of the most successful consolidators in the sector, performed well in retaining valuation over the period February 2008 to June 2009. By contrast, inability to participate in mergers can be costly. Deutsche Börse was one of the big valuation losers in 2008–09 and again in 2009–10.

Consolidation and new entities going public yield a changing mix of companies in the exchange sector. The BOVESPA BM&F case offers an example of highly successful valuation around the time of its IPO.

New Entities

In October 2007 the Sao Paulo Exchange (BOVESPA) launched its IPO. The offering was a stunning success, with a 52 percent first trading day gain, and BOVESPA reaching a market valuation of 80 times earnings compared with general market multiples of 10–12.[22]

Immediately following the IPO, BOVESPA's capitalization value was $13.8 billion, more than half of NYSE Euronext, at that point the largest and most prestigious financial exchange (Table 11.5). Yet the market capitalization value of listed shares on BOVESPA was barely 6 percent of shares listed on NYSE Euronext. In the weeks following the BOVESPA IPO, news abounded regarding an IPO by Brazil's Bolsa Mercadorias e Futuros SA (BM&F), the options and commodities exchange. This included expectation of a share swap between BM&F and CME Group.[23] The BM&F IPO was slightly smaller than that of BOVESPA.

By late February a two-way consolidation affecting the Brazilian exchanges was under way. First, BM&F and CME Group engaged in a share swap with a value of $700 million. In this swap BM&F received a 2 percent stake in CME Group, whereas CME gained a 10 percent stake in BM&F. Second, BOVESPA and BM&F agreed to a merger. Both deals represent further consolidation in a sector experiencing rapid consolidation.

A combined BOVESPA and BM&F would be second only in the Americas to CME Group, and ahead of the NYSE Euronext exchange group (Table 11.4). Many specific strengths accrue to the combined BOVESPA BM&F, including the following:

1 It is a global exchange where local (Brazilian) companies do not have to list overseas to get low cost capital. By contrast Russian companies find it necessary to list overseas to attract lower cost foreign capital. Brazil is able to attract low cost capital from foreign investors.
2 Brazil's macro-indicators reflect moderate perceived risk levels.
3 Brazil is much better off in terms of corporate governance than countries like Russia and China, according to Roberto Teixeira da Costa, former chairman

Table 11.5 Comparison of BOVESPA and NYSE Euronext Capitalization Value (October 2007)

	Capitalization value of exchange	*Market capitalization of listed shares*
BOVESPA	$13.8 billion	$1,200 billion
NYSE Euronext	$24 billion	$20,000 billion

Source: J. Wheatley, "Traders Stunned by Power of Bovespa IPO," *Financial Times*, October 29, 2007, p. 19.

of Brazil's securities regulatory commission, and a leading figure in its capital markets.[24]

4 Inflation has been under control in Brazil.
5 Brazil has reduced its net debtor status and is on the verge of becoming a net creditor.

As a result of these strengths, the combined BOVESPA BM&F ranked third and fourth in February 2008 and June 2009 respectively (Table 11.4).

More recently, the Brazilian exchange has opened offices in Shanghai, New York, and London. These aim at establishing contacts with institutional traders. Technology upgrades are moving on course at a steady pace. Finally, the Brazilian exchange has joined the trend to "co-location" in which big customers can install computer servers inside the exchange's data centers to make high speed automated trades exploiting opportunities to arbitrage between different asset classes.[25]

A final note is to observe that the stock exchanges located in the top world financial centers, New York and London, have not performed very well in retaining relative valuation. At the four time points depicted in Table 11.4, the LSE share of aggregate valuation of leading exchanges declined from 7.2 percent in 2004, to 5.0 percent in 2008, to under 4 percent in 2009, and under 3 percent in 2010. The NYSE Euronext went from 11.6 percent in 2008 to 8.0 percent in 2009 and 7 percent in 2010. Both exchanges have become the prey of alternative trading systems (ATSs) that target various pieces of NYSE and LSE trading. ATS targets include trading of blue chip shares, and institutional traders requiring algorithmic trading services.

We consider Hong Kong as the world's third leading financial center. The Hong Kong Exchange supports that evaluation. As can be observed in Table 11.4, the Hong Kong Exchange ranked third, fourth, second, and first in 2004, 2008, 2009, and 2010 respectively in market valuation. Its share of aggregate valuation rose from 13.8 percent in 2008 to 18.4 percent the following year, and to 24 percent in 2010.

Fast Forward on Valuation

Competitive Model for Valuation

Our discussion of exchange sector valuation covers the period 2004–10. It reveals a fairly simple model of exchange valuation. This model has three components:

1 consolidation and creative destruction;
2 entry of new entities as publicly owned and listed companies;
3 business model revision to grow revenues and expand profitability.

Exchanges will continue to merge, and also form alliances and share cross-holdings. These cross-holdings will, in some cases, lead to closer ties such as technology partnerships or even full merger. A Schumpeterian process of creative destruction has been going on in this sector for two decades, and will continue into the future. Consolidation should lead to efficiencies, greater control over market sectors, and revenue gains.

Continued entry of new listed financial exchanges will enlarge the business and trading base that supports exchange valuations, but it also will increase competition for that enlarged base. The net result may be less growth in overall sector valuation than expected by unflinching optimists. However, the Brazil case suggests that considerable value accretion can take place in the sector.

Exchanges continue to create new products and expand in existing service areas. Their respective business models will reflect this in areas such as data and information, clearing services, and simultaneous trading of underlying securities (stocks and bonds) and related derivative instruments.

Non-Competing Groups

Two categories of non-competing groups must be considered in the analysis of valuation. These non-competing groups are: a) exchanges operating as mutual organizations, and based in countries where country risk factors repel competitors from other locations, for example Poland, Turkey, and South Africa; and b) exchanges which are listed and operating in apparently competitive environments, but gaining preferential business flow from "protected areas," for example Hong Kong Exchanges and Clearing.

In the previous chapter we described the Hong Kong–Shanghai nexus. The HKEx derives considerable benefits from this singular relationship, in the form of extraordinary listings and the ability to play the role of "free market" arbiter in price discovery of Mainland China company listings whose share prices in Shanghai require a comparative certification through a Hong Kong listing.

We believe that HKEx's special role will continue and possibly expand in importance. This should support the high relative valuation achieved by HKEx for several years. Danger signals to its valuation role could take the form of a shift toward a freer market valuation of the renminbi, and easing of China's comprehensive currency exchange control system.

Future Challenges

Financial exchanges face a future in which institutional traders will exert greater demands, conduct more complex trading, and require an enlarged product range. Exchanges will respond by introducing new trading products, more diverse services (particularly related to data and analytics), and market venues capable of services and order execution not dreamed of a decade ago. In this final section we comment on these future challenges, understanding that the future may be only a few milliseconds away.

Challenges for Institutional Traders

If we decompose the trade cycle into its typical trilogy, front, middle, and back office functions and activities, what we observe is most enlightening. Here we examine rapid changes in front office needs and practices, reflected in how institutional traders are revising their market data and analytics, and the growing need for computer interfaces and gateways that lead to greater success in determining buy–sell orders and the proper routing of these orders.

As described by Skeete, buy-side institutions find it critical to implement direct market access. They require more sophisticated electronic facility support to access liquidity as well as aggregate it. With direct market access institutional traders "are renting a broker's infrastructure . . . controlling orders" and saving a lot of commission money.[26] Exchanges play an important role in providing institutional traders with non-intermediated trading, in which proprietary traders have no ability to see order flow, and trading becomes more like a peer-to-peer operation.

Buy-side traders increasingly are using smart order management systems, a front office activity. In this process a buy-side trader utilizes computer processed information and analytics to consider what trade strategy to follow. This includes: a) possible portfolio changes, b) timing, price, or other factors that favor any particular strategy, and c) how best to route trade orders.

The routing of trade orders has become more complicated. Traditionally, an order would be run through a broker, paying brokerage commissions and depending on the broker to secure best execution. Changes in front office technology have carried trading away from that practice. Now buy-side traders, employed by the institution whose portfolio manager wishes to initiate trades, route orders, saving commissions and preserving anonymity. In turn, anonymous trading can lower or prevent market impact trading costs.

According to Benn Steil at the Council on Foreign Relations, the buy side has adopted smart order management and execution systems.[27] The portfolio manager decides on a change (buying or selling a large position—hundreds of thousands of shares). This information is put into the order management system, and communicated to the buy-side trader. The buy-side trader does not reveal he intends to make the large size trade. In fact, he breaks the trade into small pieces and dribbles these onto the exchange. Smart order management systems obviate the need to disguise the order.

Steil sees two significant changes in the order management system. First, algorithmic trading removes the human element from trading. Increasingly, computers parcel small orders from large, timed to 1) avoid disclosing a large unfilled order, and 2) preserve anonymity and avoid disclosure of who is trading what securities. Second, updated trading software is being built into order management systems that facilitate block trades through dark pools. These dark pools (Liquidnet) attract order flow, match large trades, and reduce trading costs. They relocate trading power and discretion back to the front office component of the trade cycle, the portfolio manager.

Challenges for Exchanges

As securities traders revise their organizational systems and strategies, they will interface with market venues in new and novel ways. Financial exchanges will respond in ways that enhance their ability to draw more traders into closer working ties and intensify trader utilization of exchange services. Exchanges inevitably will adjust the capacities of their trading platforms, recruit trading platform participants who are more innovative, and extend the range of securities and tradable bundles.

By way of example, the NYSE has signed on a new specialist firm, which signals a new direction on the Big Board's historic trading floor. Early in 2010, Getco LLC indicated it would take a key specialist role on the New York Stock Exchange. Chicago based Getco operates as a proprietary trading firm, and is one of the largest electronic market makers on a number of financial exchanges around the world. Despite the increasing dominance of screen based trading on NYSE, the entry of a high profile electronic trading firm such as Getco gives weight to the New York exchange's assertion that it supports hybrid trading. Getco intends to develop a floor trading presence on NYSE, despite the increasing role of electronic trading.

In recent years the number of designated market makers (specialists) on NYSE has declined. Getco becomes the fifth specialist firm, gaining oversight of 350 securities held by Barclays Capital, which the UK bank purchased in January 2010 from LaBranche & Co. While the number of specialists on NYSE has shrunk from thirty-five in 2000 to five early in 2010, their share of trading has edged up, accounting for 9 percent of NYSE trading volume in fourth quarter 2009, compared with 4 percent in September 2008.[28]

Since its inception in 1999 Getco has joined the ranks of the five biggest traders of US equities, and also is active in bonds, derivatives, and foreign exchange trading. Getco already is active in the LIFFE US futures exchange, and will move into a specialist role in NYSE Euronext's AMEX platform.

Getco's new role on the NYSE and AMEX indicates that exchanges may be in the process of rejuvenating floor trading, as well as hybrid platforms, for equity trading. But there are other drivers of market change and expansion. These include efforts to facilitate joint trading of different asset classes simultaneously and on the same platform. For this to succeed, exchanges will need to list non-equity securities (bonds and/or derivatives) on common platforms with equities. Early in 2010 it was announced that two of the UK's largest banks were ready to open the corporate bond market to a wider audience. Royal Bank of Scotland (RBS) was preparing to issue a bond on the London Stock Exchange's electronic retail bond trading platform, with Barclays Bank expected to follow. Such issuance would: 1) improve price transparency, 2) reduce bid–offer spreads, and 3) open the bond market to retail investors who until this initiative were shut out of a market where bonds were available only in amounts of £50,000 or more.[29]

On the European Continent (Germany, France, Italy, Spain), retail bond issuance has been commonplace for many years. RBS will become a market maker to the new platform. The LSE estimates that, of the 10,000 corporate bonds outstanding in the UK, less than 200 are available in retail denominations. RBS was the first to tap the new market, with a £100 denomination issue. Initially, the new LSE platform will trade ten corporate bonds from household UK names, including Tesco, British Telecom, and government bonds (gilts) in denominations as small as £1.

Investors trade through private client brokers, who place orders in the same way as for stock trading.[30] As exchanges add different asset classes to their trading platforms, it becomes easier for securities traders to conduct more complex trades and develop more electronic trading strategies. To meet this rising demand of traders and asset managers to carry out complex trades, investment banks and brokerage units are developing greater skills and capacities to service these and related needs.

For example, Citigroup has developed a unit based at Canary Wharf, London for this purpose. Also, Goldman Sachs and Morgan Stanley have already merged their various trading operations. Some banks emphasize integration of securities services at the trading level but not at the sales level.[31] In general, American banks are somewhat more advanced than their European counterparts in merging derivatives together with cash trading and risk management. In overhauling its London trading operation Citigroup has developed unified cash and derivatives trading. As a result, different types of assets (equities, bonds, derivatives) can be traded against each other more effectively. Hedge funds and asset managers have been important drivers of this trend. As described above, financial exchanges are responding in several ways. These include: 1) adding more asset classes to platforms that allow easier linkage of trading between underlying securities and derivatives, 2) improving data flow and availability (CME purchase of the Dow Jones information unit early in 2010), 3) facilitating reduced latency through upgrades in trading platforms and co-location, and 4) providing more flexible trading platform access via improved exchange gateway linkages.

Opaque Trades

While stock market participants have been employing electronic trading to increase the efficiency and effectiveness of their own trading activities, the effects of these practices on market efficiency may be subject to question. In March 2010 Randall Dodd, a senior financial market expert at the IMF's Monetary and Capital Markets Department, published a report asserting that three market trading practices "may pose some public interest concerns because of their effect on stability."[32] These market microstructure innovations include high frequency trading (HFT), flash trading, and dark pools. All three innovations rely on trading on alternative trading systems.

High Frequency Trading

High frequency trading is also called black box trading. It uses high speed computers governed by algorithms. Algorithms are instructions to the computer that: 1) analyze data, 2) identify trading opportunities, and 3) manage order flow to the markets. An estimated 90 percent of orders by high frequency traders are canceled. Tabb Group, a financial research firm, has estimated that profits from HFT aggregated $21 billion in 2008. High ranking broker-dealers such as Goldman Sachs, and hedge funds such as Citadel invest substantial amounts in supercomputers and software designed for high frequency trading. Sharp competition has developed for HFT business, leading to broker-dealers and large institutions seeking advantage via co-location of their computer servers.

Public policy issues come to the fore regarding HFT. The 1987 stock market crash and the more recent May 6, 2010 plunge are cases in point. Also, HFT could make the playing field less competitive, putting dealers at a disadvantage compared to other market participants. Customer orders have priority over those submitted by dealers. This is based on the principle that markets operate primarily for clients. Dealers are expected to provide trading liquidity and to maintain a two-sided market for the benefit of the trading public.

Flash Trading

The national market system (NMS) aims to give all equity market participants equal access to public orders. Offers to buy and sell equity securities are submitted to an exchange or alternative trading system. Each order is automatically matched with a standing or incoming order from the opposite side of the market.

Public orders can be observed by all market participants. However, so-called flash trades work differently. In the case of flash trading, an incoming order to an exchange or ATS is made visible (or flashed) just before it is sent to the national market system. If a trader can match the best bid or offer in the system, that trader can complete the transaction before other market participants can see it. This results in a flash trade.

Formerly, the NYSE permitted specialists (designated dealers) to benefit from this first look at incoming orders. The NYSE ended this practice to allow all market participants equal access. The NYSE rationale for ending this practice was to create a more level playing field. However, many ATSs have adopted flash trades as a means of pulling business away from the exchanges.

The Dodd analysis asserts that flash trading creates a privileged market segment. This segment trades ahead of the rest of the market and contravenes the principle of market fairness. Further, it discourages market makers from posting quotes.

Dark Pools

Dark pools are used by broker-dealers, institutional investors, and hedge funds to negotiate large securities transactions, beyond formal and accepted exchange trading rules. Rules that require public disclosure of bid and ask prices do not necessarily apply on private and members only trading systems. Dark pools allow large volume, or block trades, to be conducted on non-transparent venues, protecting participants from adverse market impact trading costs.

Dark pools may be owned by exchanges, independently, or by broker-dealers. From a public policy perspective, dark pools separate information about trading volume and bid–ask quotations from the price discovery process taking place on regulated exchanges. A differential access to market information develops when dark pool participants possess greater information than others. Further, the public market is deprived of the data inputs which become hidden within dark pool trading systems.

Both the Securities Exchange Commission and the Commodity Futures Trading Commission have increasing concerns over the three innovations described above. The SEC is preparing rules to limit flash trading and to subject dark pool trading to increased disclosure. The CFTC has commenced a study of these new trading methods. Also, the CFTC is examining methods to ensure that all investors have fair access to markets and that market stability is not threatened.

The May 6 Plunge

On Thursday, May 6, 2010, the US stock market experienced the biggest single intraday drop, shattering confidence in the world's largest capital market. A congressional committee held hearings to explain what had happened and why. Clearly, equity markets did not function properly. In the twenty-minute market melee, the S&P 500 fell 4 percent, and then plunged another 4.6 percent in just a few minutes of trading. Three stocks demonstrated especially high volatility: Procter & Gamble, Accenture, and Apple each fell 8–10 percent during this hectic period.

It is not easy to identify a specific trigger for the May 6 market plunge. Technology has evolved rapidly in recent years, and trading is quicker than the blink of an eye. Also, competition between a greater number of trading venues

Table 11.6 Fragmented US Equity Trading, September 2009 (Percentage Share of Trading Volume)

I Exchange trading:	
NASDAQ	19.4%
NYSE	14.7
NYSE Arca	13.2
Subtotal	47.3%
II Electronic communication networks (ECNs)*	
BATS**	9.5%
Direct Edge	9.8
NASDAQ OMX BX	3.3
Dark pools	7.8
Other ECNs	1.0
Subtotal	31.5%
III OTC	
Broker-dealers	17.5%
Other brokerage	3.7
Subtotal	21.2%

Source: Jeremy Grant, "Plunge Places Focus on Safety of the Share Markets," *Financial Times*, May 11, 2010, p. 23.

Notes

* Ownership of ECNs is diverse, including private ownership, banks, and stock exchanges.

** Technically BATS is now an exchange. It is included among ECNs owing to its business model largely adhering to ECN style.

has yielded more fragmented market pockets, subject to pressure from spurts in trading volume. US equity trading now is scattered across thirty or more venues (Table 11.6). Many of these venues are opaque, complicating and even inhibiting a rational price discovery process.

A similar picture prevails in Europe, where pro-competitive regulation is driving equity trading into a larger number of venues, each suffering from reduced liquidity. Fragmented markets make for segmented and smaller liquidity pools, less able to withstand market pressures when traders seek to shift portfolio holdings at a rapid pace.

The SEC has been reviewing how American equity markets function. In April 2010 it released a fourteen-page document requesting comments from market participants on how technology innovations affect investor interests. Also, the SEC seeks comments on whether liquidity shifts are exerting a negative influence on the national market system.[33]

The SEC also is looking into the application of market circuit breakers. Shortly after the May 6 plunge, the SEC met with representatives of the main stock exchanges to review how their circuit breakers have operated in the past and how they might be modified to better deal with market meltdowns.[34] More flexible use of circuit breakers could become a more important weapon in the battle of the bourses to sustain improved price stability.

Notes

1 World Capital Markets

1 Anatole Kaletsky, *Capitalism 4.0*, Perseus Group, 2010, pp. 23–24.
2 According to Pagano and Steil, in the period 1988–93 the LSE share of trading in Continental (German and French) shares rose from 12.9 percent to 20.6 percent. Benn Steil, *The European Equity Markets*, Brookings Institution, 1996, pp. 5–6.
3 E. Flowers and F. Lees, *The Euro, Capital Markets, and Dollarization*, Rowman & Littlefield, 2002, pp. 208–212.
4 *The Economist*, "Stuck in Neutral," August 15, 2009, pp. 65–66.
5 Tony Golding, *The City: Inside the Great Expectation Machine*, Prentice Hall/Financial Times, 2003, pp. 140–141.
6 This point among others is brought out in K. Abohokwah and G. Sofianos, "Execution Quality at the New, Fast NYSE," *Journal of Trading*, Winter 2008, pp. 29–33.
7 Michael MacKenzie, "Flash Crash Inquiry Focuses on High Frequency Traders," *Financial Times*, May 21, 2010, p. 20.
8 Henry Sender, "BlackRock in Trading Plan," *Financial Times*, September 12, 2009, p. 1.
9 W. Buiter, "Forget the Tobin Tax: There Is a Better Way to Curb Finance," *Financial Times*, September 2, 2009, p. 9.

2 Financial Centers and Exchanges

1 M.J. Clayton, B.N. Jorgensen, and K.A. Kavajecz, "On the Presence and Market Structure of Exchanges Around the World," *Journal of Financial Markets*, February 2006, pp. 27–28.
2 Stephen Mahlow-Smith, "Swaps Future Holds Few Parallels With Japan's Past," *Financial Times*, September 7, 2010, p. 22.
3 John Plender, "Rules Will Decide New York vs. London Battle," *Financial Times*, April 7, 2010, p. 20.
4 The time of writing this section is the final quarter of 2010.
5 Gillian Tett, "School Is Out, but Does the Final Bell Also Toll for London?" *Financial Times*, July 9, 2010, p. 20.
6 James Wilson, "Shadows Over a Symbol of Stability," *Financial Times*, July 29, 2010, p. 1.
7 Liam Denning, "Selling Petrobras and GM," *Wall Street Journal*, September 25, 2010, p. B14.
8 Brooke Masters, "Hong Kong Closes in on Financial Top Spot," *Financial Times*, September 20, 2010, p. 6.
9 K. Brown and S. Tucker, "A High-Flying Rivalry," *Financial Times*, April 26, 2010, p. 7.
10 Yasheng Huang, "Lessons on Creating a Favorable Business Climate," *Financial Times*, April 30, 2009, p. 4, special section on Shanghai.

11 McKinsey & Co., *Sustaining New York's and the US Global Financial Services Leadership*, January 2007, 131 pages.
12 Robert E. Grady, "The Sarbox Monster," *Wall Street Journal*, April 26, 2007, p. A19.
13 Arthur Levitt, *Take on the Street*, Random House-Pantheon, 2002, pp. 244–247.
14 Robert Pozen, "How to Strengthen Wall Street's Global Share," *Financial Times*, April 26, 2007, p. 13.
15 M. Livingston and L. Zhou, "The Impact of Rule 144a Debt Offerings Upon Bond Yields and Underwriter Fees," *Financial Management*, Winter 2002, pp. 5–27, and *Wall Street Journal*, "A Capital Idea," April 4, 2007, p. A18.
16 Robert E. Grady, "The Sarbox Monster," *Wall Street Journal*, April 26, 2007, p. A19.
17 Ibid.
18 H. Williamson and R. Atkins, "Call to Resist Anglo-American Model of Short-Termism," *Financial Times*, April 26, 2007, p. 2.
19 R. Atkins and H. Williamson, "Germans Urged to Advance Economic Reforms," *Financial Times*, April 26, 2007, p. 2.

3 Changing Exchanges

1 *The Economist*, April 21, 2004.
2 R. Aggarwal and S. Dahiya, "Demutualization and Public Offerings of Financial Exchanges," *Journal of Applied Corporate Finance*, Summer 2006, p. 97.
3 P. Tolmunen and S. Torstila, "Cross-Listings and M&A Activity: Transatlantic Evidence," *Financial Management*, Spring 2005, pp. 124–141.
4 Euronext, *Annual Report 2005*, pp. viii–ix.
5 OMX Group, *Experts in the Exchange Industry*, 2005 Annual Report, pp. 19–20.
6 OMX Group, *Annual Report 2006*, pp. 8–13.
7 OMX Group, *Annual Report 2007*, pp. 14–19.
8 Joanna Chung, "Quartet of Global Interests That Are Reshaping Trends in Financial World," *Financial Times*, October 9, 2007, p. 27.
9 Larry Harris, *Trading and Exchanges*, Oxford University Press, 2003, p. 390.
10 S. Scholtes, "Atlantic Divide Over E-Trading," *Financial Times*, October 5, 2006, p. 25.
11 Carl Carone, "Illuminating the New Dark Influence on Trading and US Market Structure," *Journal of Trading*, Winter 2008, p. 40.
12 H. Mittal, "Are You Playing in a Toxic Dark Pool?" *Journal of Trading*, Summer 2008, pp. 20–29.
13 J. Grant, "Furse Takes Issue With Bluster About LSE," *Financial Times*, May 23, 2008, p. 17.
14 S. Patterson and A. Lucchetti, "Dark Pools Being Spoiled by Success: Glut Dims Their Allure for Big Traders," *Wall Street Journal*, May 8, 2008, p. C1.
15 J. Chung and A. Gangahar, "SEC to Turn Spotlight on Dark Pools," *Financial Times*, June 19, 2009, p. 16.
16 J. Grant, "Regulators Keen to Shine a Light Into Dark Pools," *Financial Times*, June 21, 2009, p. 15.
17 W.R. Smyser, *The German Economy*, St. Martin's Press, 1993, p. 75. W. Meyer-Larsen, *Germany Inc.*, Wiley, 2000, pp. 90–96.
18 W. Megginson and D. Scarnapuco, "The Financial and Economic Lessons of Italy's Privatization Program," *Journal of Applied Corporate Finance*, Summer 2006, pp. 56–63.
19 P. Smith and N. Cohen, "Record $150 bn of Delistings," *Financial Times*, January 2, 2007, p. 1.
20 N. Cohen and P. Smith, "Upsurge in IPOs and Private Deals," *Financial Times*, January 2, 2007, p. 15.
21 J.M. Hill, "Equity Trading Capacity Revisited: Growth, Fragmentation, and Fluidity," *Journal of Trading*, Spring 2007, pp. 22–24.
22 Ibid.

4 Business Models

1 M.W. Johnson, C.M. Christensen, and H. Kagermann, "Reinventing Your Business Model," *Harvard Business Review*, December 2008, pp. 51–59.
2 M.J. Clayton, B.N. Jorgensen, and K.A. Kavajecz, "On the Presence and Market Structure of Exchanges Around the World," *Journal of Financial Markets*, February 2006, pp. 28–29.
3 Ibid., pp. 33–35.
4 Marc Levinson, *Guide to Financial Markets*, Bloomberg Press, 2006, pp. 150–155.
5 Ibid., pp. 170–171.
6 M. Gorham and N. Singh, *Electronic Exchanges*, Elsevier Press, 2009, pp. 193–197.
7 Lynn Strongin Dodds, "Offshore Exchanges," *FTSE Global Markets*, March–April 2008, p. 90.
8 Bourse de Luxembourg, *Factbook*, 2008, p. 13.
9 Luxembourg Stock Exchange, *The Luxembourg Stock Exchange: A Prime Location for Listing*, PricewaterhouseCoopers, 2010, pp. 2–3.
10 Ibid., pp. 4–5.
11 H.E. Teitelbaum, "Exchanges in Europe Lead the World in IPOs," *Wall Street Journal*, July 2, 2007, p. C8.
12 Martin Arnold, "Buyout Deals Accelerate as Banks Increase Their Lending," *Financial Times*, September 27, 2010, p. 20. Robert Cookson, "HK Eclipses Rivals as the Place to List," *Financial Times*, October 7, 2010, p. 24.
13 Liam Denning, "Selling Petrobras and GM," *Wall Street Journal*, September 25, 2010, p. B14. J. Wheatley, "Record Petrobras Share Offer Increased," *Financial Times*, September 19, 2010, p. 1.
14 Luxembourg Stock Exchange, *Annual Report for 2008*, pp. 19–27.
15 Ibid., pp. 68–70.
16 P. Tolmunen and S. Torstila, "Cross-Listings and M&A Activity: Transatlantic Evidence," *Financial Management*, Spring 2005, pp. 123–140.
17 S. Peng, K. Wang, and Y. Huang, "International Cross-Listings, Valuation Effects and Company Characteristics, Evidence From Taiwan," *Journal of Emerging Markets*, Fall–Winter 2007, pp. 7–20.
18 C. Doidge, G.A. Karolyi, and R. Stulz, *Has New York Become Less Competitive in Global Markets? Evaluating Foreign Listing Choices Over Time*, NBER Working Paper, 2007.
19 National Bureau of Economic Research, "Why Do Foreign Firms Leave US Equity Markets?" *NBER Digest*, July 2009, p. 4.
20 Deutsche Bundesbank, *Monthly Report*, October 2008, pp. 24–25.
21 According to J. Amner, S. Holland, D. Smith, and F. Warnock, countries can attract a larger volume of foreign investors to their stock markets by improving disclosure required by their own publicly traded firms. See National Bureau of Economic Research (NBER) Working Paper 12500, *Look at Me Now: What Attracts US Shareholders*? August 2006, pp. 29–30.
22 Clara Furse, "Speak up to Keep Clearing Houses Competitive," *Financial Times*, April 16, 2008, p. 11.
23 W.M. Clarke, *How the City of London Works*, Sweet & Maxwell, Sixth Edition, 2004, pp. 96–97.
24 J. Grant, "LSE Chief in Warning Over Vertical Silos," *Financial Times*, April 16, 2008, p. 19.
25 N. Tait and J. Grant, "EU Gives Clearing Houses Last Chance," *Financial Times*, April 21, 2008, p. 22.
26 J. Grant, "LCH.Clearnet Faces a Clutch of Challenges," *Financial Times*, April 29, 2008, p. 20.
27 J. Grant, "DTCC in Talks on Transatlantic Tieup," *Financial Times*, April 29, 2008, p. 20.

28 P. Mazzilli, D. Maister, and D. Perlman, "Fixed Income ETFs: Over 60 ETFs Enable Portfolios of Bonds to Be Traded Like Stocks," *Exchange Traded Funds*, Institutional Investor, 2008, pp. 58–73.

5 Restructuring via Mergers

1 Bruce Wasserstein, *Big Deal*, Warner Books, 1998, p. 3.
2 These are: in the United States, SEC Regulation NMS; and in Europe, Regulation MIFID.
3 T.O. Miller and M.S. Pagano, "Who Wants to Dance? Some Possible Exchange Partners," *Journal of Trading*, Spring 2007, p. 63.
4 Ibid., p. 70.
5 OMX Group, *OMX: Experts in the Exchange Industry*, 2007 Report, pp. 12–29.
6 OMX, "CEO's Comments," *Annual Report 2007*, pp. 10–12.
7 NYSE Group, *Prospectus*, May 4, 2006, filed with SEC, pp. 5–6.
8 Ibid., p. 69.
9 Larry Harris, *Trading and Exchanges*, Oxford University Press, 2003, p. 543.
10 N. Nakamoto, J. Burton, and D. Cameron, "TSE Buys $303m Stake in Singapore Exchange," *Financial Times*, June 16, 2007, p. 8.
11 A. Morse, "Tokyo Stock Exchange Acquires Stake in Singapore Market Is First for Asia," *Wall Street Journal*, June 16, 2007, p. B3.
12 A. Morse, "NYSE's Designs on Tokyo," *Wall Street Journal*, January 12, 2007, p. C3.
13 *Economist*, "The Hunt for Liquidity," July 28, 2001, p. 65.
14 Ibid.
15 E. Pretzlik, "LIFFE Staff and Management May Net £35m," *Financial Times*, October 4, 2001, p. 20.
16 V. Boland, "Exchanges Life Volume as Bid Battle Looms," *Financial Times*, October 4, 2001, p. 20.
17 V. Boland, "LSE Plans New Technology System in LIFFE Bid," *Financial Times*, October 24, 2001, p. 28.
18 V. Boland and E. Pretzlik, "Deutsche Börse Joins Race to Acquire LIFFE," *Financial Times*, October 18, 2001, p. 23.
19 V. Boland and C. Pretzlik, "Euronext Deals L550m Knockout Blow in Takeover Battle for LIFFE," *Financial Times*, October 30, 2001, p. 19.
20 *Financial Times*, "A New Stage of LIFFE," October 30, 2001, p. 16.
21 Kevin Brown, "Exchanges' $8.3bn Bid a Test for Asian Consolidation," *Financial Times*, October 27, 2010, p. 21.
22 *Wall Street Journal*, "Singapore Exchange Bids for ASX," October 25, 2010, p. C1.
23 J. Grant and P. Smith, "SGX Offers Premium for ASX," *Financial Times*, October 25, 2010, p. 16.
24 J. Grant and P. Smith, "SGX Shares Slip on ASX Takeover Plan," *FT.com*, October 24, 2010.
25 Kevin Brown, Jeremy Grant, and Peter Smith, "Canberra Key on SGX Bid for ASX," *Financial Times*, October 26, 2010, p. 16.

6 Transatlantic Mergers

1 A. Lucchetti, "NYSE Considers Its Next Move," *Wall Street Journal*, April 13, 2006, p. C3.
2 J.C. Francis, A. Harel, and G. Harpaz, "Exchange Mergers and Electronic Trading," *Journal of Trading*, Winter 2009, p. 39.
3 These points are abstracted from *Form 425*, NYSE Group Inc.—NYX, Filed June 2, 2006 with SEC.

4 Charles Gasparino, *King of the Club*, HarperCollins, 2007, pp. 286–287.
5 Ibid., p. 317.
6 NYSE Group, *Public Offering Prospectus*, May 4, 2006, p. 1.
7 Ibid., p. 117.
8 L. Boni and M. Rosen, "Hello Hybrid, Goodbye Price Improvement," *Journal of Trading*, Spring 2007, p. 98.
9 Ibid., p. 100.
10 J. Grant, "Regulators' Boundaries May Soon Start to Blur," *Financial Times*, June 19, 2007, p. 17.
11 A. Gallari, "Euronext Creator Reaches for New Deal," *Wall Street Journal*, May 30, 2006, pp. C1, C5.
12 Lex Column, "Pooling Rank," *Financial Times*, June 21, 2006, p. 16.
13 A. Gangahar, "A $14bn Deal Was Won by Compromise," *Financial Times*, December 23, 2006, p. 11.
14 Ibid.
15 A. Gangahar, "NYSE Euronext to Buy Rival AMEX for $260m," *Financial Times*, January 18, 2008, p. 14.
16 A. Lucchetti, "NYSE AMEX Finally Merging," *Wall Street Journal*, January 18, 2008, p. C3.
17 J. Spence, "NYSE to Gain an Edge With AMEX Deal," *Wall Street Journal*, January 21, 2008, p. C3.
18 A. Lucchetti, "NYSE Deal May Force AMEX to Eliminate 75% of Staff," *Wall Street Journal*, May 5, 2008, p. C1.
19 J.C. Francis, A. Harel, and G. Harpaz, "Exchange Mergers and Electronic Trading," *Journal of Trading*, Winter 2009, p. 39.
20 S. Kerr and J. Grant, "NYSE Euronext Buys 25% of Qatar Exchange," *Financial Times*, June 25, 2008, p. 1.
21 D. Ambucca and S. Ng, "NYSE, Deutsche Börse Resume Deal Talks," *Wall Street Journal*, April 24, 2009, p. C3.
22 *Economist*, "Three-Dimensional Chess," August 6, 2005, pp. 60–61.
23 M. Santoli, "Death of the Floor," *Barron's*, November 20, 2006, pp. 27–30.
24 M. Santoli, "The Big Board's Shrinking World," *Barron's*, July 16, 2007, p. 26.
25 Ibid.
26 Jacob Bunji, "NYSE Adjusts Charges in Bid to Draw Traders," *Wall Street Journal*, February 3, 2009, p. C5.
27 J. Grant, "NASDAQ OMX Europe Slashes Costs," *Financial Times*, May 1, 2009, p. 23.
28 Carolyn Cui, "NYSE Plans to Launch Stock Index Contracts," *Wall Street Journal*, May 27, 2009, p. C3.
29 A. Gangahar, "NYSE Euronext in Tech Partnership," *Financial Times*, June 10, 2008, p. 25.
30 S. Ng and G. Rogow, "NYSE Speeds Trades to Meet Competition," *Wall Street Journal*, March 2, 2009, p. C3.
31 Serena Ng, "NYSE's New Kid on Blocks," *Wall Street Journal*, January 29, 2009, p. C5.
32 *International Directory of Company Histories*, Volume 92, 2008, St. James Press, pp. 256–259.
33 *Forbes*, "Faster, Cheaper, Smarter," January 12, 2009, pp. 57–60.
34 Larry Harris, *Trading and Exchanges*, Oxford University Press, 2003, p. 132.
35 A. Gangahar, "NASDAQ Counts the Cost of LSE Bid," *Financial Times*, April 17, 2009, p. 16.
36 A. Lucchetti and A. MacDonald, "Browsing but No Buyers for an LSE Stake," *Wall Street Journal*, August 18, 2007, p. C3.
37 D. Iblson, "Börse Dubai Makes $4bn. Bid for OMX," *Financial Times*, August 18, 2007, p. 8. J. Clevstrom and A. MacDonald, "Was NASDAQ Outbid in Sweden?" *Wall Street Journal*, August 18, 2007, p. B3.

38 N. Lohide and A. MacDonald, "NASDAQ's Bid to Purchase OMX Hits a Snag," *Wall Street Journal*, August 10, 2007, p. C3.
39 A. MacDonald and J. Singer, "Börse Dubai's Vision," *Wall Street Journal*, August 13, 2007, p. C3.
40 A. Lucchetti and A. MacDonald, "NASDAQ Lands OMX for $3.7bn," *Wall Street Journal*, May 26, 2007, p. B3.
41 S. Kerr and N. Cohen, "Qatar Eyes NASDAQ's LSE Stake," *Financial Times*, September 5, 2007, p. 18.
42 A. Lucchetti and S. Craig, "NASDAQ Chief Turns Page," *Wall Street Journal*, February 25, 2008, pp. C1, C4.
43 A. Gangahar and N. Cohen, "NASDAQ to Acquire Boston Stock Exchange," *Financial Times*, October 3, 2007, p. 17.
44 *Forbes*, "Faster, Cheaper, Smarter," January 12, 2009, pp. 57–60.
45 Stacy-Marie Ishmael, "NASDAQ Talks to PHLX About Possible Takeover Bid," *Financial Times*, November 7, 2007, p. 18.
46 M. Gorham and N. Singh, *Electronic Exchanges*, Elsevier, 2009, pp. 136–138.
47 Doug Cameron, "NASDAQ OMX Takes a Rest After a String of Mergers," *Wall Street Journal*, August 20, 2008, p. C3.
48 A. Lucchetti and D. Kardos, "NASDAQ OMX Net Income Jumps More Than Sixfold," *Wall Street Journal*, May 9, 2008, p. C3.
49 A. Gangahar, "Crosswell Leads NASDAQ OMX's European Push," *Financial Times*, May 15, 2008, p. 21.
50 Serena Ng, "NASDAQ OMX Is Ready to Go," *Wall Street Journal*, September 8, 2008, p. C3.
51 Tom Fairless, "New Platforms Nip at Old Guard," *Wall Street Journal*, May 18, 2009, p. C6.
52 Mary Anastasia O'Grady, "Is the Stock Exchange Obsolete?" *Wall Street Journal*, October 31, 2009, p. A17.
53 J. Nunge and R. Smith, "Extreme Makeover: Big Board Edition," *Wall Street Journal*, October 8, 2009, p. C1.
54 J. Grant, "NYSE Euronext Picks IBM Veteran Cerutti," *Financial Times*, October 2, 2009, p. 20.
55 Jonathan Spicer, "NYSE Aims for Human Touch as It Modernizes," *International Herald Tribune*, August 5, 2009, p. 15.
56 A. Gangahar, "NASDAQ Chief Says Sector Will Fragment," *Financial Times*, January 8, 2009, p. 17.
57 A. Gangahar, "NASDAQ to Launch Dark Liquidity Pool," *Financial Times*, March 18, 2009, p. 23.
58 Richard Thaler, "The Price Is Not Always Right and Markets Can Be Wrong," *Financial Times*, August 5, 2009, p. 7.
59 T. Tracy, "BOX Ratchets up Rivalry in ETF Space," *Wall Street Journal*, June 24, 2009, p. C5.
60 Michael Mackenzie, "Flash Crash Inquiry Focuses on High-Frequency Traders," *Financial Times*, May 21, 2010, p. 20.
61 The joint report is titled *Preliminary Findings Regarding the Market Events of May 6, 2010*, Report of the Staffs of the CFTC and SEC to the Joint Advisory Committee on Emerging Regulatory Issues, May 18, 2010.
62 Securities and Exchange Commission and Commodity Futures Trading Commission, *Preliminary Findings Regarding the Market Events of May 6, 2010*, May 18, 2010, p. 4.
63 Aline Van Duyn and Talis Demis, "Flash Crash: Market Reform Examined," *Financial Times*, October 5, 2010, p. 27.
64 *Financial Times*, "Flash Crash Report Leaves Key Questions Unanswered," October 2, 2010, p. 3.

65 Graham Bowley, "Lone Sale of $4.1bn. in Contracts Led to Flash Crash," *New York Times Business Day*, October 2, 2010, pp. B1, B2.
66 N. Mehta, L. Thomasson, and P.M. Barrett, "The Machines That Ate the Market," *Bloomberg Business Week*, May 24, 2010, p. 53.
67 Michael Mackenzie and Aline Van Duyn, "Flash Crash Sparked by $4.1bn. Sale of Futures in 20 Minutes, a Report Says," *Financial Times*, October 2, 2010, p. 1.

7 London Calling

1 *Euromoney*, "London Should Sell at the Highest Price," June 2000, pp. 34–36.
2 *Euromoney*, "Modernizer Plots London Takeover," October 2000, pp. 42–48.
3 London Stock Exchange, *Annual Report 2006*, p. 6.
4 Philip Stafford, "LSE Claims Top Spot for Foreign Flotations," *Financial Times*, December 28, 2007, p. 13.
5 D. Blackwell and B. Masters, "Slowdown in AIM Listings Takes a Heavy Toll on Brokers' Profits," *Financial Times*, July 12, 2007, p. 17.
6 J. Mackintosh, "LSE Plans Light Touch Market," *Financial Times*, May 20, 2008, p. 22.
7 A. MacDonald, "LSE Puts Its Stock in Speed," *Wall Street Journal*, June 19, 2007, p. C2.
8 Janette Rutterford, *Stock Exchange Investment*, Macmillan, 1993, pp. 11–12.
9 Stephen Valdez, *An Introduction to Global Financial Markets*, Macmillan, 2000, pp. 173–174.
10 Tony Golding, *The City: Inside the Great Expectation Machine*, FT Prentice Hall, 2003, p. 85.
11 The EuroNM markets included: Nouveau Marché (Paris), Neuer Markt (Frankfurt), EuroNM (Brussels), and Nuovo Mercato (Milan). E. Flowers and F. Lees, *The Euro, Capital Markets, and Dollarization*, Rowman & Littlefield, 2002, pp. 167–168, 220.
12 LSE, *Annual Report 2006*, p. 6.
13 Ibid., p. 7.
14 LSE, *Annual Report 2007*, p. 12.
15 Luke Clancy, "AIM on the Up," *World Mining Stocks*, May 2, 2006, p. 1. Luke Clancy, "In-Bocus Aim," *World Mining Stocks*, May 2006, pp. 12–14.
16 Nick Davis, "A Leading Position for Memory Crystal," *World Mining Stocks*, May 2006, p. 23.
17 Lina Saigol and Megan Murphy, "Pressures on Banks to Build up Broker Share," *Financial Times*, October 8, 2010, p. 19.
18 LSE, *Annual Report 2007*, p. 23.
19 A. Lucchetti and D. Reilly, "London Exchange Rebuffs a Bid From NASDAQ," *Wall Street Journal*, March 11, 2006, p. B1.
20 A. Postelnucu and D. Blackwell, "Take Aim and Outshine the Competition," *Financial Times*, September 3, 2005, p. 9.
21 J. Authers, "Platforms Hold Key to Merger Savings," *Financial Times*, March 16, 2006, p. 21.
22 A. MacDonald and H. Teitelbaum, "NASDAQ Declines to Raise Its Bid for LSE," *Wall Street Journal*, January 27, 2007, p. B3.
23 A. MacDonald, "LSE Holder Raises Its Stake," *Wall Street Journal*, January 5, 2007, p. C3.
24 N. Cohen, "LSE Sails Into a Period of Relative Calm," *Financial Times*, February 10, 2007, p. 9.
25 A. MacDonald, "LSE Available Again, May Seek New Partner," *Wall Street Journal*, February 13, 2007, p. C.2.
26 Jeremy Grant, "Case for Change Heard Loud and Clear," *Financial Times*, February 9, 2009, p. 16.

27 A. MacDonald and A. Mecenni, "LSE Adds Dimension as Holders Back Deal," *Wall Street Journal*, August 9, 2007, p. C3.
28 Lex Column, "LSE and Borsa Italia," *Financial Times*, June 22, 2007, p. 12.
29 A. Mocenni and E. Taylor, "NYSE Makes Rival Bid for Borsa Italiana," *Wall Street Journal*, June 22, 2007, p. C2.
30 A. MacDonald, "LSE Begins Talks With Milan on Tie-Up," *Wall Street Journal*, June 21, 2007, p. C2.
31 These include JPMorgan, Deutsche Bank, and IMI.
32 N. Cohen, "Defensive Logic Behind LSE's Aggressive Italian Manoeuvre," *Financial Times*, June 23, 2007, p. 9.
33 H.E. Teitelbaum and C. Emsden, "LSE to Gain Italy IPO Pipeline," *Wall Street Journal*, July 12, 2007, p. C2.
34 N. Cohen and M. Wang, "Sure NASDAQ Does Not Have Power to Halt Borsa Exchange Deal," *Financial Times*, June 26, 2007, p. 15.
35 Neal Shah and Vladimir Gevarra, "London Exchange Maps Strategy," *Wall Street Journal*, July 16, 2009, p. C5.
36 J. Grant, "Baikal to Spearhead LSE's Europe Drive," *Financial Times*, June 17, 2009, p. 17.
37 Lex Column, "Ole Rolet," *Financial Times*, September 17, 2009, p. 14.

8 Derivatives Dominate

1 K. Chan, "A Further Analysis of Lead–Lag Relationships Between the Cash Market and Index Futures Market," *Review of Financial Studies*, 1992, pp. 123–152.
2 S. Fung and S. Tsai, "Interrelationships Between Options, Futures and Stock Markets: Evidence From Taiwan's Derivatives Markets," *Journal of Emerging Markets*, Summer 2008, pp. 7–14.
3 Harvard Business School, "Bringing OTC Back to the Exchange," Case Studies in Business Series, March 2004.
4 MF Global, *Annual Report 2008*, pp. 10–11.
5 *Economist*, "Global OTC Derivatives," May 31, 2008, p. 102.
6 W.M. Clarke, *How the City of London Works*, Sweet & Maxwell, 2004, pp. 15–16.
7 Javier Blas, "£1.6 m is top price to join the LME," *Financial Times*, July 12, 2007, p. 26.
8 Javier Blas, "LME Seeks a Profitable Billet With Steel Contracts," *Financial Times*, January 16, 2008, p. 25.
9 Alex MacDonald, "LME Launches Steel Futures," *Wall Street Journal*, February 25, 2008, p. C2.
10 LME, "A Day in the Ring," *Ringsider*, 2008, pp. 114–116.
11 LME, "Select Trading," *Ringsider*, 2008, p. 125.
12 A. Lucchetti and A. Davis, "A Commodities Behemoth," *Wall Street Journal*, January 29, 2008, pp. C1, C2.
13 M. Chambers, "ICE Could Benefit from NYMEX Plan," *Wall Street Journal*, January 8, 2007, p. C4.
14 These included American Electric Power, Aquila Energy, Duke Energy, El Paso Energy, Reliant Energy, and Southern Company.
15 A. Lucchetti and B. Wysocki, "Futures Fight: Upstart Makes Play for the CBOT," *Wall Street Journal*, March 16, 2007, pp. C1–C2.
16 A. Lucchetti, "Newcomer ICE, Chicago Merc. Try to Sell Rival Bids to CBOT," *Wall Street Journal*, March 21, 2007, p. C3.
17 FI stands for fixed income, C for currency, and C for commodity trading.
18 K. Griffin, "We Must Overturn the Status Quo in Derivatives," *Financial Times*, October 27, 2009, p. 7.
19 Kent Cherry and Ben Craig, "Credit Default Swaps and Their Market Function," *Economic Commentary*, Federal Reserve Bank of Cleveland, July 2009, p. 2.

20 *Wall Street Journal*, "AIG and Systemic Risk," November 20, 2009, p. 26.
21 Burton Malkiel, "Finding a Way to Regain Trust in the Battered Financial System," *Financial Times*, November 13, 2008, p. 26. S. Lynch and J. Bunge, "Derivative Clearing: Making It the Law?" *Wall Street Journal*, December 9, 2008, p. C4.
22 S. O'Connor and F. Guerrera, "Geithner in Push on Derivatives Regulation," *Financial Times*, May 14, 2009, p. 1.
23 S. Lynch and S. Ng, "US Moves to Regulate Derivatives Trade," *Wall Street Journal*, May 14, 2009, p. C1.
24 David G. Mayes (editor), *The Future of Financial Markets*, Palgrave Macmillan, 2006, pp. 102–104.
25 M. Gorham and N. Singh, *Electronic Exchanges*, Elsevier, 2009, pp. 205–206.
26 Aline Van Duyn, "ICE to Begin Clearing as Regulators Approve Plan for Credit Default Swaps," *Financial Times*, March 7, 2009, p. 17.
27 Hal Weitzmann, "ICE Forges Ahead With Central CDS Clearing," *Financial Times*, November 4, 2009, p. 27.
28 S. Tucker and R. Cookson, "CME Head Backs Derivatives Program," *Financial Times*, October 9, 2009, p. 16.
29 J. Grant, "Caution Over OTC Clearing as Dealers Flex Their Muscles," *Financial Times*, November 13, 2009, p. 24.
30 Aline Van Duyn, "Pressure Increases on Derivatives Traders to Use Central Clearing," *Financial Times*, January 14, 2010, p. 25.
31 Aline Van Duyn and J. Grant, "Use of Clearers to Rein in OTC Derivatives Poses Fresh Dilemma," *Financial Times*, January 15, 2010, p. 2.
32 Y.E. Simaan and L. Wu, "Price Discovery in the US Stock Options Market," *Journal of Trading*, Winter 2008, p. 70.
33 S.M. Sears, "A Bull Market in Exchanges," *Barron's*, April 7, 2008, p. M6.
34 E. Lambert, "Up From the Pits," *Forbes*, January 28, 2008, pp. 65–69.
35 J. Thomas, "CBOT–CME Deal Is Done at Last," *Wall Street Journal*, July 10, 2007, p. C3.
36 Doug Cameron, "New All-Chicago Exchange Fears Challenges After CBOT Battle," *Financial Times*, July 10, 2007, p. 1.
37 A. Lucchetti, "In CBOT Fight, It All Adds up to Derivatives," *Wall Street Journal*, March 20, 2007, pp. C1, C2.
38 A. Gangaher and N. Cohen, "Three Names as NYMEX Merger Talk Starts," *Financial Times*, June 16, 2007, p. 8.
39 A. Lucchetti, "CME Group Swallows NYMEX," *Wall Street Journal*, August 28, 2008, p. C3.
40 H.N. Moore, "NYMEX Blinked in CME Battle," *Wall Street Journal*, August 18, 2008, p. C3.
41 CBOE Holdings Inc., *Prospectus*, June 2010, p. 3.
42 Ibid., p. 84.
43 Ibid., pp. 92–98.
44 Ibid., pp. 97–99.

9 Asia Pacific Exchanges

1 John King, "Asia Keeps the West's Betrayed Faith," *Financial Times*, July 22, 2009, p. 9.
2 Thomas Schiller, "How Asia Could Have Vibrant Capital Markets," *Financial Times*, April 25, 2007, p. 11.
3 Ibid.
4 Federal Reserve Bank of Dallas, "Miracle to Malaise: What's Next for Japan?" *Economic Letter*, January 2006, pp. 1–8.
5 *Economist*, "Why Japan Keeps Failing," February 22, 2008, pp. 33–35.

6 M. Nakamoto, "Japan Told to Improve Its Corporate Governance," *Financial Times*, May 22, 2008, p. 24.
7 M. Nakamoto, "Modernizers Span a Cultural Divide," *Financial Times*, May 22, 2008, p. 14.
8 J.R. Laing, "Is the Sun Setting on Japan?" *Barron's*, September 28, 2009, pp. 25–26.
9 Murc Dickie, "A Fiscal Frailty," *Financial Times*, August 4, 2009, p. 5.
10 *Wall Street Journal*, "Baby Bundle: Japan's Cash Incentive for Parenthood," October 8, 2009, p. A19.
11 D. Pilling, "OECD Urges Japan to Raise Taxes," *Financial Times*, April 8, 2008, p. 6.
12 J.R. Laing, "Is the Sun Setting on Japan?" *Barron's*, September 28, 2009, pp. 25–26.
13 *Economist*, "Under Pressure," March 8, 2008, pp. 71–72.
14 Peter Tasker, "Japan's Future Is in the Hands of Its Small Companies," *Financial Times*, July 9, 2009, p. 20.
15 *Economist*, "Power Struggles," May 31, 2008, pp. 67–68.
16 *Economist*, "Japan's Pension Pot: Thinking," July 26, 2008, p. 87.
17 D. Pilling, "Tokyo Looks at Public Pensions Revamp," *Financial Times*, May 23, 2008, p. 25.
18 L. Lucas, "Behemoth Limbers up," *Financial Times*, Supplement on Japan Banking, Finance and Investment, September 14, 2007, p. 3.
19 M. Nakamoto, "It's Time to Leave Home Again," *Financial Times*, Supplement on Japan Banking, Finance and Investment, September 12, 2008, p. 1.
20 Yuka Hayeshi, "Tokyo Plan for Japan Post Slows," *Wall Street Journal*, June 15, 2009, p. A8. R. Harding, M. Nakamoto, and L. Whipp, "Pragmatism Drives Stance on Japan Post," *Financial Times*, June 6, 2010, p. 3.
21 Murc Dickie, "DPJ Seeks to Unlock Consumer Savings," *Financial Times*, October 9, 2009, p. 6.
22 Tokyo Stock Exchange, *Annual Report 2007*, p. 1.
23 Ibid., p. 8.
24 Tokyo Stock Exchange, *Factbook 2008*, pp. 70–78.
25 A. Tomisara, "For the Chief of TSE, Life Under Siege," *Wall Street Journal*, September 2, 2010, p. C5.
26 Tokyo Stock Exchange, *Annual Report 2008*, p. 14.
27 L. Whipp, "Tokyo AIM Looks to Niche Role to Get Ahead of Rivals," *Financial Times*, July 1, 2009, p. 20.
28 L. Whipp, "Co-location to Get Tokyo up to Speed," *Financial Times*, November 2, 2009, p. 16.
29 L. Whipp, "TSE Seeks Boost to Trade From Launch of Platform," *Financial Times*, January 4, 2010, p. 19.
30 Kevin Brown, "Spate of Multinationals Eye Listing in Singapore," *Financial Times*, April 27, 2010, p. 23.
31 J. Grant and S. Tucker, "SGX Is Determined to Punch Above Its Weight," *Financial Times*, June 12, 2008, p. 14.
32 J. Grant, "SGX to Pursue Role in OTC Clearing," *Financial Times*, June 16, 2009, p. 21.
33 Kevin Brown, "Singapore Exchange Eyes Global Trading Opportunities," *Financial Times*, February 22, 2010, p. 16. Kevin Brown, "SGX to Offer OTC Derivatives Clearing," *Financial Times*, September 21, 2010, p. 25.
34 James Campbell, "Singapore Getting New Player in Futures," *Wall Street Journal*, August 18, 2010, p. C2.
35 Sameer Mohandara and James Campbell, "Singapore Futures Trading Heats up," *Wall Street Journal*, September 1, 2010, p. C3.
36 Sarah Sparks, "Collins Stewart Moves to Tap AIM Rival," *Financial Times*, January 3, 2008, p. 15.
37 SGX Group, *Annual Report 2007*, p. 22.
38 Ibid., p. 48.

39 S. Tucker, "Oz Finds Its Pot of Gold," *Financial Times*, Australia Finance Supplement, September 6, 2006, p. 1.
40 Virginia Marsh, "Compulsory Pensions Fund Super Pool," *Financial Times*, Australia Finance Supplement, September 6, 2006, p. 2.
41 Louise Lucas, "Exchange Expands at Home So It Can Make Its Mark Abroad," *Financial Times*, Australia Finance Supplement, September 6, 2006, p. 4.
42 Jim Bain, *A Financial Tale of Two Cities*, University of New South Wales Press, 2007, pp. 96–99.
43 Ibid., p. 102.
44 Ibid., pp. 236–237.

10 Hong Kong–Shanghai Nexus

1 H.-g. Fung and Q.W. Liu, "China's Qualified Foreign Institutional Investor and Qualified Domestic Institutional Investor Programs," in K.C. Chan, H.-g. Fung and Q.W. Liu (editors), *China's Capital Markets*, Edward Elgar, 2007, pp. 218–219.
2 Henry Sender, "China's Listed Banks Are Still at the Behest of the State," *Financial Times*, December 10, 2010, p. 24.
3 A.S. Douglas and A.G. Huang, "Investment Banking in China: Past, Present and Future," in K.C. Chan, H.-g. Fung and Q.W. Liu (editors), *China's Capital Markets*, Edward Elgar, 2007, pp. 139–140.
4 G. Zhang, "China's Foreign Exchange Market," in K.C. Chan, H.-g. Fung and Q.W. Liu (editors), *China's Capital Markets*, Edward Elgar, 2007, pp. 182–183.
5 Geoff Doyen, "Paulson in Last Stand Against Weak Renminbi," *Financial Times*, December 4, 2008, p. 3.
6 J.T. Areddy, "Beijing Signals Inflation Focus as It Lets Yuan Rise," *Wall Street Journal*, April 11, 2008, p. A8.
7 A. Tang and P. Gavinan, "New Forex Controls in China to Combat Hot Money," *Financial Times*, August 8, 2008, p. 23.
8 Henry Sender, "Hong Kong Faces Heat in Dollar Peg," *Financial Times*, November 4, 2010, p. 26.
9 T. Mitchell and J. Lau, "A Breakthrough for Renminbi Bonds," *Financial Times*, January 12, 2007, p. 21.
10 Ibid.
11 Shai Oster, Dinny McMahon, and Tom Lauricella, "Yuan Trading Is Taking off on Global Exchange Markets," *Wall Street Journal*, December 14, 2010, pp. A1, A12.
12 Robert Cookson, "ADB Raises Its First Dim Sum Bond," *Financial Times*, October 20, 2010, p. 27.
13 Zhiwu Chen, "Privatization Would Enrich China," *Financial Times*, August 8, 2008, p. 9.
14 Chen's point is supported by the low consumer spending and high saving rate in China.
15 Tom Mitchell, "Hong Kong Celebrates 25 Years of the US Dollar Peg," *Financial Times*, October 17, 2008, p. 24.
16 J. Cheung, "Hong Kong Chief Considers Currency Link With China," *Wall Street Journal*, March 25, 2009, p. C12.
17 J. Lau, "Tycoons Who Aim to Keep It in the Family," *Financial Times*, Hong Kong Supplement, June 30, 2008, p. 4.
18 Sundeep Tucker, "HK to Challenge the Big Two?" *Financial Times*, March 17, 2007, p. 12.
19 Hong Kong Exchanges and Clearing Limited, *2007 Annual Report*, p. 2.
20 Ibid., p. 9.
21 Ibid., p. 11.

22 Ibid., p. 15.
23 Ibid., p. 15.
24 Ibid., p. 26.
25 J. Grant and J. Lau, "Bourses in Brazil and HK Leap up Global Rankings," *Financial Times*, June 15, 2009, p. 16.
26 *Bloomberg Businessweek*, "In China, a Stock Market Where Startups Thrive," November 28, 2010, pp. 59–60.
27 K.C. Chan, H.-g. Fung, and J.S. Kwok, "Chinese Stock Market: Perspectives in Institutional Structure, Regulations and Performance," in K.C. Chan, H.-g. Fung and Q.W. Liu (editors), *China's Capital Markets*, Edward Elgar, 2007, pp. 28–29.
28 Ibid., pp. 33–34.
29 Lex Column, "Chinese Stock Market," *Financial Times*, December 28, 2007, p. 12.
30 R. McGregor and T. Mitchell, "A Tale of Two Exchanges Emerges From Opening Day Bonanza," *Financial Times*, January 17, 2007, p. 22.
31 Robert Cookson, "Shenzhen Takes Over as China's Listing Hub," *Financial Times*, October 19, 2010, p. 24.
32 Carl Walter and Fraser Howie, *Privatizing China*, John Wiley, 2006, pp. 113–121.
33 David Blackwell, "Chinese Groups Take Fresh Look at AIM," *Financial Times*, October 7, 2010, p. 20.
34 Leslie Hook, "Ambition to Build China's Futures," *Financial Times*, October 29, 2010, p. 20.
35 Robert Cookson, "Wealthy Traders Fuel Mania for Chinese Financial Futures," *Financial Times*, April 29, 2010, p. 26.
36 Patti Waldmeir, "Stock Index Futures Are Launched in China," *Financial Times*, April 16, 2010, p. 19.
37 John Jannarone and Andrew Peaple, "China Controls Leap Into Futures," *Wall Street Journal*, April 23, 2010, p. C12.
38 S. Oster, "China Iron-Ore Price Pact Could Color Future Deals," *Wall Street Journal*, August 18, 2009, p. A10.
39 J. Cheng, "Hong Kong Plans to Open Commodities Exchange," *Wall Street Journal*, June 25, 2008, p. C2.

11 Looking Forward

1 Robert Kimmitt, "Public Footprints in Private Markets," *Foreign Affairs*, January–February 2008, p. 119.
2 Thai Larsen, "Foreign Funds Put Cash in the Banks," *Financial Times*, November 28, 2007, p.19. Robin Wigglesworth, "Sovereign Wealth Funds Start to Open up Their Books," *Financial Times*, March 18, 2010, p. 5.
3 Kristin Halvorsen, "Norway's Sovereign Fund Sets an Ethical Example," *Financial Times*, February 15, 2008, p. 9.
4 John Burton, "Buying Quest Takes Temasek West," *Financial Times*, December 22, 2007, p. 9.
5 R. Carew and T. Wright, "China Sovereign Fund Bets Big in Resources," *Wall Street Journal*, September 24, 2009, pp. C1, C2.
6 David Oakley and Gillian Tett, "Sovereign Wealth Funds Courted in Debt Sales," *Financial Times*, March 25, 2010, p. 23.
7 Alan Murray, "Ascent of Sovereign Wealth Funds Illustrates New World Order," *Wall Street Journal*, January 18, 2008, p. A2.
8 A.A. Rehman, *Dubai & Co.*, McGraw-Hill, 2008, pp. 22–29, 45–49.
9 The Levant includes Iraq, Jordan, Lebanon, Syria, the Palestine Territory, and Israel. North Africa includes Egypt, Sudan, Libya, Tunisia, Algeria, and Morocco.
10 A.A. Rehman, *Dubai & Co.*, McGraw-Hill, 2008, p. 67.

11 David Blair, "LNG Producer Aims to Build on Early Lead," *Financial Times*, Special Report on Qatar, November 13, 2010, p. 4.
12 Digby Lidstone, "Competition for Dwindling Gas Supplies," *Financial Times*, Special Report on Bahrain, November 10, 2010, p. 4.
13 A.A. Rehman, *Dubai & Co.*, McGraw-Hill, 2008, pp. 221–224.
14 Robin Wigglesworth, "Saudi Bourse Poised to Exercise More Global Appeal," *Financial Times*, September 2, 2010, p. 23.
15 Riz Khan, *Alwaleed: Businessman, Billionaire, Prince*, Harper-Collins, 2004, pp. 240–241. Khan provides a detailed description of the business strategy behind the success of Kingdom Holding Company.
16 Robin Wigglesworth, "Saudi Bourse Poised to Exercise More Global Appeal," *Financial Times*, September 2, 2010, p. 23.
17 This is based on information reported by Mondo Visione, which reports periodically on market valuations of exchanges, and the changing population of these marketplaces.
18 Jonathan Wheatley, "Brazil Basks in Petrobras Spotlight," *Financial Times*, September 25, 2010, p. 9.
19 *Financial Times*, "Brazil Dazzles Global Finance," September 28, 2010, p. 12.
20 In Chapter 4, "Defining Ownership," Walter and Howie note China's securities laws create uncertainties regarding legal status of company shares vis-à-vis the many types of shares that have not been given formal recognition. Carl Walter and Fraser Howie, *Privatizing China*, Wiley, 2006, pp. 67–106.
21 J. Grant, "Clearers Step Into Limelight," *Financial Times*, Exchanges and Trading Supplement, October 20, 2008, p. 4.
22 J. Wheatley, "Traders Stunned by Power of Bovespa IPO," *Financial Times*, October 29, 2007, p. 19.
23 A. Regalado, "Brazilian Exchanges May Merge After IPO," *Wall Street Journal*, November 29, 2007, p. C4.
24 J. Wheatley, "Brazil Exchange Executives Get Into Global Party Mind," *Financial Times*, February 29, 2008, p. 20.
25 J. Wheatley and J. Grant, "Brazil Quick to Make up for Its Slow Start," *Financial Times*, June 29, 2009, p. 16.
26 Herbie Skeete, *The Future of the Financial Exchanges*, Elsevier and Mondo Visione, 2009, p. 55.
27 Ibid., pp. 4–5.
28 K. Peterson and J. Bunge, "Getco Becomes NYSE Market Maker," *Wall Street Journal*, February 12, 2010, p. C5.
29 S. Johnson, "UK Plan to Open up Bond Trade," *Financial Times*, Fund Management Supplement, February 1, 2010, p. 1.
30 J. Hughes, A. Gray, and M. Vincent, "New Products Set for LSE Bond Platform," *Financial Times*, February 2, 2010, p. 23.
31 M. Serdarevic, "Barriers Falling Between Traders," *Financial Times*, February 2, 2010, p. 22.
32 Randall Dodd, "Opaque Trades," *Finance and Development*, March 2010, International Monetary Fund, pp. 26–28.
33 J. Grant, "Plunge Places Focus on Safety of the Share Markets," *Financial Times*, May 11, 2010, p. 23.
34 Michael Mackenzie, "Trading Circuit Breakers Considered," *Financial Times*, May 11, 2010, p. 23.

Index

Made in the USA
Las Vegas, NV
19 September 2026

46d8d660-00fb-4c73-abbd-4a7bc11ea19eR01